Dragon Eye
Volume 4

Kairi Fujiyama

Translated and adapted by Mari Morimoto

Lettered by North Market Street Graphics

Ballantine Books • New York

Dragon Eye volume 4 is a work of fiction. Names, characters, places, and incidents are the products of the author's imagination or are used fictitiously. Any resemblance to actual events, locales, or persons, living or dead, is entirely coincidental.

A Del Rey Manga/Kodansha Trade Paperback Original

Published in the United States by Del Rey Books, an imprint of The Random House Publishing Group, a division of Random House, Inc., New York.

DEL REY is a registered trademark and the Del Rey colophon is a trademark of Random House, Inc.

Publication rights arranged through Kodansha Ltd.

First published in Japan in 2006 by Kodansha Ltd., Tokyo

ISBN 978-0-345-50132-5

Printed in the United States of America

www.delreymanga.com

9 8 7 6 5 4 3 2 1

Translator/Adaptor—Mari Morimoto
Lettering: NMSG

Contents

Honorifics Explained v

Dragon Eye, volume 4 1

Translation Notes 198

When I heard the editor in chief
mention the word "Dracule," my
first thought was "I can't believe
a mature adult just used that
word." I thought the same thing
when I heard editor M.S.-san say it.
I wonder why, when I'm the one
drawing this manga.

Honorifics Explained

Throughout the Del Rey Manga books, you will find Japanese honorifics left intact in the translations. For those not familiar with how the Japanese use honorifics and, more important, how they differ from American honorifics, we present this brief overview.

Politeness has always been a critical facet of Japanese culture. Ever since the feudal era, when Japan was a highly stratified society, use of honorifics—which can be defined as polite speech that indicates relationship or status—has played an essential role in the Japanese language. When you address someone in Japanese, an honorific usually takes the form of a suffix attached to one's name (example: "Asuna-san"), is used as a title at the end of one's name, or appears in place of the name itself (example: "Negi-sensei," or simply "Sensei!").

Honorifics can be expressions of respect or endearment. In the context of manga and anime, honorifics give insight into the nature of the relationship between characters. Many English translations leave out these important honorifics and therefore distort the feel of the original Japanese. Because Japanese honorifics contain nuances that English honorifics lack, it is our policy at Del Rey not to translate them. Here, instead, is a guide to some of the honorifics you may encounter in Del Rey Manga.

-*san:* This is the most common honorific and is equivalent to Mr., Miss, Ms., or Mrs. It is the all-purpose honorific and can be used in any situation where politeness is required.

-*sama:* This is one level higher than "-san." It is used to confer great respect.

-*dono:* This comes from the word "tono," which means "lord." It is an even higher level than "-sama" and confers utmost respect.

-kun: This suffix is used at the end of boys' names to express familiarity or endearment. It is also sometimes used by men among friends, or when addressing someone younger or of a lower station.

-chan: This is used to express endearment, mostly toward girls. It is also used for little boys, pets, and even among lovers. It gives a sense of childish cuteness.

Bozu: This is an informal way to refer to a boy, similar to the English terms "kid" and "squirt."

Sempai/Senpai: This title suggests that the addressee is one's senior in a group or organization. It is most often used in a school setting, where underclassmen refer to their upperclassmen as "sempai." It can also be used in the workplace, such as when a newer employee addresses an employee who has seniority in the company.

Kohai: This is the opposite of "sempai" and is used toward underclassmen in school or newcomers in the workplace. It connotes that the addressee is of a lower station.

Sensei: Literally meaning "one who has come before," this title is used for teachers, doctors, or masters of any profession or art.

-[blank]: This is usually forgotten in these lists, but it is perhaps the most significant difference between Japanese and English. The lack of honorific means that the speaker has permission to address the person in a very intimate way. Usually, only family, spouses, or very close friends have this kind of permission. Known as *yobisute*, it can be gratifying when someone who has earned the intimacy starts to call one by one's name without an honorific. But when that intimacy hasn't been earned, it can be very insulting.

Dragon Eye

Kairi Fujiyama

4

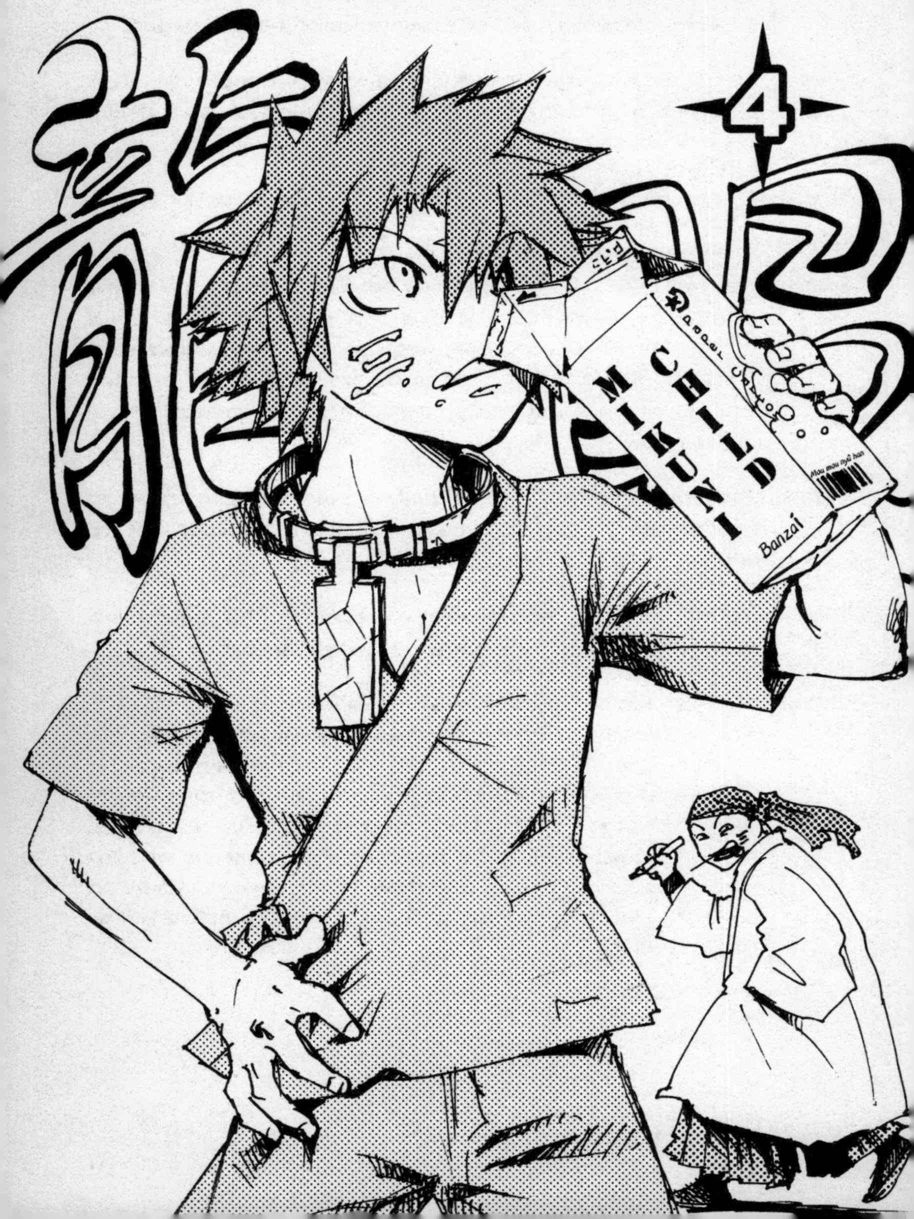

The Story of DRAGON EYE

龍眼物語

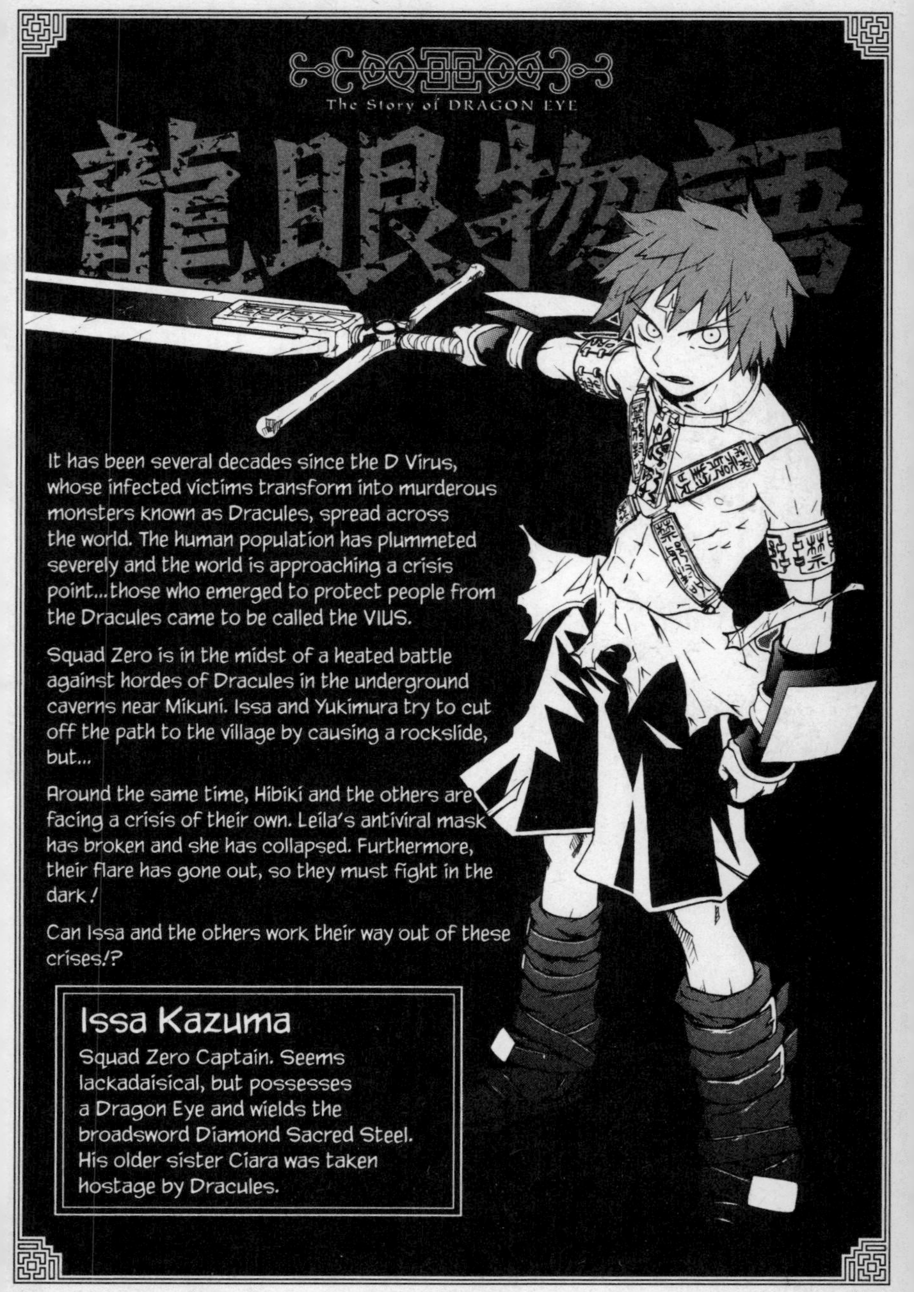

It has been several decades since the D Virus, whose infected victims transform into murderous monsters known as Dracules, spread across the world. The human population has plummeted severely and the world is approaching a crisis point...those who emerged to protect people from the Dracules came to be called the VIUS.

Squad Zero is in the midst of a heated battle against hordes of Dracules in the underground caverns near Mikuni. Issa and Yukimura try to cut off the path to the village by causing a rockslide, but...

Around the same time, Hibiki and the others are facing a crisis of their own. Leila's antiviral mask has broken and she has collapsed. Furthermore, their flare has gone out, so they must fight in the dark!

Can Issa and the others work their way out of these crises!?

Issa Kazuma

Squad Zero Captain. Seems lackadaisical, but possesses a Dragon Eye and wields the broadsword Diamond Sacred Steel. His older sister Ciara was taken hostage by Dracules.

Sôsei Yukimura

A former Squad Five member currently on temporary reassignment to Squad Zero. Believes Issa killed his twin sister—and so he wields twin blades in her memory and secretly plots for vengeance.

Leila Mikami

Newly inducted VIUS member. When she was little both her parents were killed by Dracules, and she alone survived. Her weapon of choice is the katana blade.

Kajiyama

Volunteer helper on loan from Squad Two. Uses rigged shells he invented himself that he fires from his bazooka. Has served on a mission with Issa once before.

Hibiki Masamune

Squad Six member. Volunteers as a helper on missions of the short-handed Squad Zero. Simultaneously wields the two giant blades he carries on his back in two-sword style.

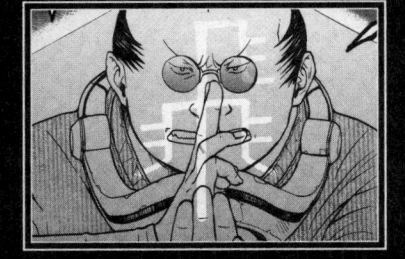

Nanbu

Volunteer helper on loan from Squad Seven. Expert at unarmed combat, but can cast certain spells as well. His short staff can serve to enhance his spell power.

Sazanami

Volunteer helper on loan from Squad Three. Wields a waistband whip containing spell power.

Mission ◉ Ten

If You Should Ever Recall This Day Someday

5

Mission ◉ Eleven

Leila's Errand

71

Mission ◉ Twelve

The Evil Plot in Motion

125

Extras

194

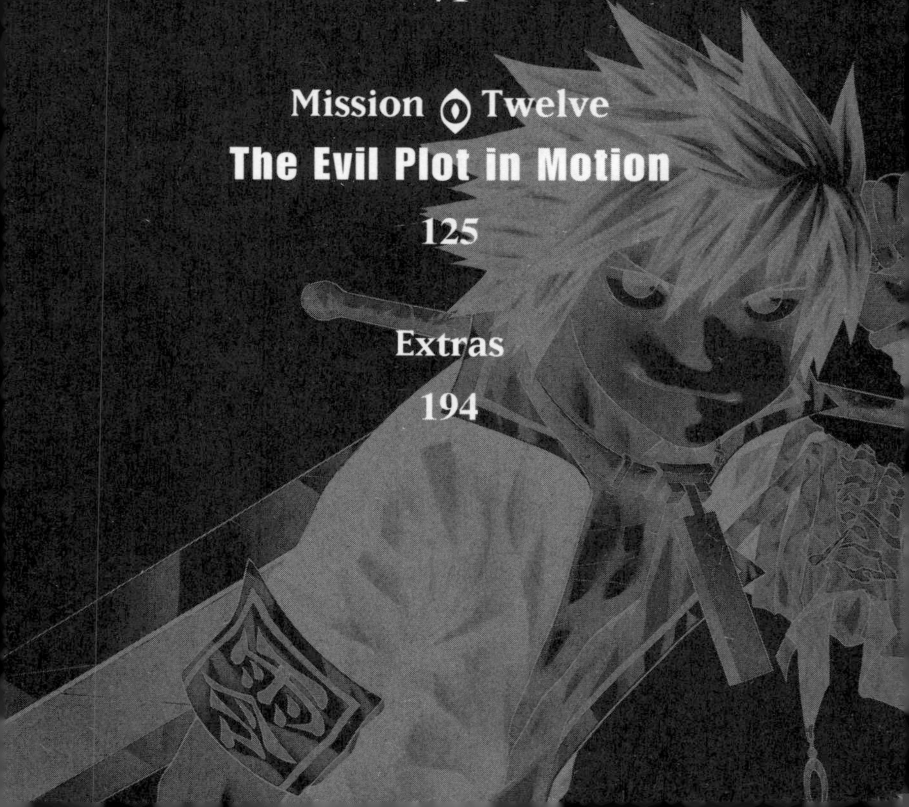

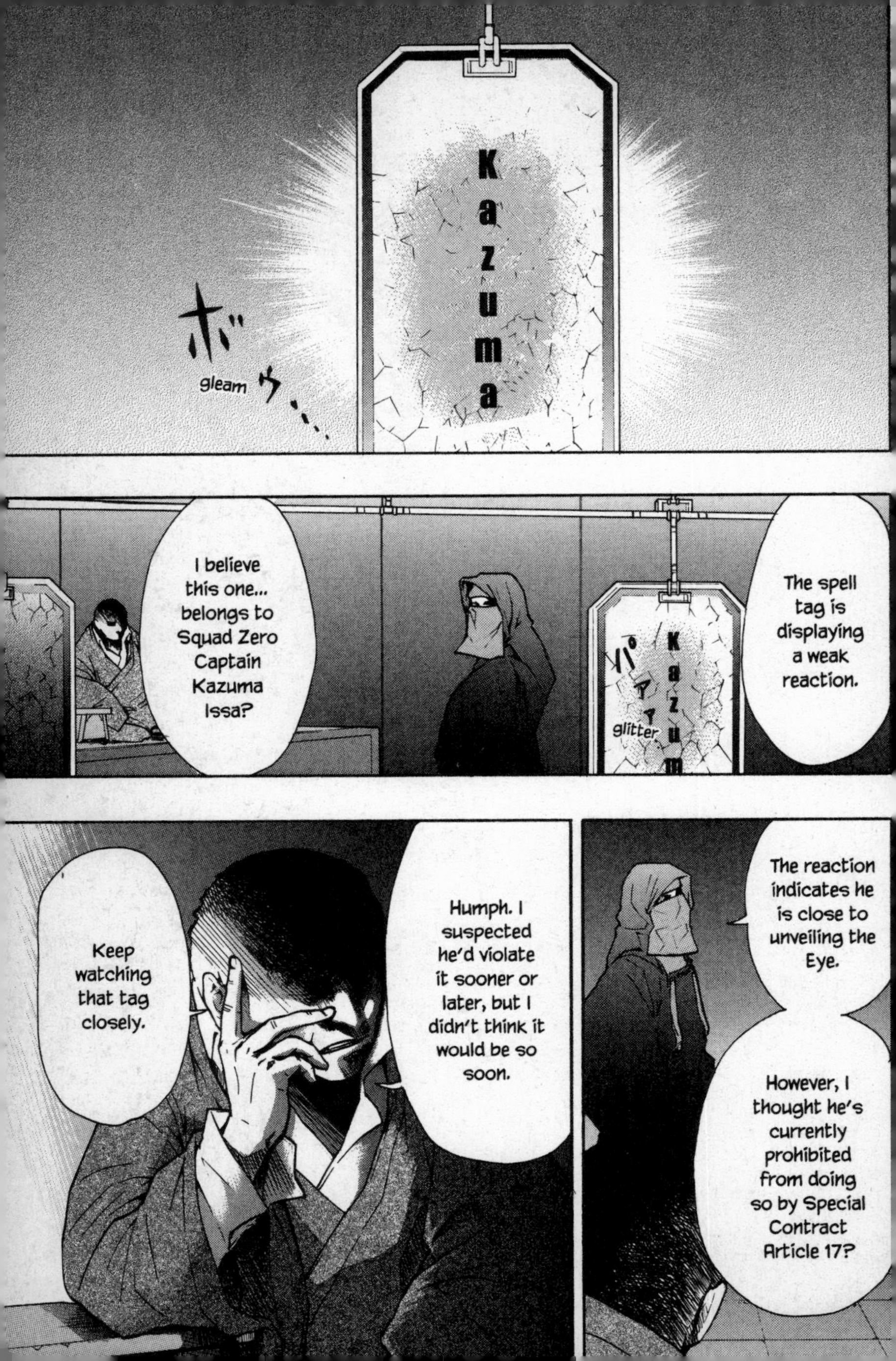
Kazuma
gleam
The spell tag is displaying a weak reaction.
glitter
I believe this one... belongs to Squad Zero Captain Kazuma Issa?
The reaction indicates he is close to unveiling the Eye.
However, I thought he's currently prohibited from doing so by Special Contract Article 17?
Humph. I suspected he'd violate it sooner or later, but I didn't think it would be so soon.
Keep watching that tag closely.

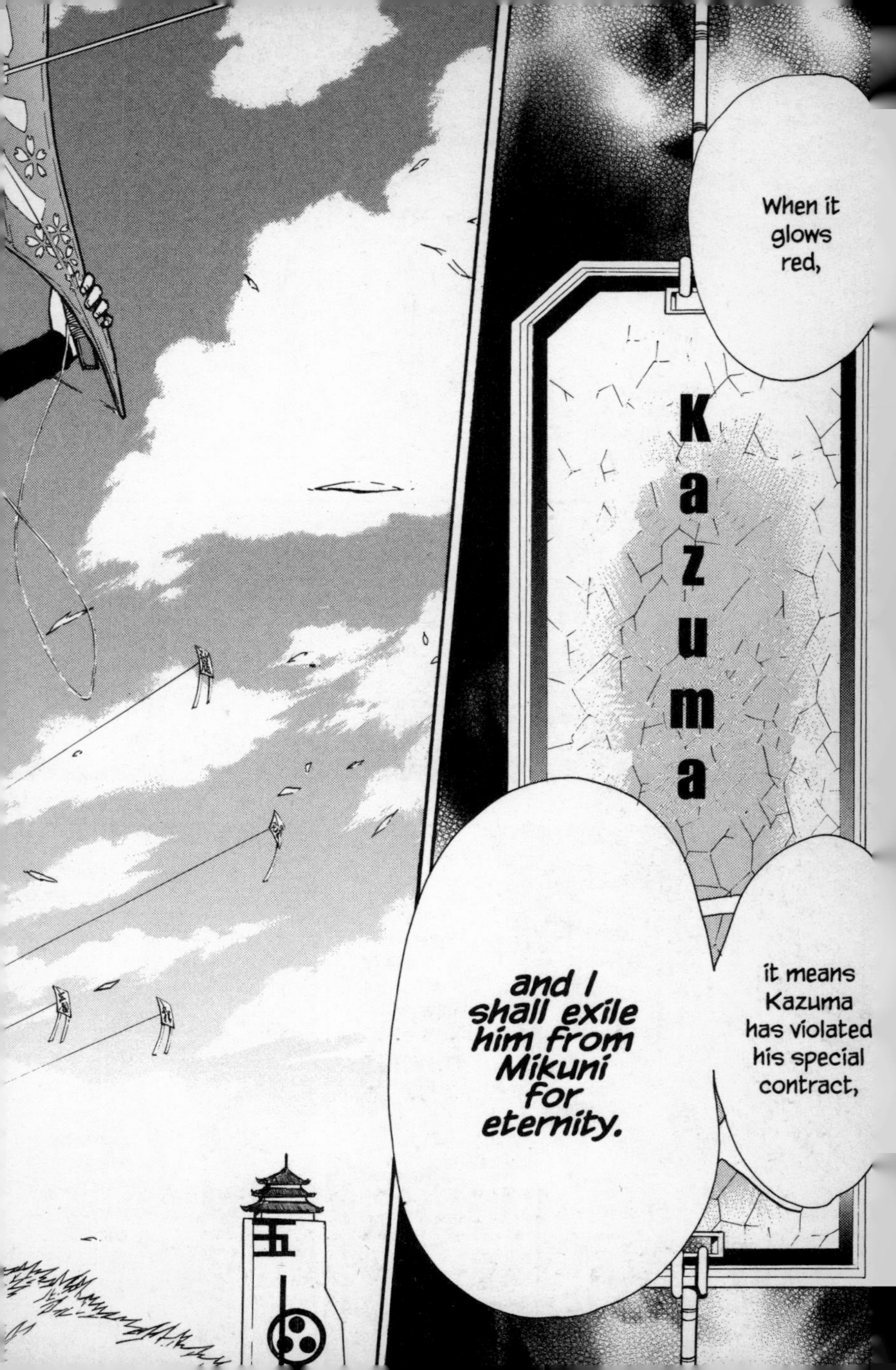
When it glows red,
Kazuma
it means Kazuma has violated his special contract,
and I shall exile him from Mikuni for eternity.

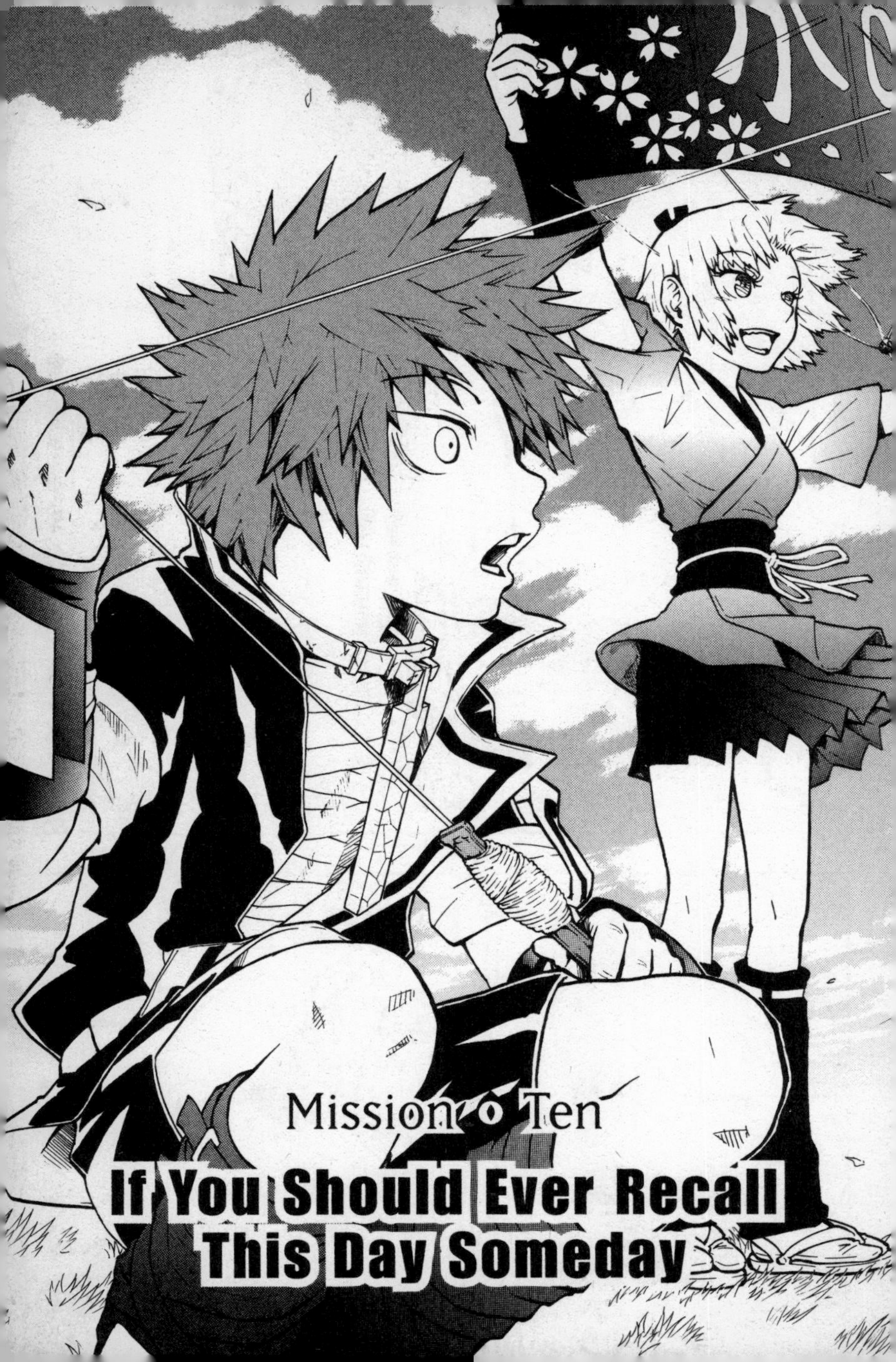
Mission ◦ Ten
If You Should Ever Recall
This Day Someday

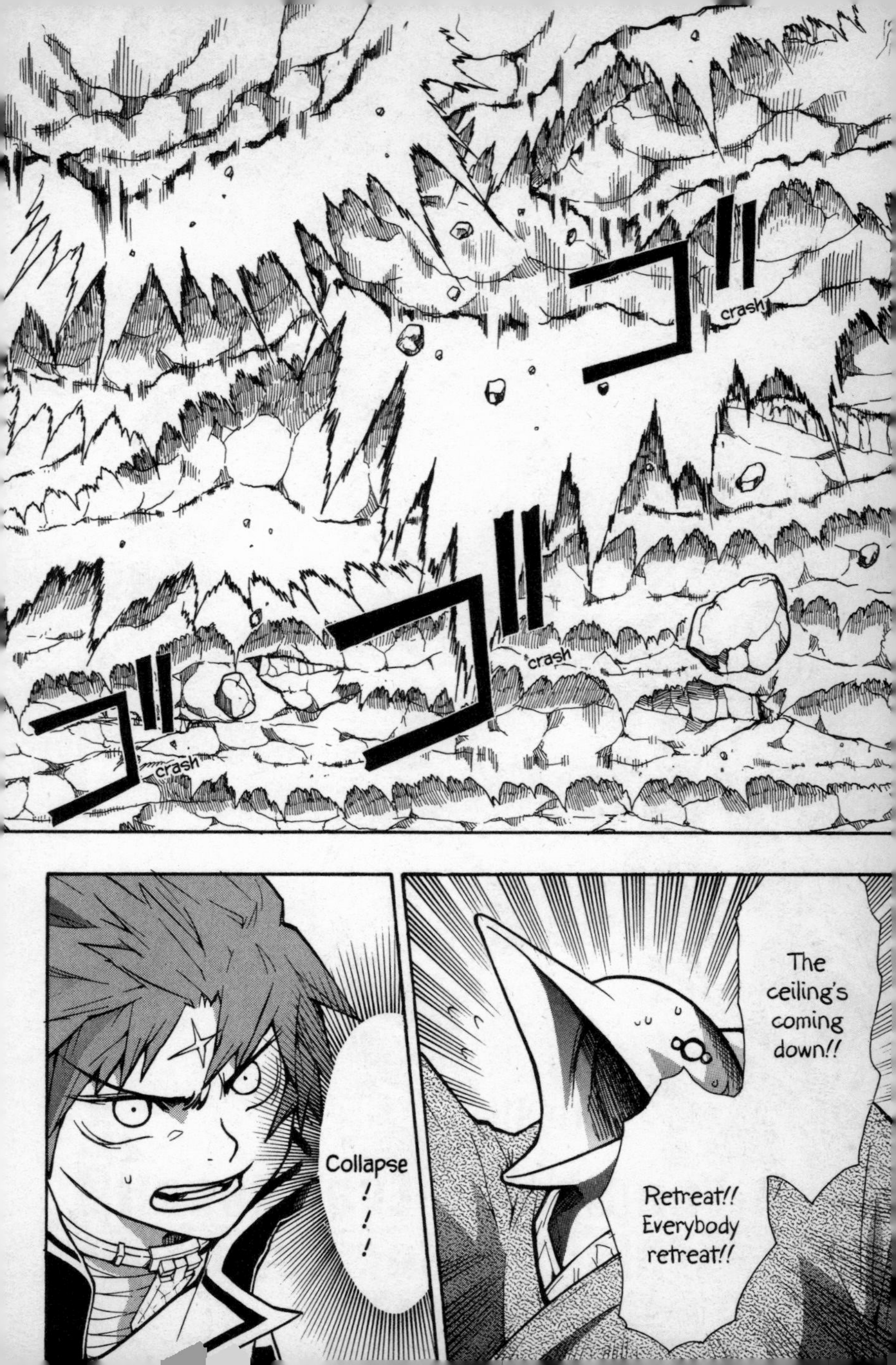
ゴ
crash
ゴ
crash
ゴ
crash
The ceiling's coming down!!
Retreat!! Everybody retreat!!
Collapse
!!!

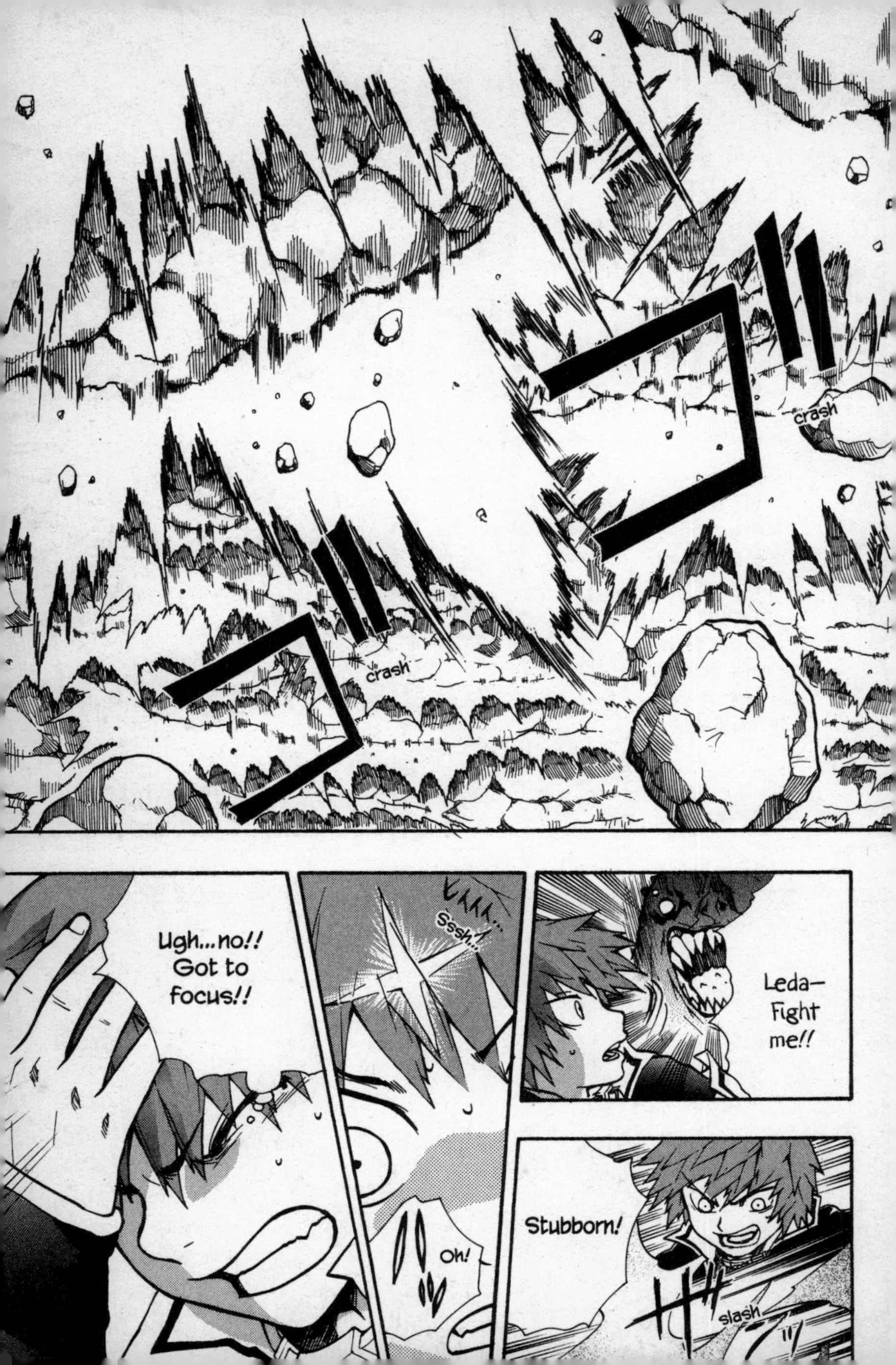
crash
crash
Leda—
Fight me!!
Stubborn!
slash
Sssh...
Oh!
Ugh...no!!
Got to
focus!!

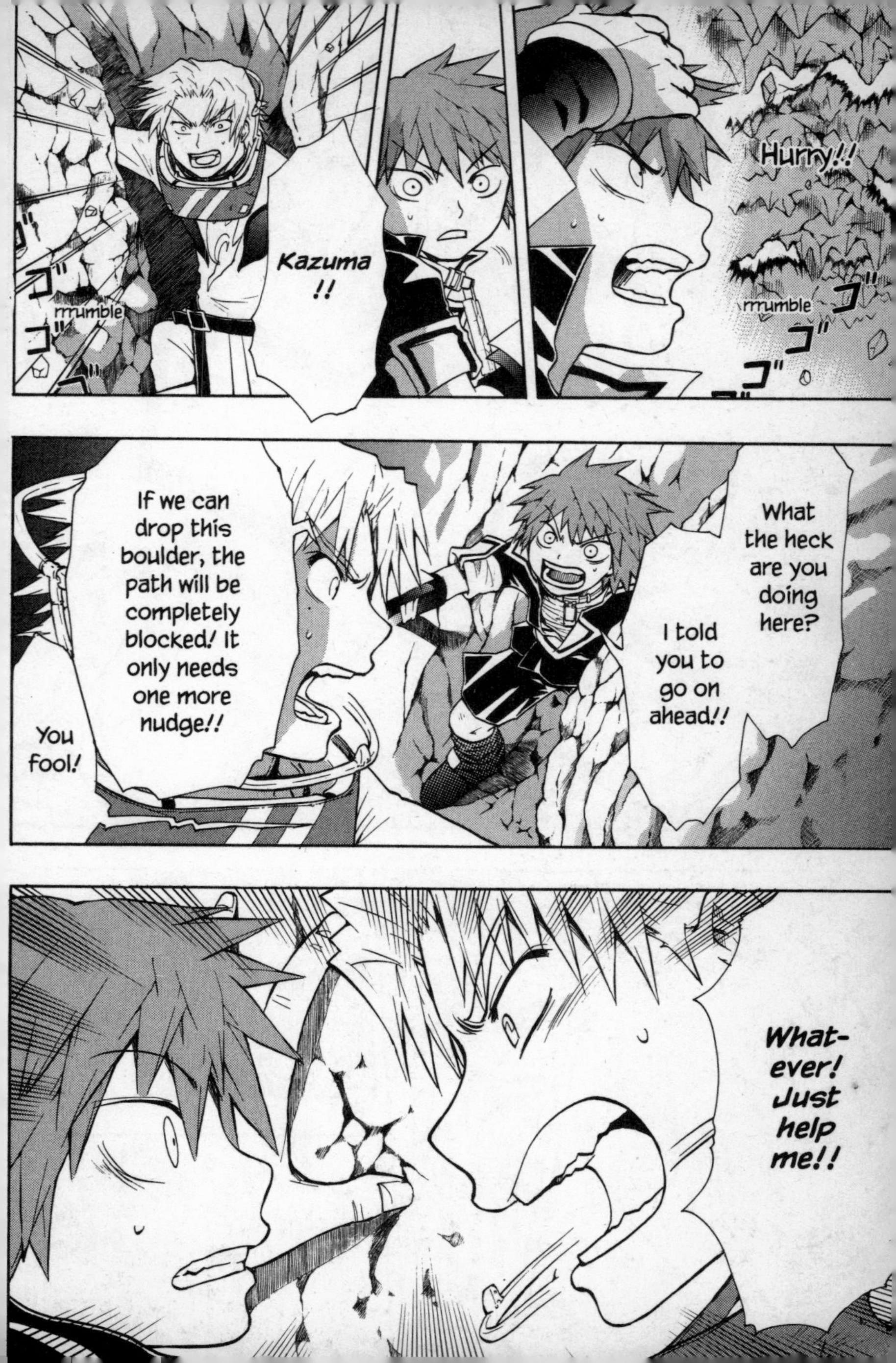
Hurry!!
rrrumble
Kazuma
!!
rrrumble
What the heck are you doing here?
I told you to go on ahead!!
If we can drop this boulder, the path will be completely blocked! It only needs one more nudge!!
You fool!
What-ever! Just help me!!

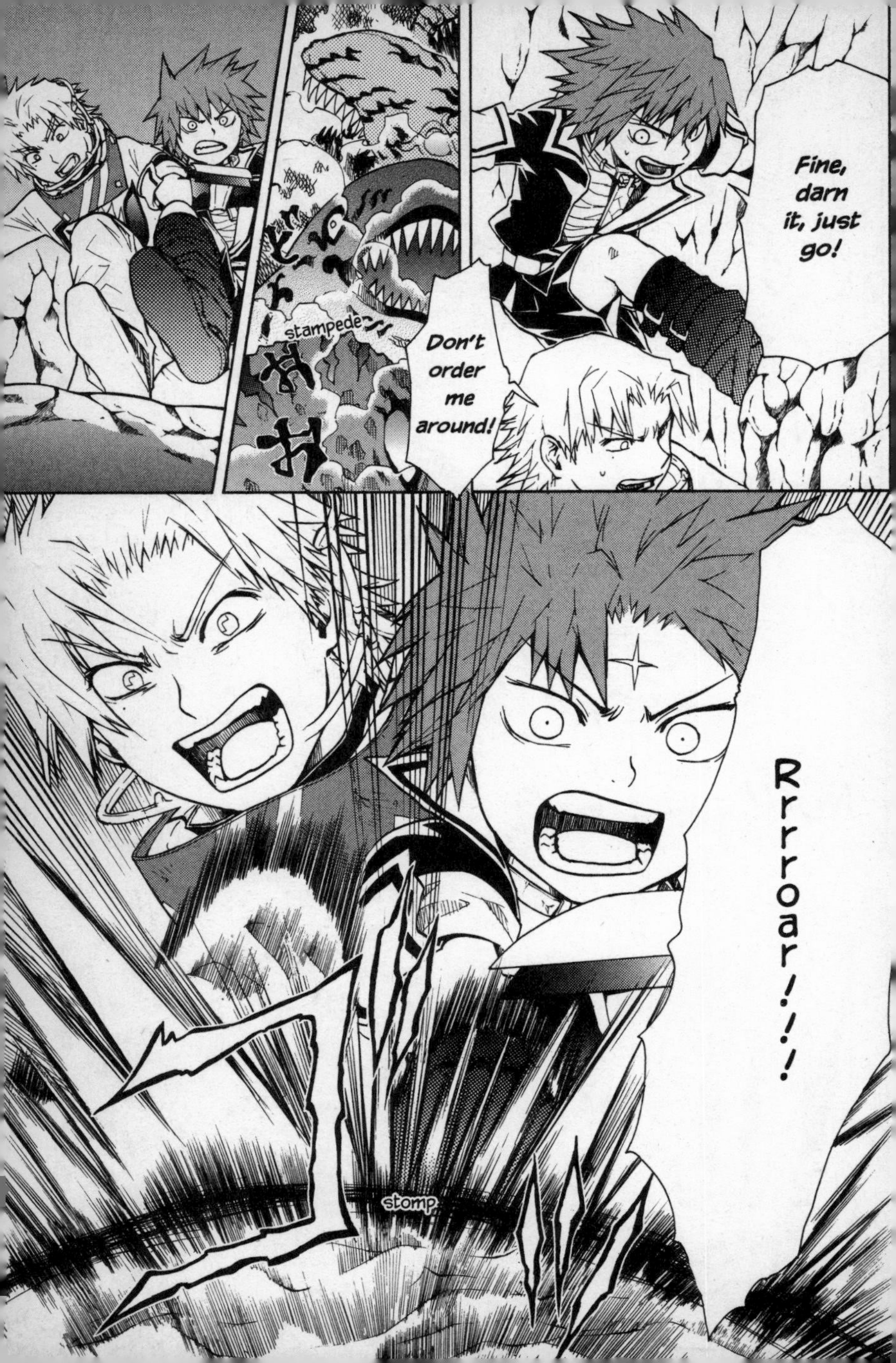
Fine, darn it, just go!
Don't order me around!
stampede
Rrroar!!!
stomp

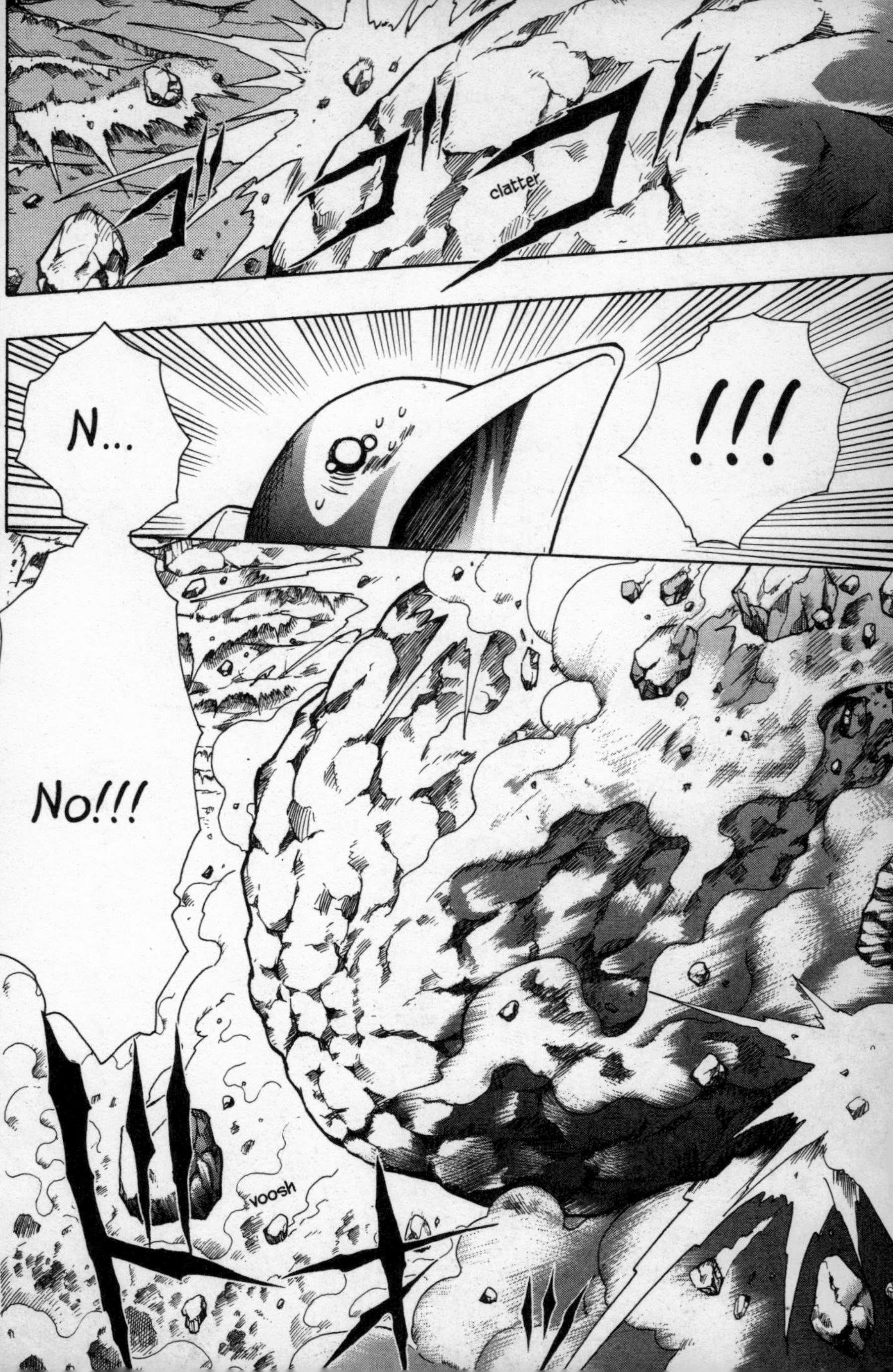
clatter
!!!
N...
No!!!
voosh

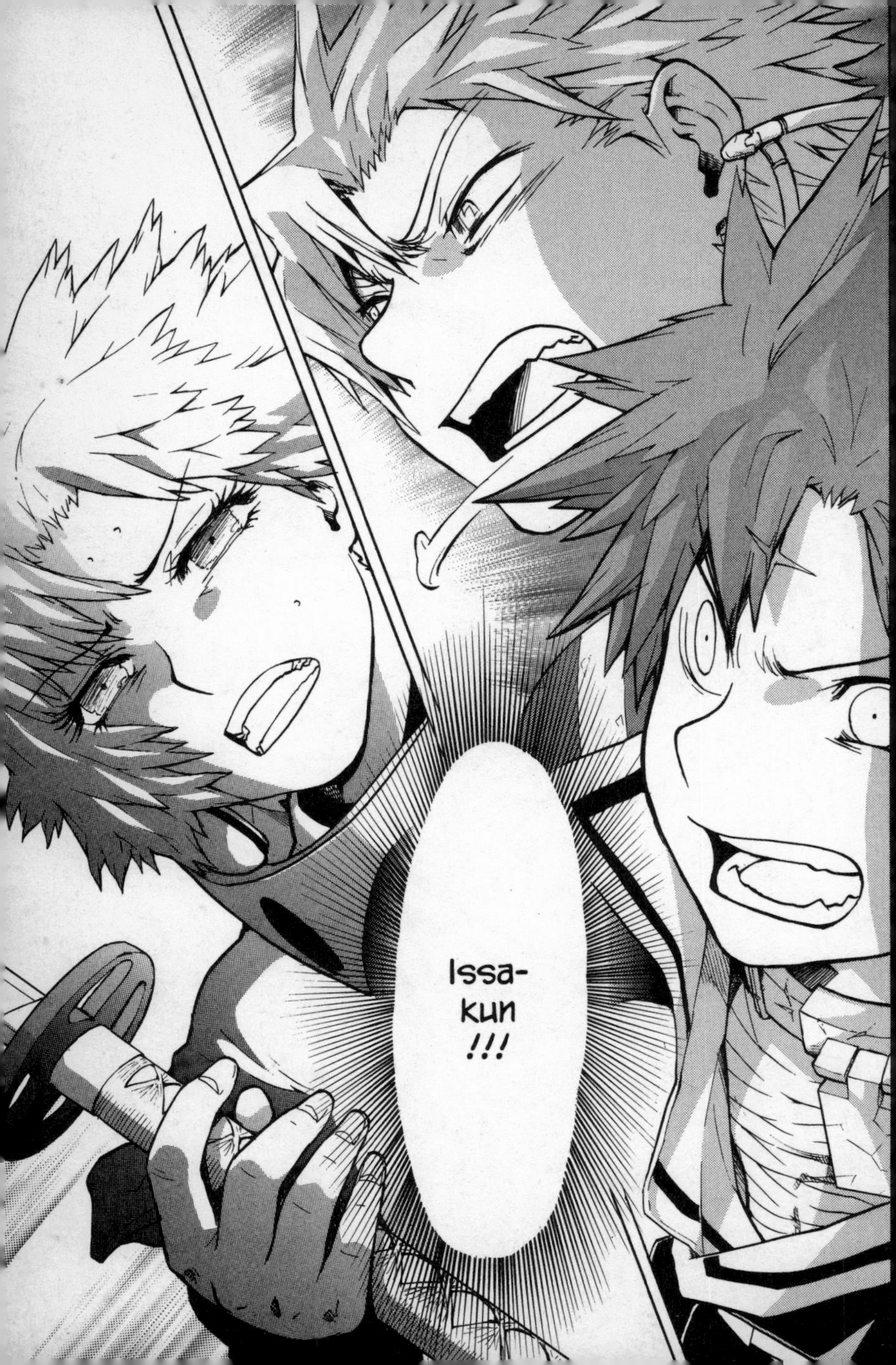
Issa-kun!!!

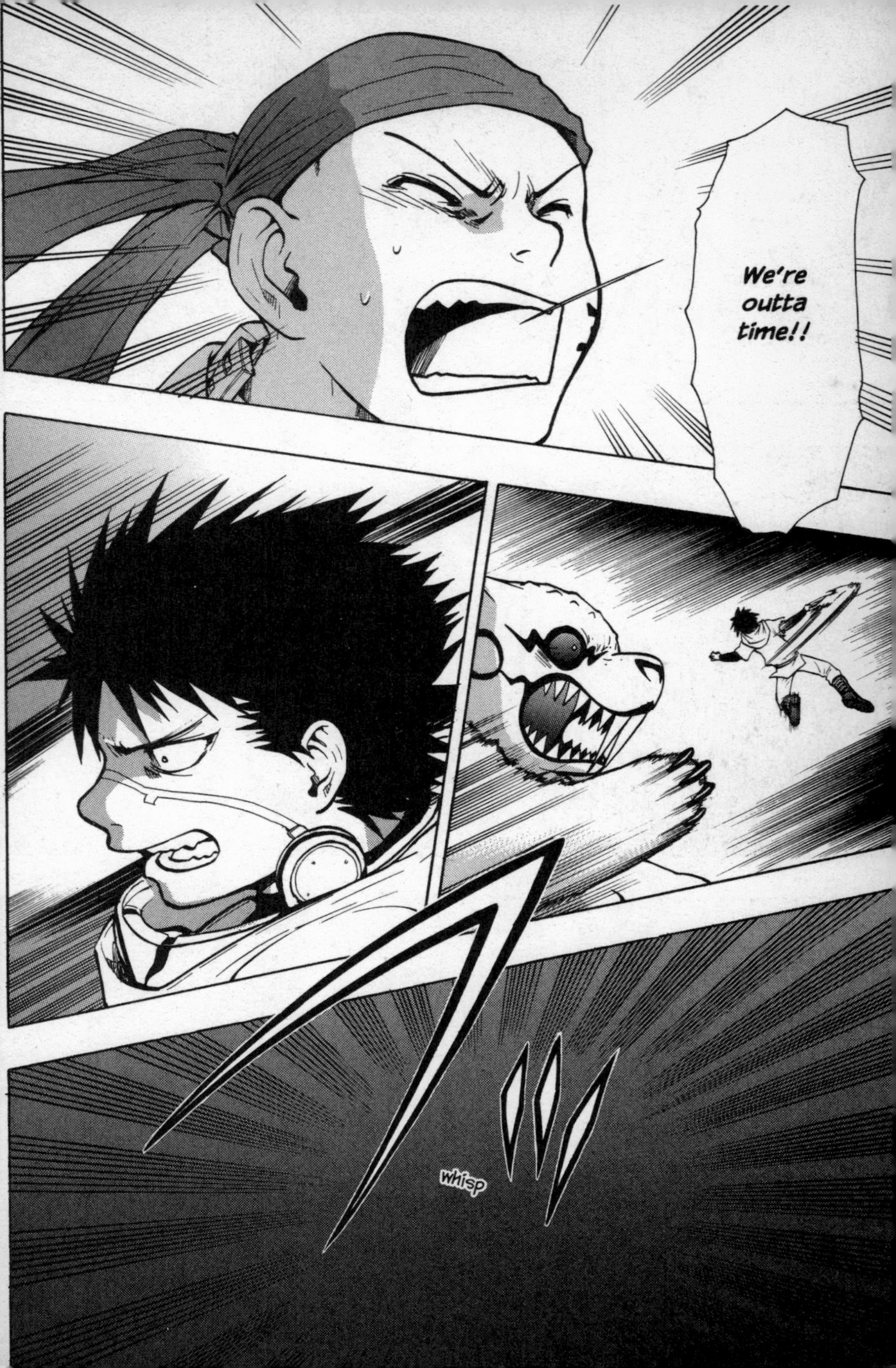
We're outta time!!
whisp

Darn it, can't see a thing!!
slash
stab
thudd
clod
Just keep cutting them down! And find a way out of here!!
slump
Why... d...does my body...
feel so stiff... faint...
Don't tell me... viral blood poisoning...

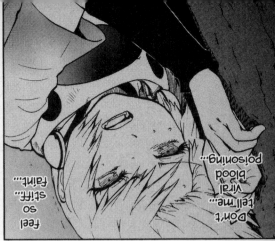

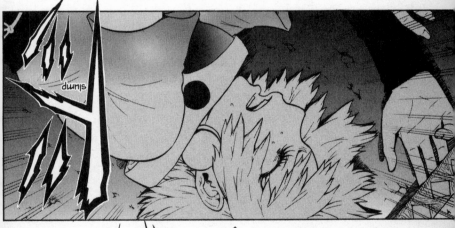

No... can't fall here, now!!
!
L...Light...
fwhoooo
outside ?
C...Can't move, even though so close...
G... Gotta tell the others...
Every-body !!
Can't... speak...!
Ah...

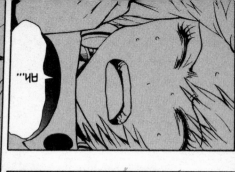

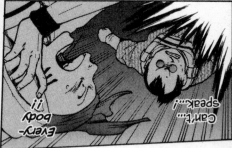

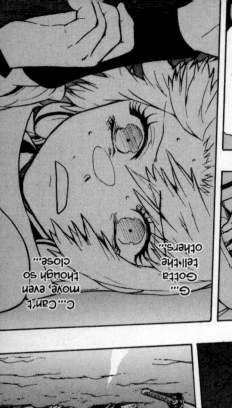

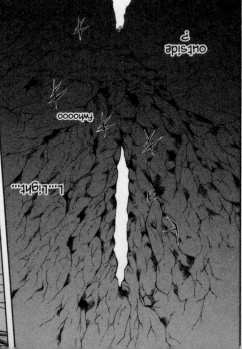

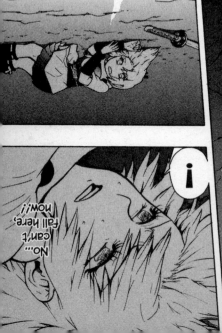

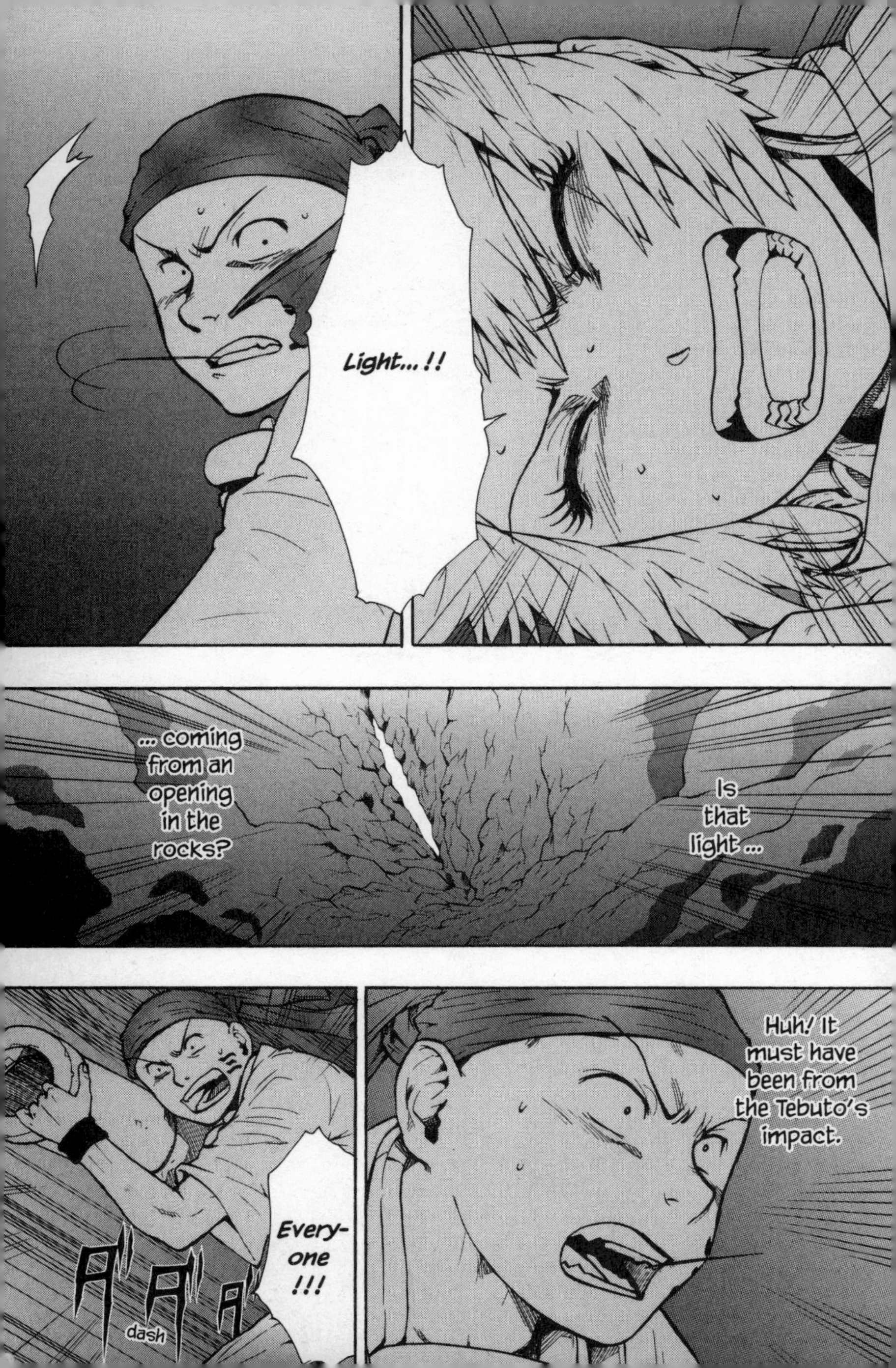
Light...!!
Is that light ...
... coming from an opening in the rocks?
Huh! It must have been from the Tebuto's impact.
Every-one !!!
dash

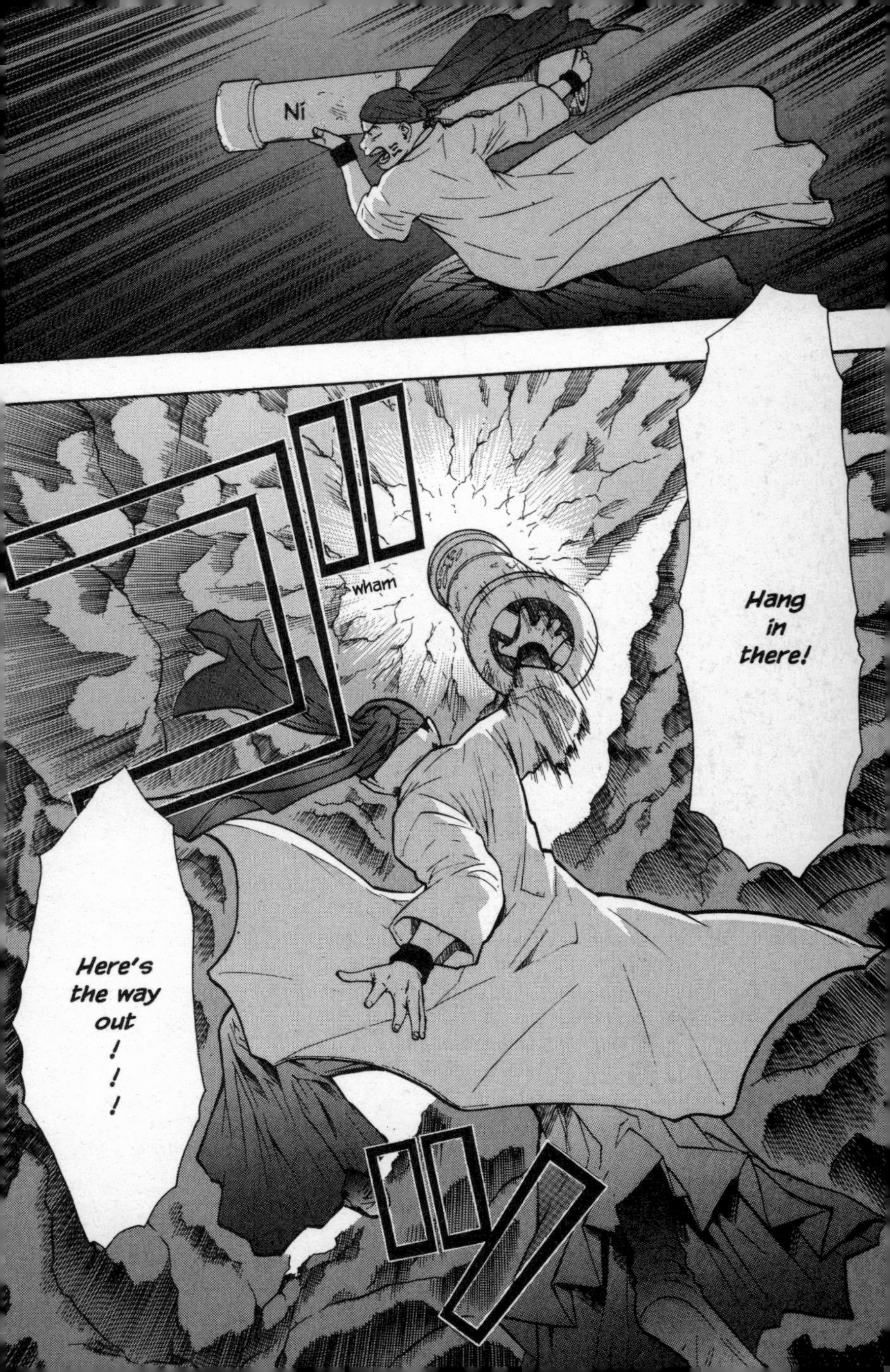
Ní
Hang in there!
wham
Here's the way out!!!

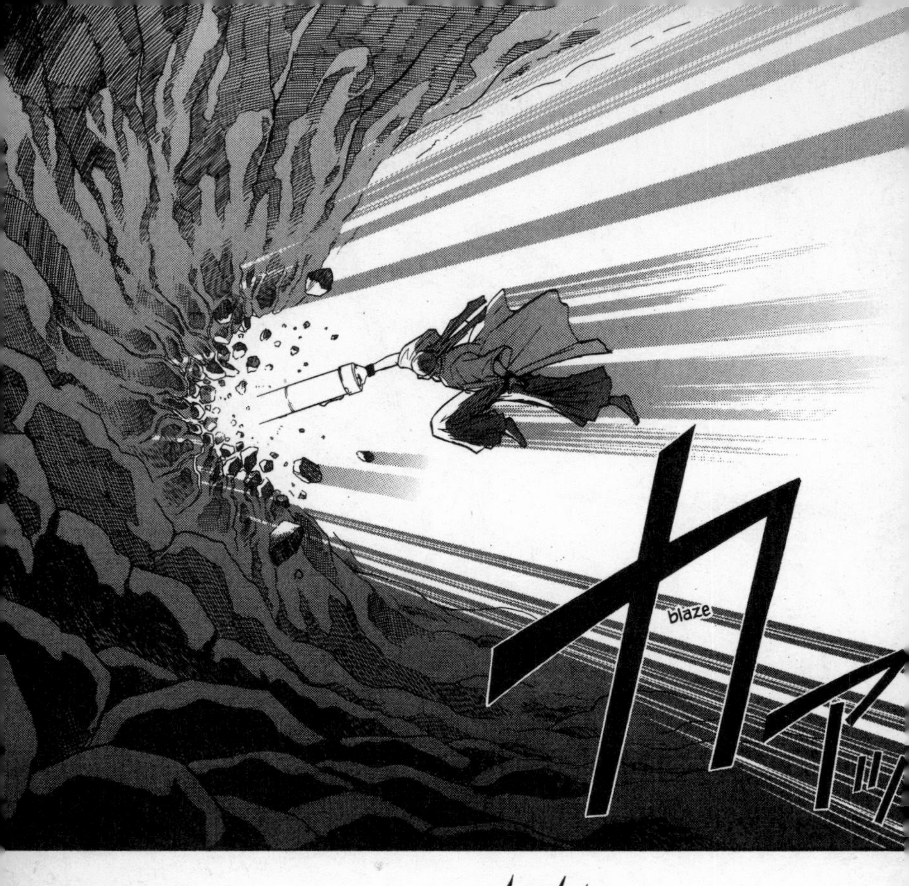
blaze
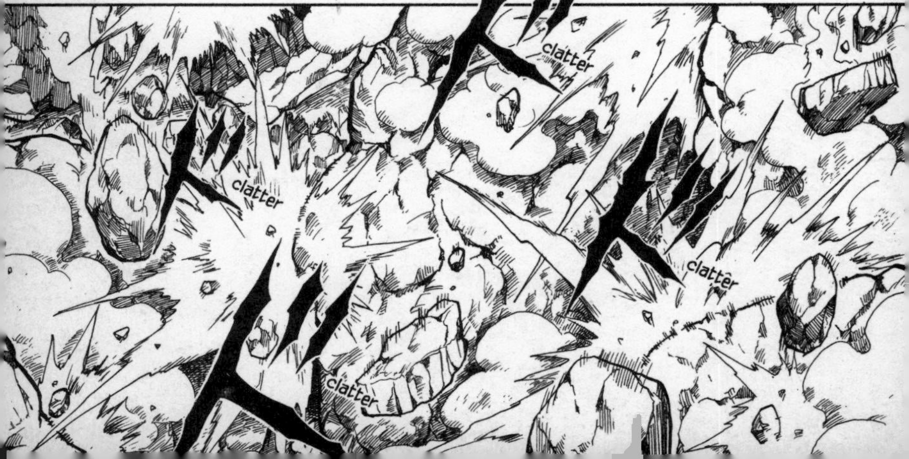
clatter
clatter
clatter
clatter

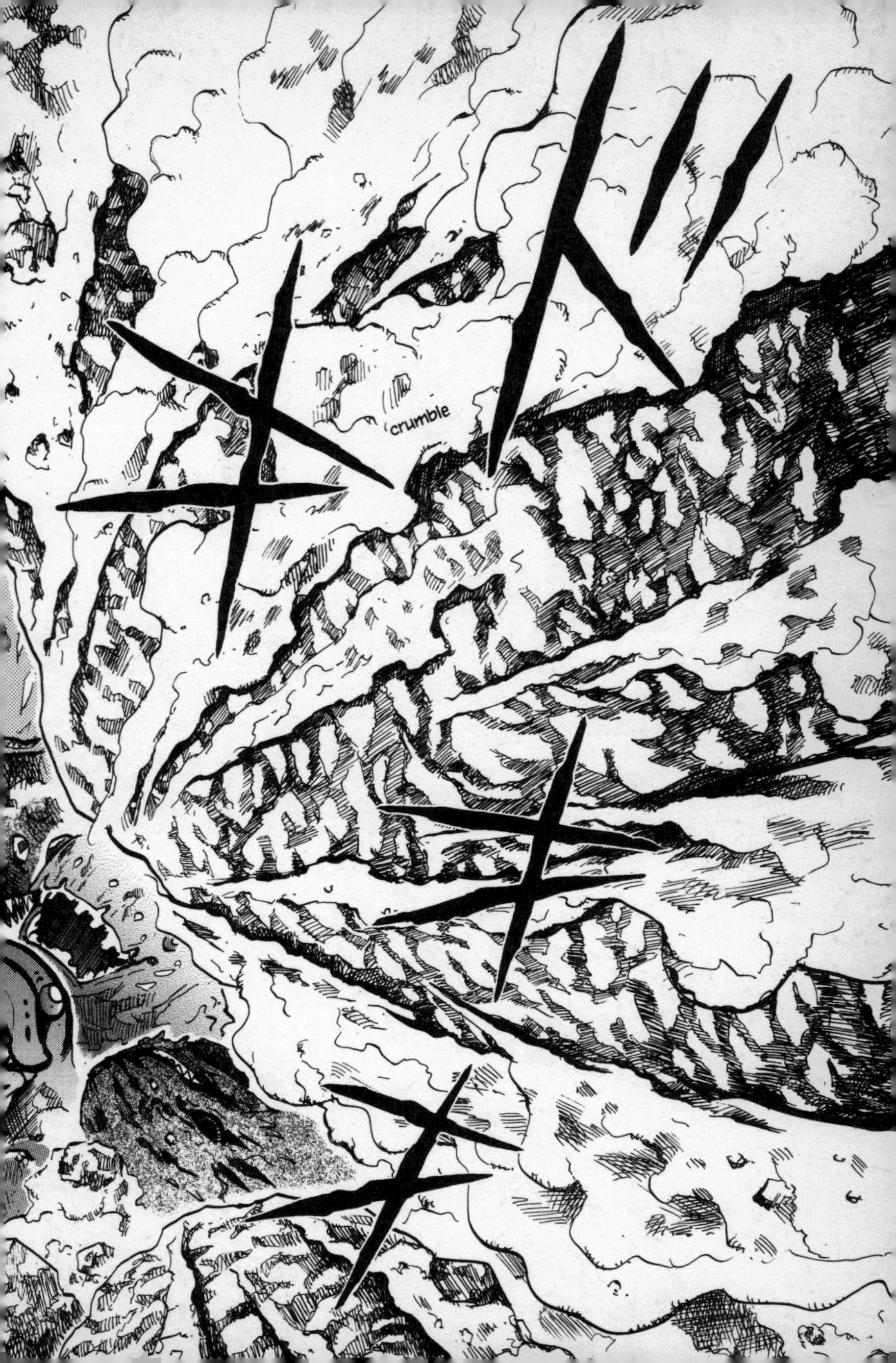
crumble

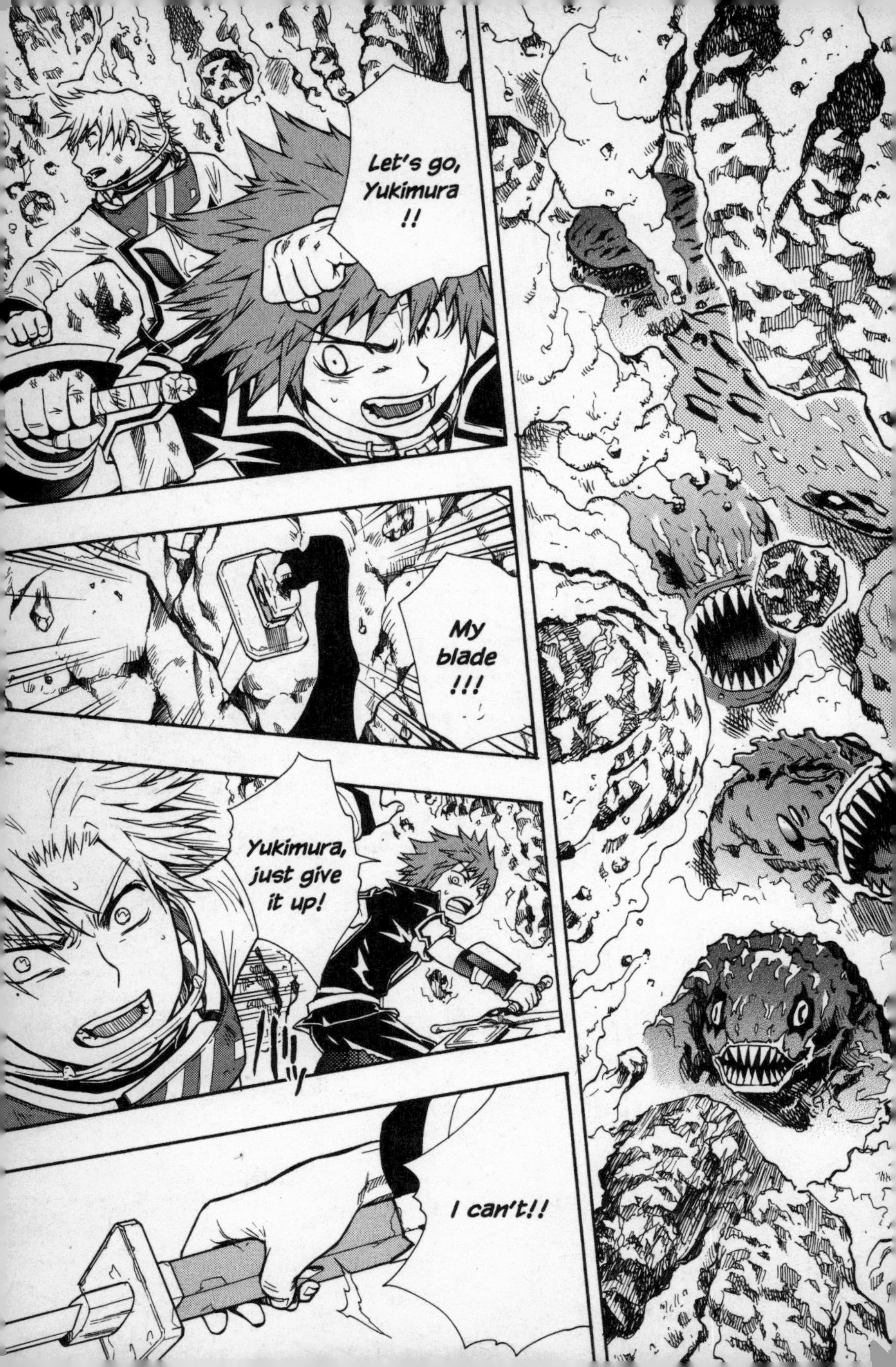
Let's go, Yukimura !!
My blade !!!
Yukimura, just give it up!
I can't!!

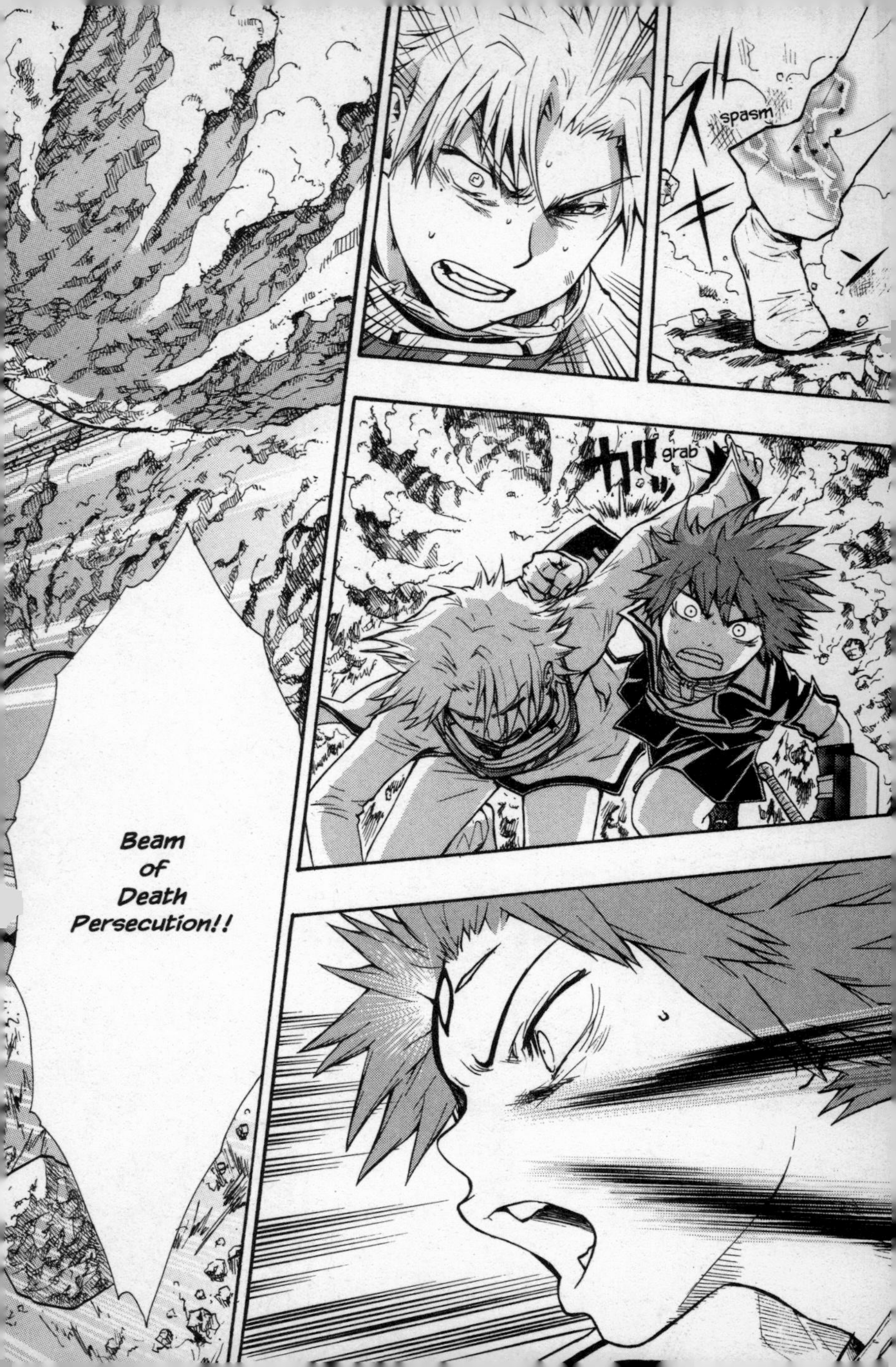
spasm
grab
Beam of Death Persecution!!

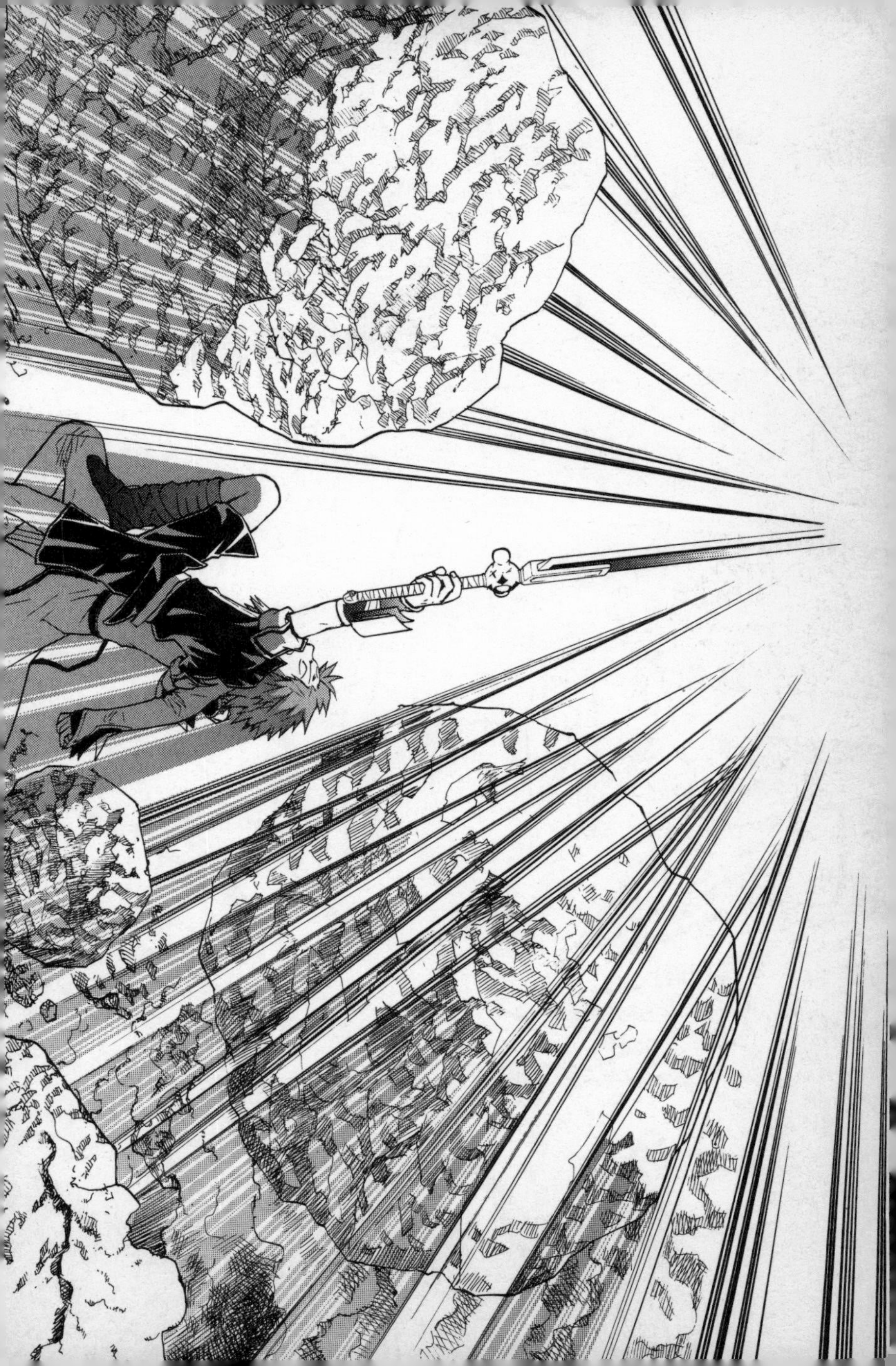

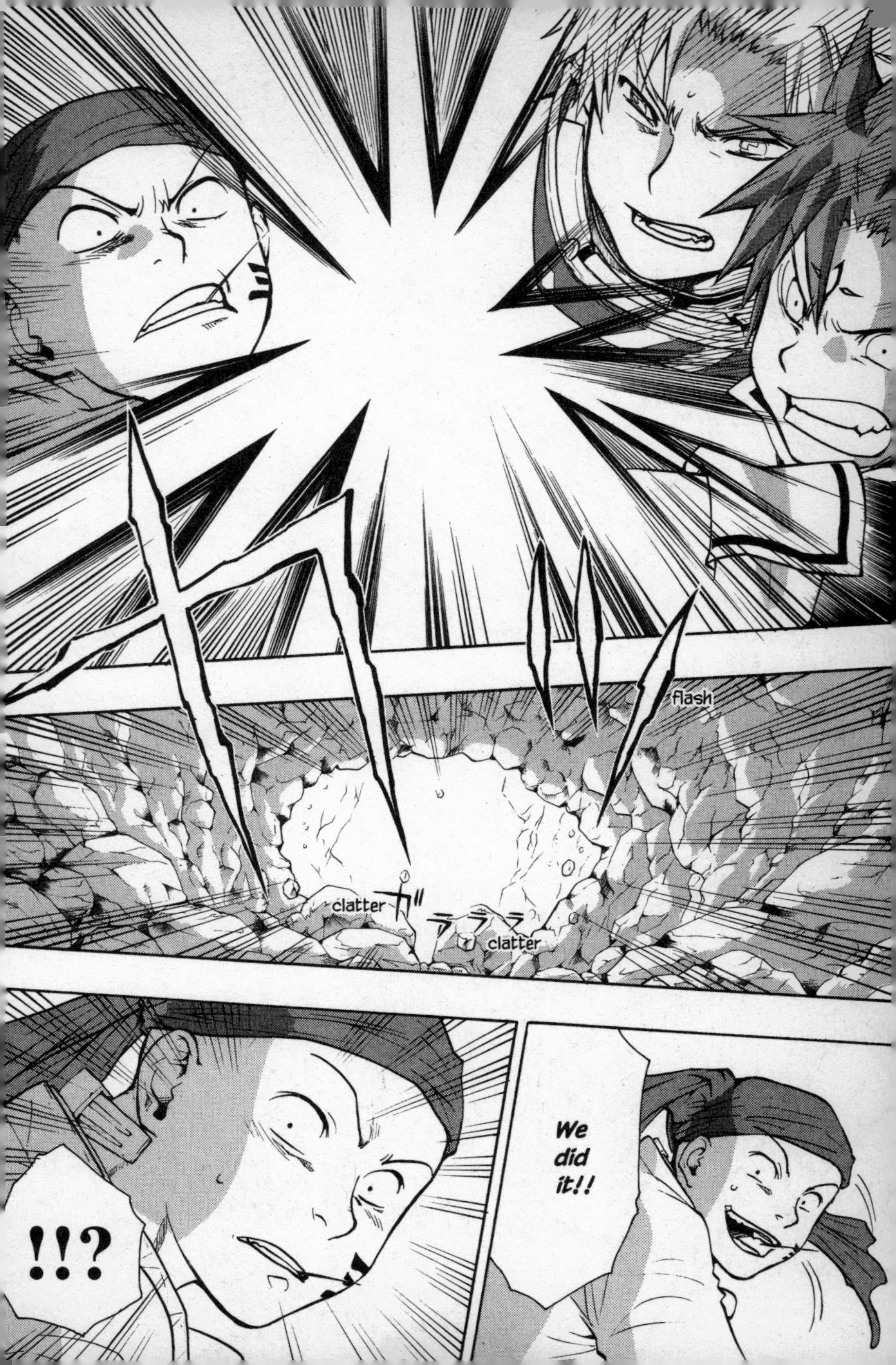
flash
clatter ガ
ラララ clatter
We did it!!
!!?

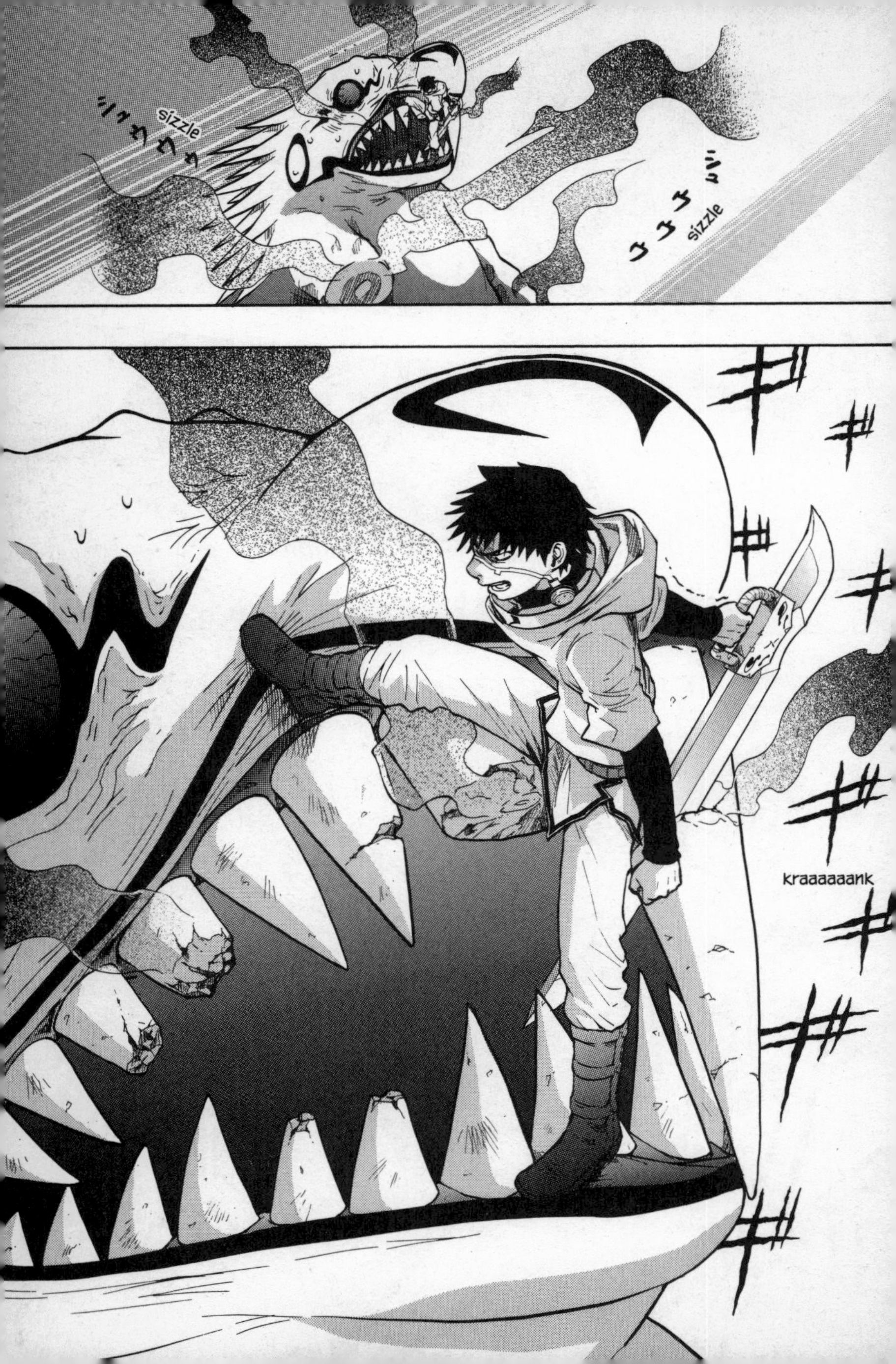
sizzle
sizzle
kraaaaaank

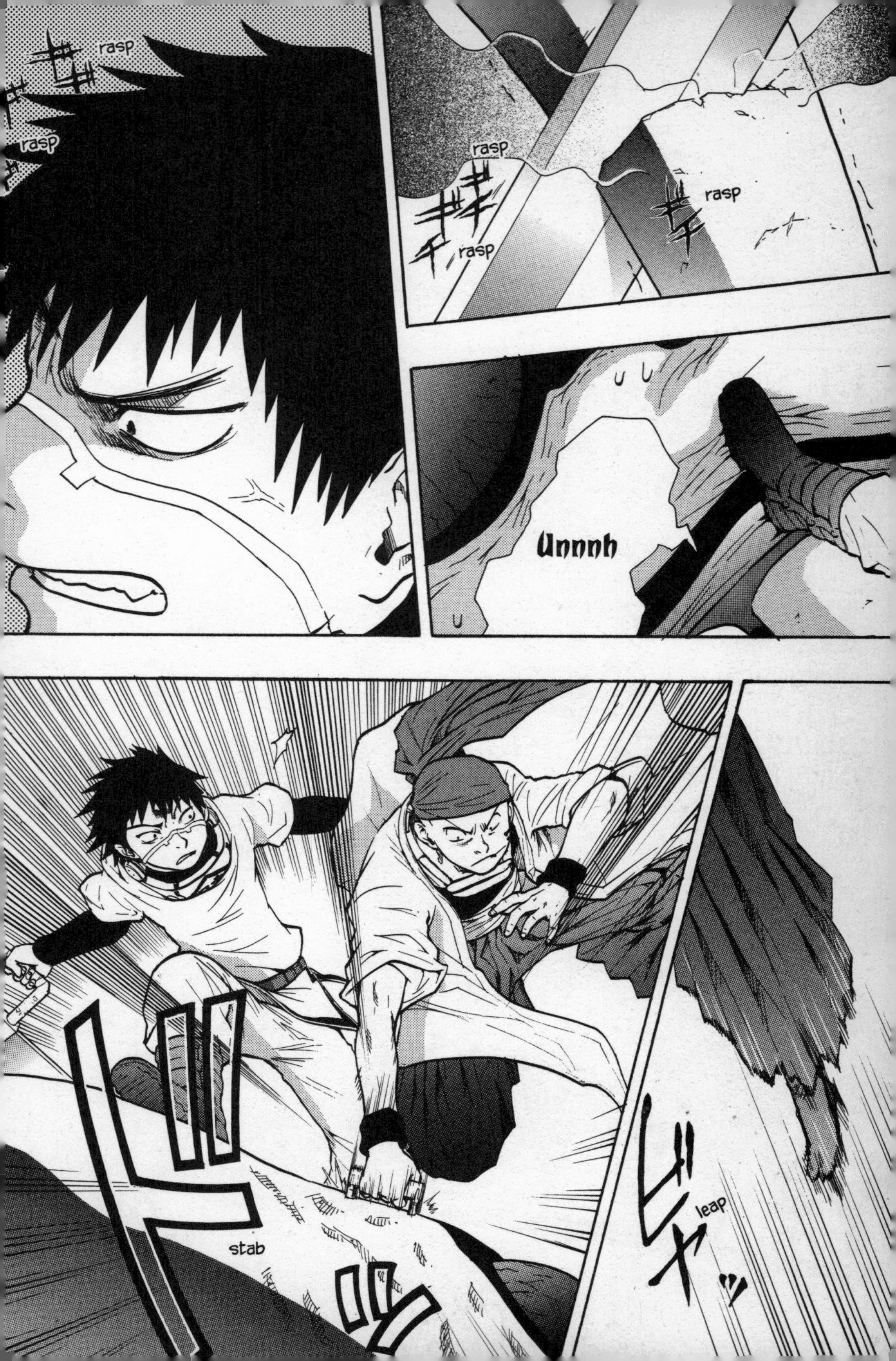
rasp
rasp
rasp
Unnnh
rasp
rasp
leap
stab

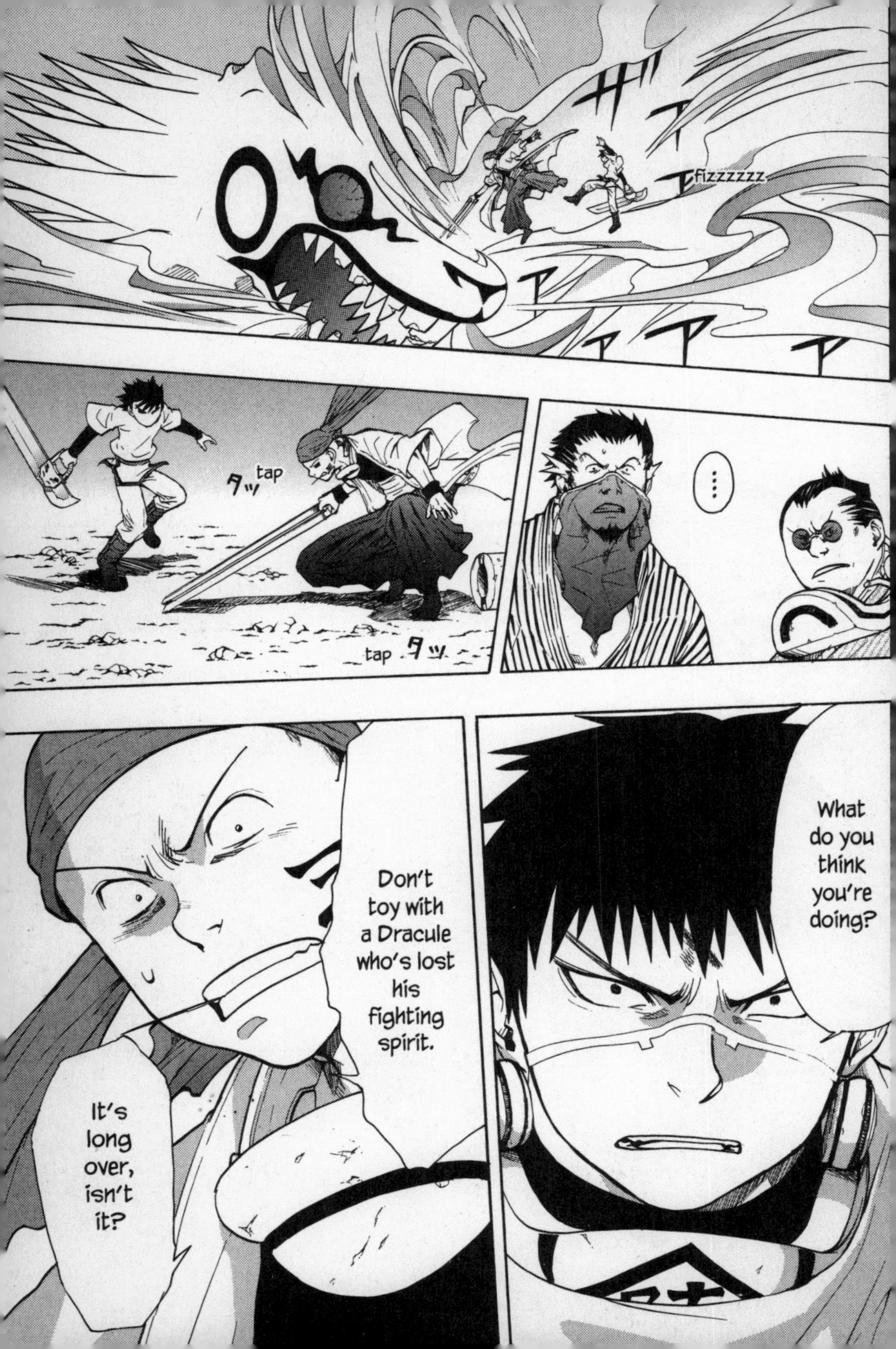

fizzzzzz
…
tap
tap
What do you think you're doing?
Don't toy with a Dracule who's lost his fighting spirit.
It's long over, isn't it?

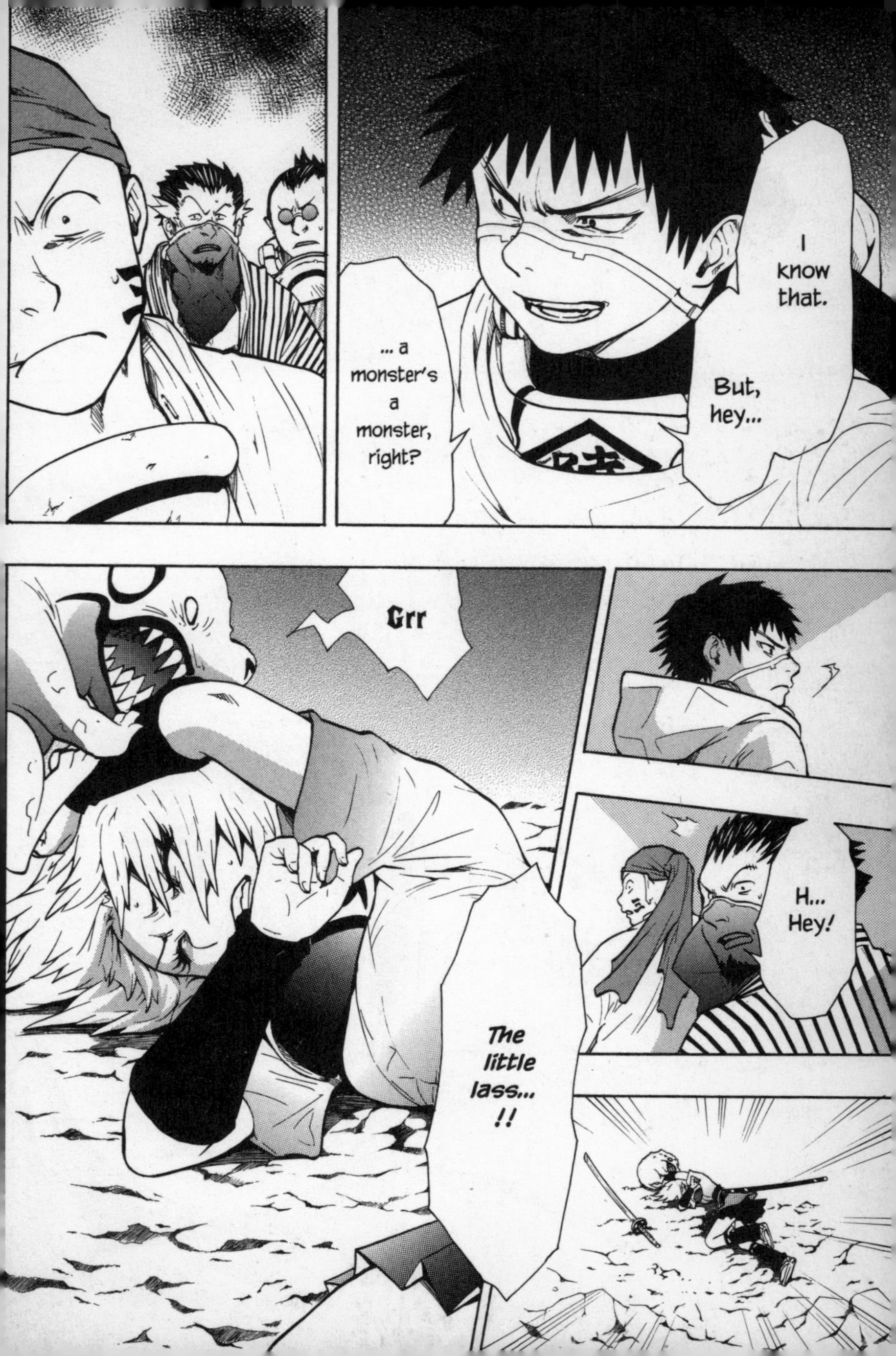
I know that.
But, hey...
... a monster's a monster, right?
H... Hey!
Grr
The little lass... !!

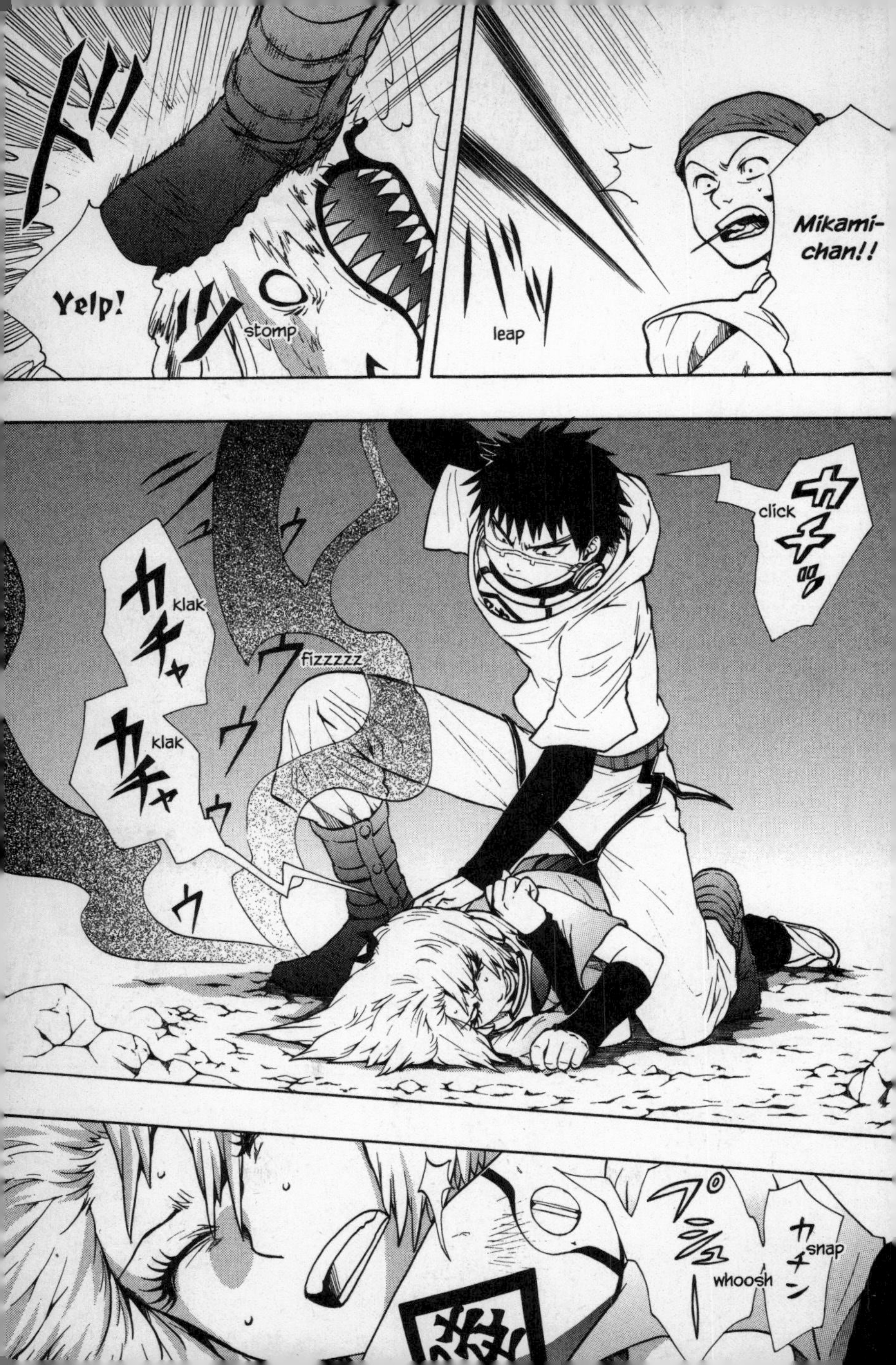
Mikami-chan!!
leap
stomp
Yelp!
click
カチャ
klak
カチャ
klak
fizzzzz
カチン
snap
whoosh

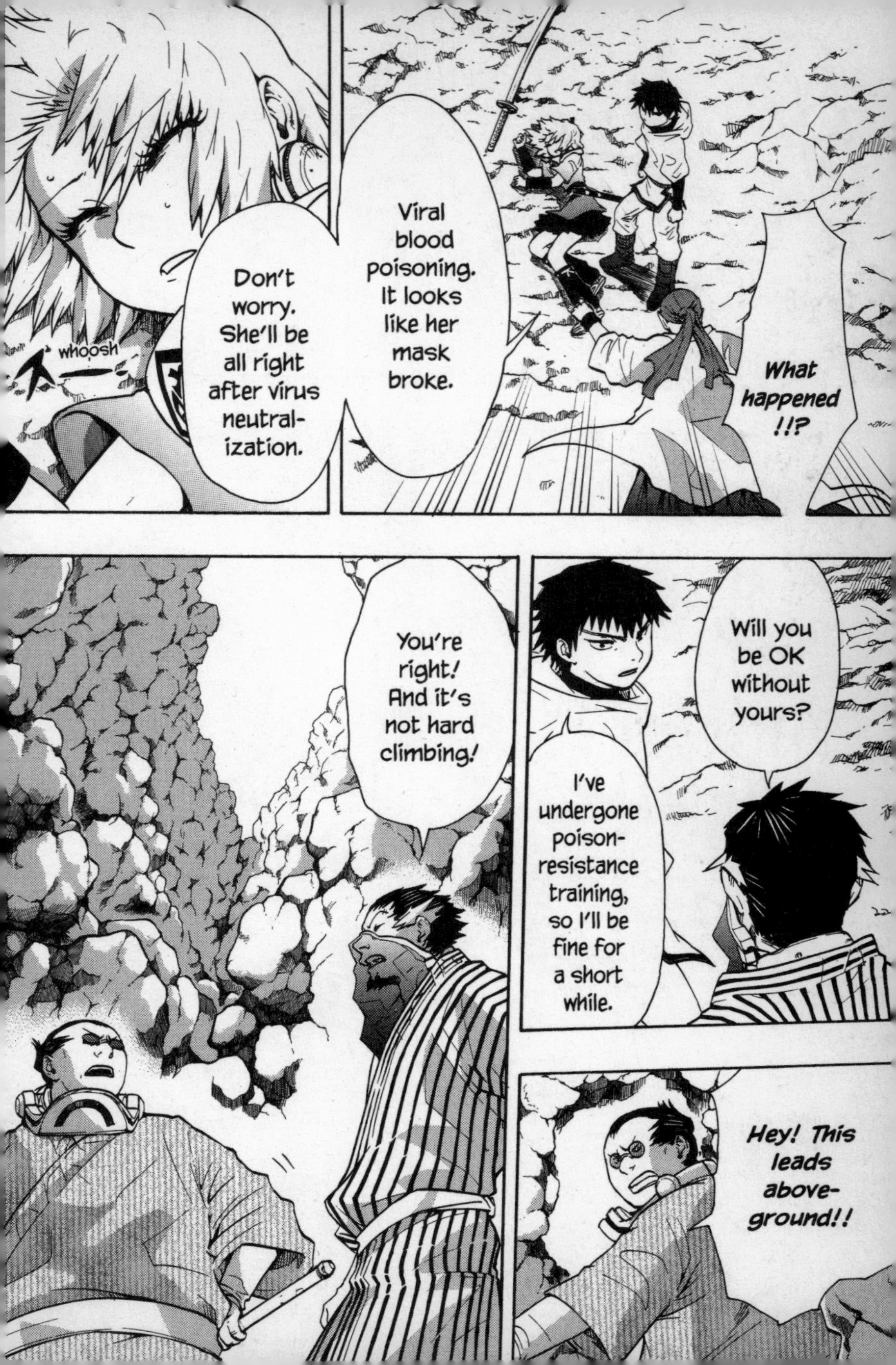
What happened!!?
Viral blood poisoning. It looks like her mask broke.
Don't worry. She'll be all right after virus neutral-ization.
whoosh
Will you be OK without yours?
I've undergone poison-resistance training, so I'll be fine for a short while.
Hey! This leads above-ground!!
You're right! And it's not hard climbing!

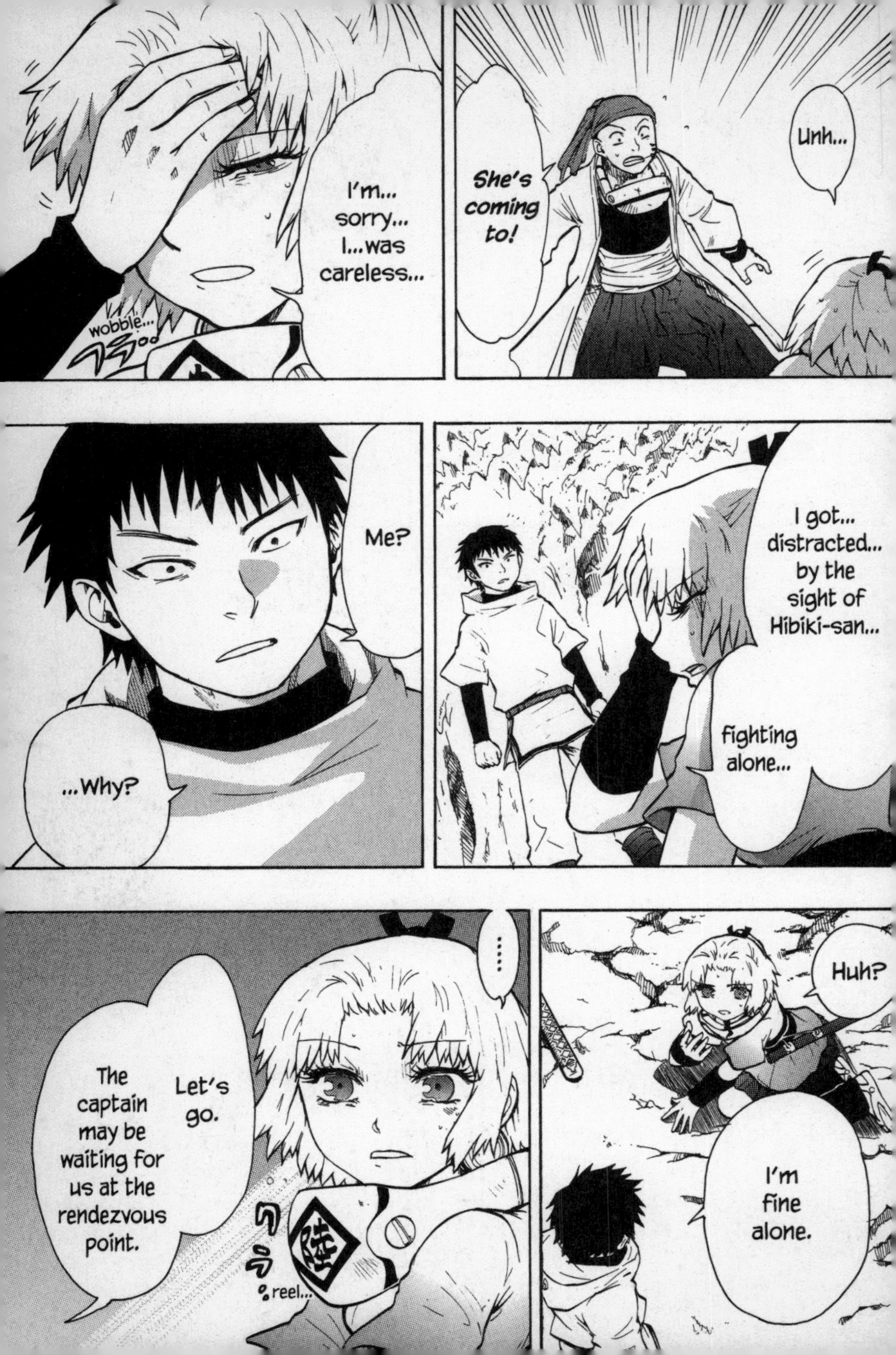
Unh...
She's coming to!
I'm... sorry... I...was careless...
wobble...
I got... distracted... by the sight of Hibiki-san...
fighting alone...
Me?
...Why?
Huh?
I'm fine alone.
.....
Let's go.
The captain may be waiting for us at the rendezvous point.
reel...

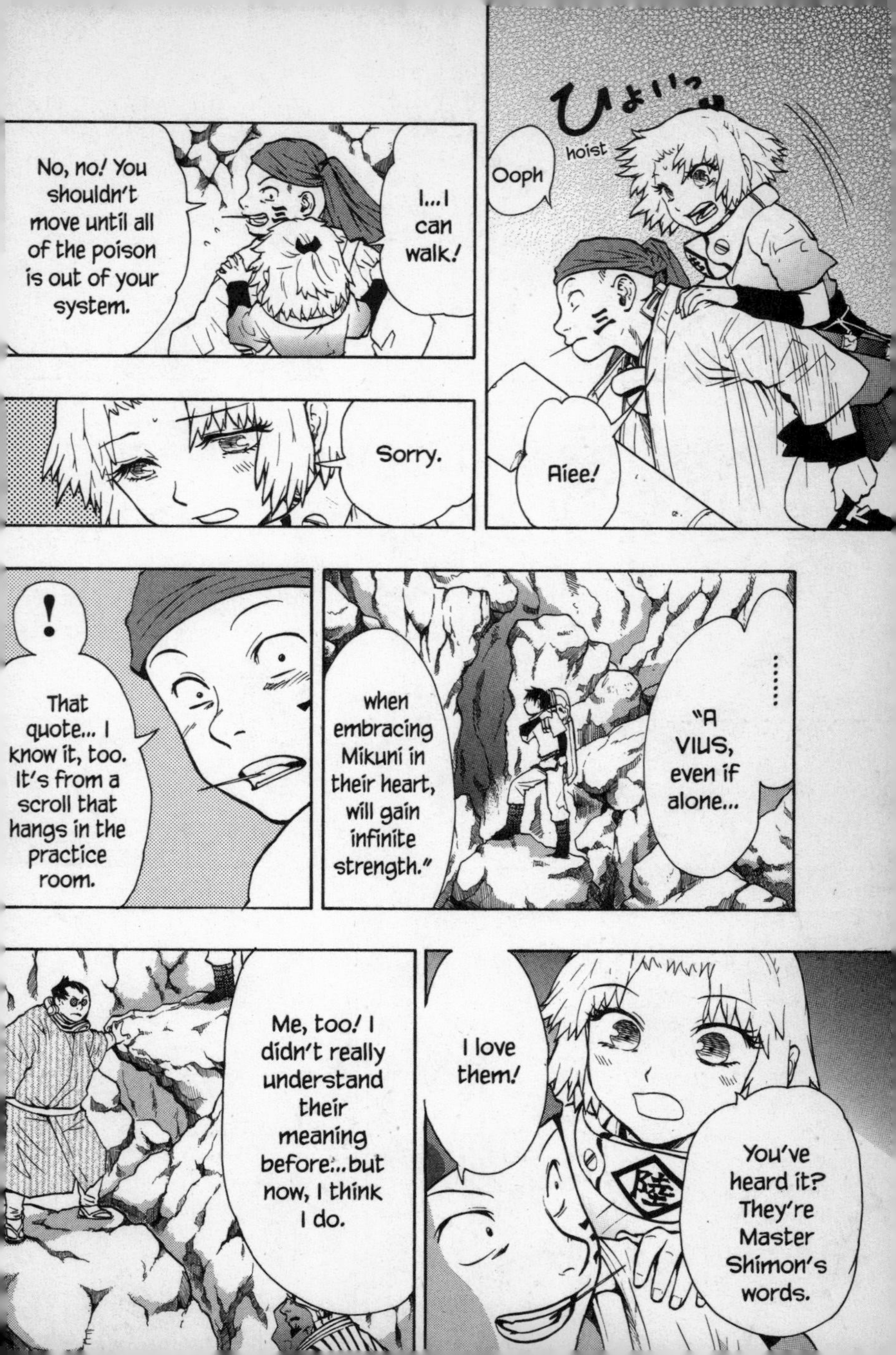
ひょいっ
hoist
Ooph
Aiee!
I...I can walk!
No, no! You shouldn't move until all of the poison is out of your system.
Sorry.
......
"A VIUS, even if alone...
when embracing Mikuni in their heart, will gain infinite strength."
!
That quote... I know it, too. It's from a scroll that hangs in the practice room.
You've heard it? They're Master Shimon's words.
I love them!
Me, too! I didn't really understand their meaning before...but now, I think I do.

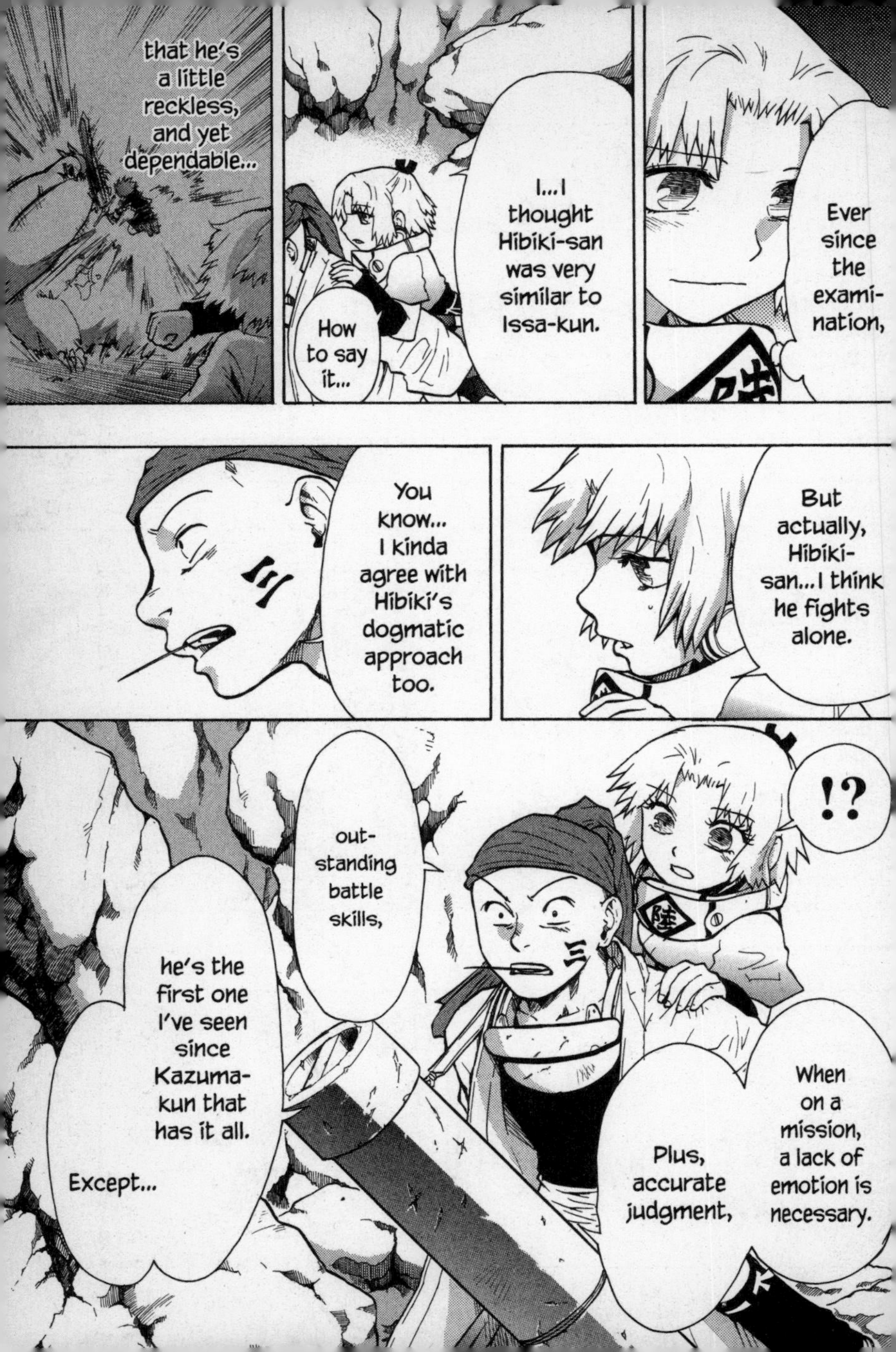
Ever since the examination,
I...I thought Hibiki-san was very similar to Issa-kun.
How to say it...
that he's a little reckless, and yet dependable...
But actually, Hibiki-san...I think he fights alone.
You know... I kinda agree with Hibiki's dogmatic approach too.
!?
When on a mission, a lack of emotion is necessary.
Plus, accurate judgment,
out-standing battle skills,
he's the first one I've seen since Kazuma-kun that has it all.
Except...

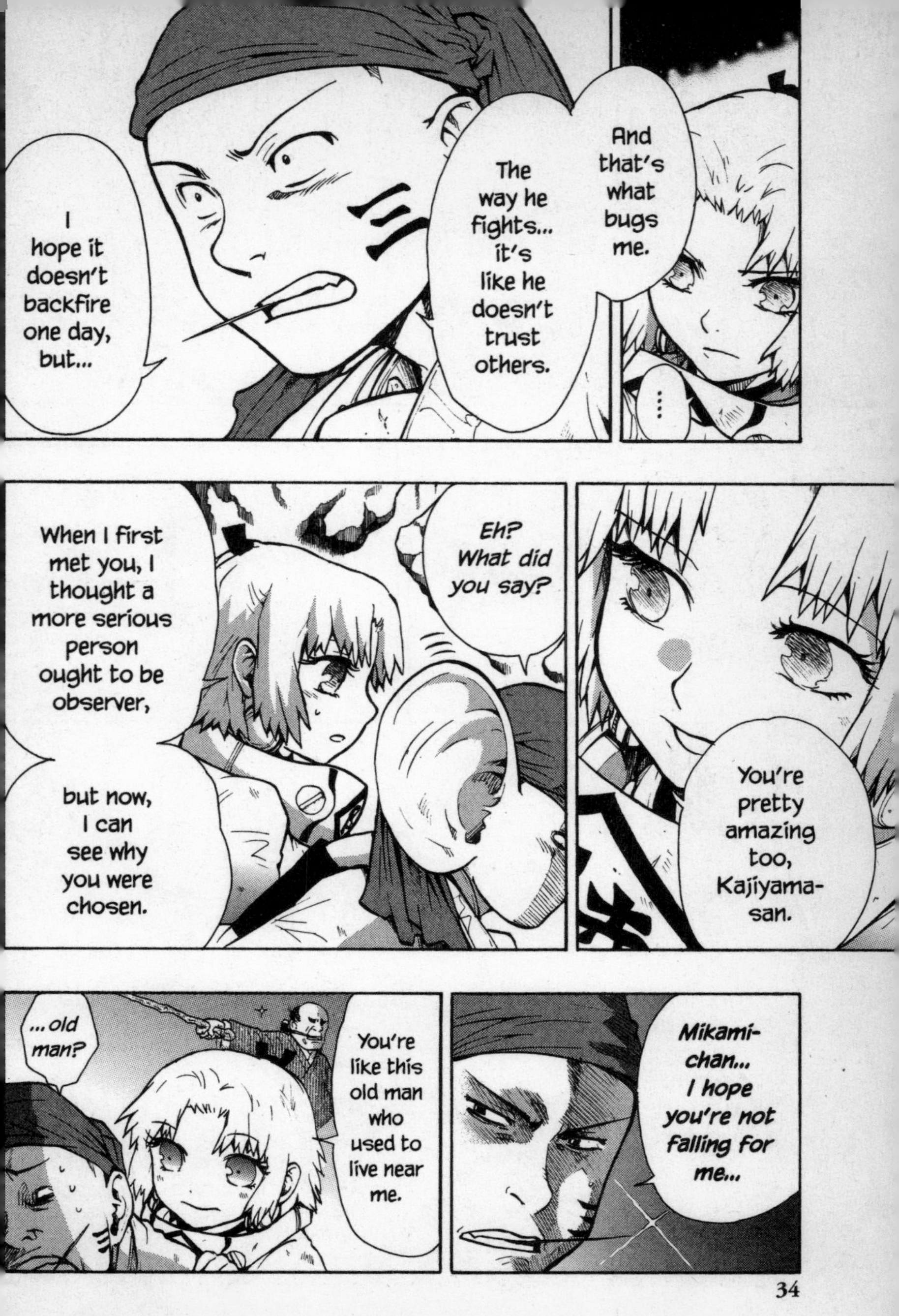
I hope it doesn't backfire one day, but...
The way he fights... it's like he doesn't trust others.
And that's what bugs me.
....
You're pretty amazing too, Kajiyama-san.
Eh? What did you say?
When I first met you, I thought a more serious person ought to be observer,
but now, I can see why you were chosen.
Mikami-chan... I hope you're not falling for me...
You're like this old man who used to live near me.
...old man?

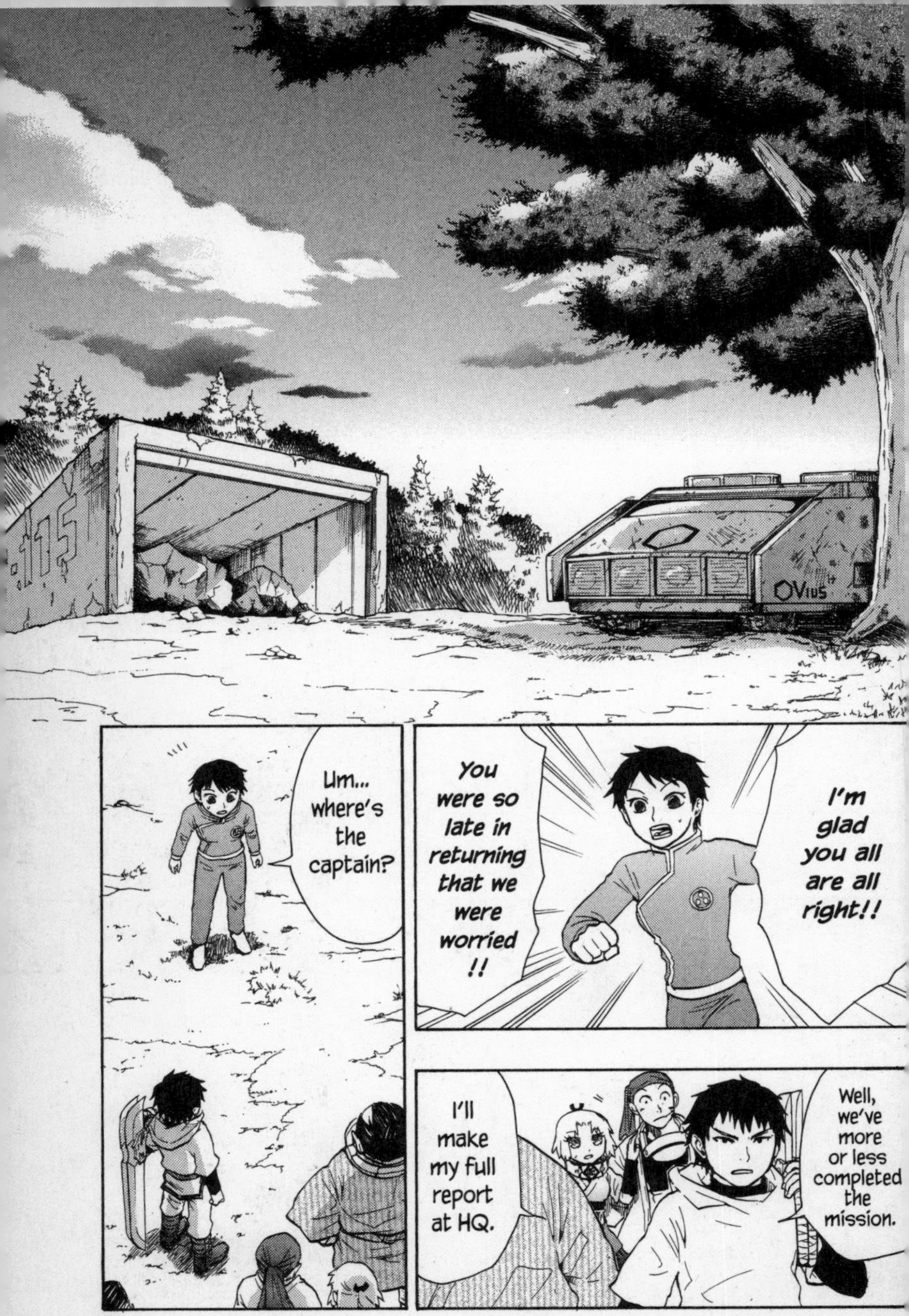
OVIUS
I'm glad you all are all right!!
You were so late in returning that we were worried!!
Well, we've more or less completed the mission.
I'll make my full report at HQ.
Um... where's the captain?

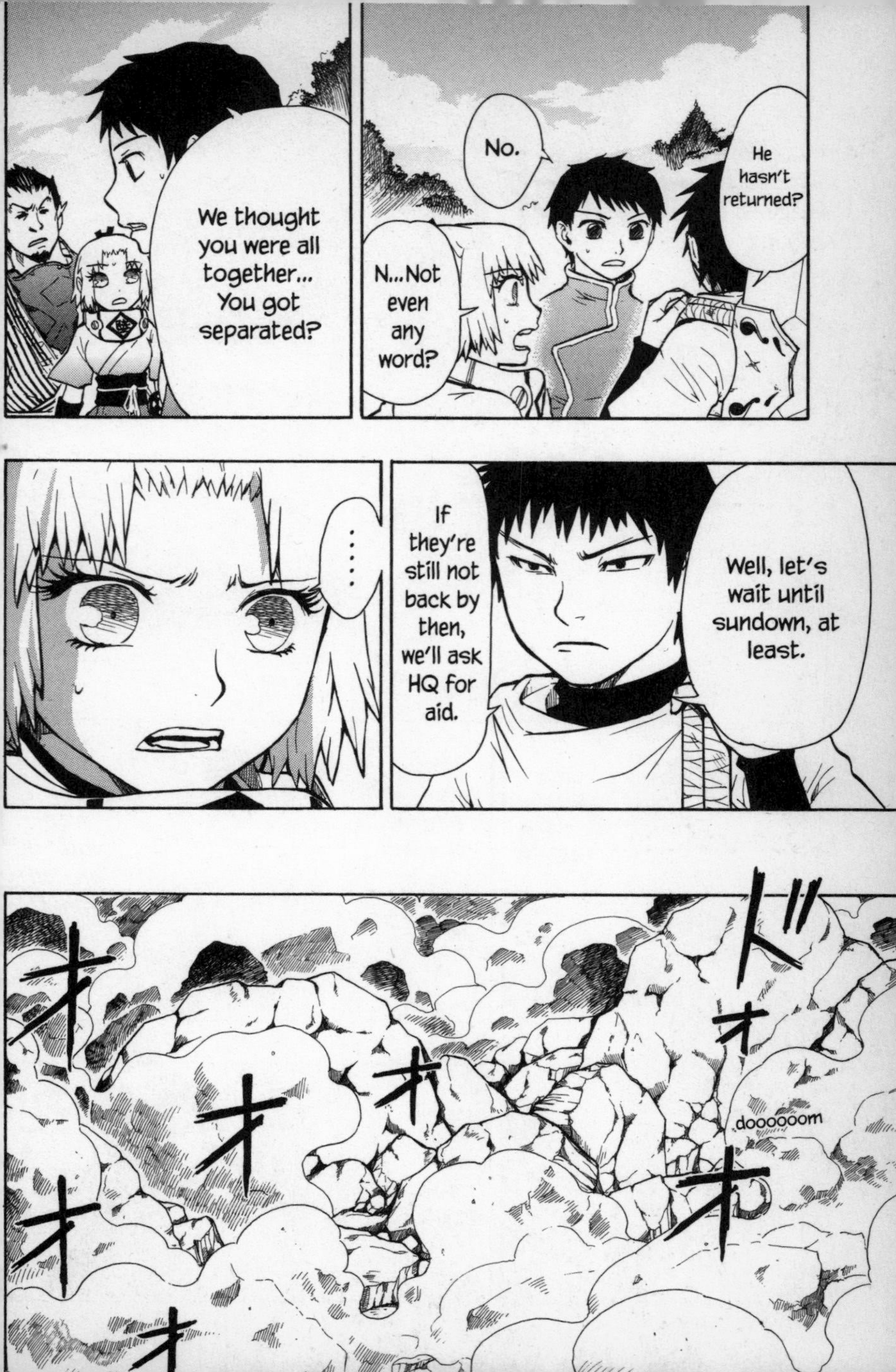
He hasn't returned?
No.
N...Not even any word?
We thought you were all together... You got separated?
Well, let's wait until sundown, at least.
If they're still not back by then, we'll ask HQ for aid.
.....
ドオオオオオオ
dooooooom

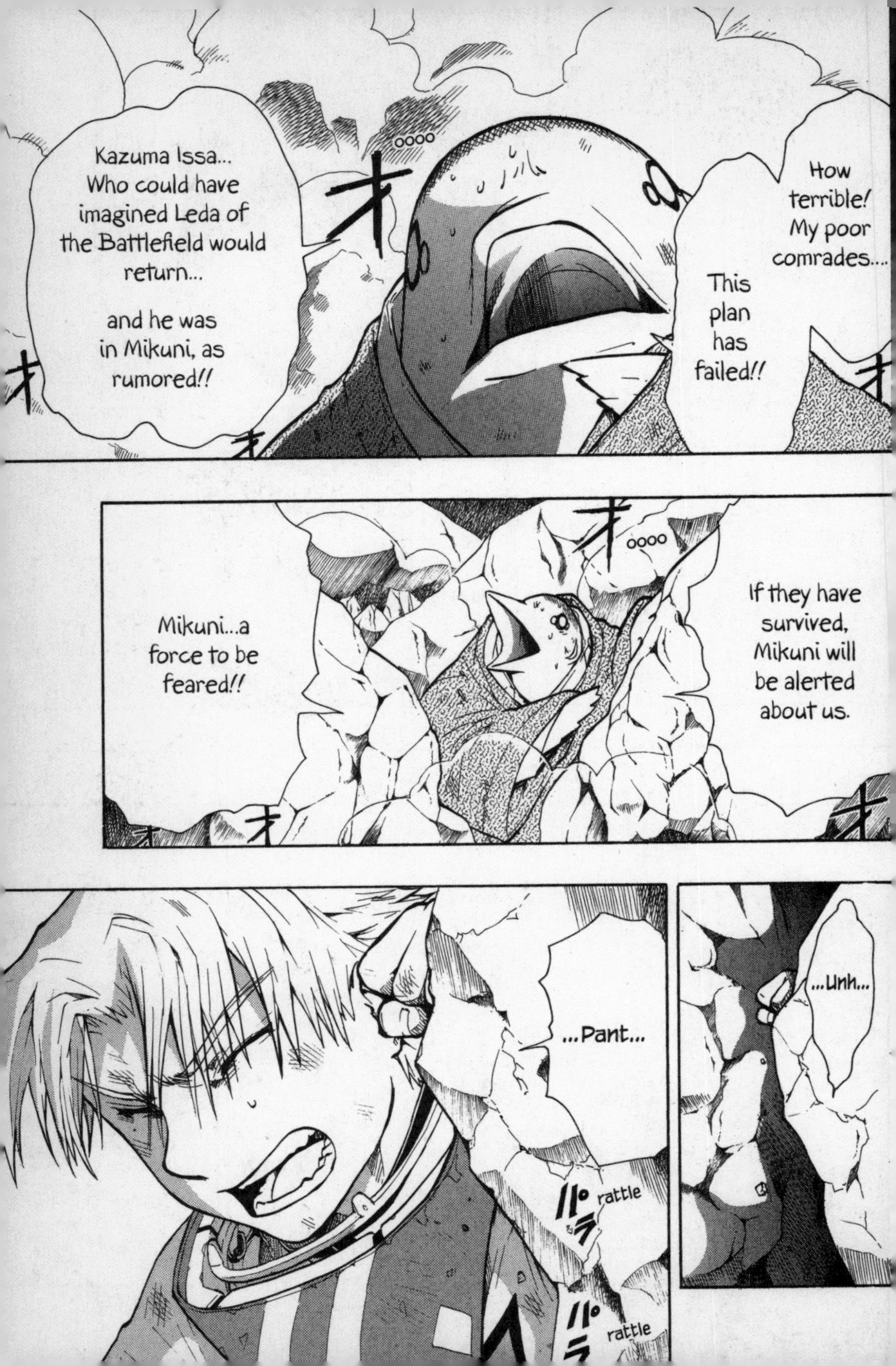
How terrible! My poor comrades....
This plan has failed!!
oooo
Kazuma Issa... Who could have imagined Leda of the Battlefield would return...
and he was in Mikuni, as rumored!!
oooo
If they have survived, Mikuni will be alerted about us.
Mikuni...a force to be feared!!
...Unh...
...Pant...
rattle
rattle

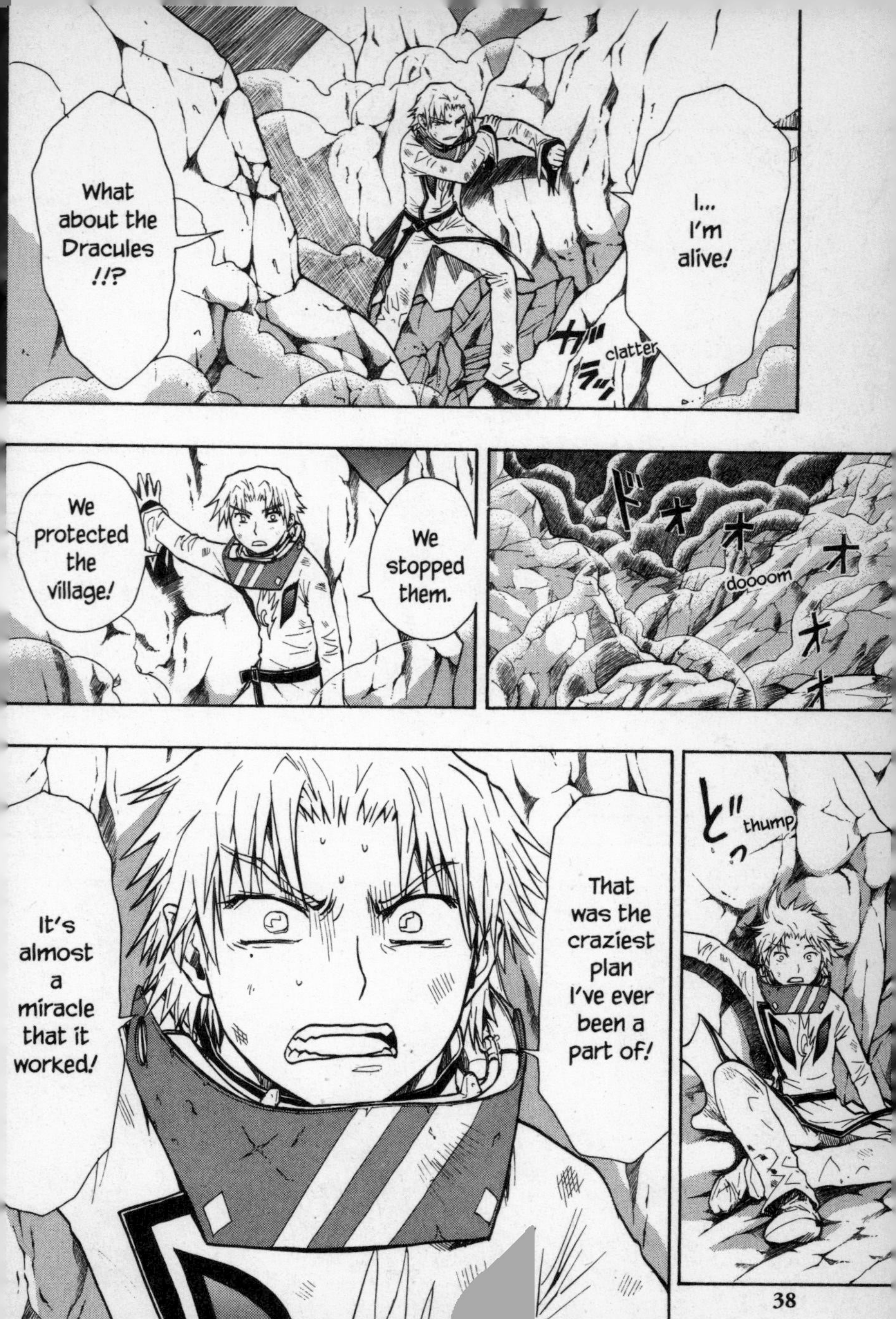
I...
I'm
alive!
clatter
What
about the
Dracules
!!?
doooom
We
stopped
them.
We
protected
the
village!
thump
That
was the
craziest
plan
I've ever
been a
part of!
It's
almost
a
miracle
that it
worked!

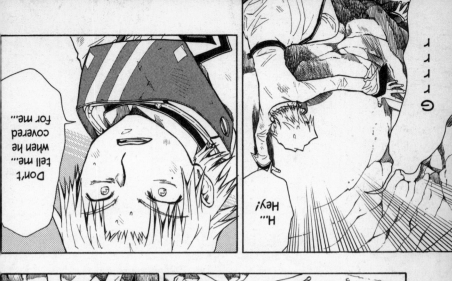

グ

H... Hey!

Don't tell me... when he covered for me...

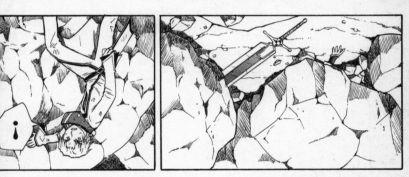

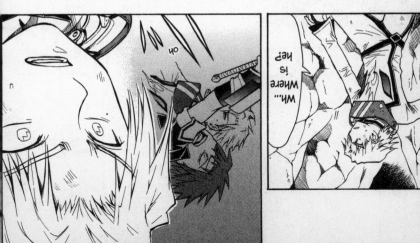

Oh

Wh... where is he?

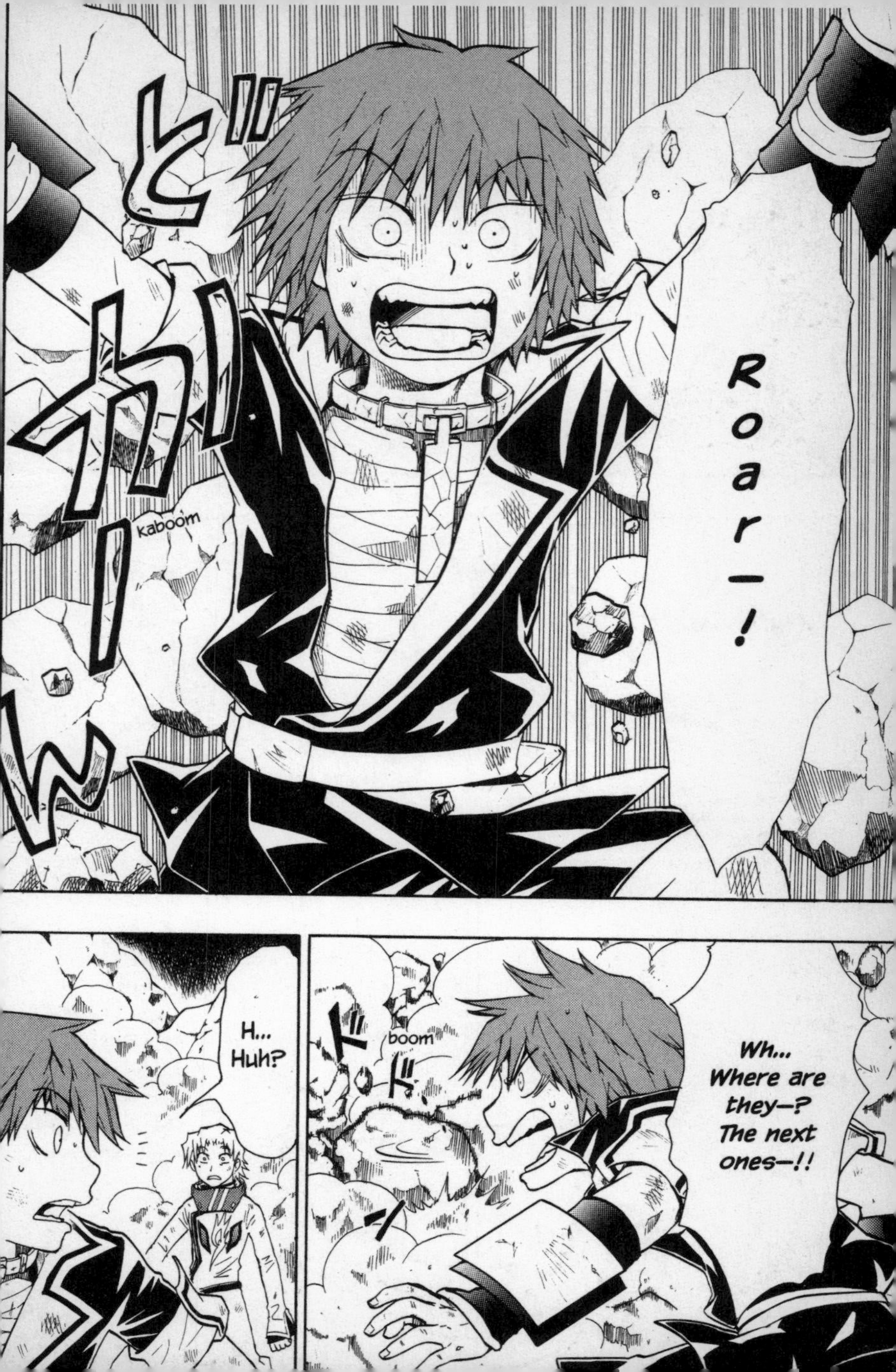
kaboom
Roar—!
Wh... Where are they—? The next ones—!!
boom
H... Huh?

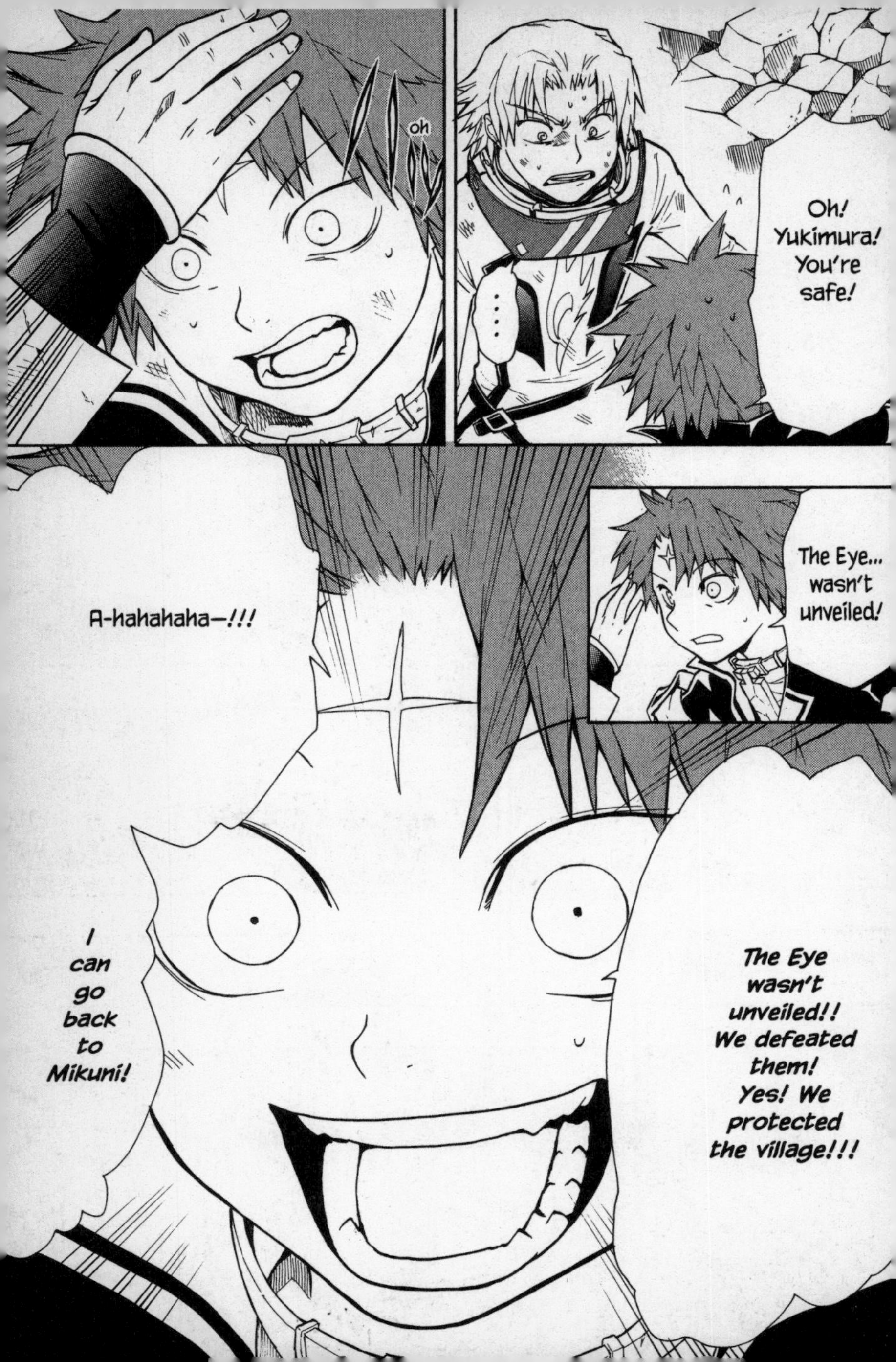
Oh! Yukimura! You're safe!
....
oh
The Eye... wasn't unveiled!
A-hahahaha—!!!
The Eye wasn't unveiled!! We defeated them! Yes! We protected the village!!!
I can go back to Mikuni!

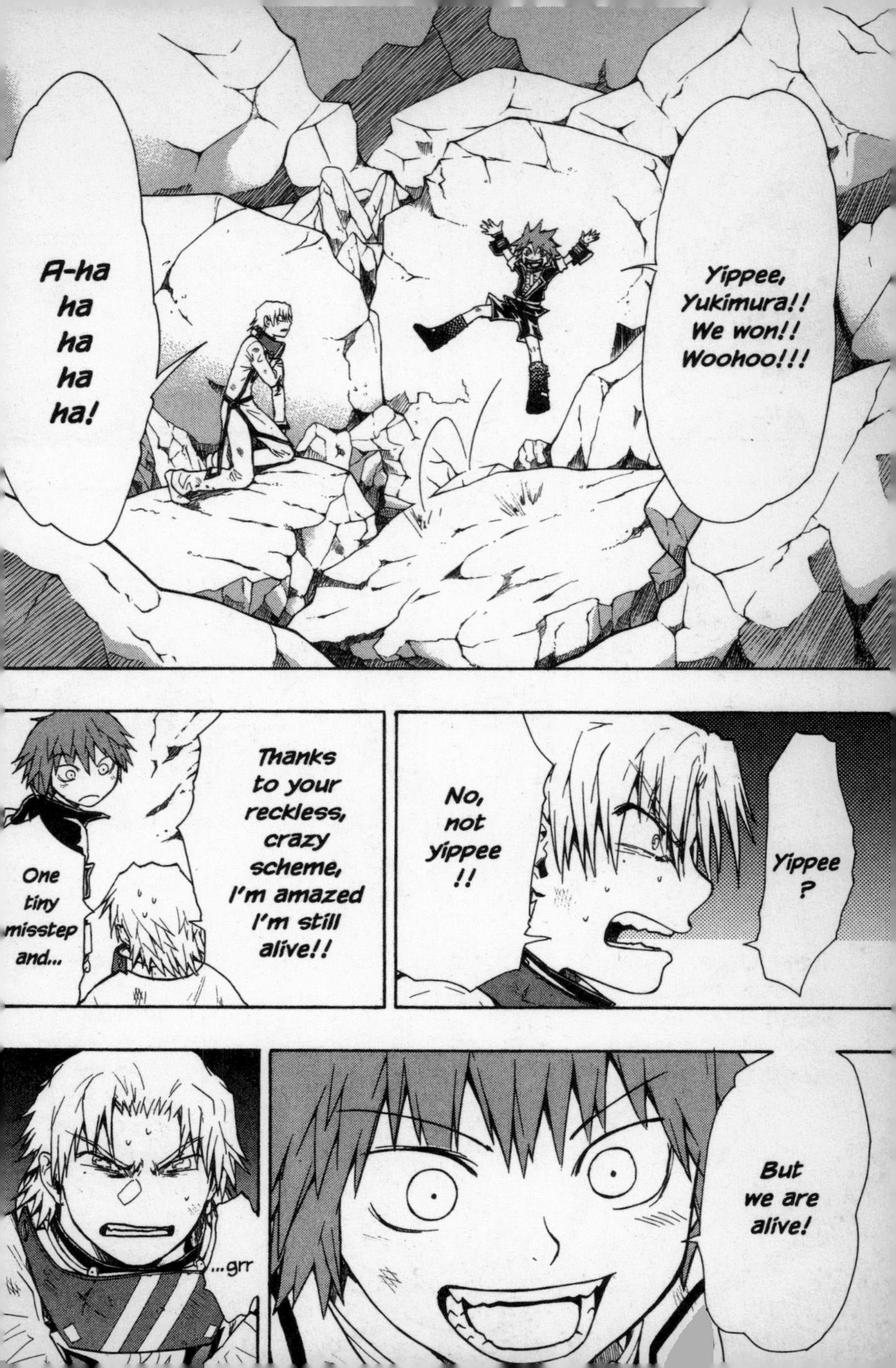
Yippee, Yukimura!! We won!! Woohoo!!!
A-ha ha ha ha ha!
Yippee ?
No, not yippee !!
Thanks to your reckless, crazy scheme, I'm amazed I'm still alive!!
One tiny misstep and...
But we are alive!
...grr

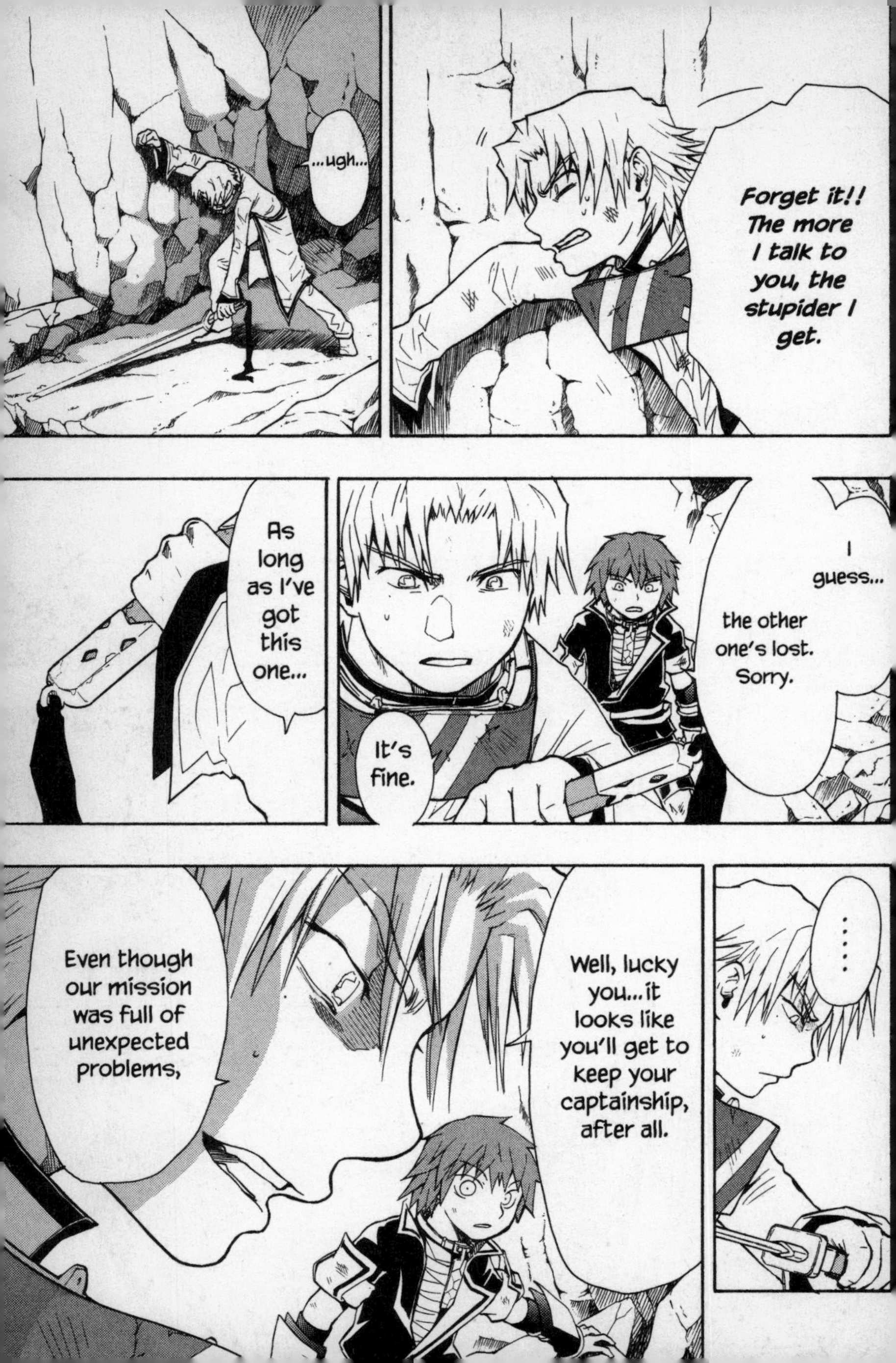
Forget it!! The more I talk to you, the stupider I get.
...ugh...
I guess... the other one's lost. Sorry.
It's fine.
As long as I've got this one...
......
Well, lucky you...it looks like you'll get to keep your captainship, after all.
Even though our mission was full of unexpected problems,

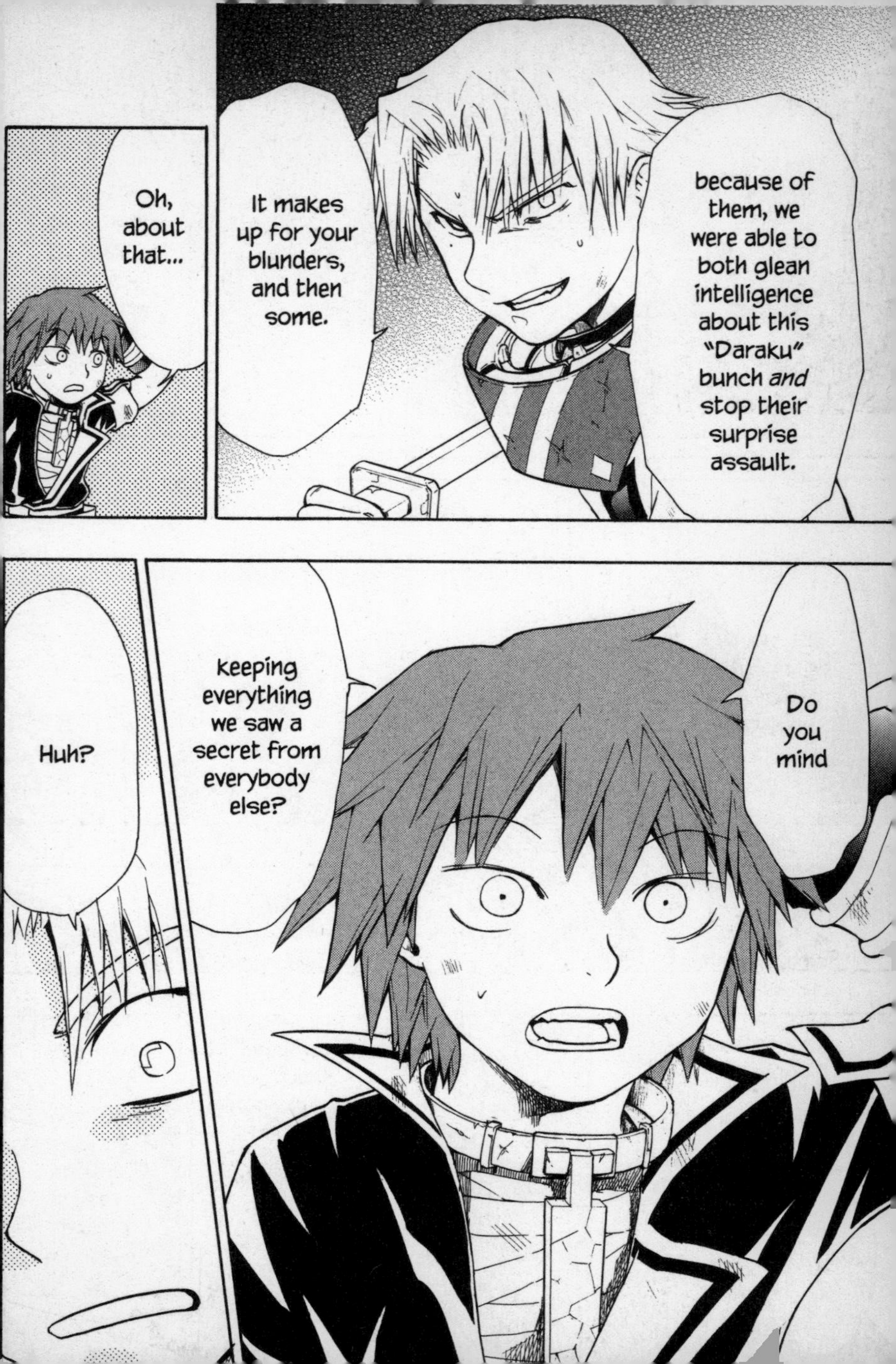
because of them, we were able to both glean intelligence about this "Daraku" bunch *and* stop their surprise assault.
It makes up for your blunders, and then some.
Oh, about that...
Do you mind
keeping everything we saw a secret from everybody else?
Huh?

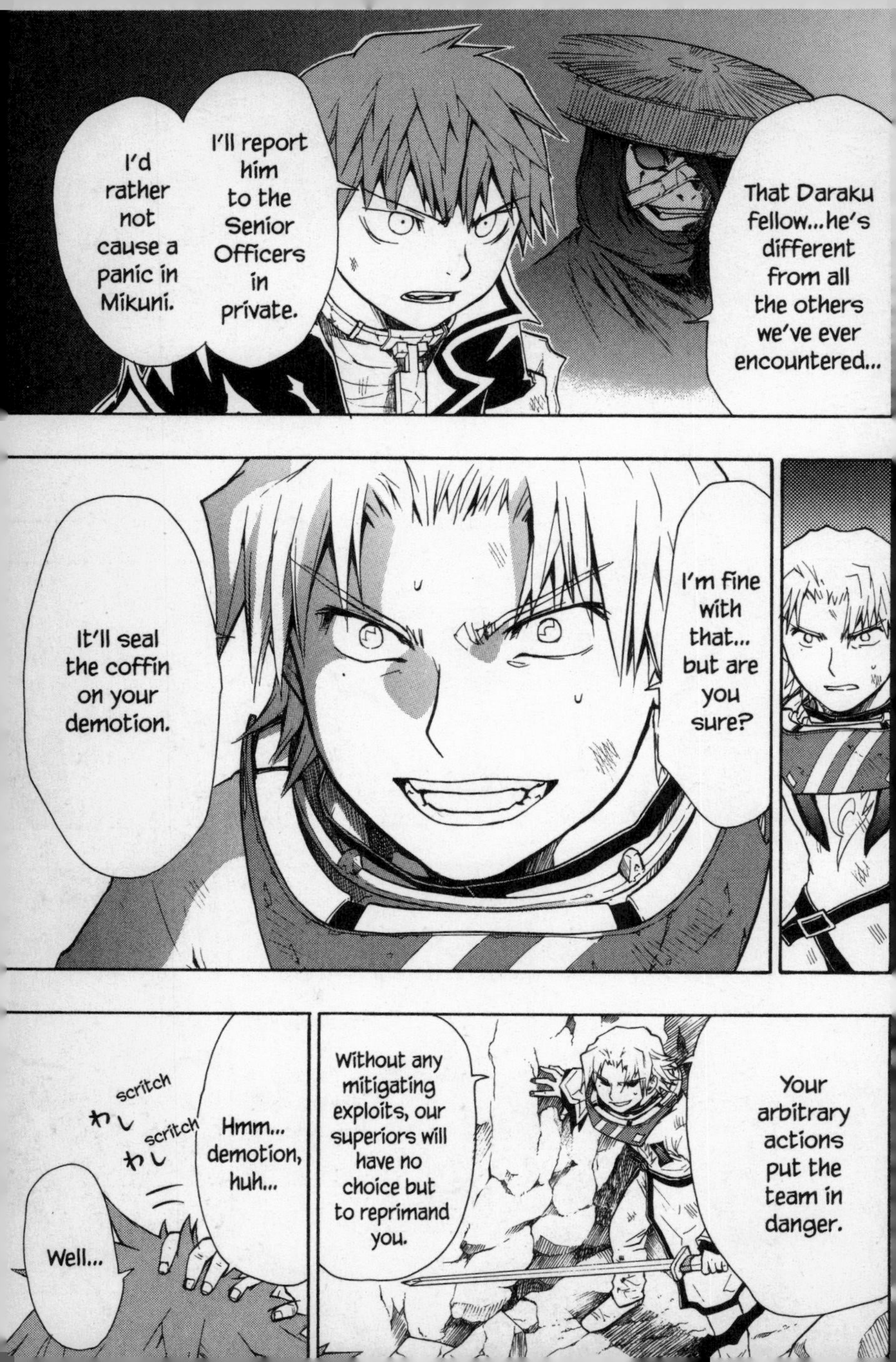
That Daraku fellow...he's different from all the others we've ever encountered...
I'll report him to the Senior Officers in private.
I'd rather not cause a panic in Mikuni.
I'm fine with that... but are you sure?
It'll seal the coffin on your demotion.
Your arbitrary actions put the team in danger.
Without any mitigating exploits, our superiors will have no choice but to reprimand you.
Hmm... demotion, huh...
scritch
scritch
Well...

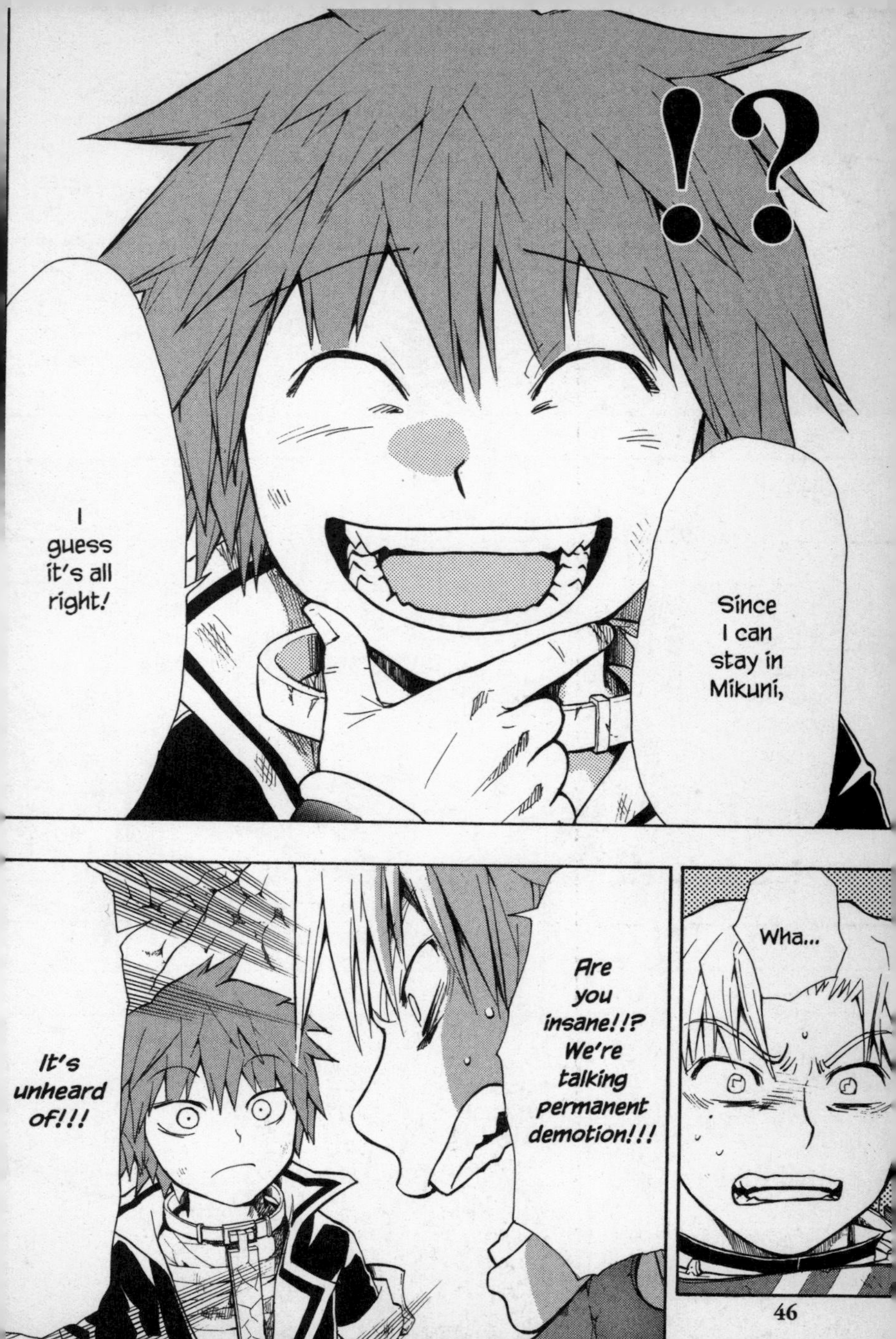
!?
Since I can stay in Mikuni,
I guess it's all right!
Wha...
Are you insane!!? We're talking permanent demotion!!!
It's unheard of!!!

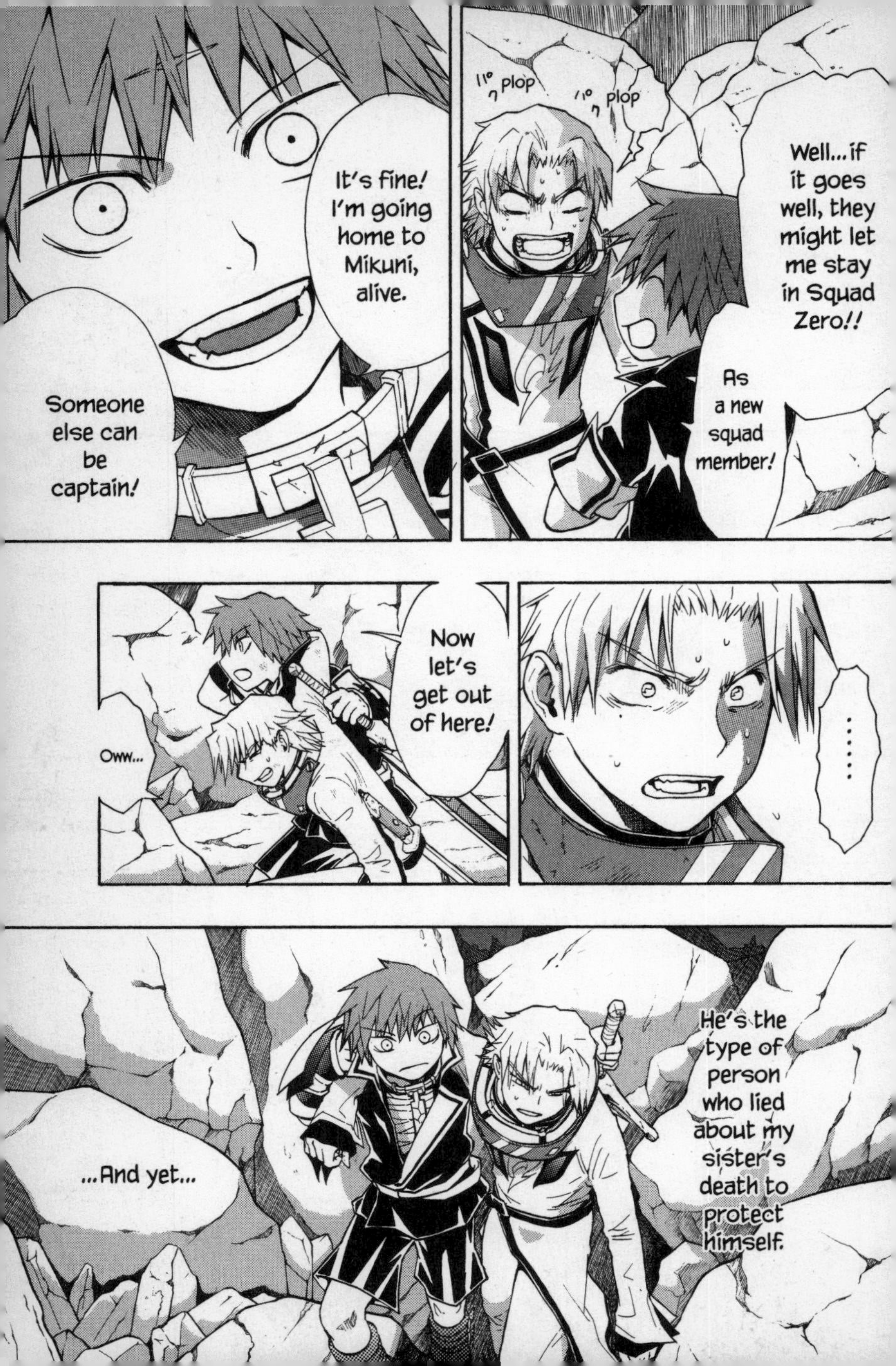
plop
plop
Well...if it goes well, they might let me stay in Squad Zero!!
As a new squad member!
It's fine! I'm going home to Mikuni, alive.
Someone else can be captain!
......
Now let's get out of here!
Oww...
He's the type of person who lied about my sister's death to protect himself.
...And yet...

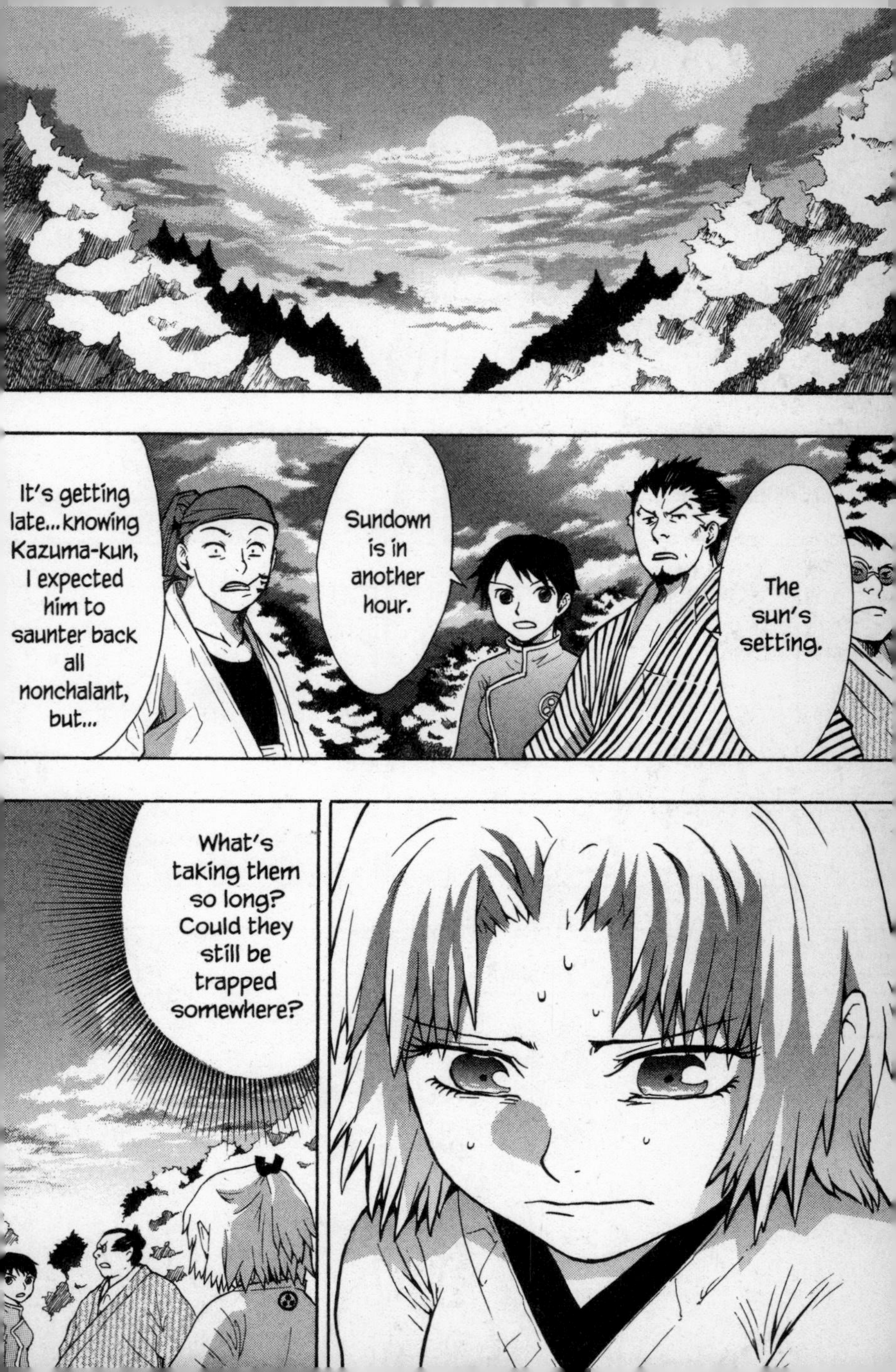
The sun's setting.
Sundown is in another hour.
It's getting late...knowing Kazuma-kun, I expected him to saunter back all nonchalant, but...
What's taking them so long? Could they still be trapped somewhere?

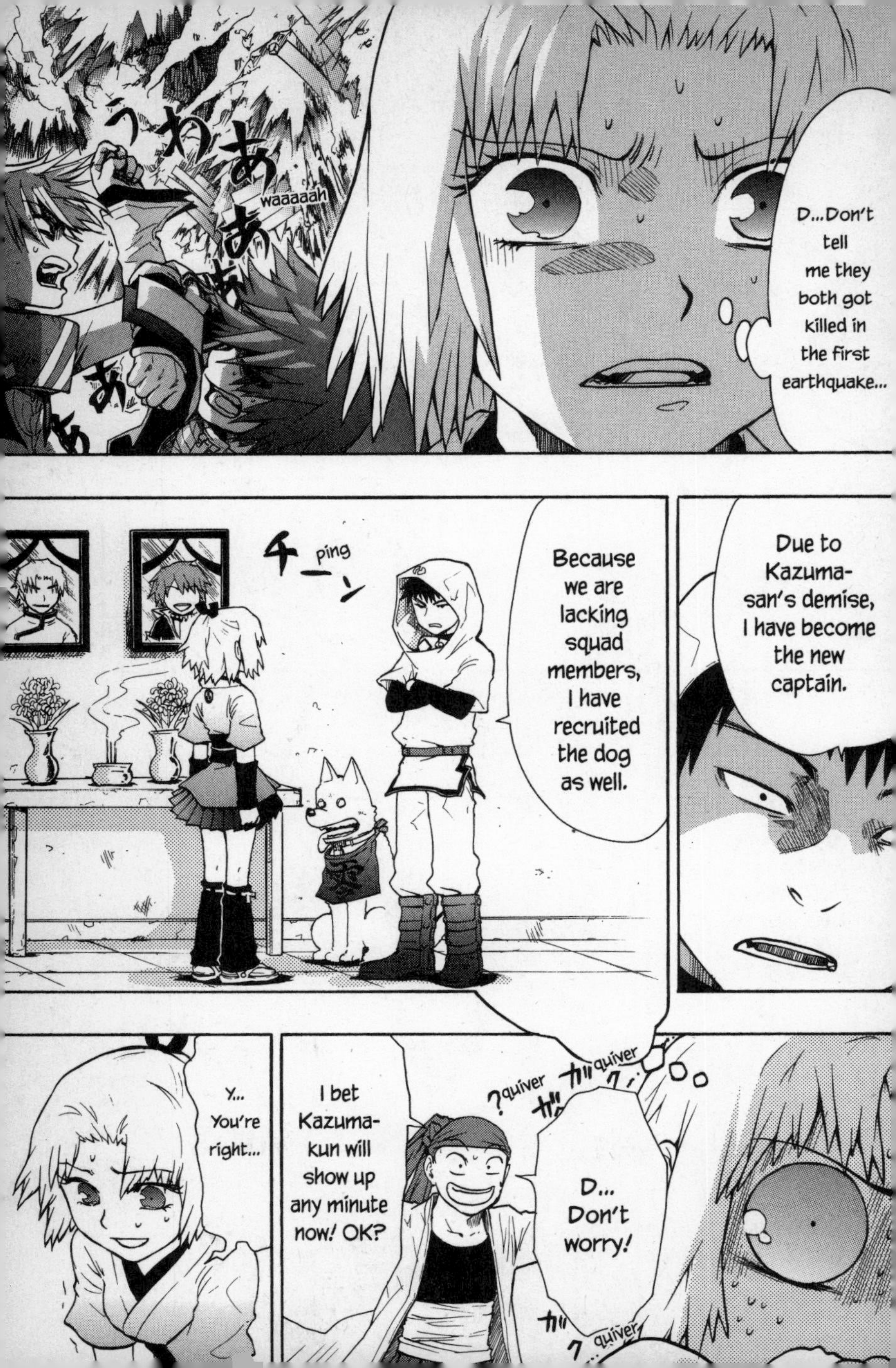
D...Don't tell me they both got killed in the first earthquake...
waaaaah
Due to Kazuma-san's demise, I have become the new captain.
Because we are lacking squad members, I have recruited the dog as well.
ping
quiver
quiver
D... Don't worry!
quiver
I bet Kazuma-kun will show up any minute now! OK?
Y... You're right...

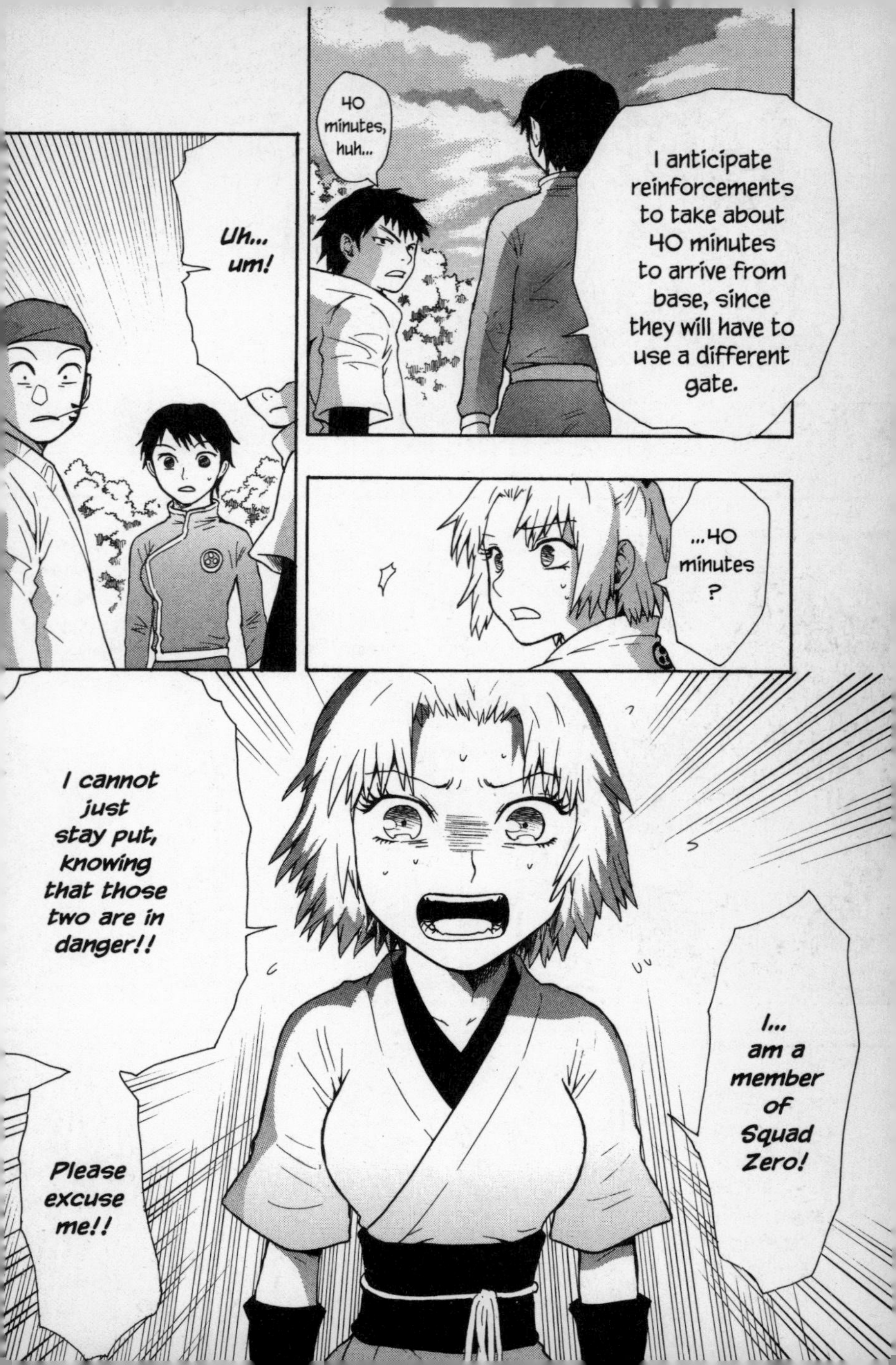
I anticipate reinforcements to take about 40 minutes to arrive from base, since they will have to use a different gate.
40 minutes, huh...
Uh... um!
...40 minutes ?
I... am a member of Squad Zero!
I cannot just stay put, knowing that those two are in danger!!
Please excuse me!!

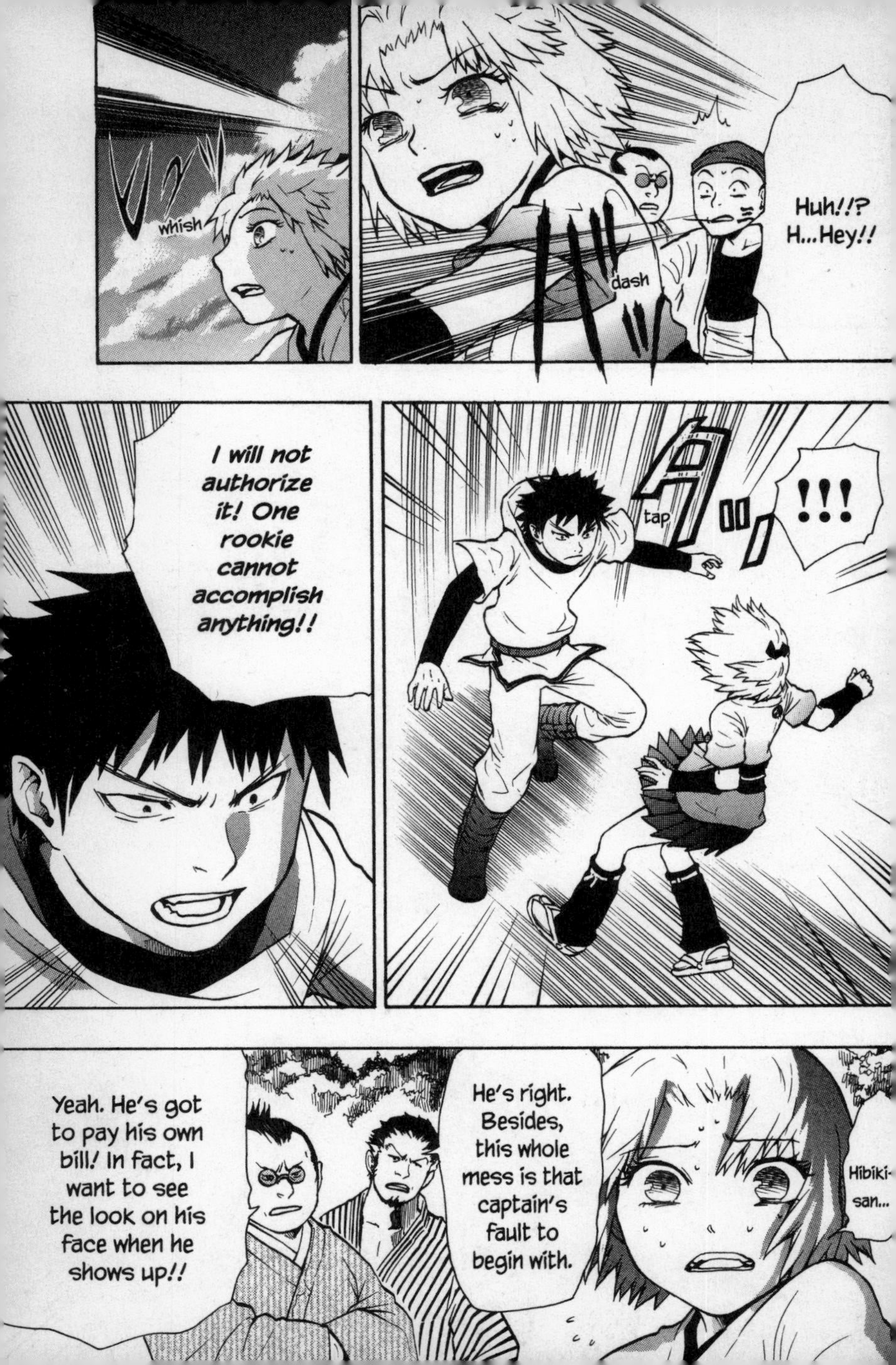
Huh!!?
H...Hey!!
dash
whish
!!!
tap
I will not authorize it! One rookie cannot accomplish anything!!
Hibiki-san...
He's right. Besides, this whole mess is that captain's fault to begin with.
Yeah. He's got to pay his own bill! In fact, I want to see the look on his face when he shows up!!

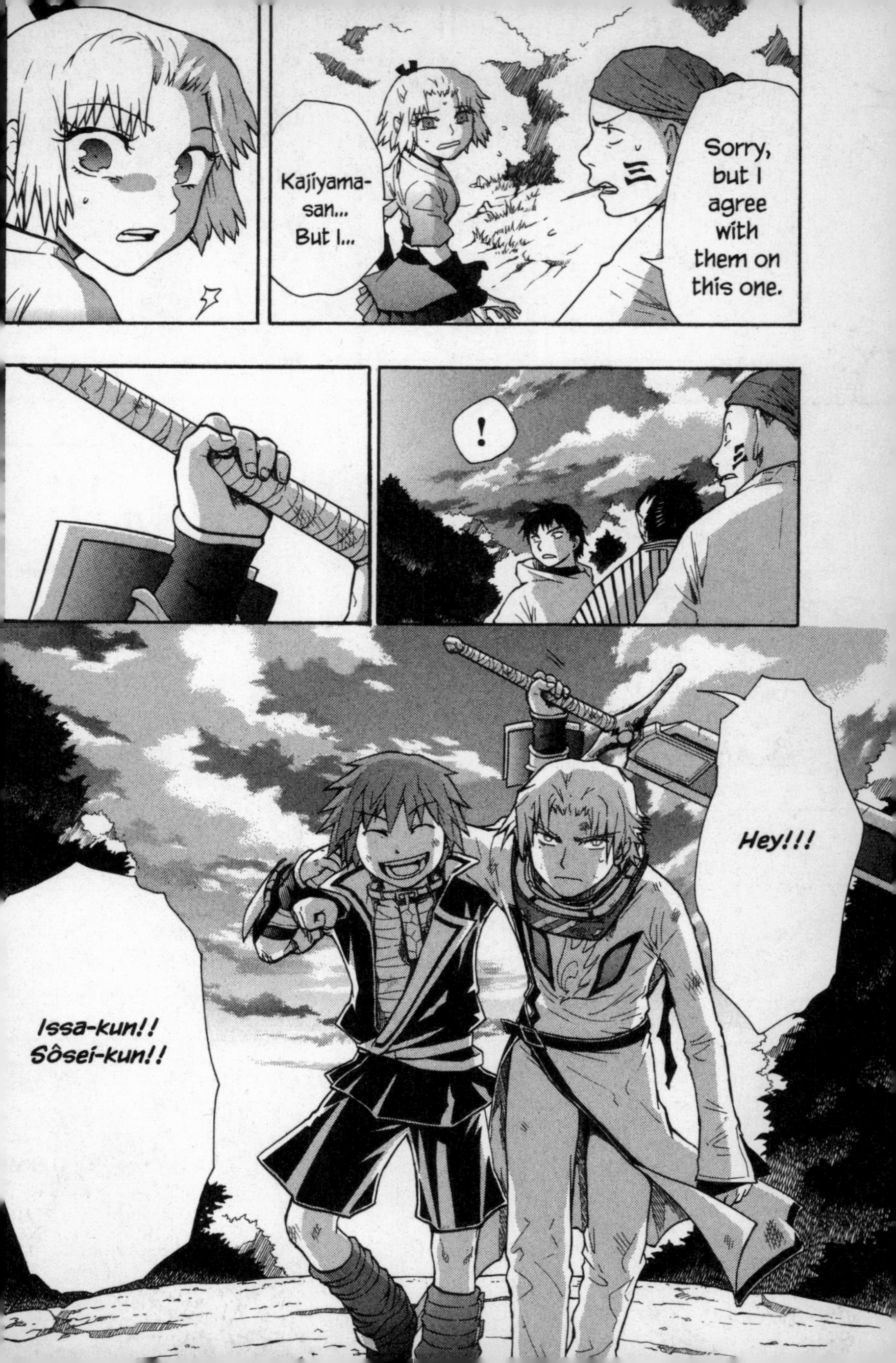
Sorry, but I agree with them on this one.
Kajiyama-san... But I...
!
Hey!!!
Issa-kun!! Sôsei-kun!!

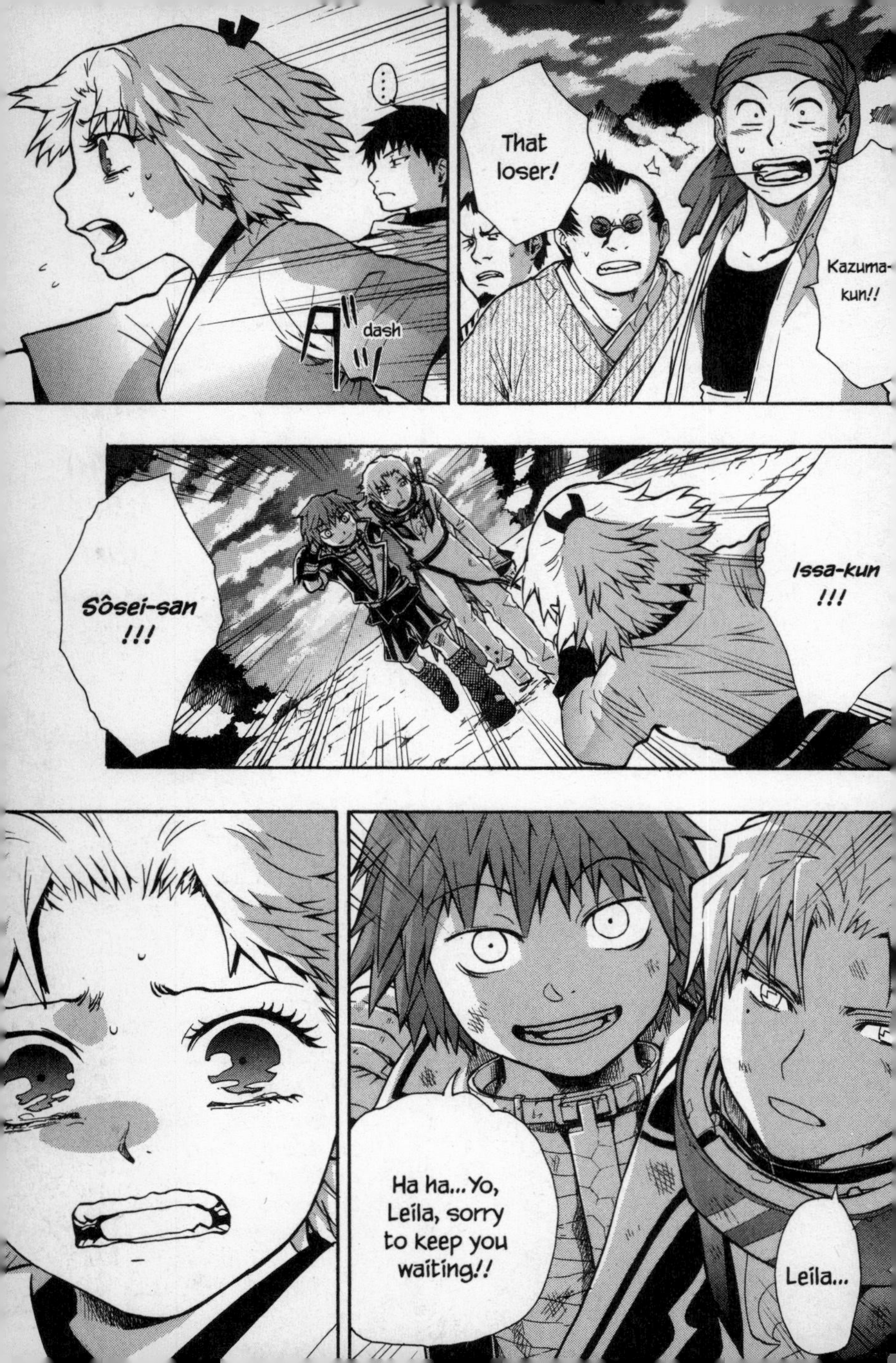
Kazuma-kun!!
That loser!
...
dash
Issa-kun !!!
Sôsei-san !!!
Leila...
Ha ha...Yo, Leila, sorry to keep you waiting!!

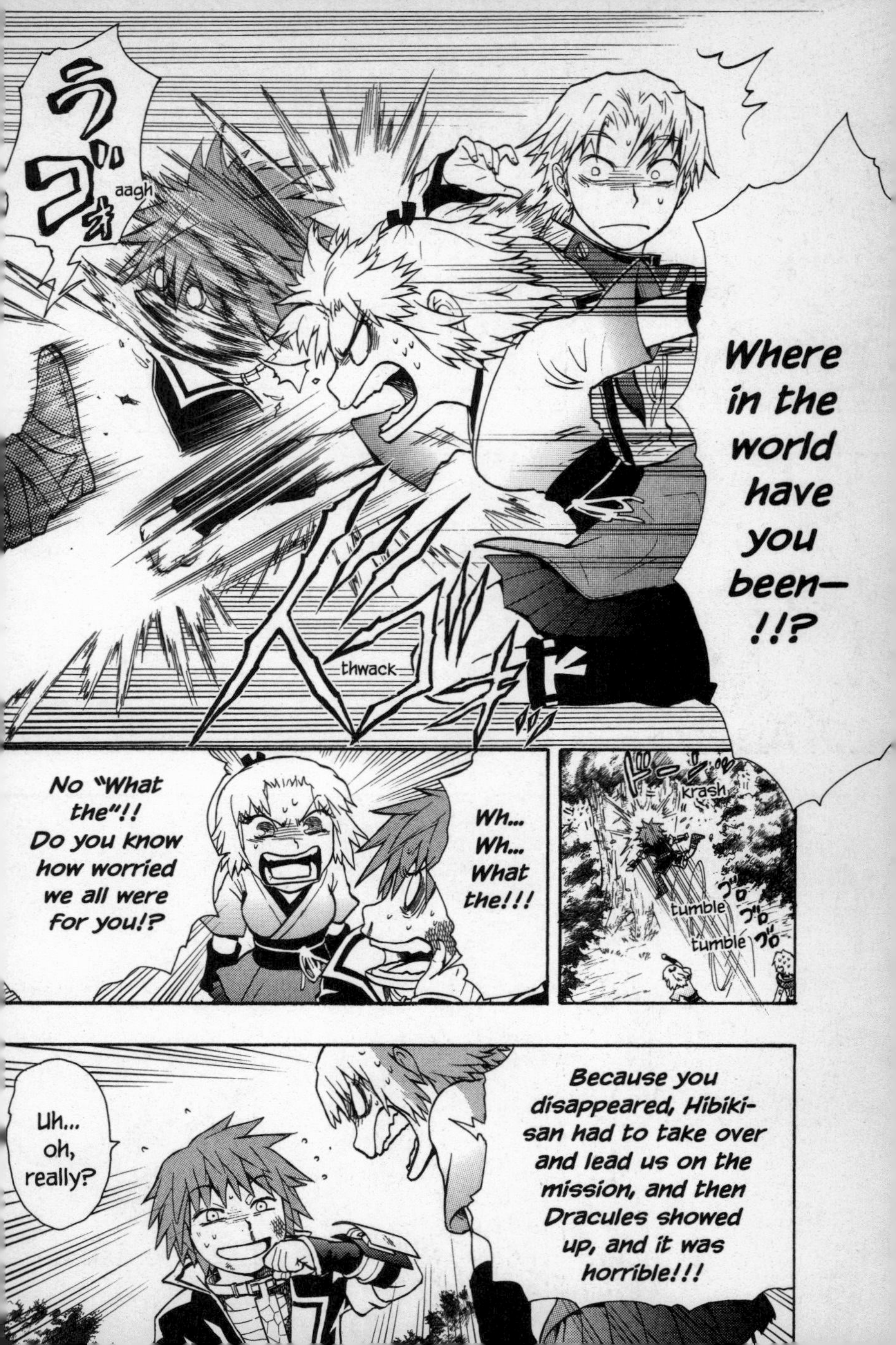
Where in the world have you been—!!?
thwack
aagh
krash
tumble
tumble
No "What the"!! Do you know how worried we all were for you!?
Wh... Wh... What the!!!
Because you disappeared, Hibiki-san had to take over and lead us on the mission, and then Dracules showed up, and it was horrible!!!
Uh... oh, really?

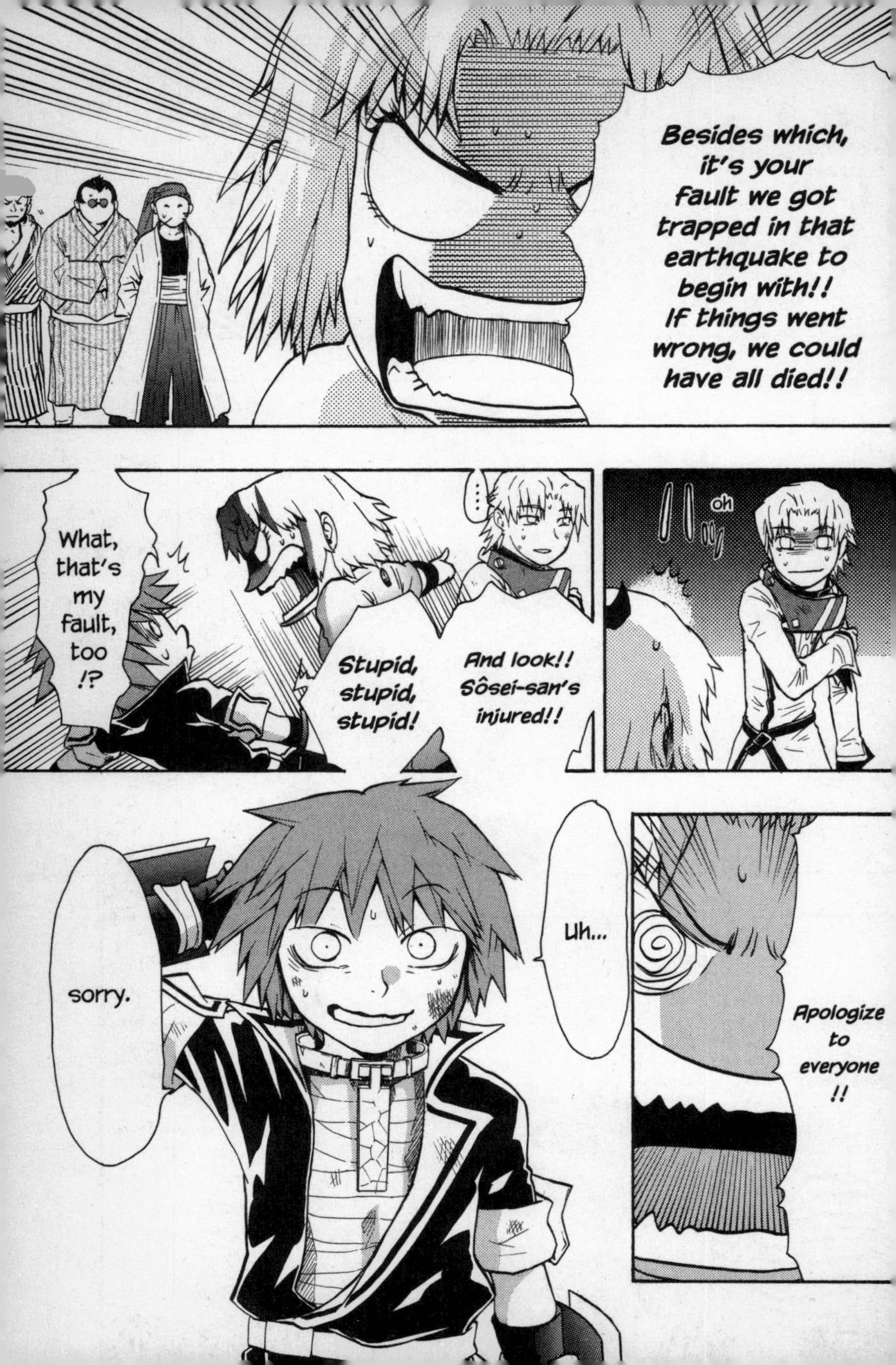
Besides which, it's your fault we got trapped in that earthquake to begin with!! If things went wrong, we could have all died!!
oh
And look!! Sôsei-san's injured!!
Stupid, stupid, stupid!
What, that's my fault, too !?
Apologize to everyone !!
Uh...
sorry.

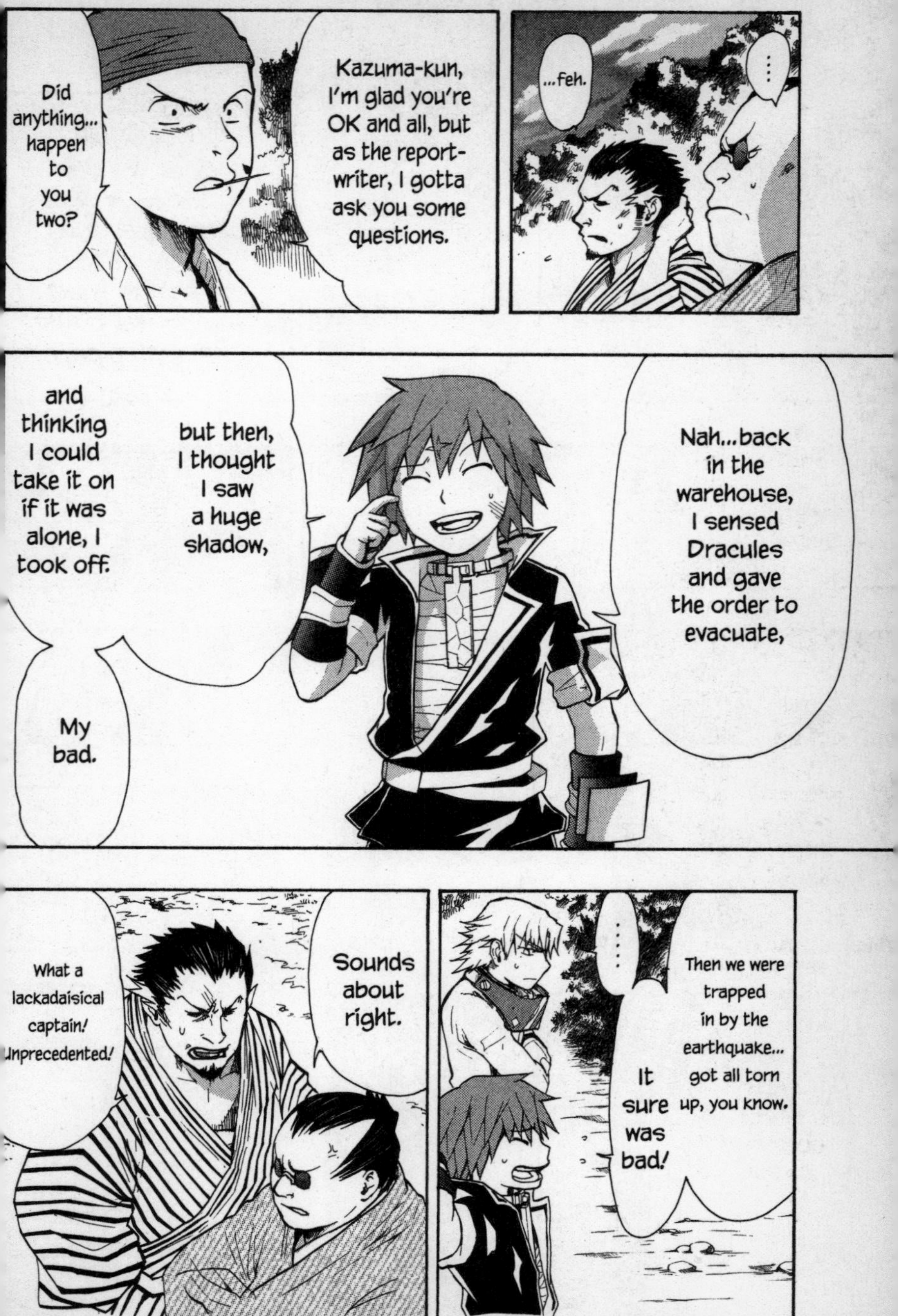
......
...feh.
Kazuma-kun, I'm glad you're OK and all, but as the report-writer, I gotta ask you some questions.
Did anything... happen to you two?
Nah...back in the warehouse, I sensed Dracules and gave the order to evacuate,
but then, I thought I saw a huge shadow,
and thinking I could take it on if it was alone, I took off.
My bad.
......
Then we were trapped in by the earthquake... got all torn up, you know.
It sure was bad!
Sounds about right.
What a lackadaisical captain! Unprecedented!

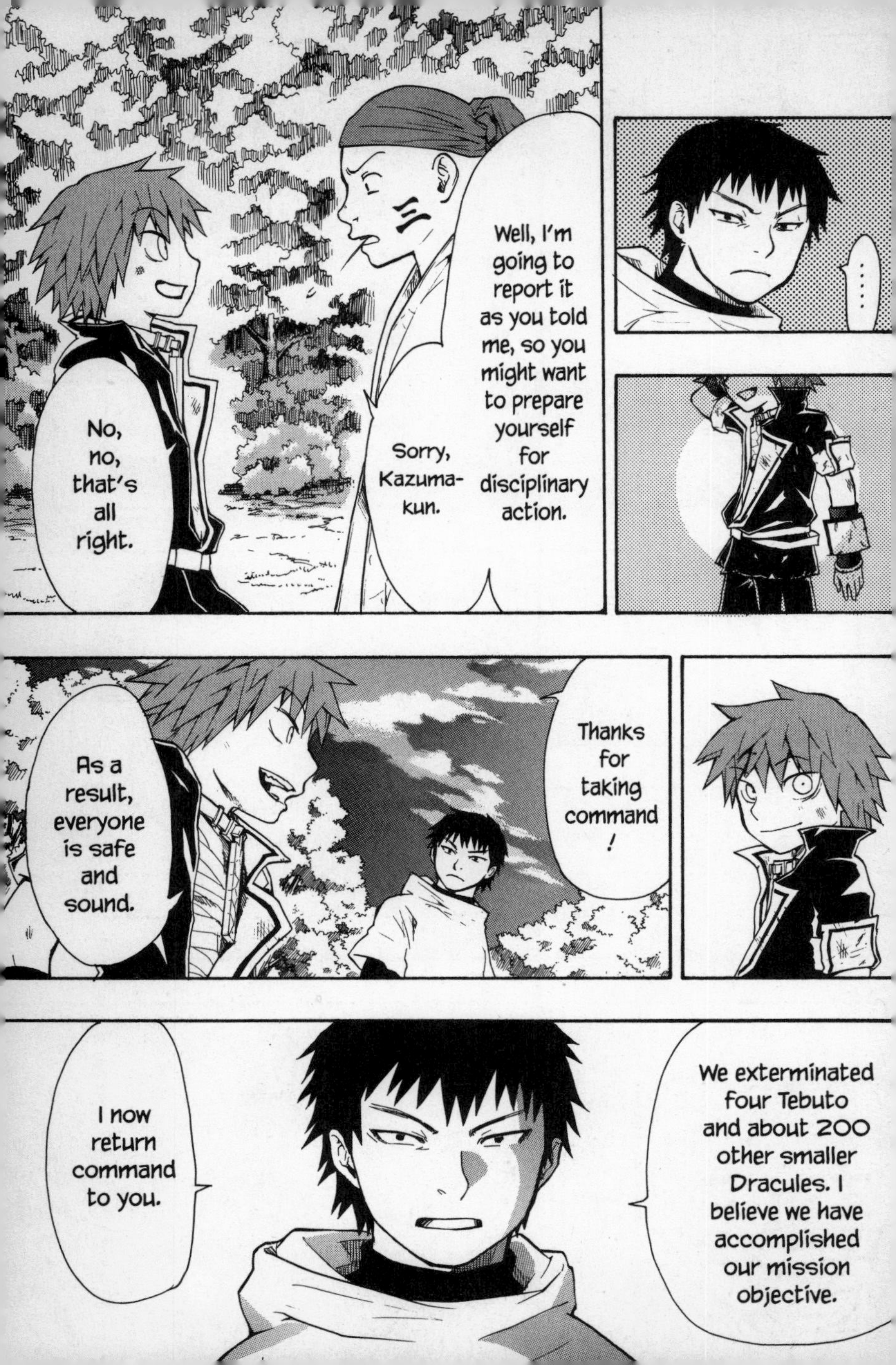
.....
Well, I'm going to report it as you told me, so you might want to prepare yourself for disciplinary action.
Sorry, Kazuma-kun.
No, no, that's all right.
Thanks for taking command!
As a result, everyone is safe and sound.
We exterminated four Tebuto and about 200 other smaller Dracules. I believe we have accomplished our mission objective.
I now return command to you.

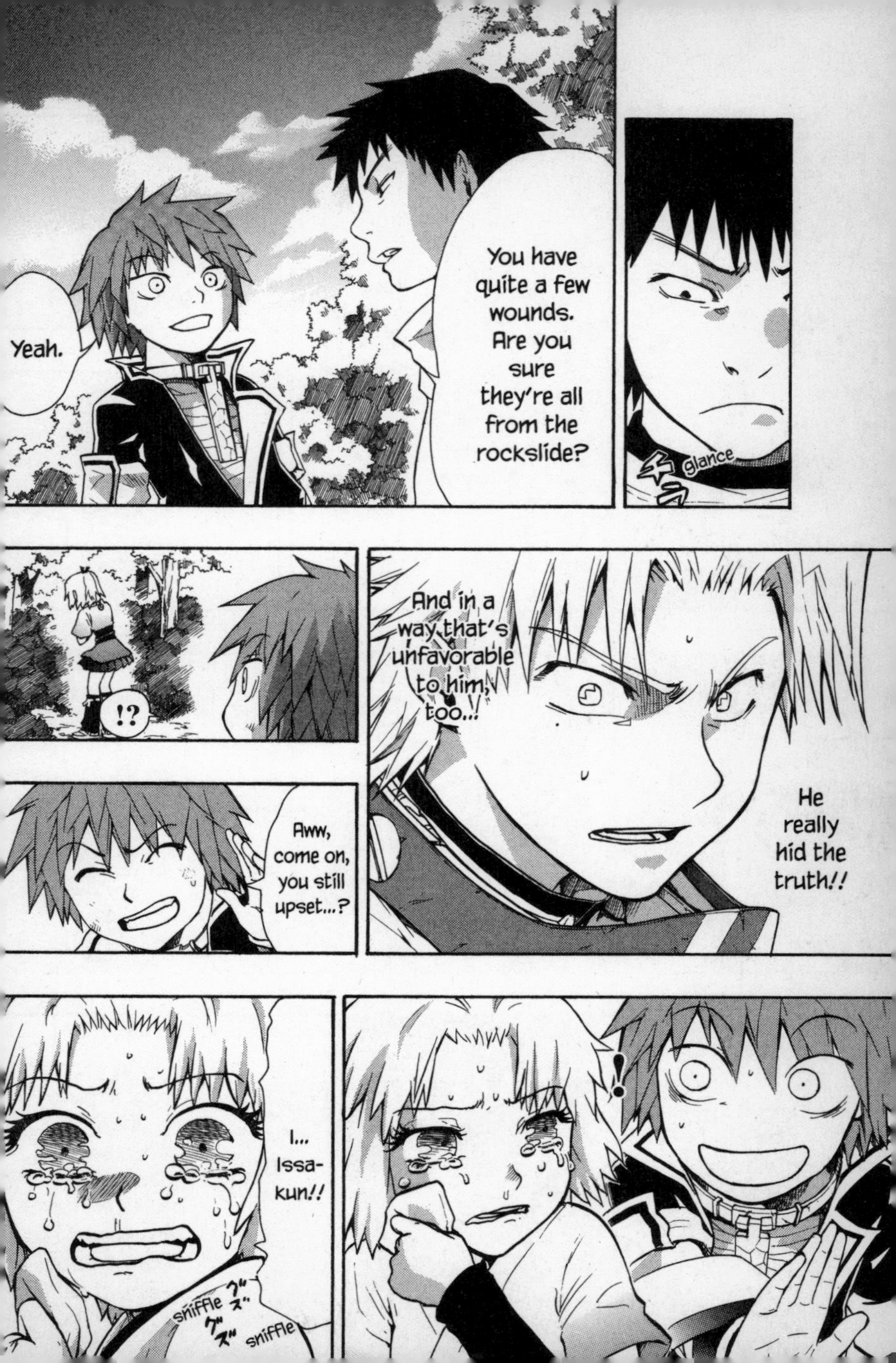
glance
You have quite a few wounds. Are you sure they're all from the rockslide?
Yeah.
He really hid the truth!!
And in a way that's unfavorable to him, too...!
!?
Aww, come on, you still upset...?
!
I... Issa-kun!!
sniffle
sniffle

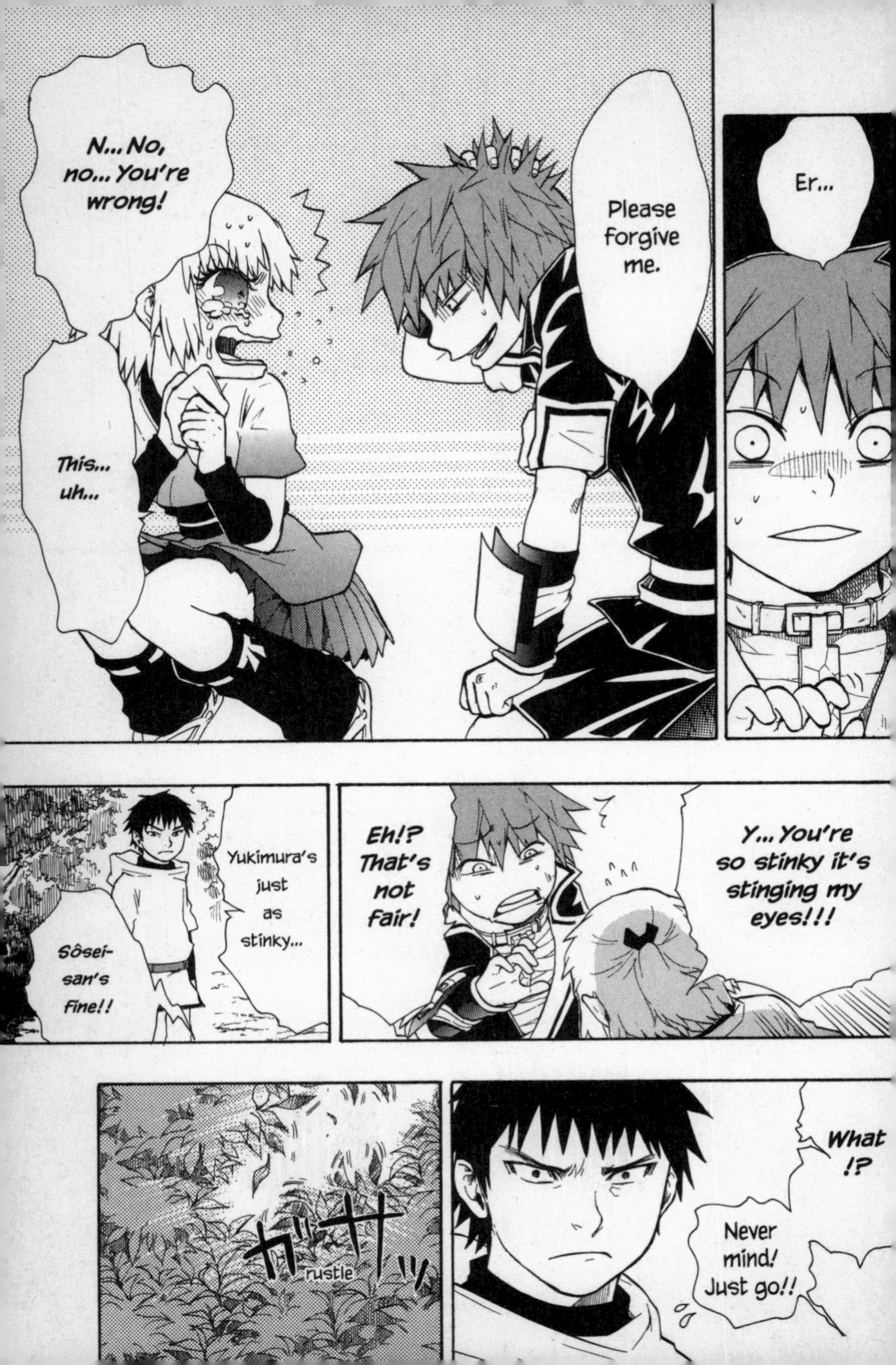
Er...
Please forgive me.
N... No, no... You're wrong!
This... uh...
Y... You're so stinky it's stinging my eyes!!!
Eh!? That's not fair!
Yukimura's just as stinky...
Sôsei-san's fine!!
What!?
Never mind! Just go!!
rustle

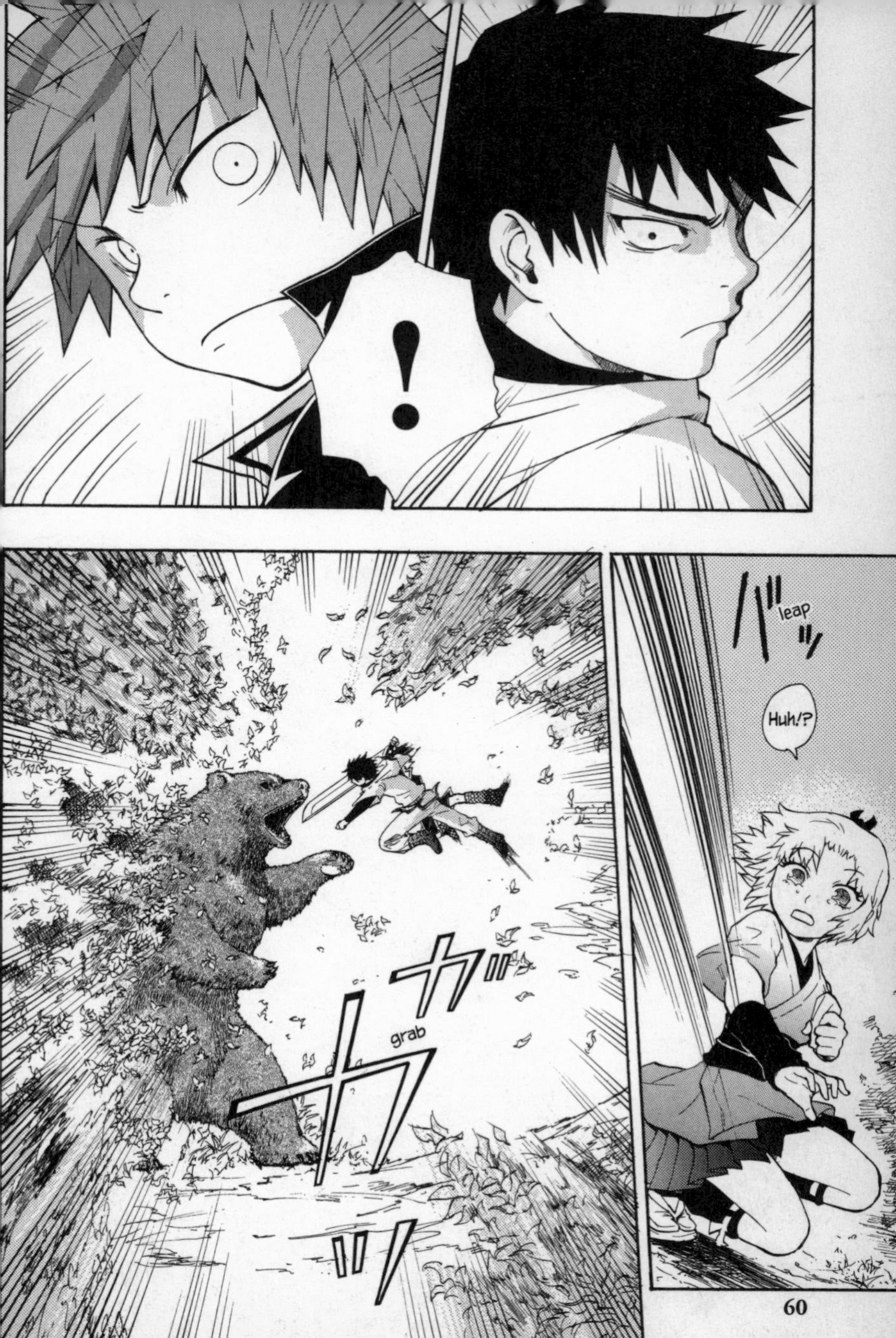
!
leap
Huh!?
grab

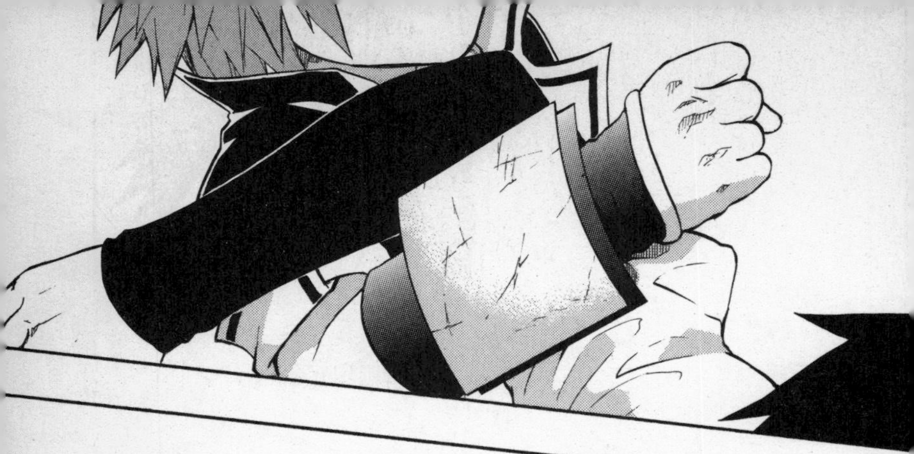

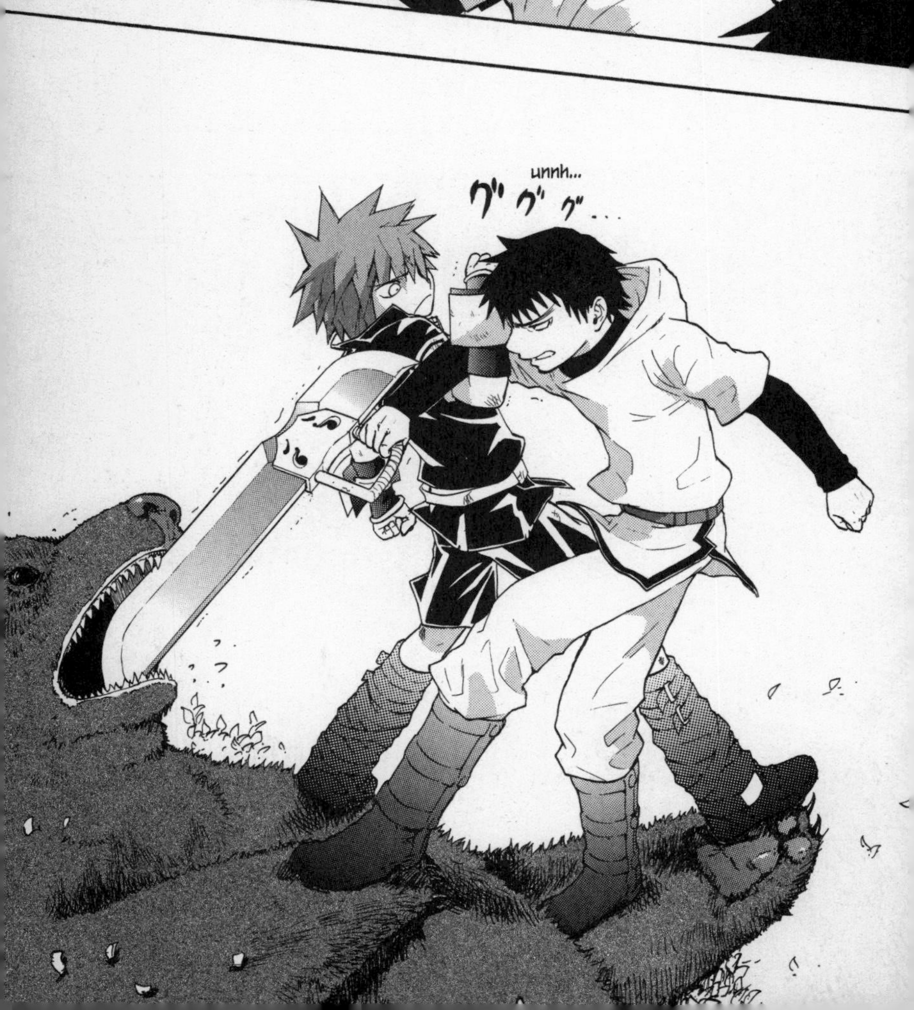
グググ...
unnh...

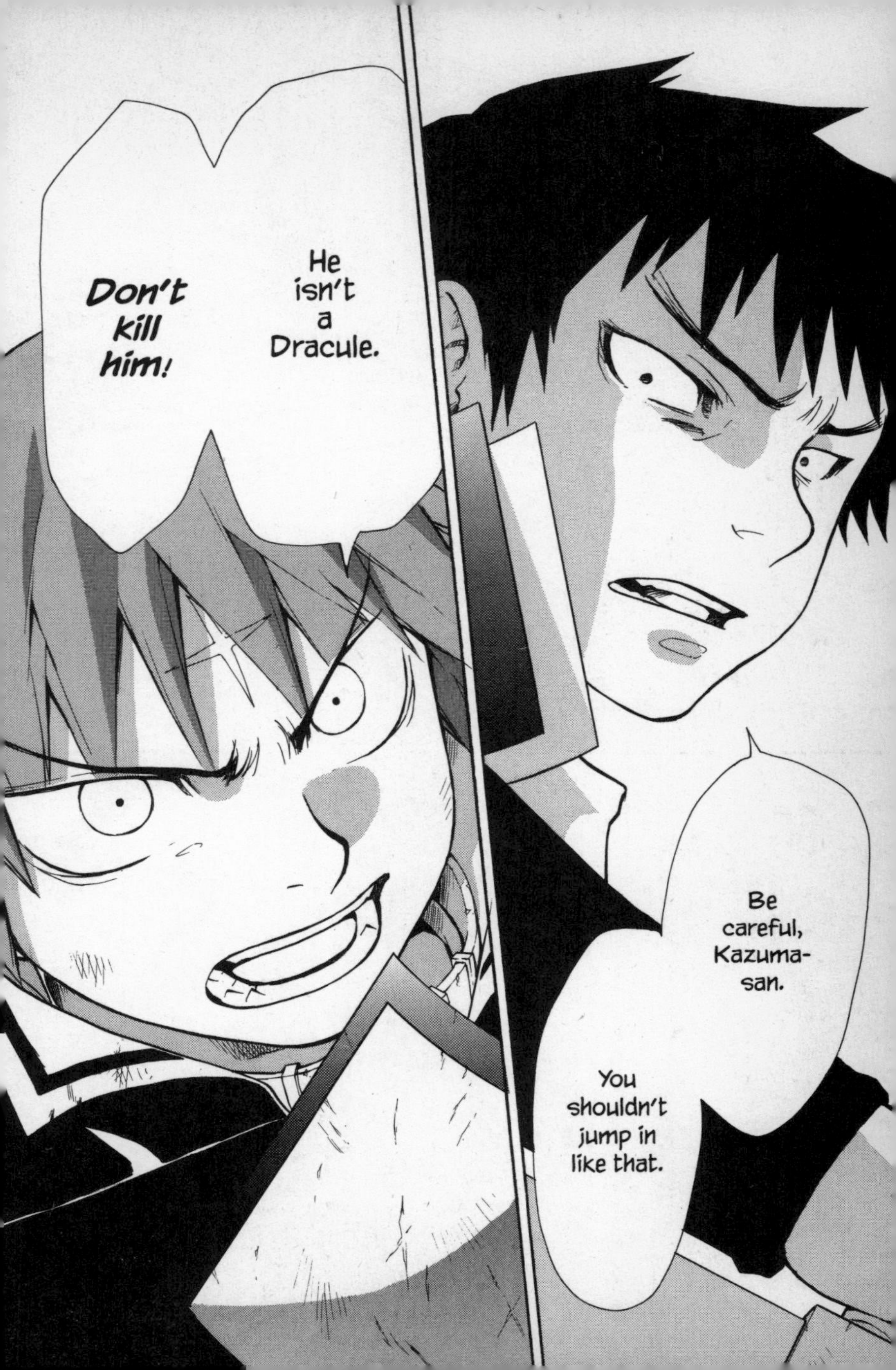
Be careful, Kazuma-san.
You shouldn't jump in like that.
Don't kill him!
He isn't a Dracule.

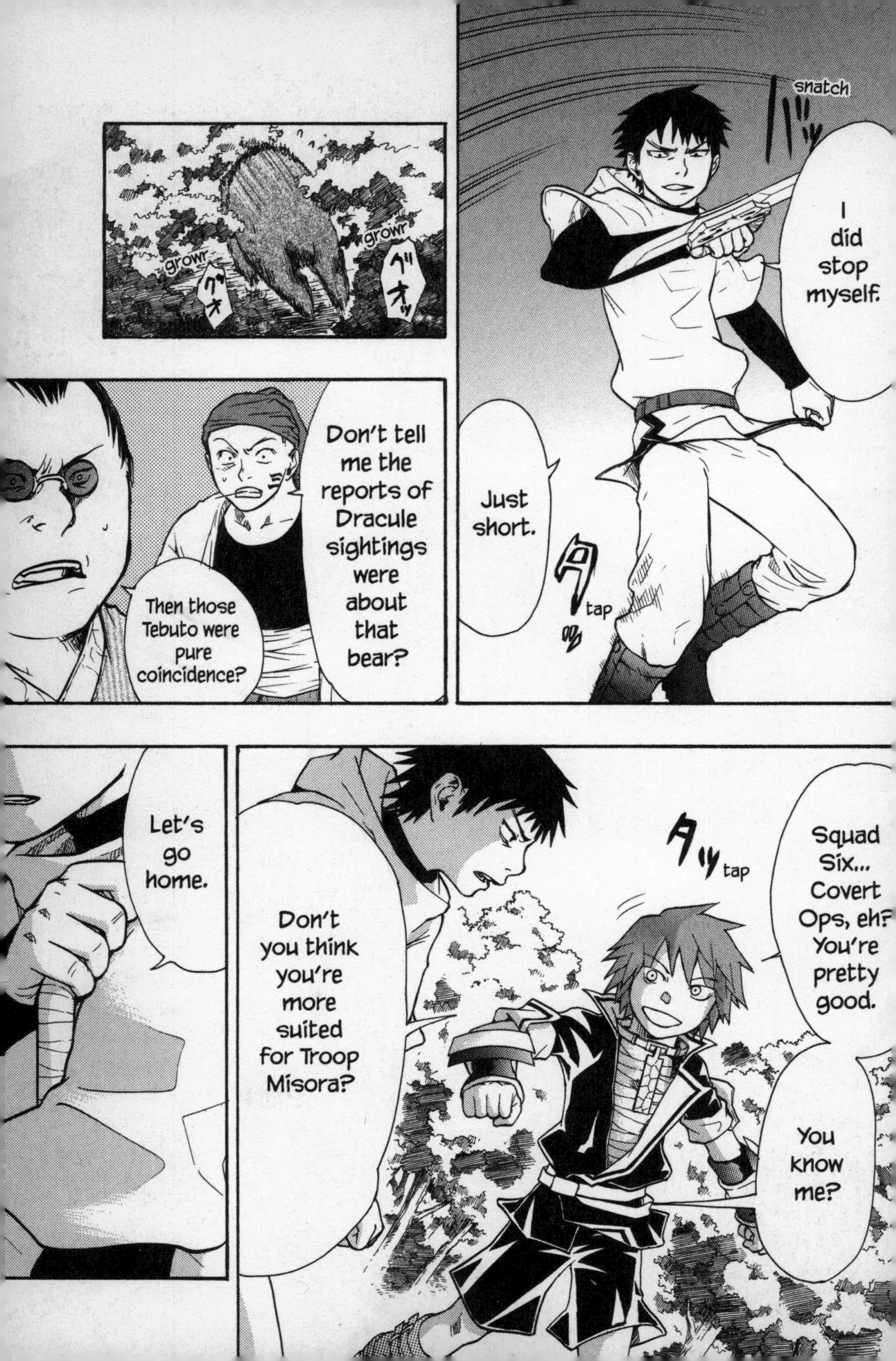
snatch
I did stop myself.
Just short.
tap
growr
growr
Don't tell me the reports of Dracule sightings were about that bear?
Then those Tebuto were pure coincidence?
Squad Six... Covert Ops, eh? You're pretty good.
You know me?
tap
Don't you think you're more suited for Troop Misora?
Let's go home.

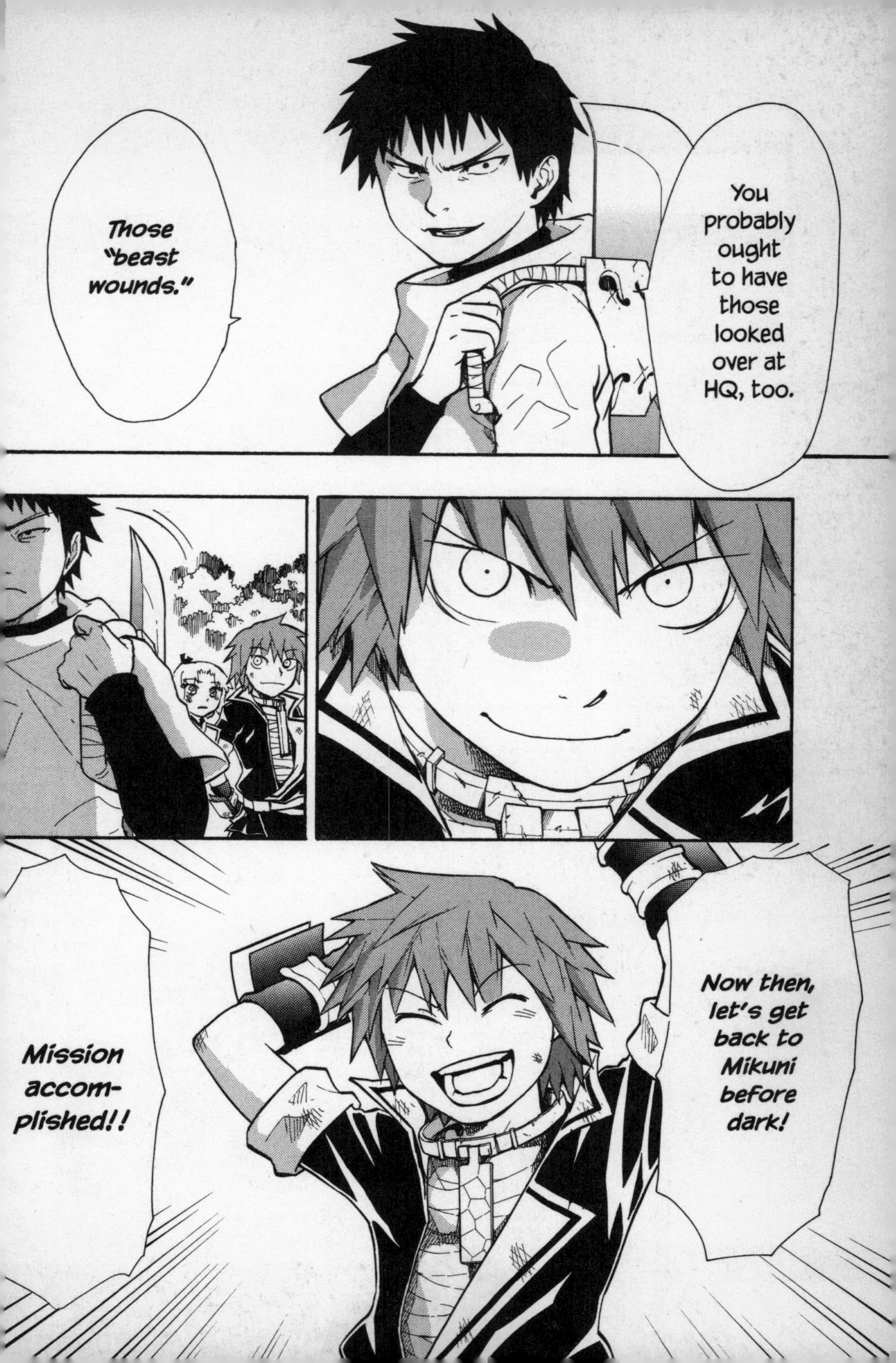
You probably ought to have those looked over at HQ, too.
Those "beast wounds."
Now then, let's get back to Mikuni before dark!
Mission accom-plished!!

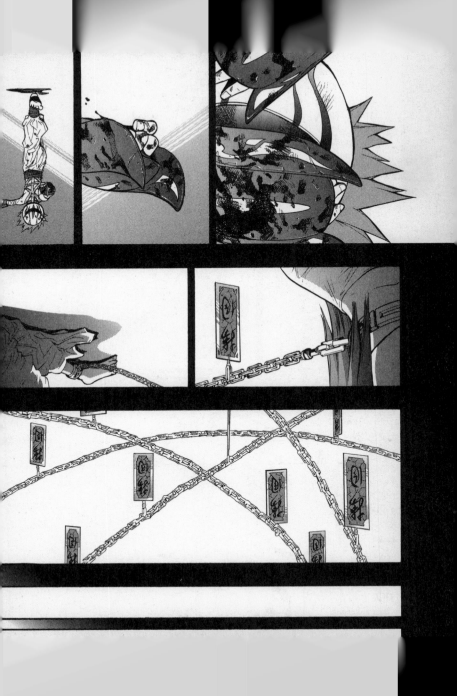

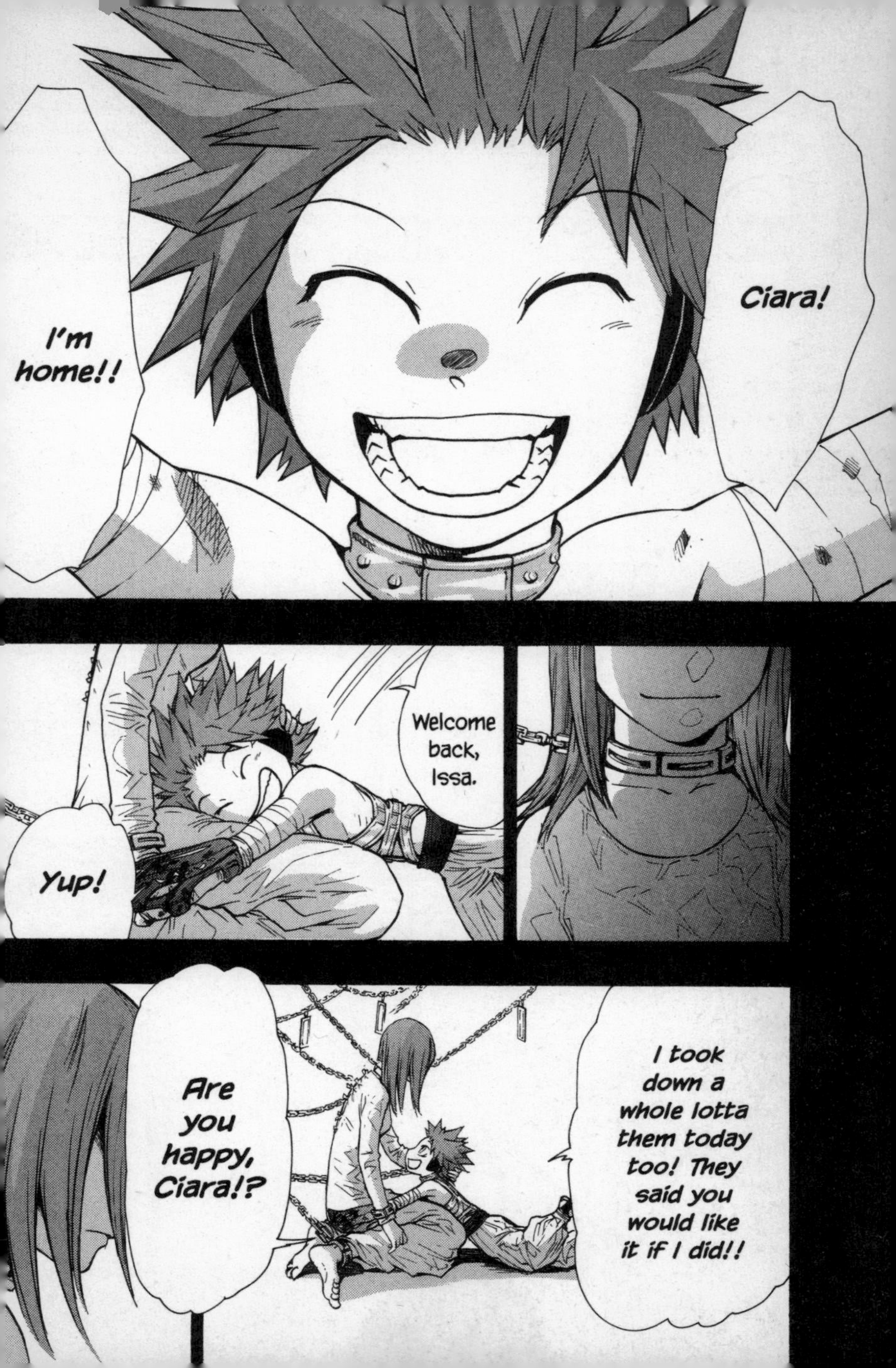
Ciara!
I'm home!!
Welcome back, Issa.
Yup!
I took down a whole lotta them today too! They said you would like it if I did!!
Are you happy, Ciara!?

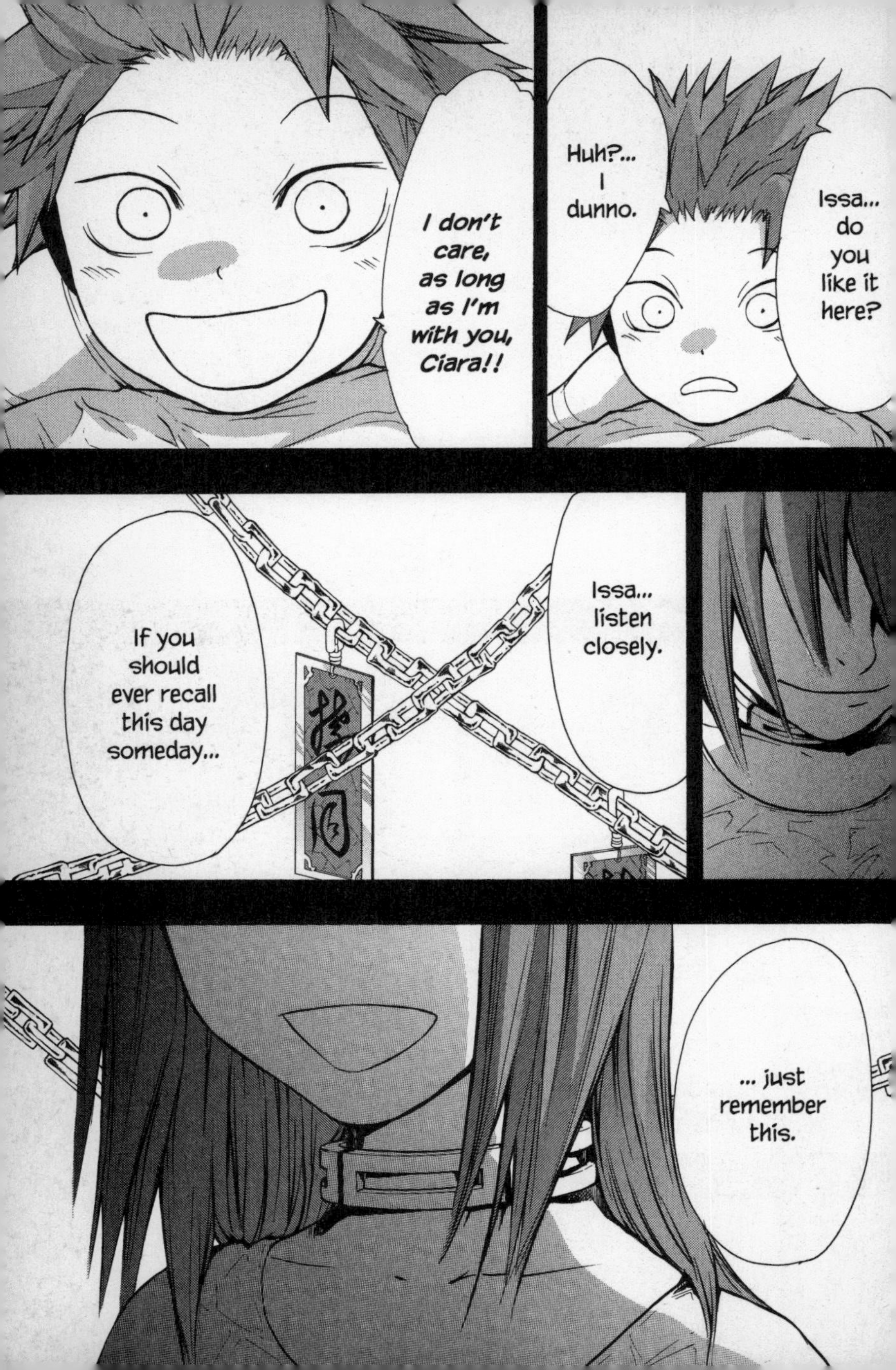
Issa... do you like it here?
Huh?... I dunno.
I don't care, as long as I'm with you, Ciara!!
Issa... listen closely.
If you should ever recall this day someday...
... just remember this.

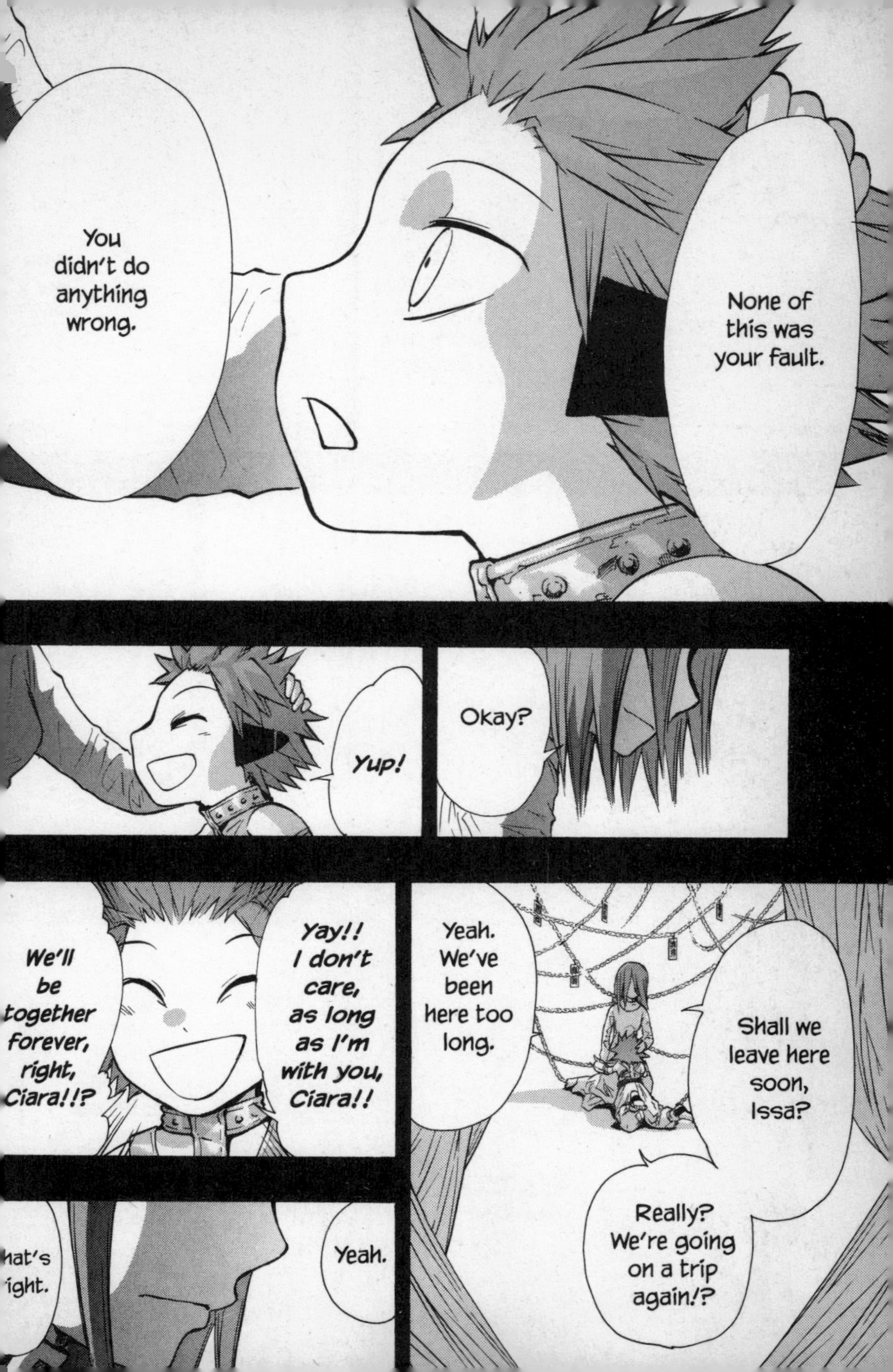
None of this was your fault.
You didn't do anything wrong.
Okay?
Yup!
Shall we leave here soon, Issa?
Really? We're going on a trip again!?
Yeah. We've been here too long.
Yay!! I don't care, as long as I'm with you, Ciara!!
We'll be together forever, right, Ciara!!?
Yeah.

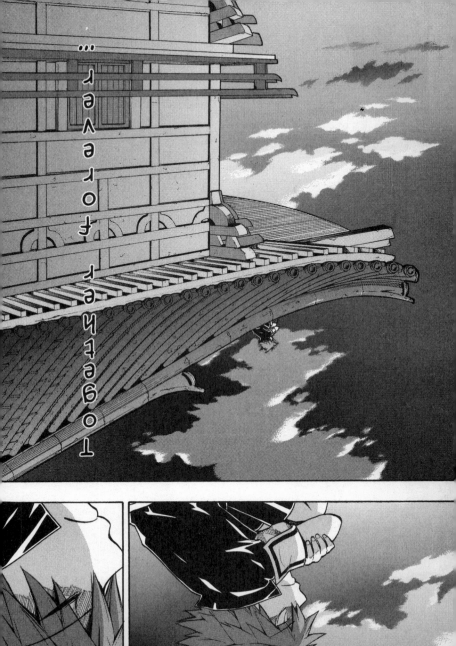

...forever together

…あぶないですよヤヅマさん とび出しちゃ
こいつはドラクル異形種じゃない
殺すな

あなたも本部で看てもらった方がいい
その獣傷…
さ…て日が落ちる前に三国に帰れるな!!
本日の任務完了オ!!

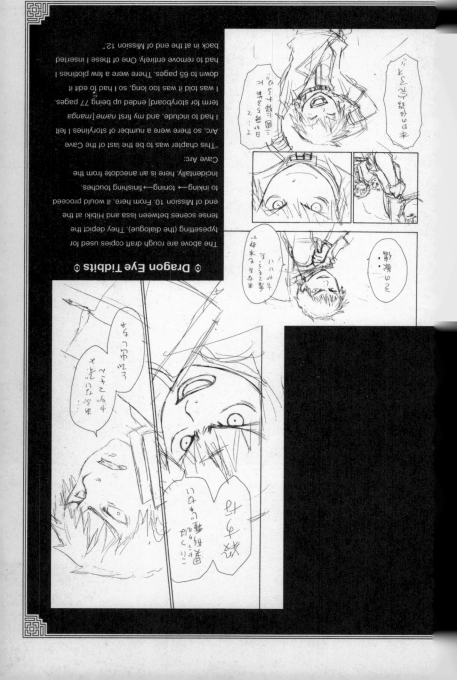

◊ Dragon Eye Tidbits ◊

The above are rough draft copies used for typesetting (the dialogue). They depict the tense scenes between Issa and Hibiki at the end of Mission 10. From here, it would proceed to inking⟶ toning⟶finishing touches.

Incidentally, here is an anecdote from the Cave Arc:

"This chapter was to be the last of the Cave Arc, so there were a number of storylines I felt I had to include, and my first *name* [*manga* term for storyboard] ended up being 77 pages. I was told it was too long, so I had to edit it down to 65 pages. There were a few plotlines I had to remove entirely. One of these I inserted back in at the end of Mission 12."

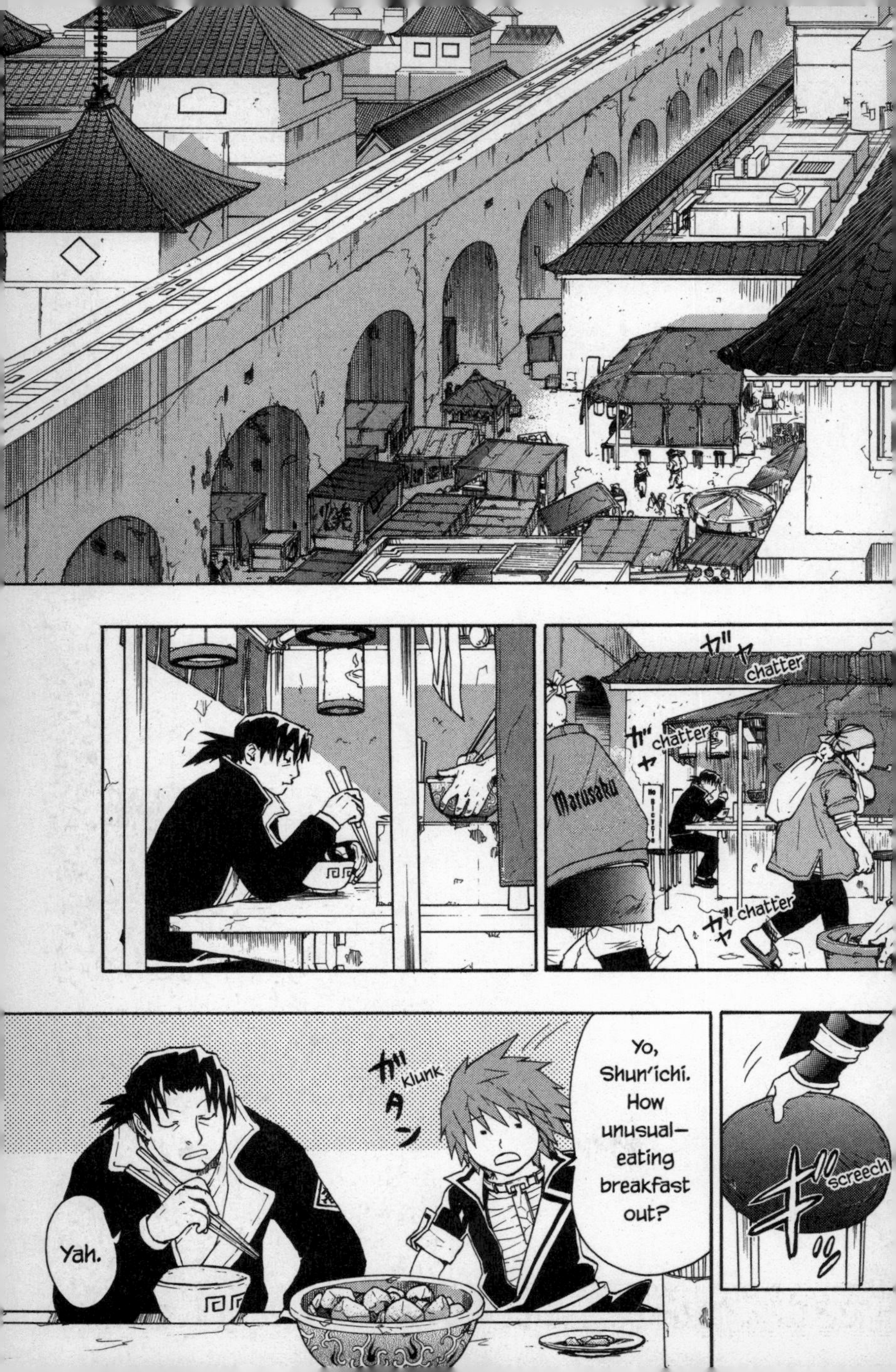
chatter
chatter
Marusaku
No Bicycles
chatter
screech
Yo, Shun'ichi. How unusual—eating breakfast out?
klunk
Yah.

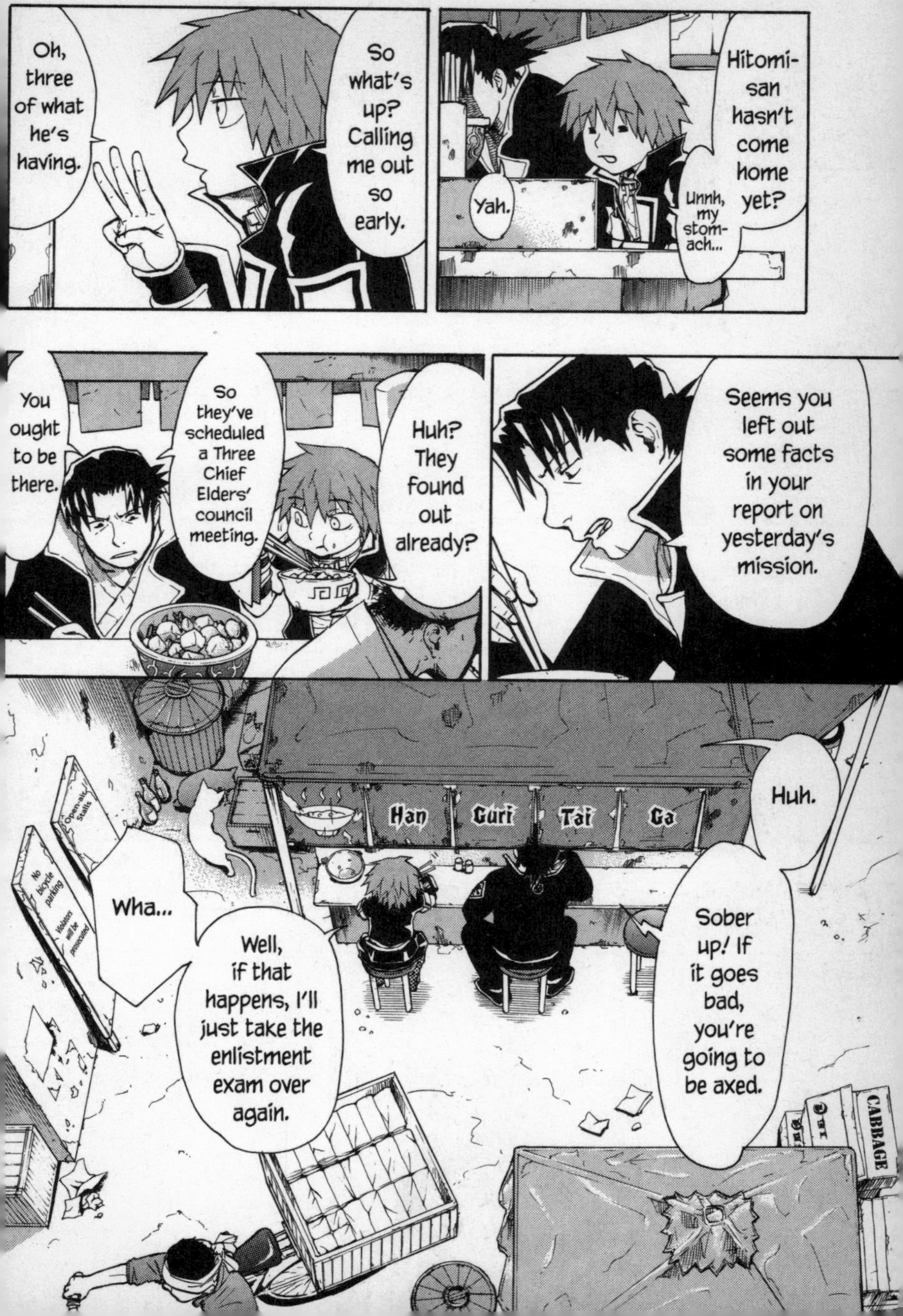
Hitomi-san hasn't come home yet?
Unnh, my stomach...
Yah.
So what's up? Calling me out so early.
Oh, three of what he's having.
Seems you left out some facts in your report on yesterday's mission.
Huh? They found out already?
So they've scheduled a Three Chief Elders' council meeting.
You ought to be there.
Huh.
Han Guri Tai Ga
Sober up! If it goes bad, you're going to be axed.
Well, if that happens, I'll just take the enlistment exam over again.
Wha...
Open-air Stalls
No bicycle parking
Violators will be prosecuted
CABBAGE

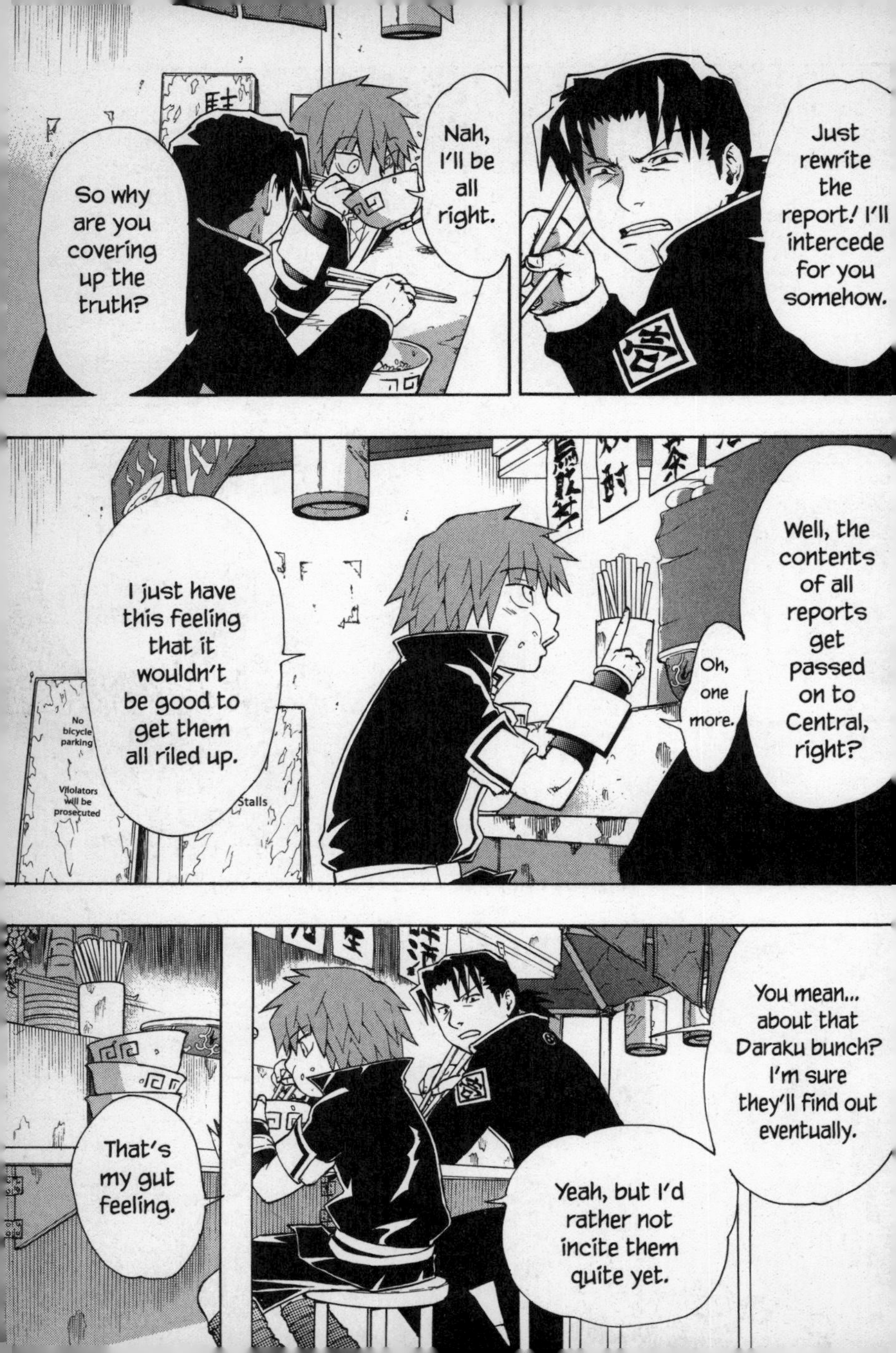
Just rewrite the report! I'll intercede for you somehow.
Nah, I'll be all right.
So why are you covering up the truth?
Well, the contents of all reports get passed on to Central, right?
Oh, one more.
I just have this feeling that it wouldn't be good to get them all riled up.
No bicycle parking
Violators will be prosecuted
Stalls
You mean... about that Daraku bunch? I'm sure they'll find out eventually.
Yeah, but I'd rather not incite them quite yet.
That's my gut feeling.

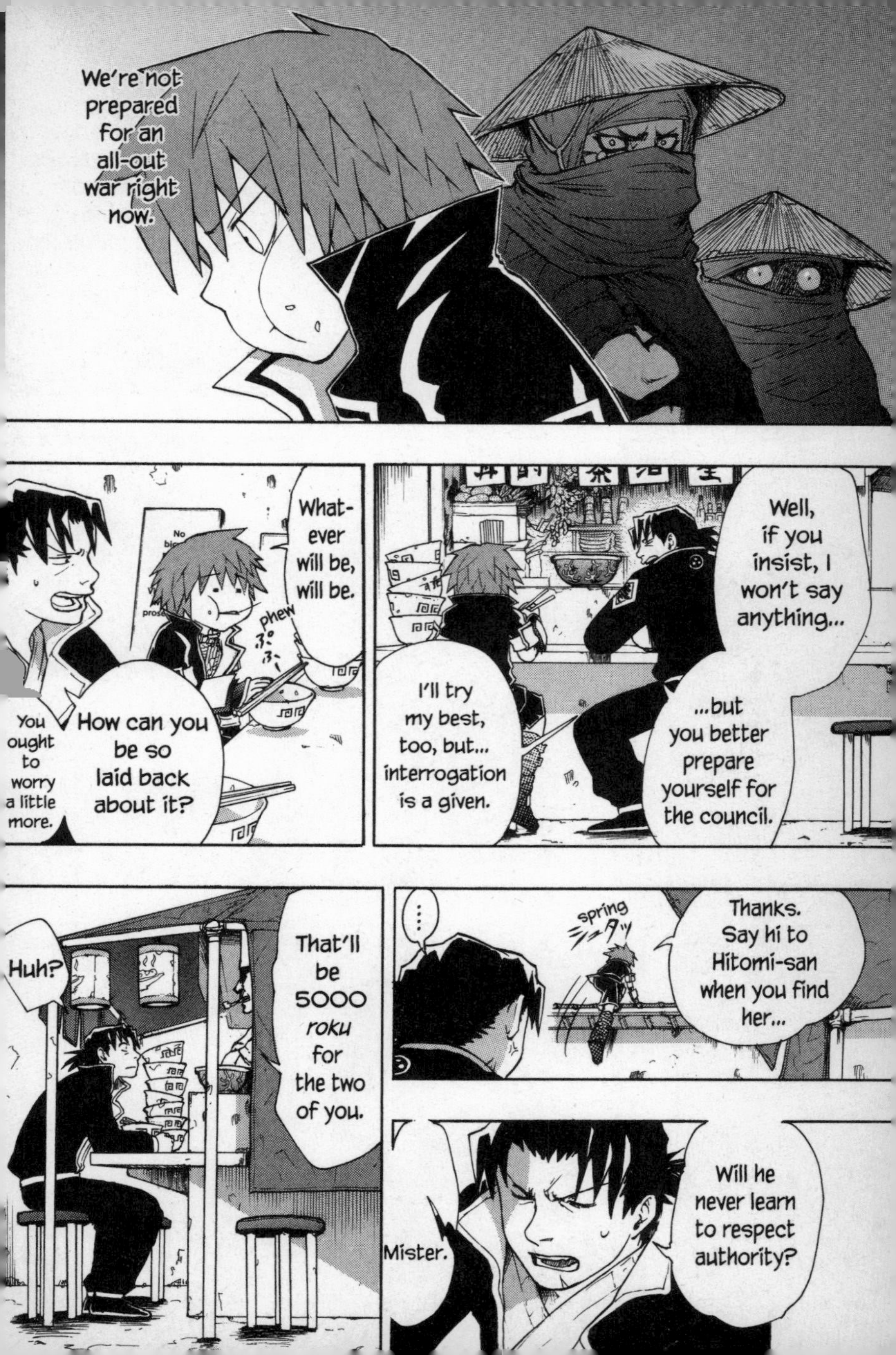
We're not prepared for an all-out war right now.
Well, if you insist, I won't say anything...
...but you better prepare yourself for the council.
I'll try my best, too, but... interrogation is a given.
What-ever will be, will be.
phew
How can you be so laid back about it?
You ought to worry a little more.
Thanks. Say hi to Hitomi-san when you find her...
spring
....
Will he never learn to respect authority?
Mister.
That'll be 5000 *roku* for the two of you.
Huh?

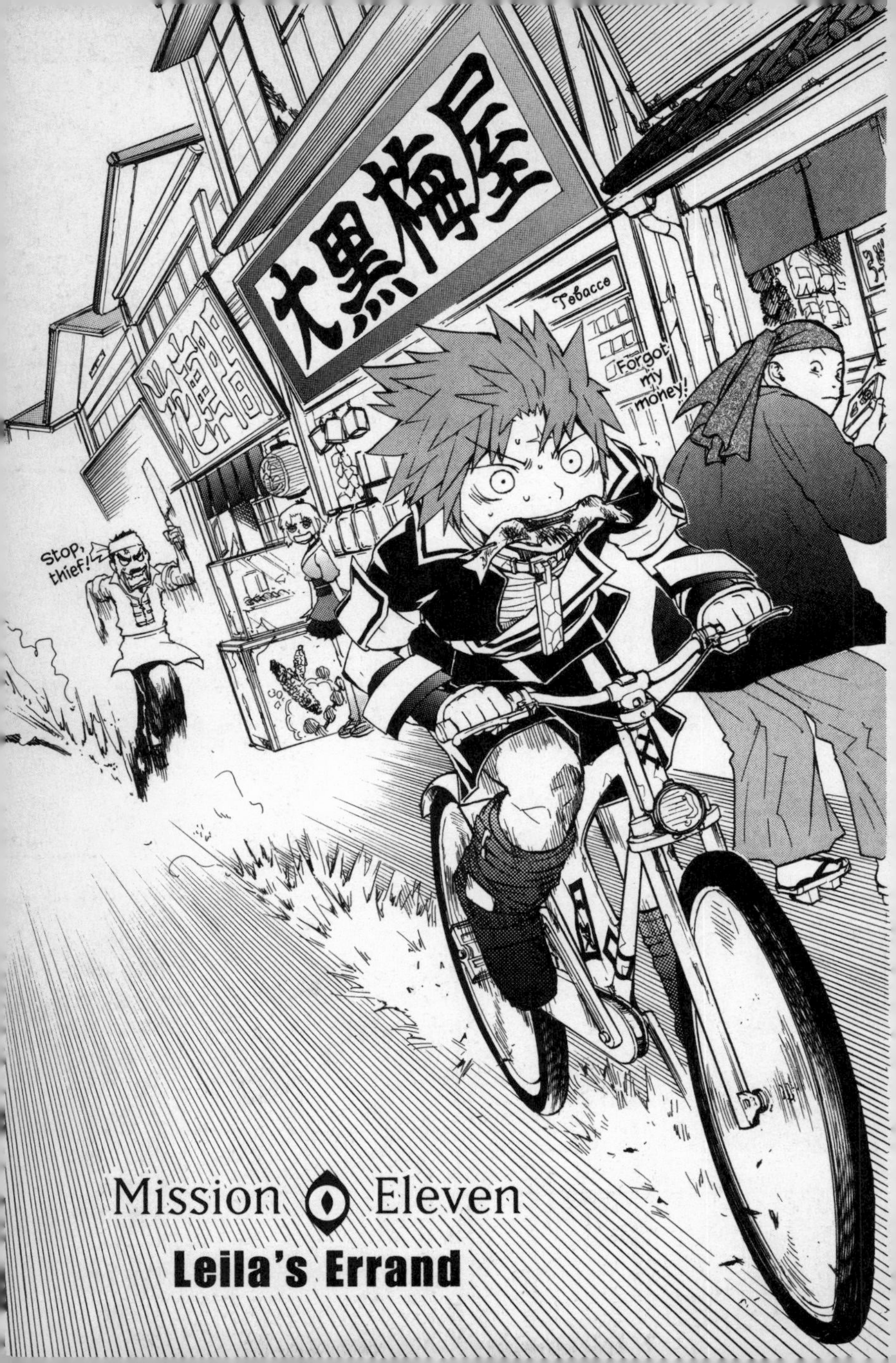
Forgot my money!
Tobacco
大黒梅屋
Stop, thief!
Mission Eleven
Leila's Errand

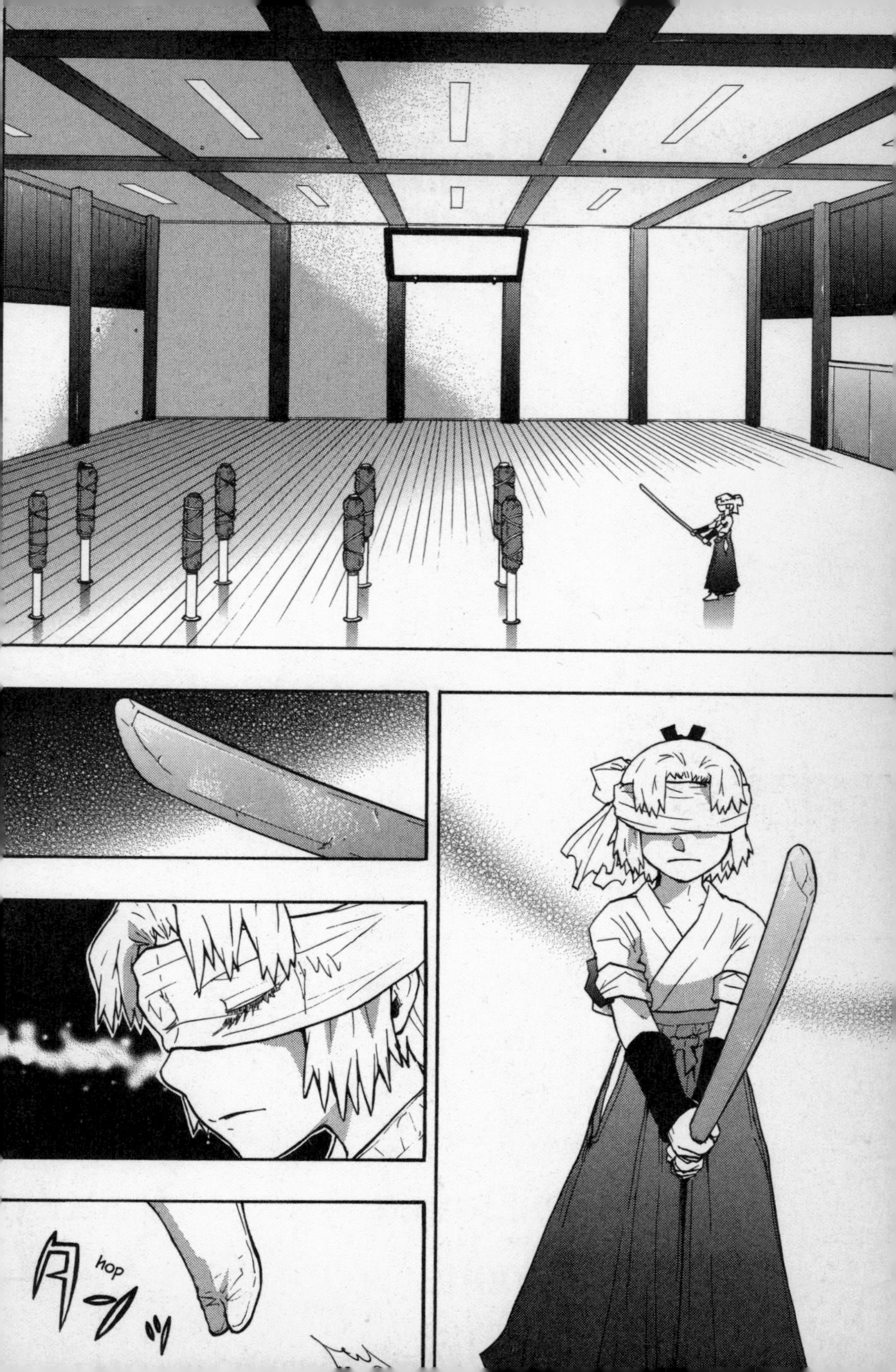
hop

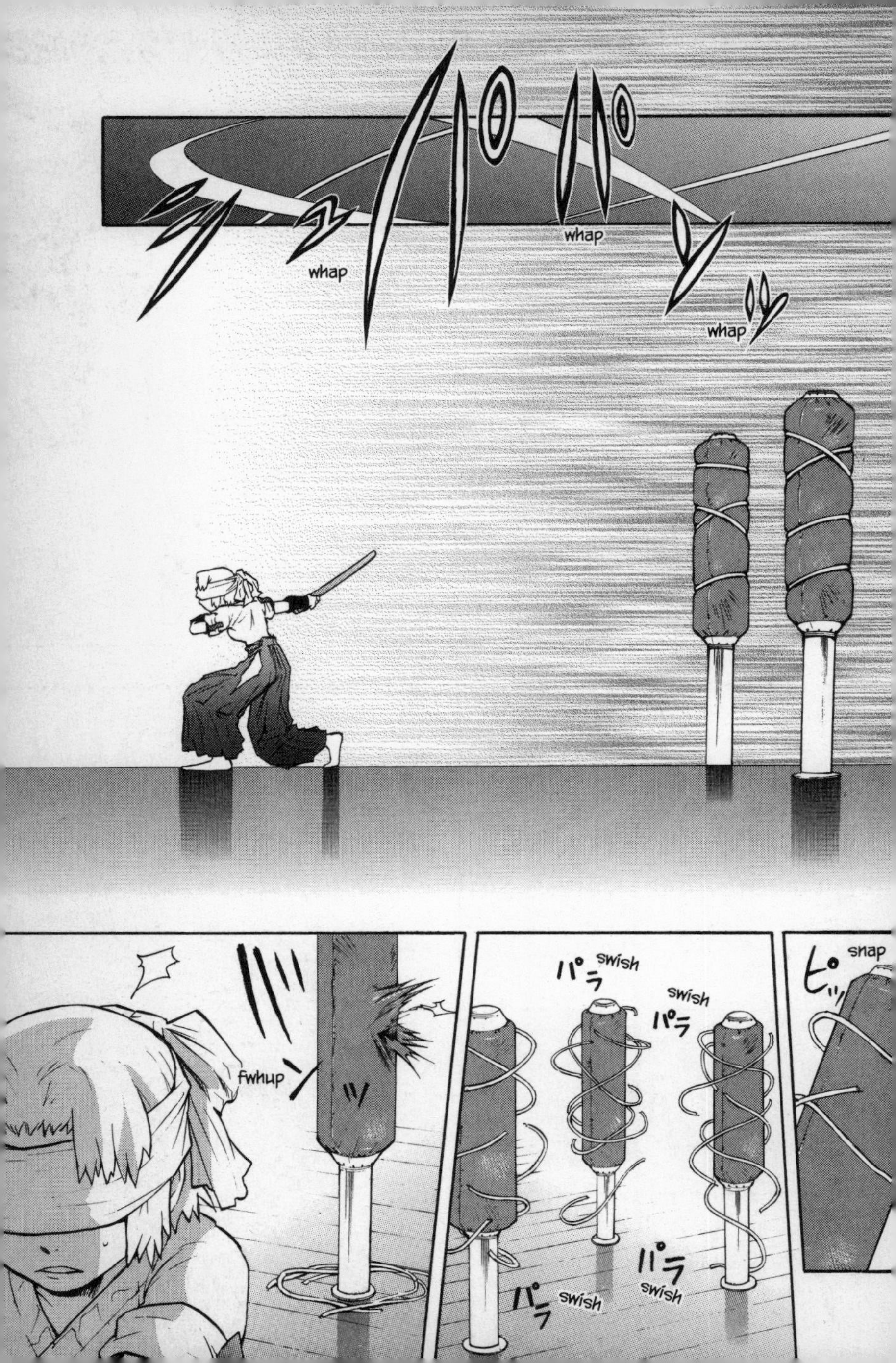
whap
whap
whap
ピッ
snap
swish
パラ
swish
パラ
swish
パラ
swish
パラ
fwhup

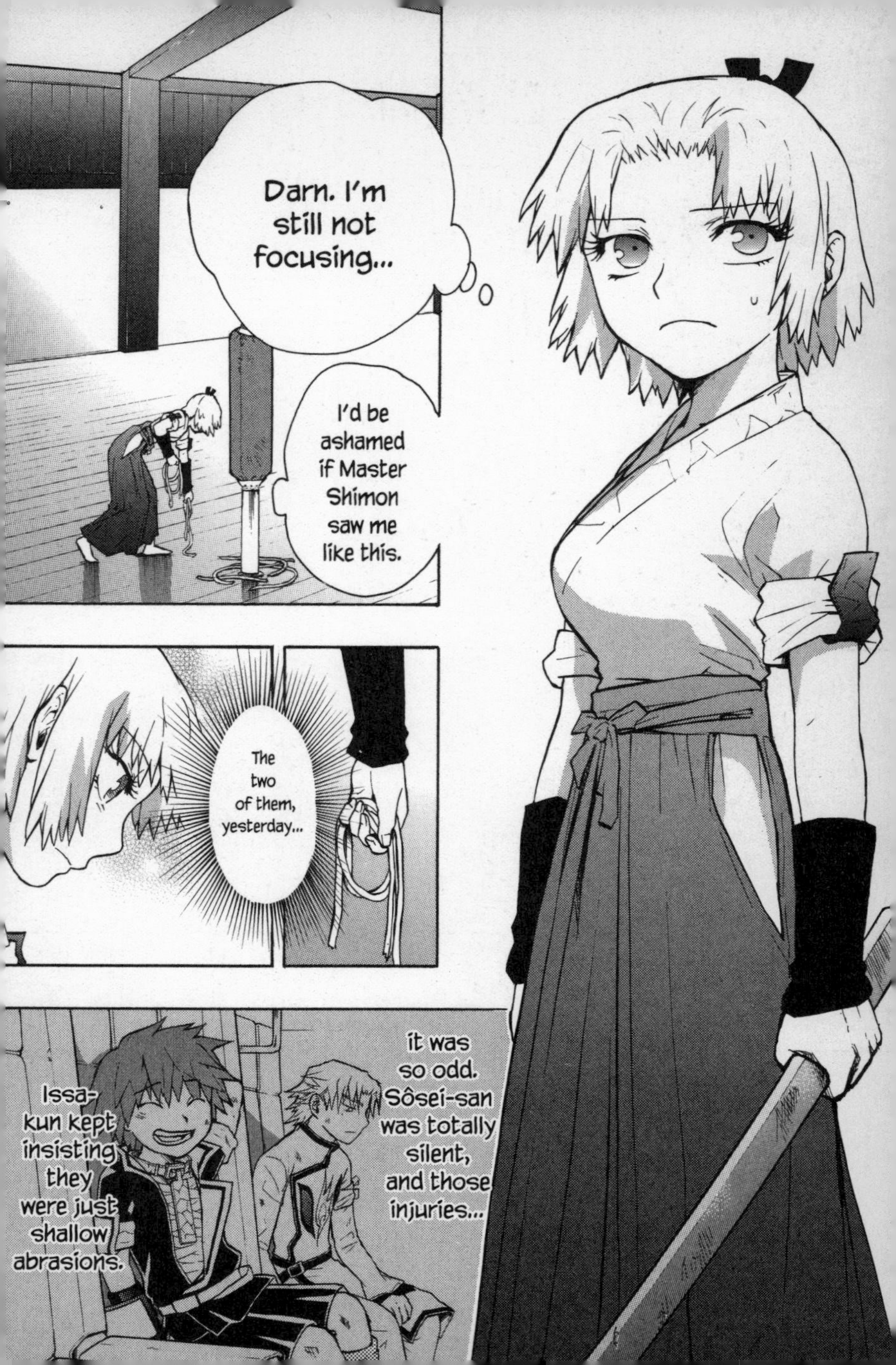
Darn. I'm still not focusing...
I'd be ashamed if Master Shimon saw me like this.
The two of them, yesterday...
it was so odd. Sôsei-san was totally silent, and those injuries...
Issa-kun kept insisting they were just shallow abrasions.

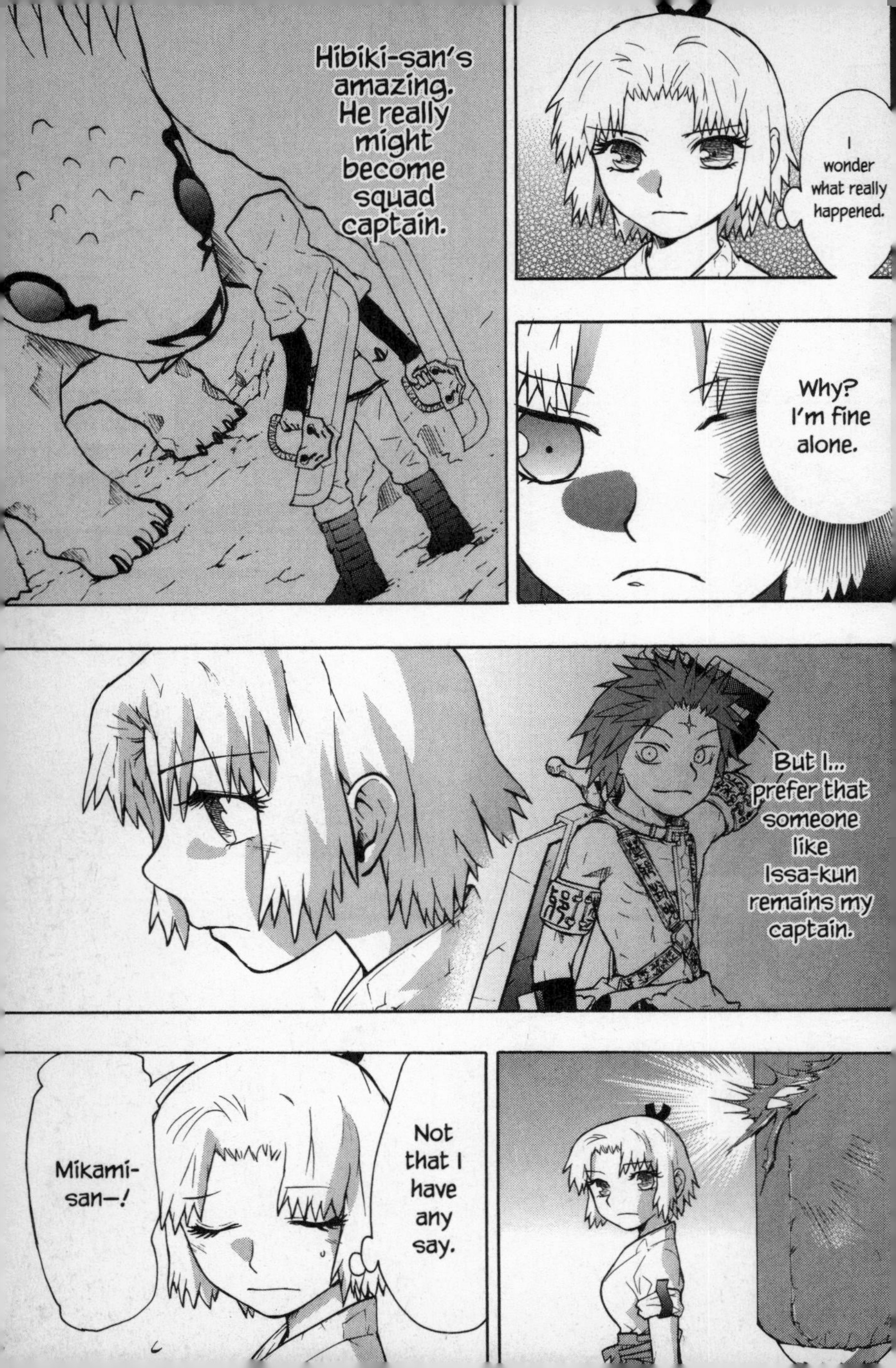
I wonder what really happened.
Why? I'm fine alone.
Hibiki-san's amazing. He really might become squad captain.
But I... prefer that someone like Issa-kun remains my captain.
Not that I have any say.
Mikami-san—!

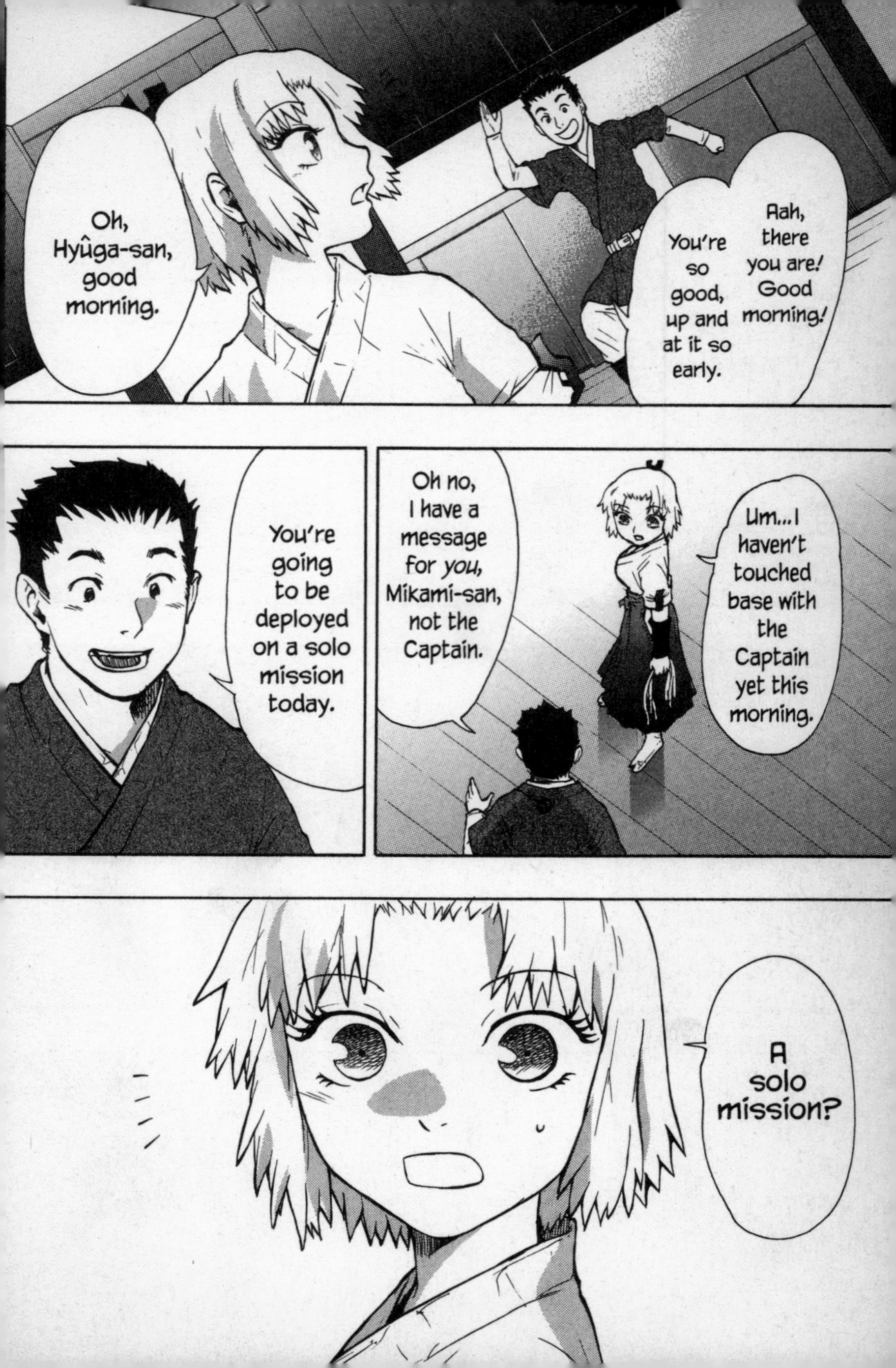
Aah, there you are! Good morning!
You're so good, up and at it so early.
Oh, Hyûga-san, good morning.
Um...I haven't touched base with the Captain yet this morning.
Oh no, I have a message for *you*, Mikami-san, not the Captain.
You're going to be deployed on a solo mission today.
A solo mission?

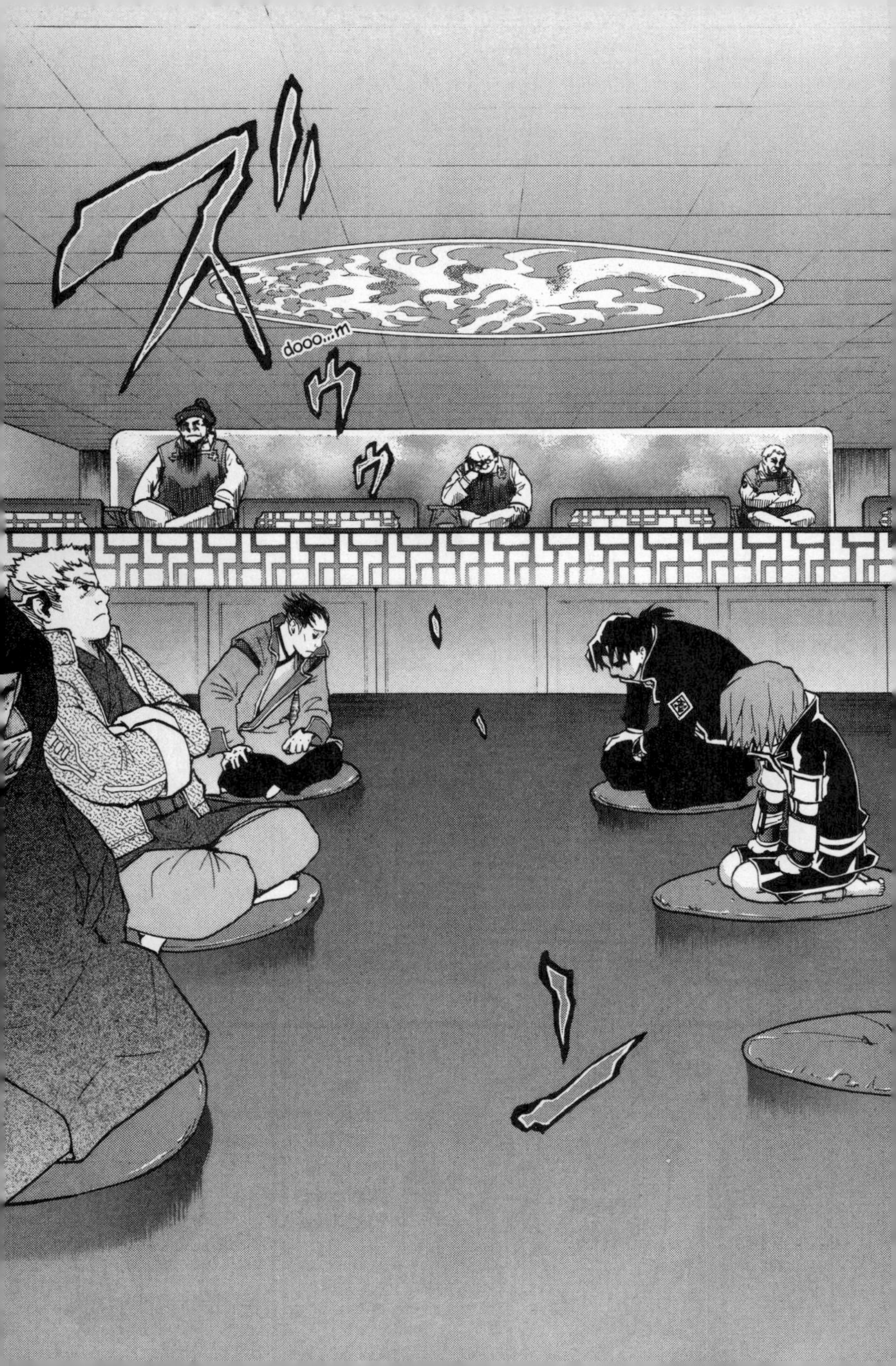
dooo...m

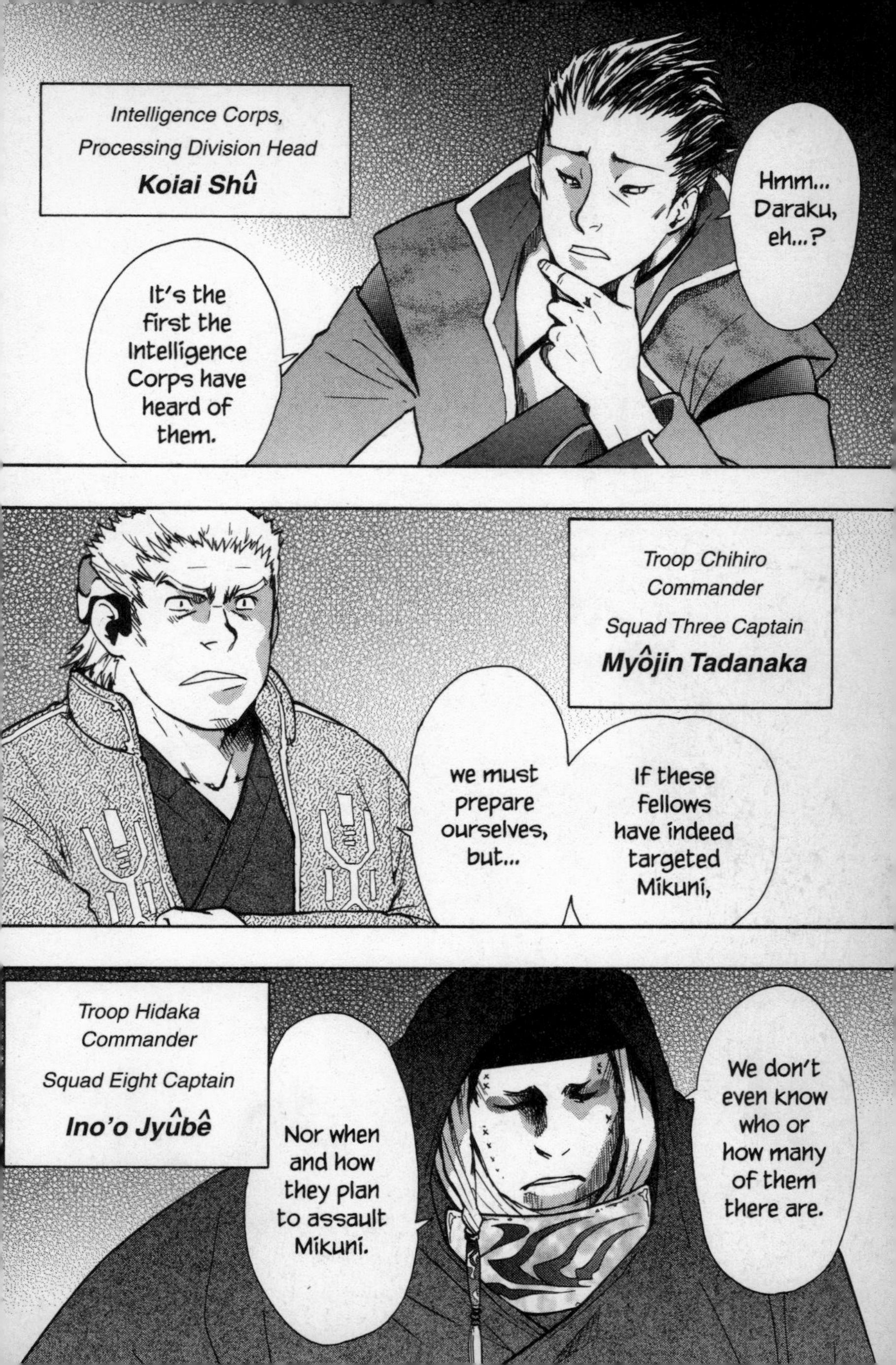
Hmm... Daraku, eh...?
Intelligence Corps, Processing Division Head Koiai Shû
It's the first the Intelligence Corps have heard of them.
Troop Chihiro Commander Squad Three Captain Myôjin Tadanaka
If these fellows have indeed targeted Mikuni,
we must prepare ourselves, but...
We don't even know who or how many of them there are.
Troop Hidaka Commander Squad Eight Captain Ino'o Jyûbê
Nor when and how they plan to assault Mikuni.

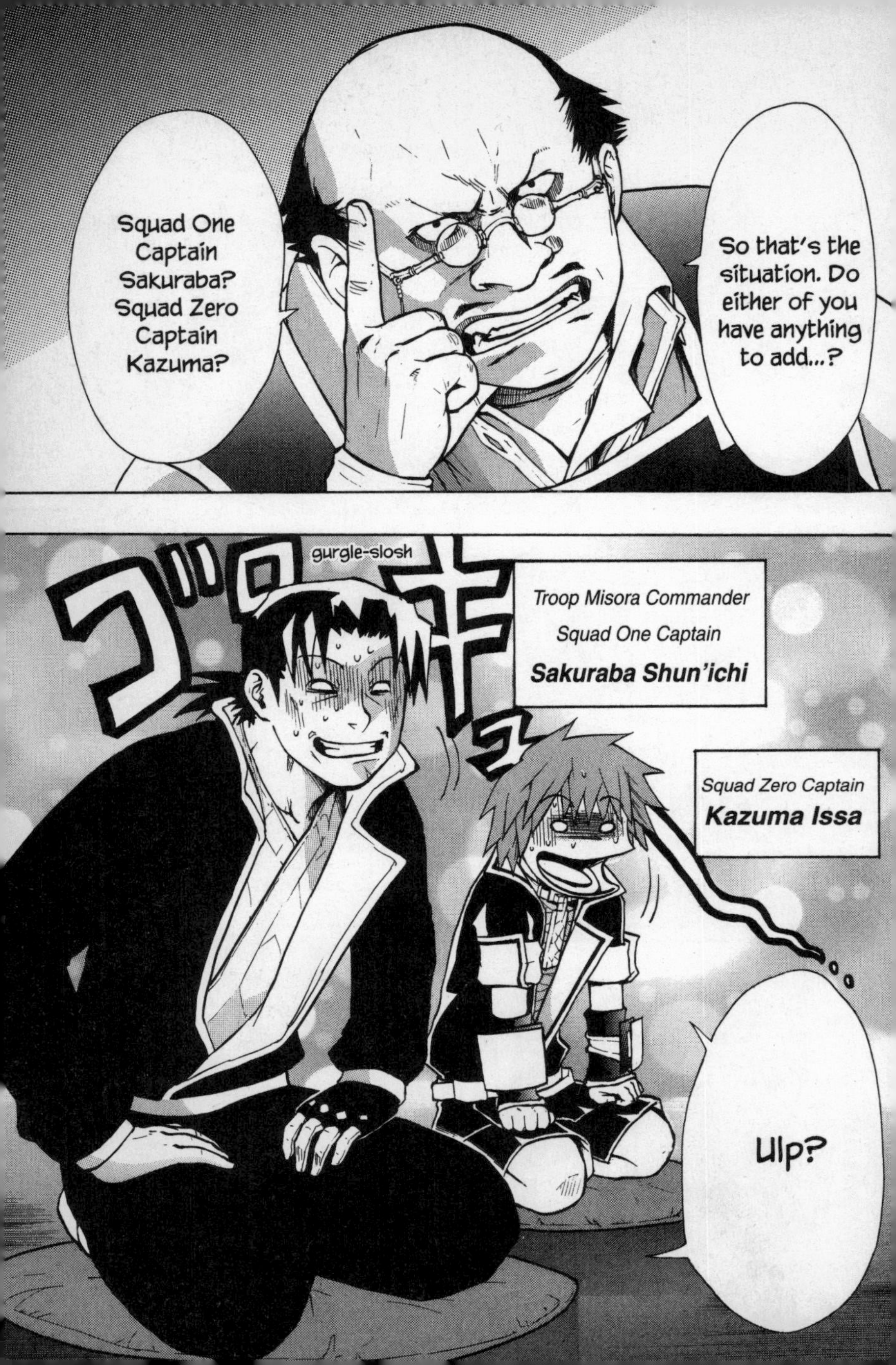
So that's the situation. Do either of you have anything to add...?
Squad One Captain Sakuraba? Squad Zero Captain Kazuma?
Troop Misora Commander Squad One Captain Sakuraba Shun'ichi
gurgle-slosh
Squad Zero Captain Kazuma Issa
Ulp?

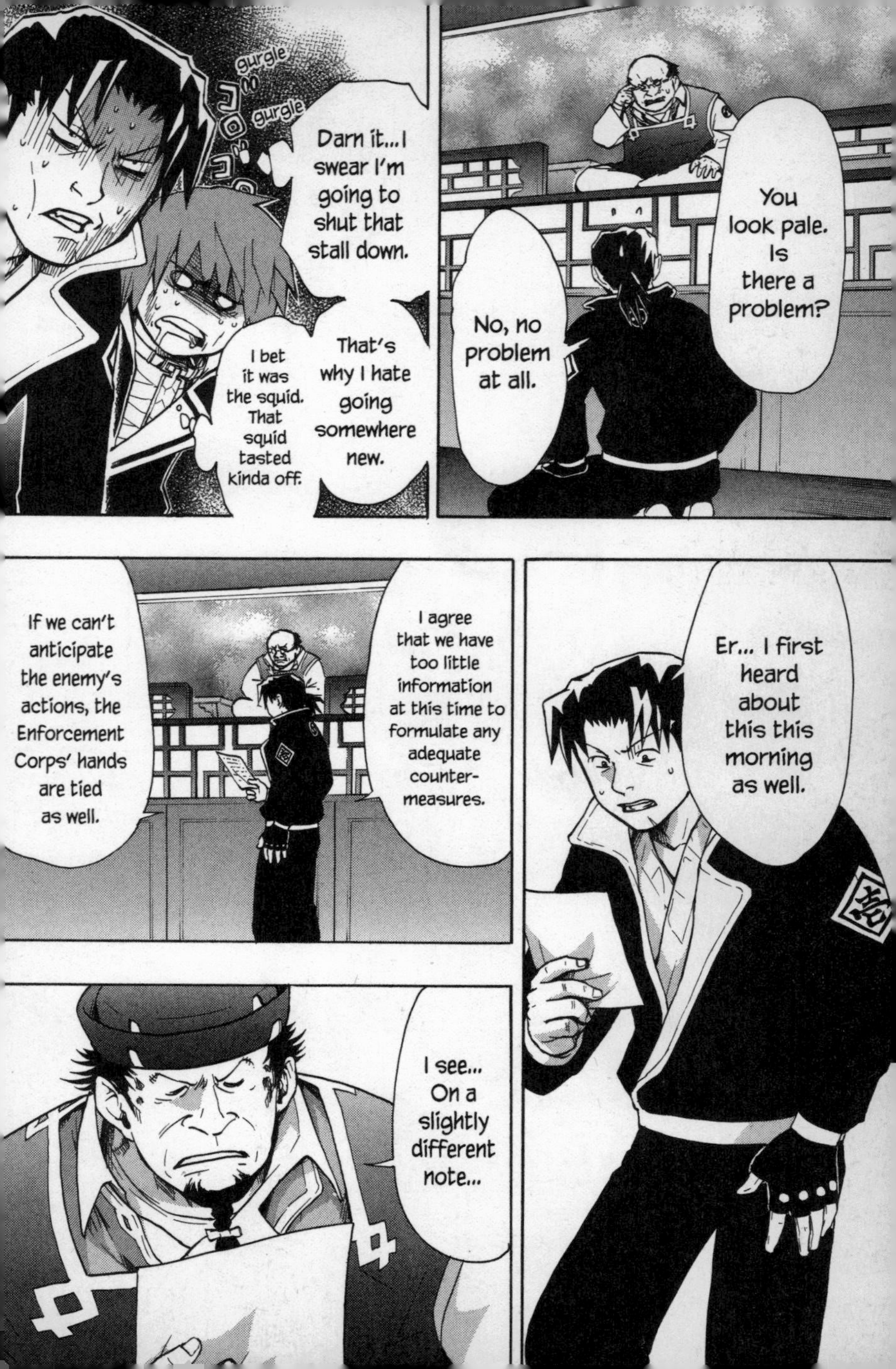
You look pale. Is there a problem?
No, no problem at all.
Darn it...I swear I'm going to shut that stall down.
gurgle
gurgle
That's why I hate going somewhere new.
I bet it was the squid. That squid tasted kinda off.
Er... I first heard about this this morning as well.
I agree that we have too little information at this time to formulate any adequate counter-measures.
If we can't anticipate the enemy's actions, the Enforcement Corps' hands are tied as well.
I see... On a slightly different note...

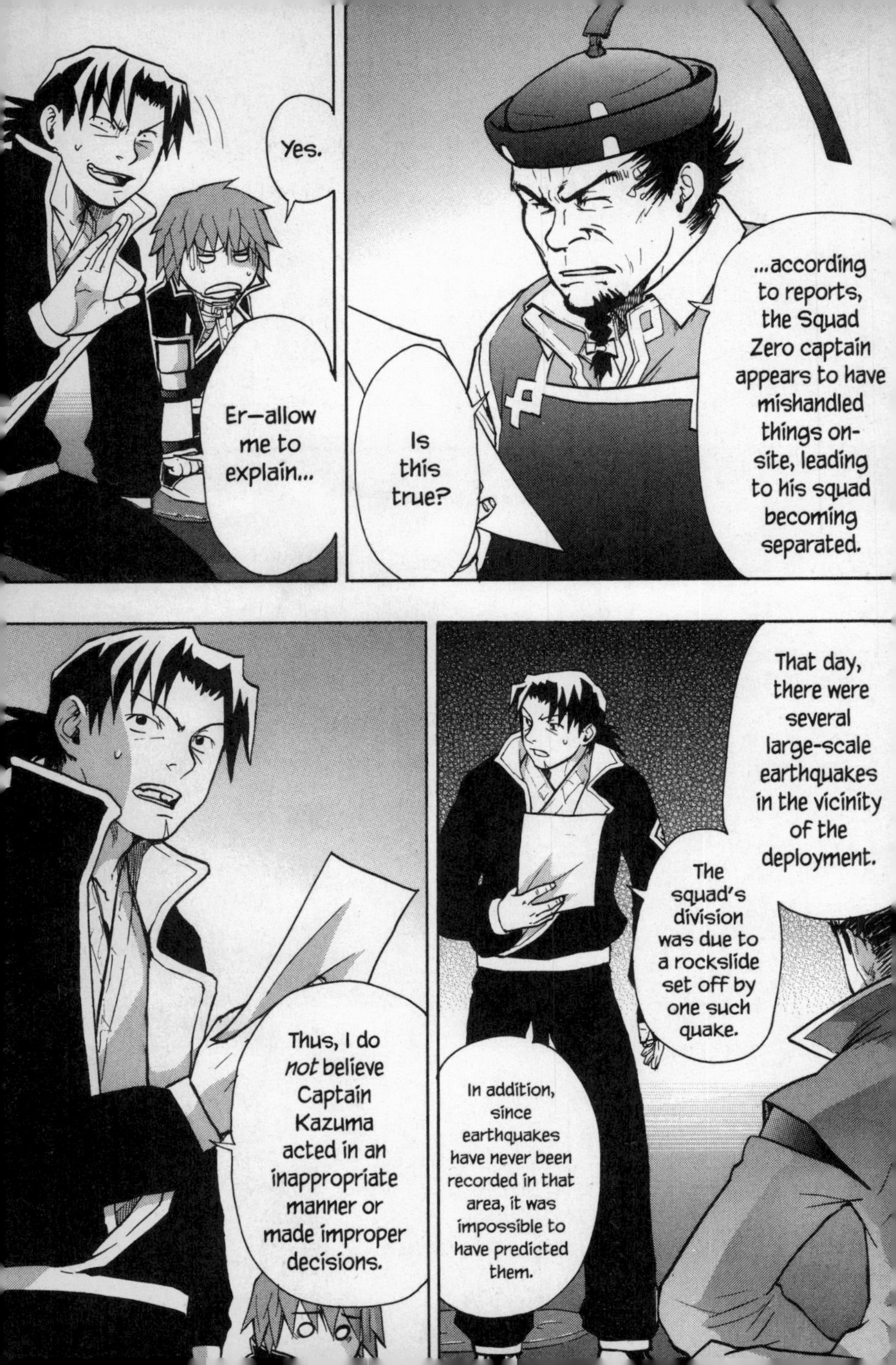
...according to reports, the Squad Zero captain appears to have mishandled things on-site, leading to his squad becoming separated.
Is this true?
Yes.
Er—allow me to explain...
That day, there were several large-scale earthquakes in the vicinity of the deployment.
The squad's division was due to a rockslide set off by one such quake.
In addition, since earthquakes have never been recorded in that area, it was impossible to have predicted them.
Thus, I do *not* believe Captain Kazuma acted in an inappropriate manner or made improper decisions.

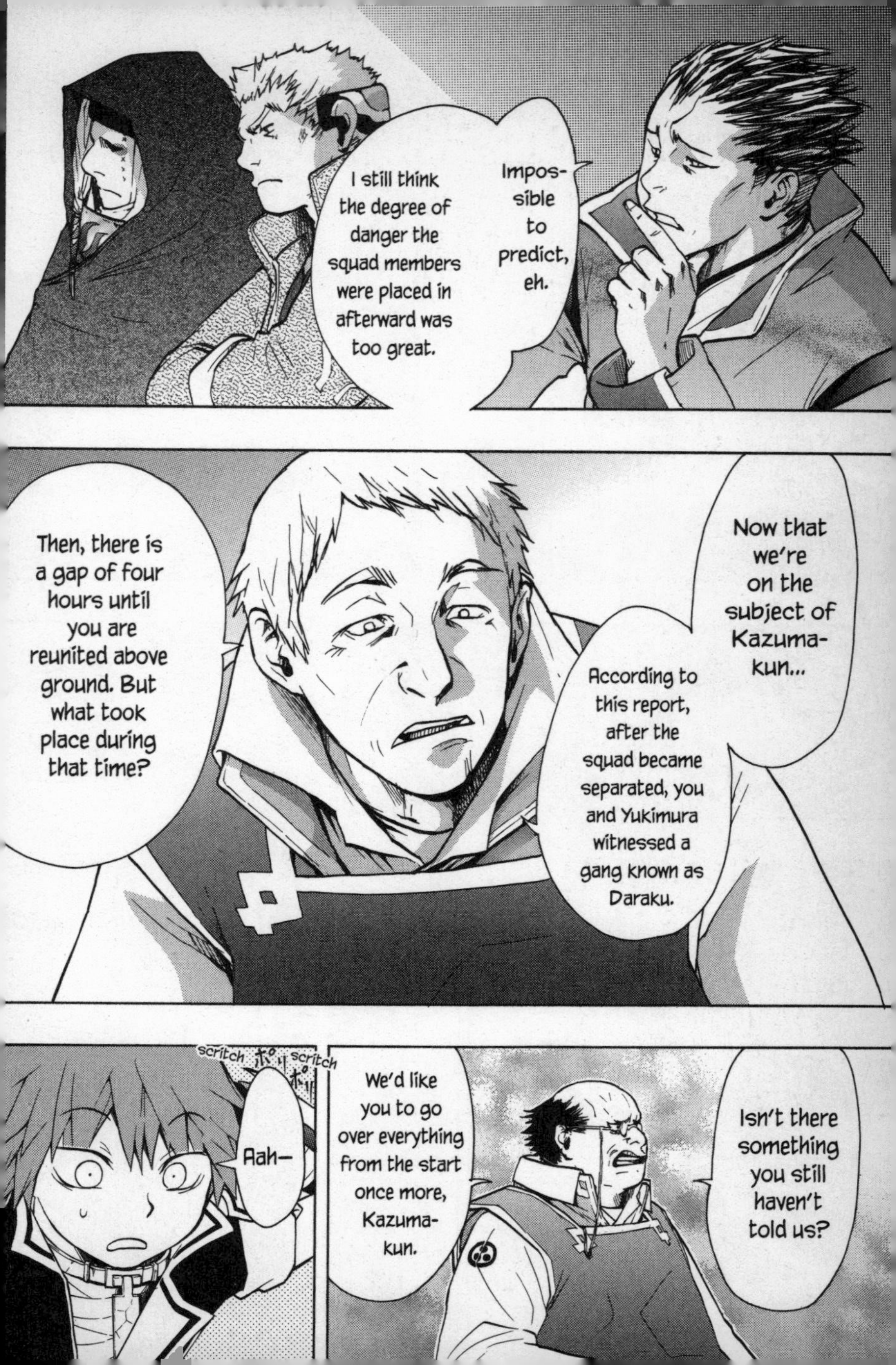
Impos-sible to predict, eh.
I still think the degree of danger the squad members were placed in afterward was too great.
Now that we're on the subject of Kazuma-kun...
According to this report, after the squad became separated, you and Yukimura witnessed a gang known as Daraku.
Then, there is a gap of four hours until you are reunited above ground. But what took place during that time?
Isn't there something you still haven't told us?
We'd like you to go over everything from the start once more, Kazuma-kun.
scritch
scritch
Aah—

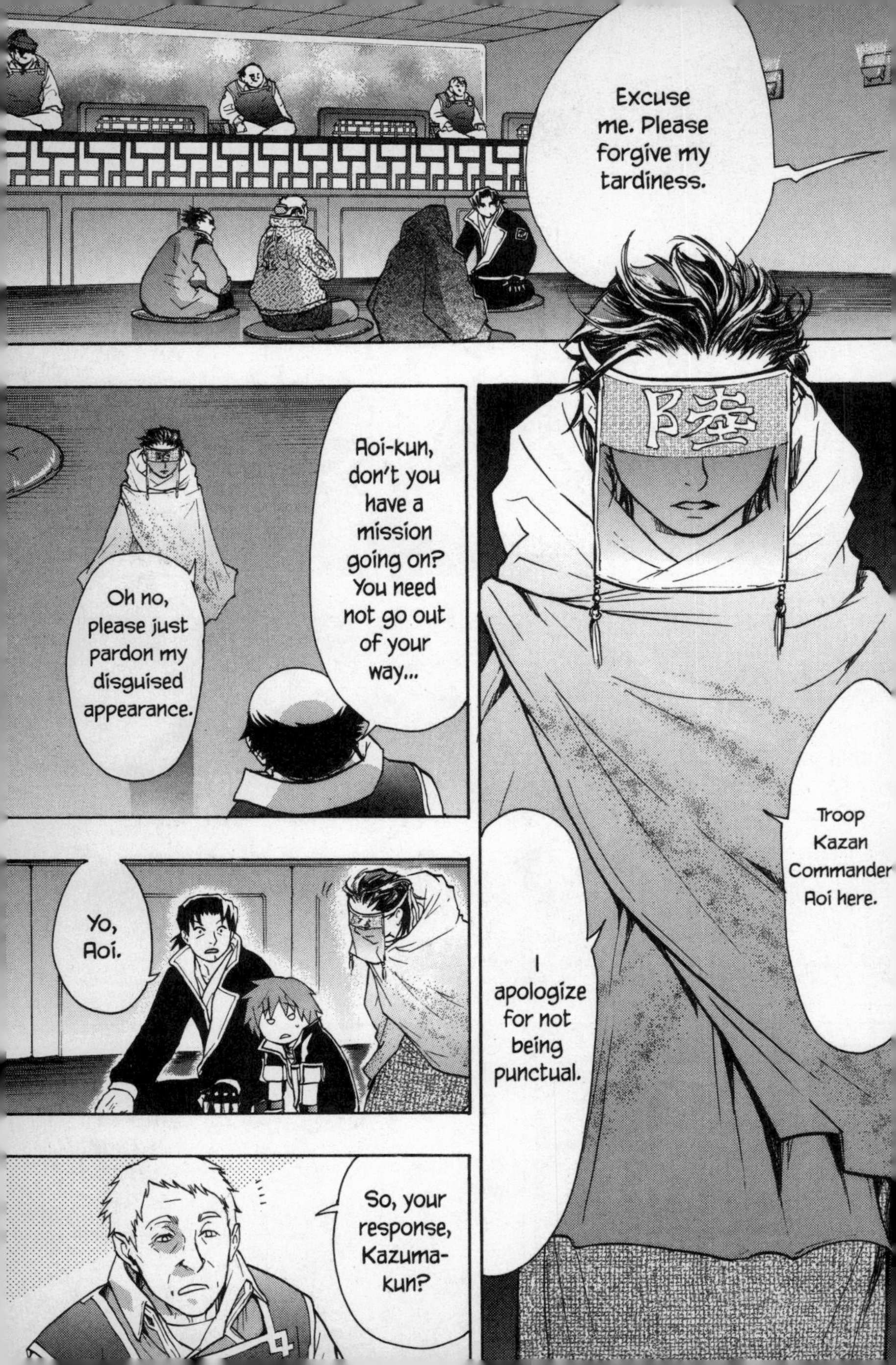
Excuse me. Please forgive my tardiness.
陸
Troop Kazan Commander Aoi here.
I apologize for not being punctual.
Aoi-kun, don't you have a mission going on? You need not go out of your way...
Oh no, please just pardon my disguised appearance.
Yo, Aoi.
So, your response, Kazuma-kun?

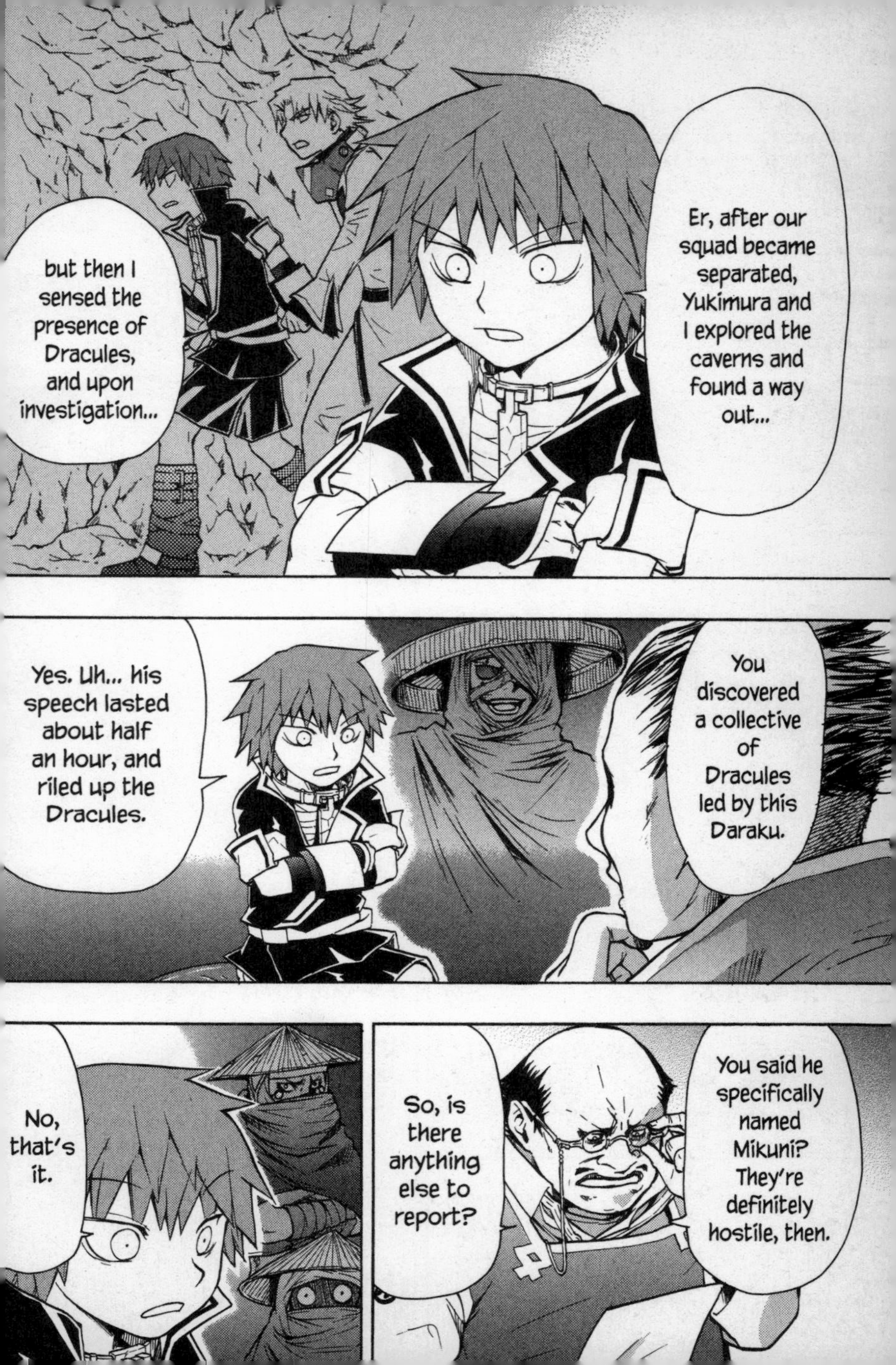
Er, after our squad became separated, Yukimura and I explored the caverns and found a way out...
but then I sensed the presence of Dracules, and upon investigation...
You discovered a collective of Dracules led by this Daraku.
Yes. Uh... his speech lasted about half an hour, and riled up the Dracules.
You said he specifically named Mikuni? They're definitely hostile, then.
So, is there anything else to report?
No, that's it.

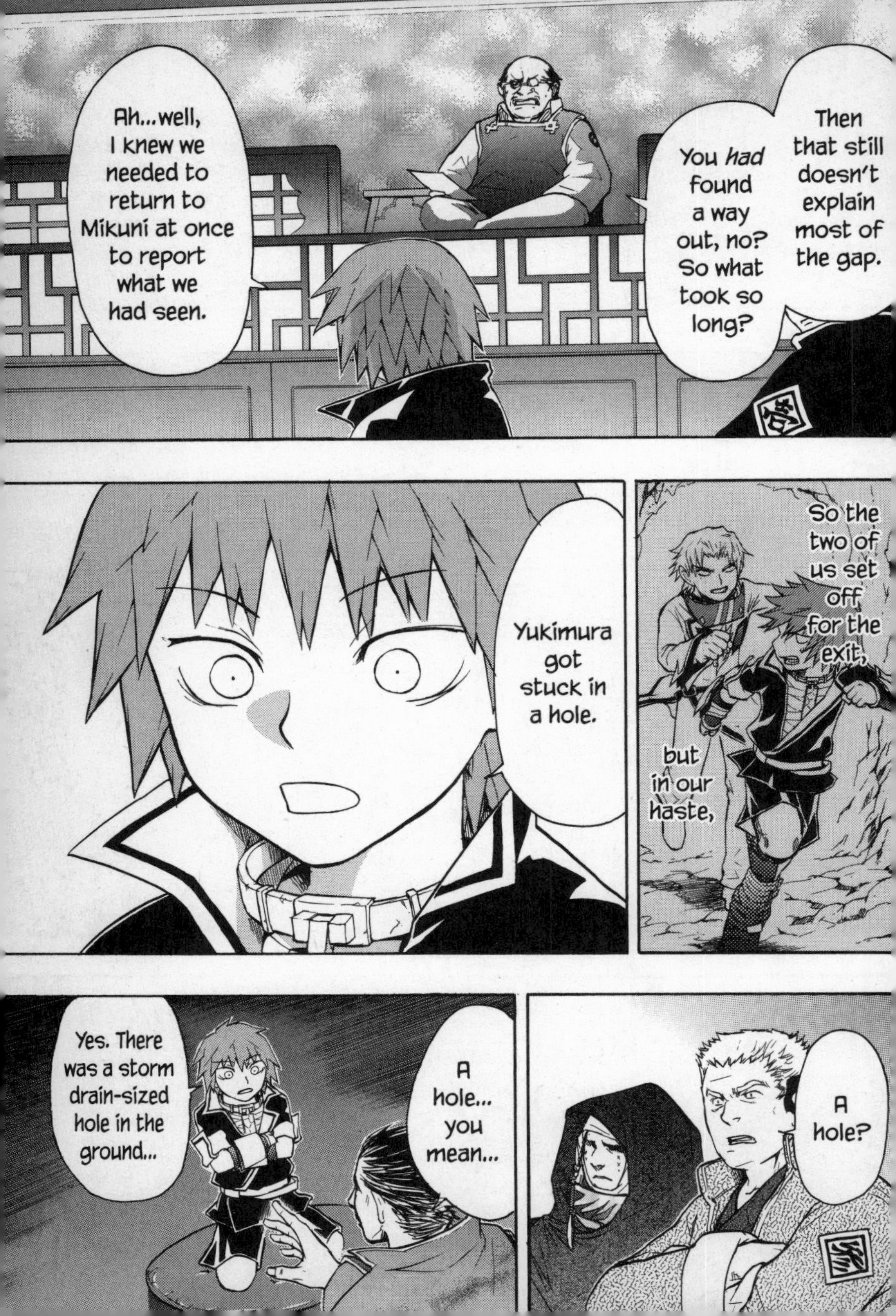
Then that still doesn't explain most of the gap.
You *had* found a way out, no? So what took so long?
Ah...well, I knew we needed to return to Mikuni at once to report what we had seen.
So the two of us set off for the exit,
but in our haste,
Yukimura got stuck in a hole.
A hole?
A hole... you mean...
Yes. There was a storm drain-sized hole in the ground...

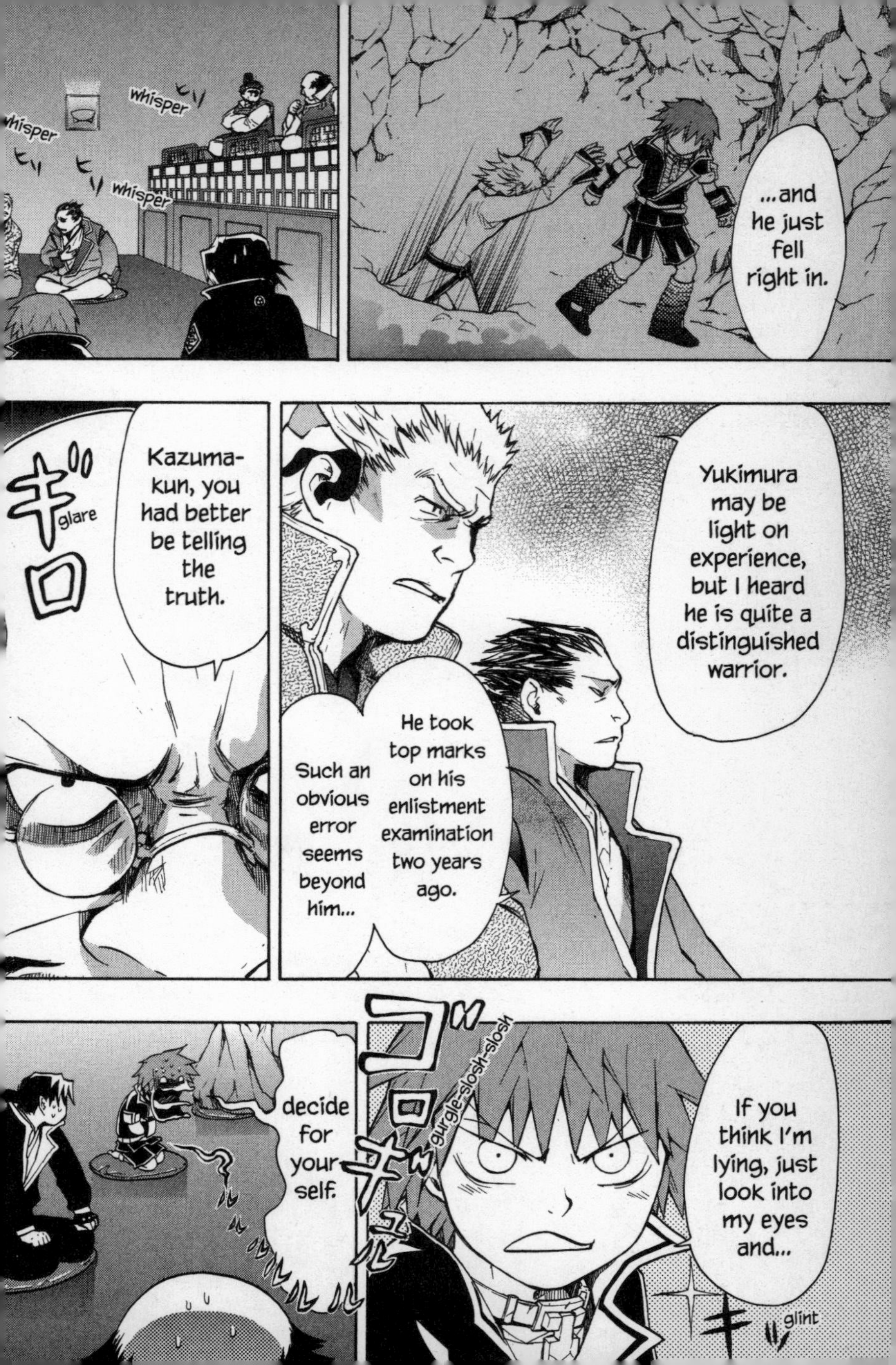
...and he just fell right in.
whisper
whisper
whisper
Yukimura may be light on experience, but I heard he is quite a distinguished warrior.
He took top marks on his enlistment examination two years ago.
Such an obvious error seems beyond him...
Kazuma-kun, you had better be telling the truth.
glare
If you think I'm lying, just look into my eyes and...
glint
gurgle-slosh-slosh
decide for yourself.

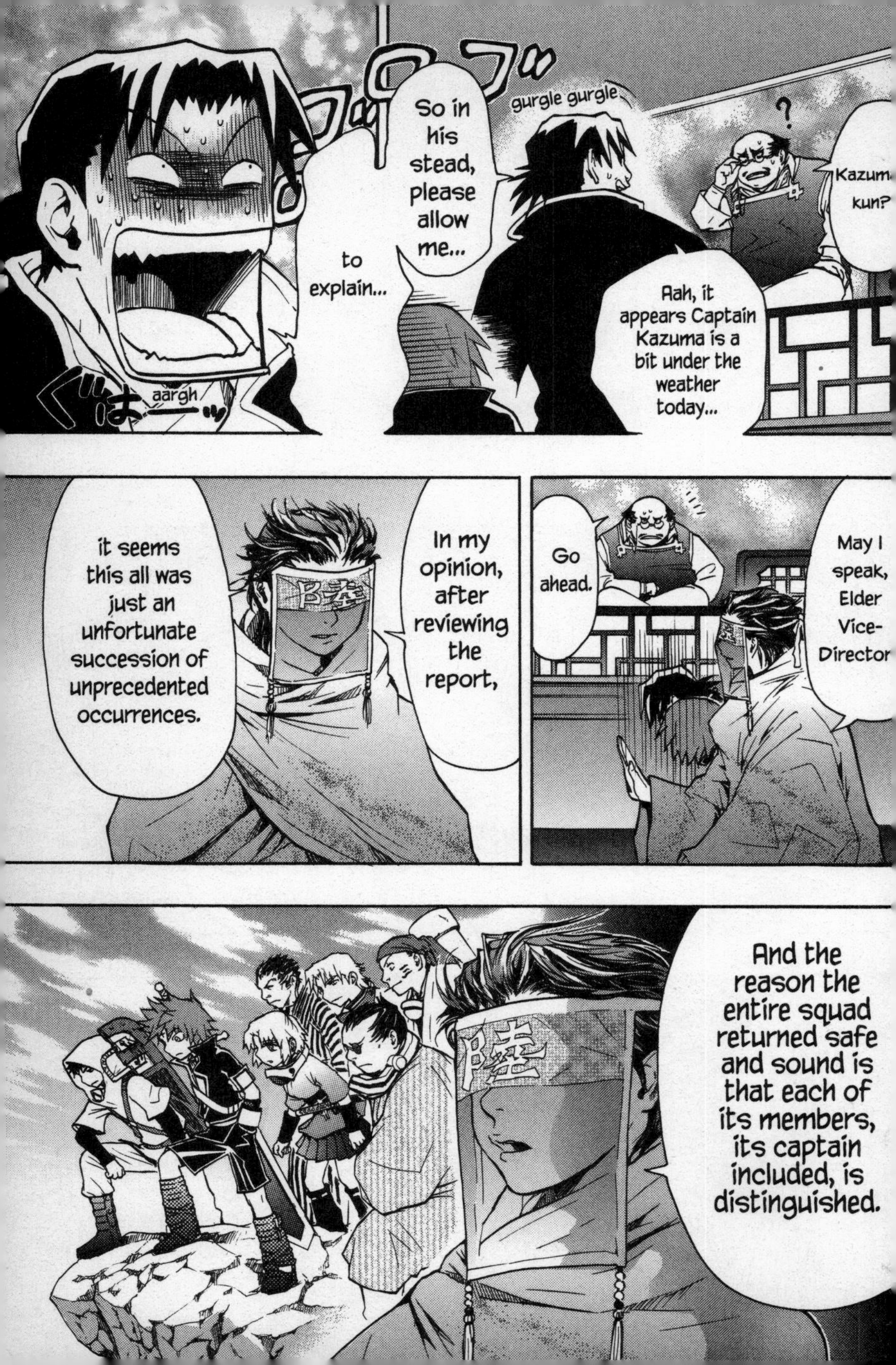
Kazuma kun?
?
Aah, it appears Captain Kazuma is a bit under the weather today...
gurgle gurgle
So in his stead, please allow me...
to explain...
aargh
May I speak, Elder Vice-Director
Go ahead.
In my opinion, after reviewing the report,
it seems this all was just an unfortunate succession of unprecedented occurrences.
And the reason the entire squad returned safe and sound is that each of its members, its captain included, is distinguished.

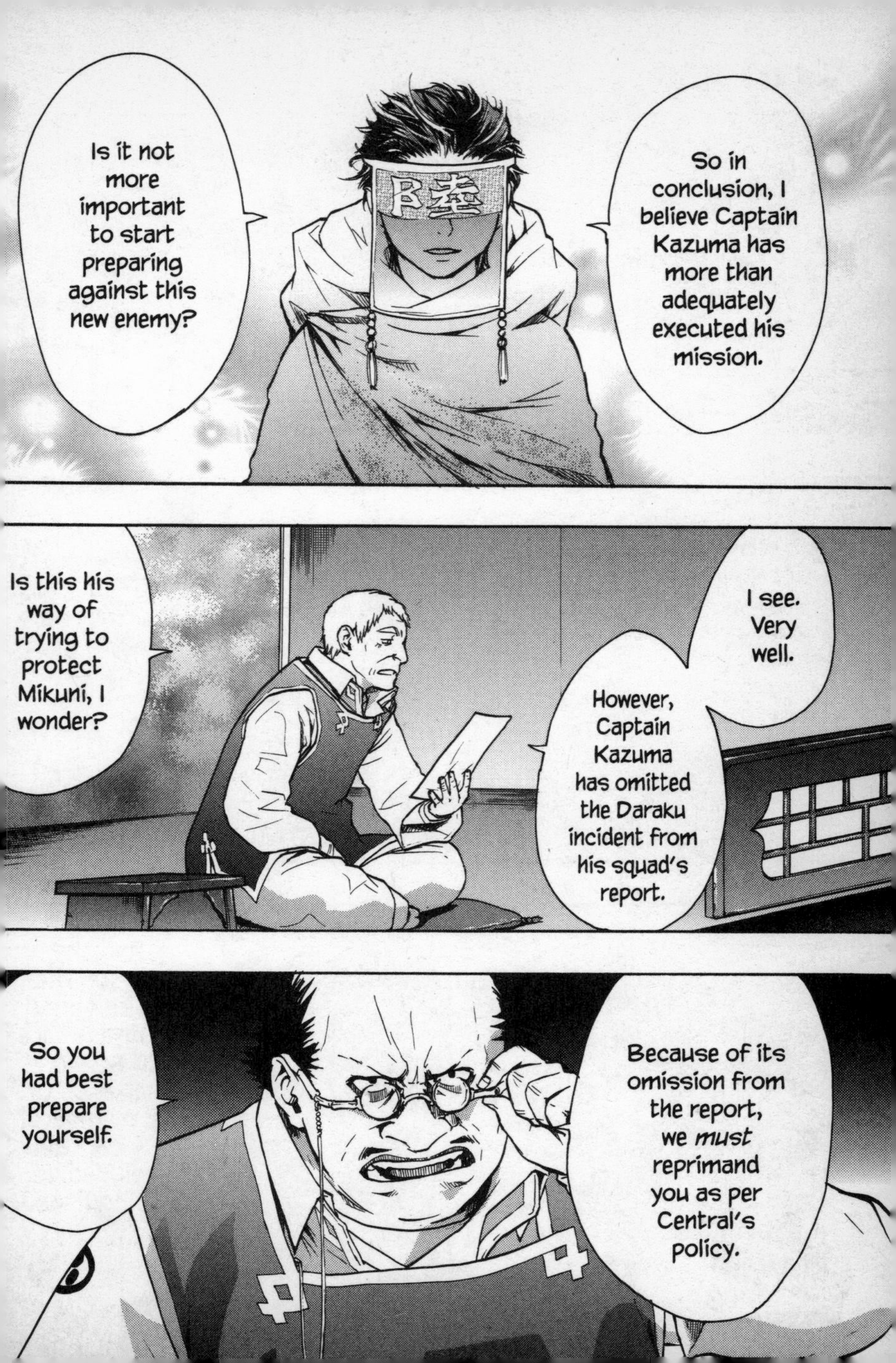
So in conclusion, I believe Captain Kazuma has more than adequately executed his mission.
Is it not more important to start preparing against this new enemy?
I see. Very well.
However, Captain Kazuma has omitted the Daraku incident from his squad's report.
Is this his way of trying to protect Mikuni, I wonder?
Because of its omission from the report, we *must* reprimand you as per Central's policy.
So you had best prepare yourself.

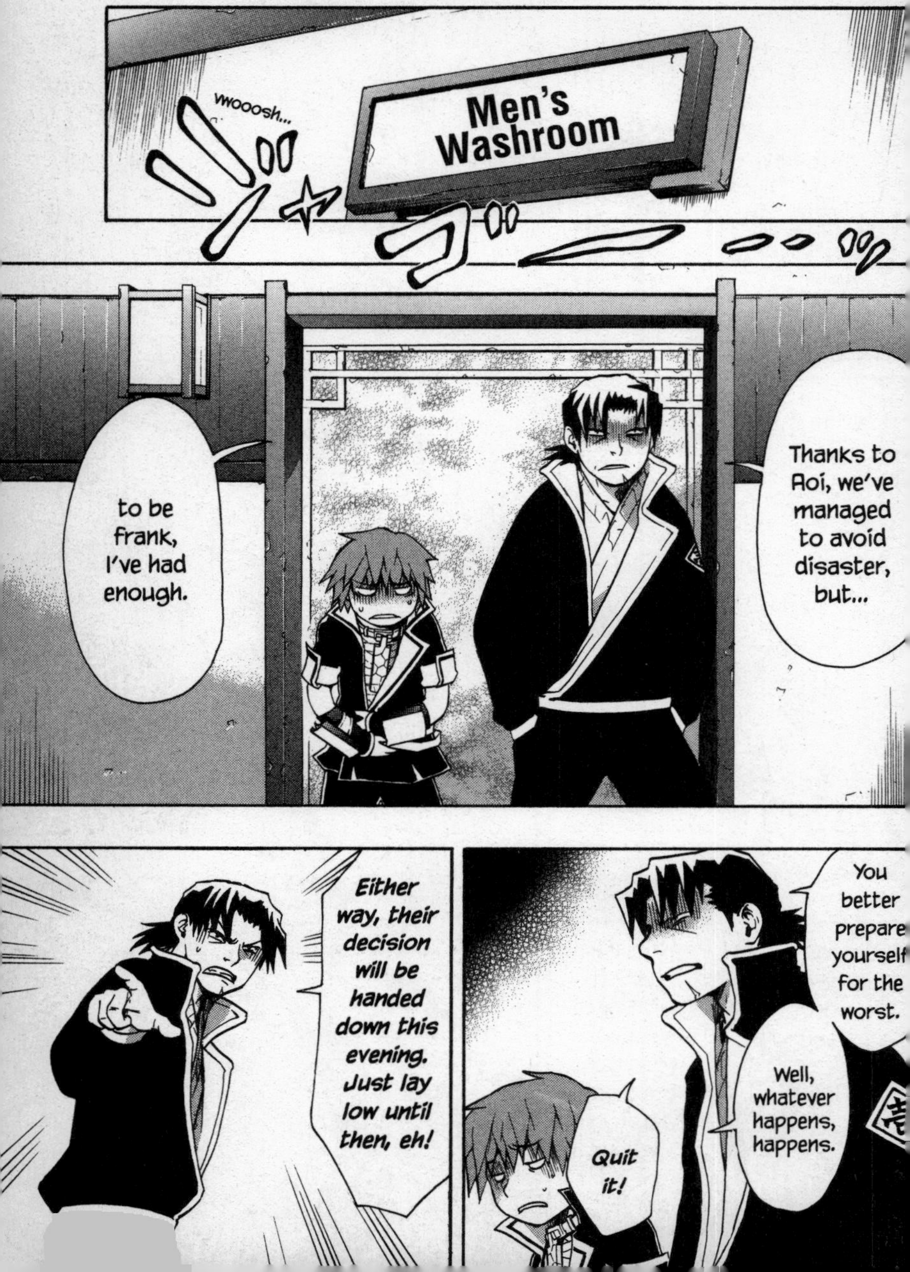
Men's Washroom
wooosh...
Thanks to Aoi, we've managed to avoid disaster, but...
to be frank, I've had enough.
You better prepare yourself for the worst.
Well, whatever happens, happens.
Quit it!
Either way, their decision will be handed down this evening. Just lay low until then, eh!

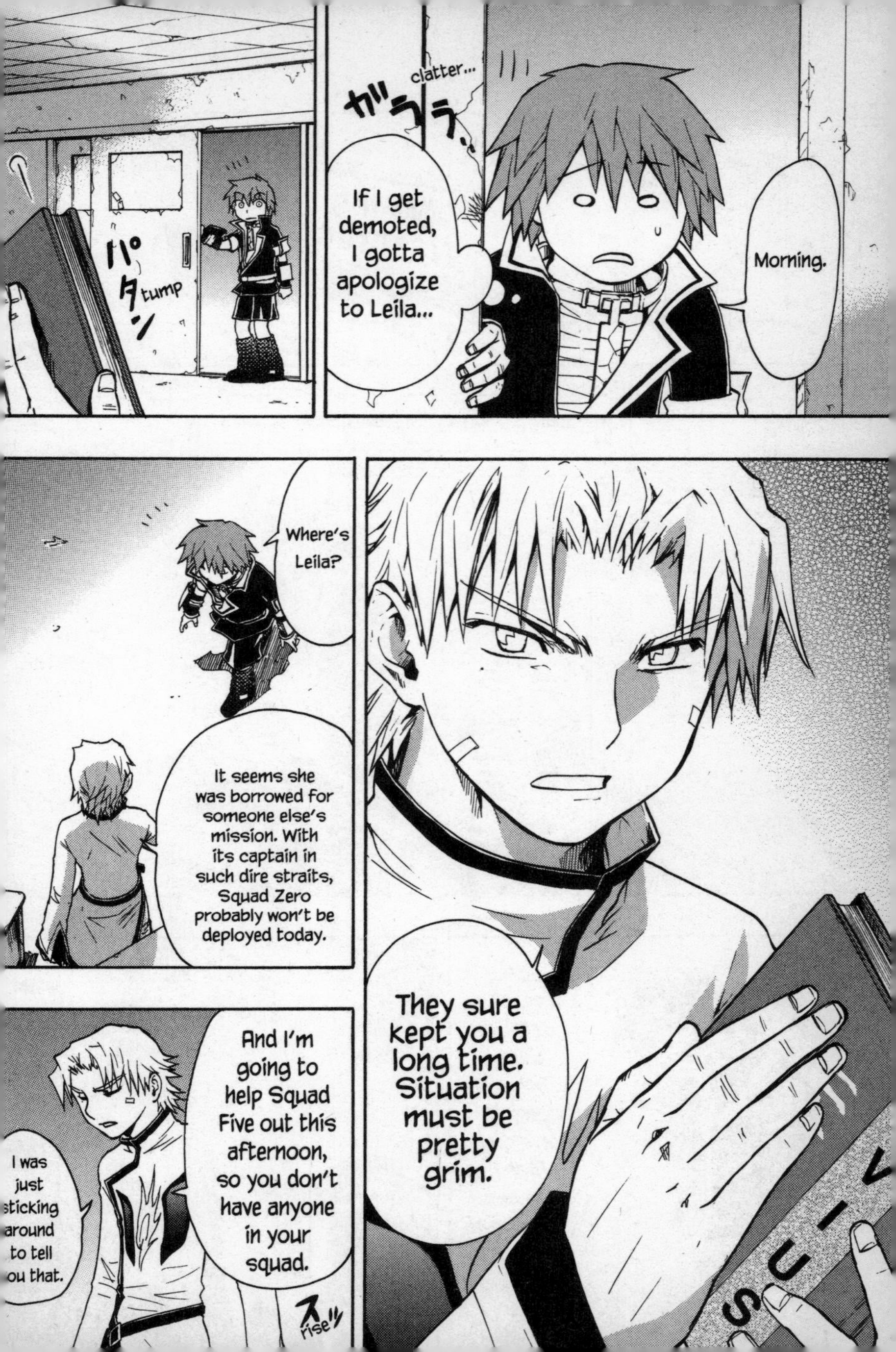
Morning.
clatter...
If I get demoted, I gotta apologize to Leila...
tump
They sure kept you a long time. Situation must be pretty grim.
Where's Leila?
It seems she was borrowed for someone else's mission. With its captain in such dire straits, Squad Zero probably won't be deployed today.
rise
And I'm going to help Squad Five out this afternoon, so you don't have anyone in your squad.
I was just sticking around to tell ou that.

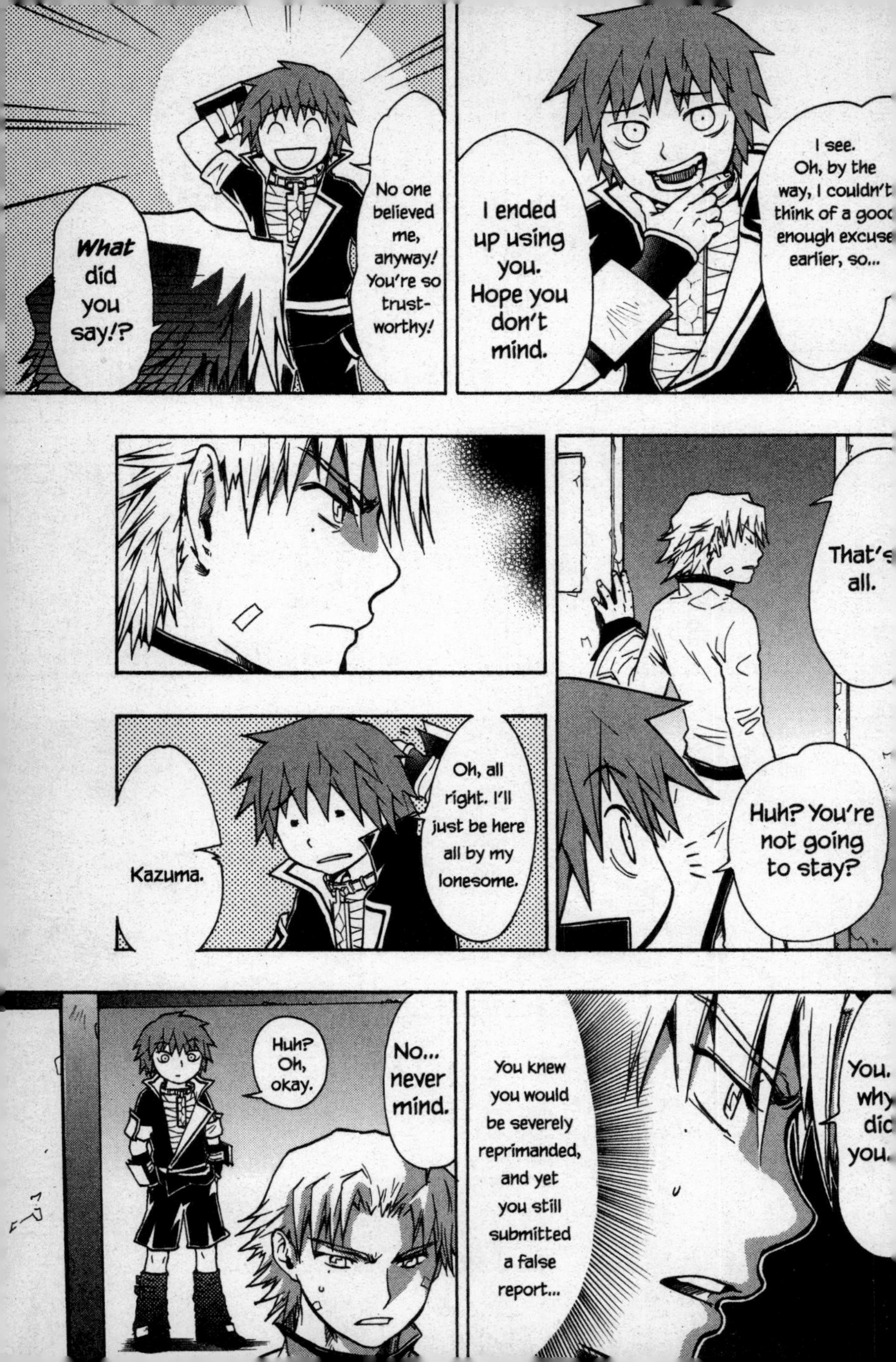
I see.
Oh, by the way, I couldn't think of a gooc enough excuse earlier, so...
I ended up using you. Hope you don't mind.
No one believed me, anyway! You're so trust-worthy!
What did you say!?
That's all.
Huh? You're not going to stay?
Oh, all right. I'll just be here all by my lonesome.
Kazuma.
You. why dic you.
You knew you would be severely reprimanded, and yet you still submitted a false report...
No... never mind.
Huh? Oh, okay.

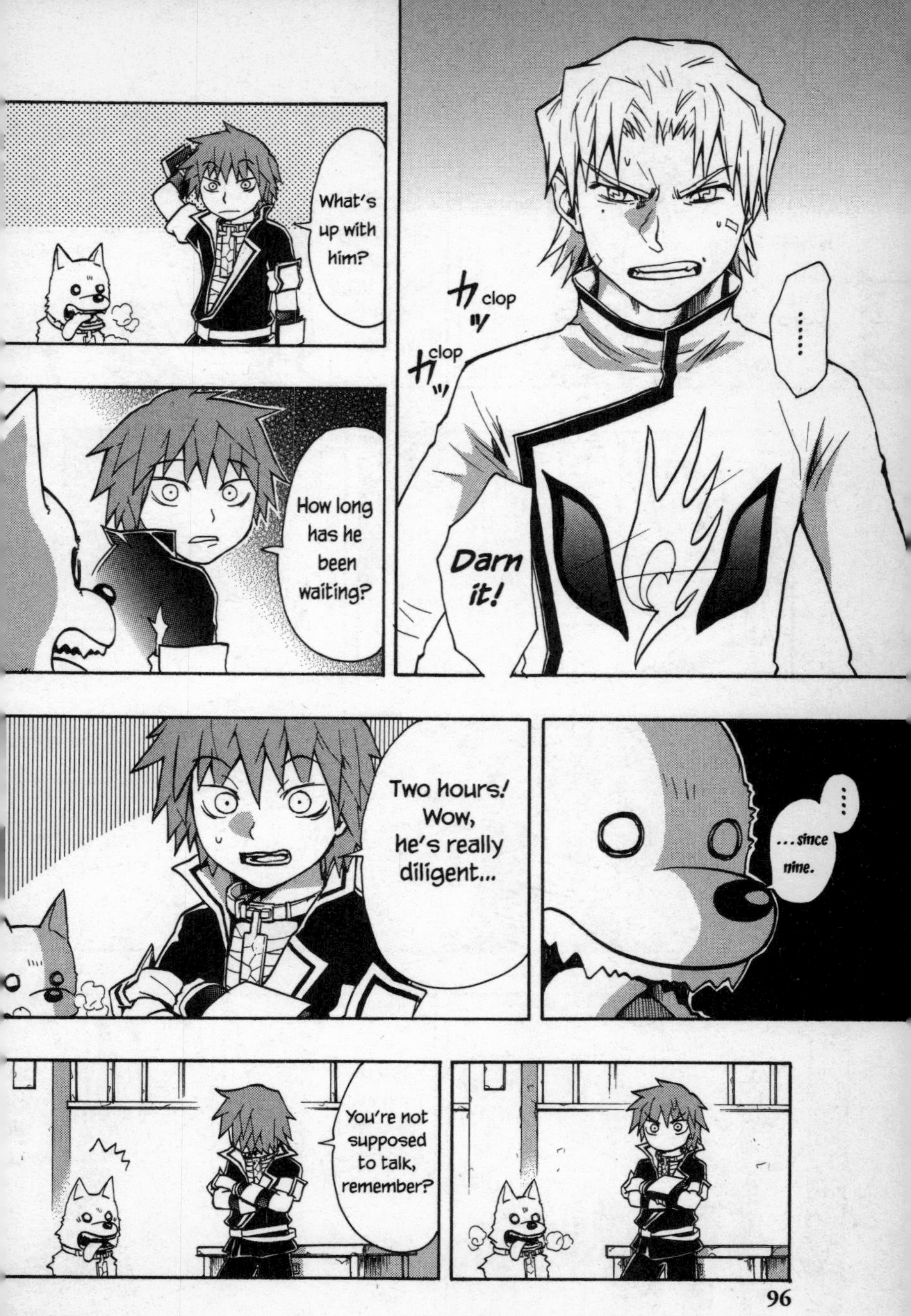
......
カッ clop
カッ clop
Darn it!
What's up with him?
How long has he been waiting?
...
...since nine.
Two hours! Wow, he's really diligent...
You're not supposed to talk, remember?

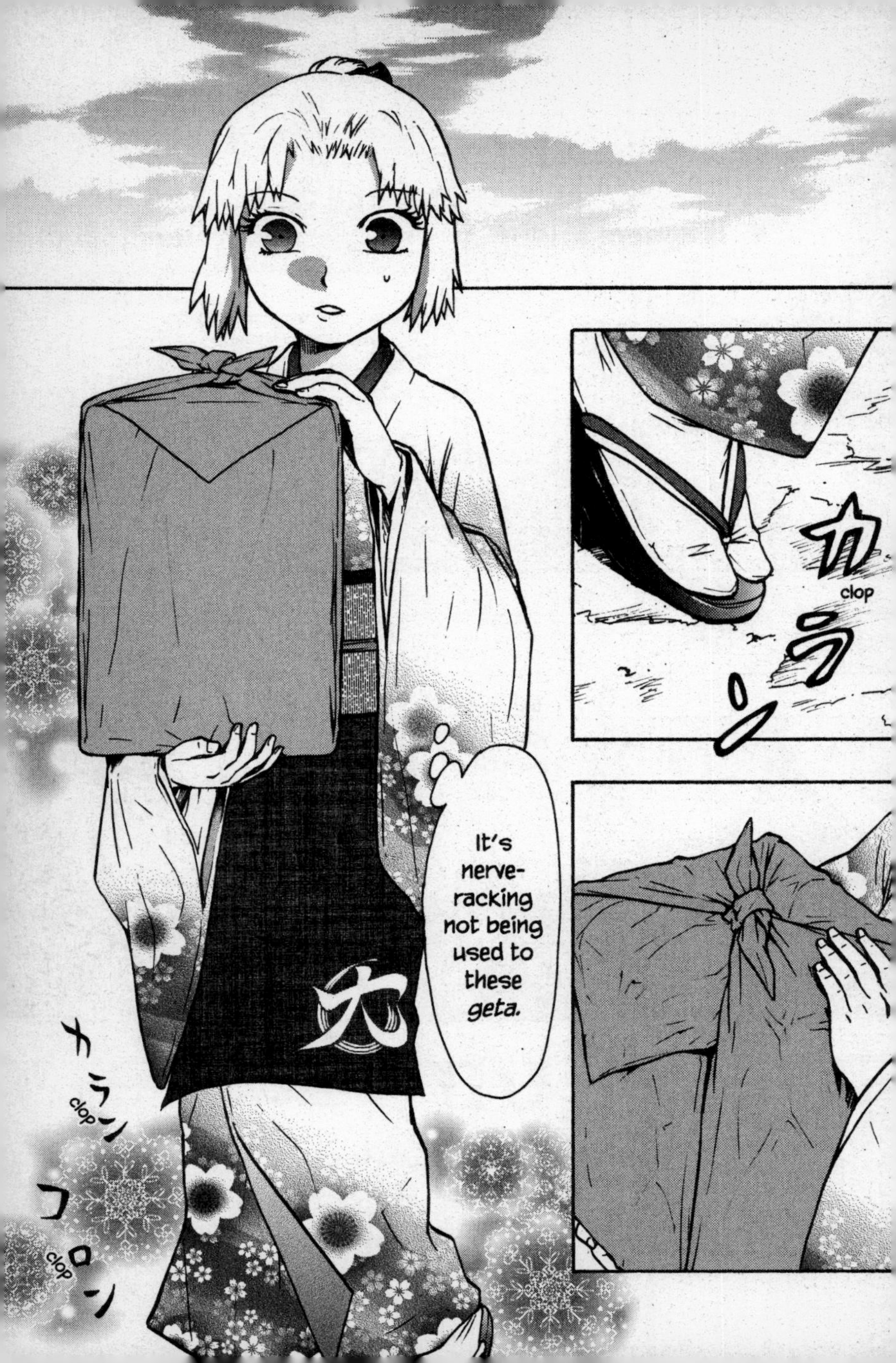
カラン
clop
It's nerve-racking not being used to these *geta.*
カラン
clop
コロン
clop

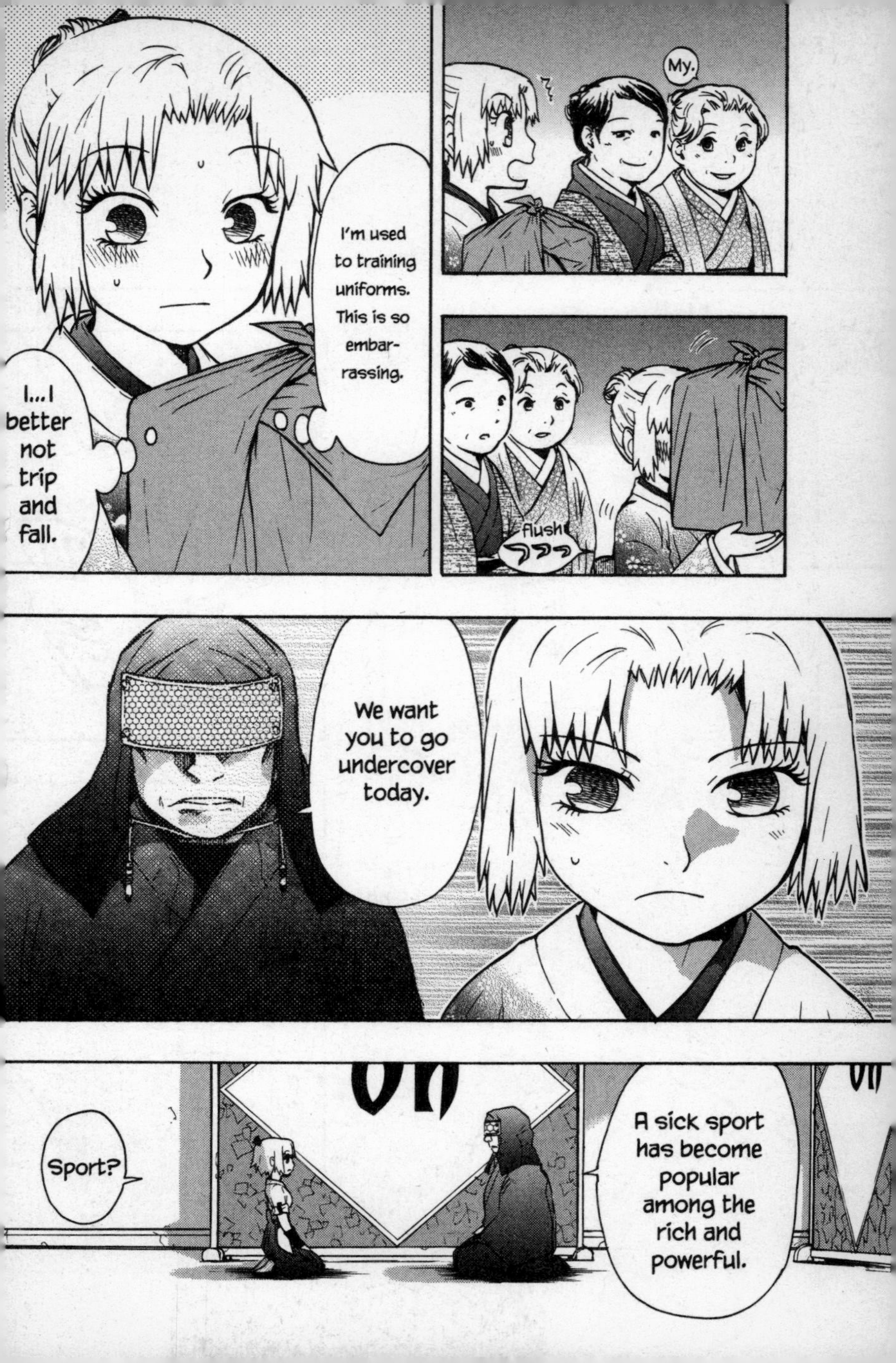
My.
flush
I'm used to training uniforms. This is so embar-rassing.
I...I better not trip and fall.
We want you to go undercover today.
A sick sport has become popular among the rich and powerful.
Sport?

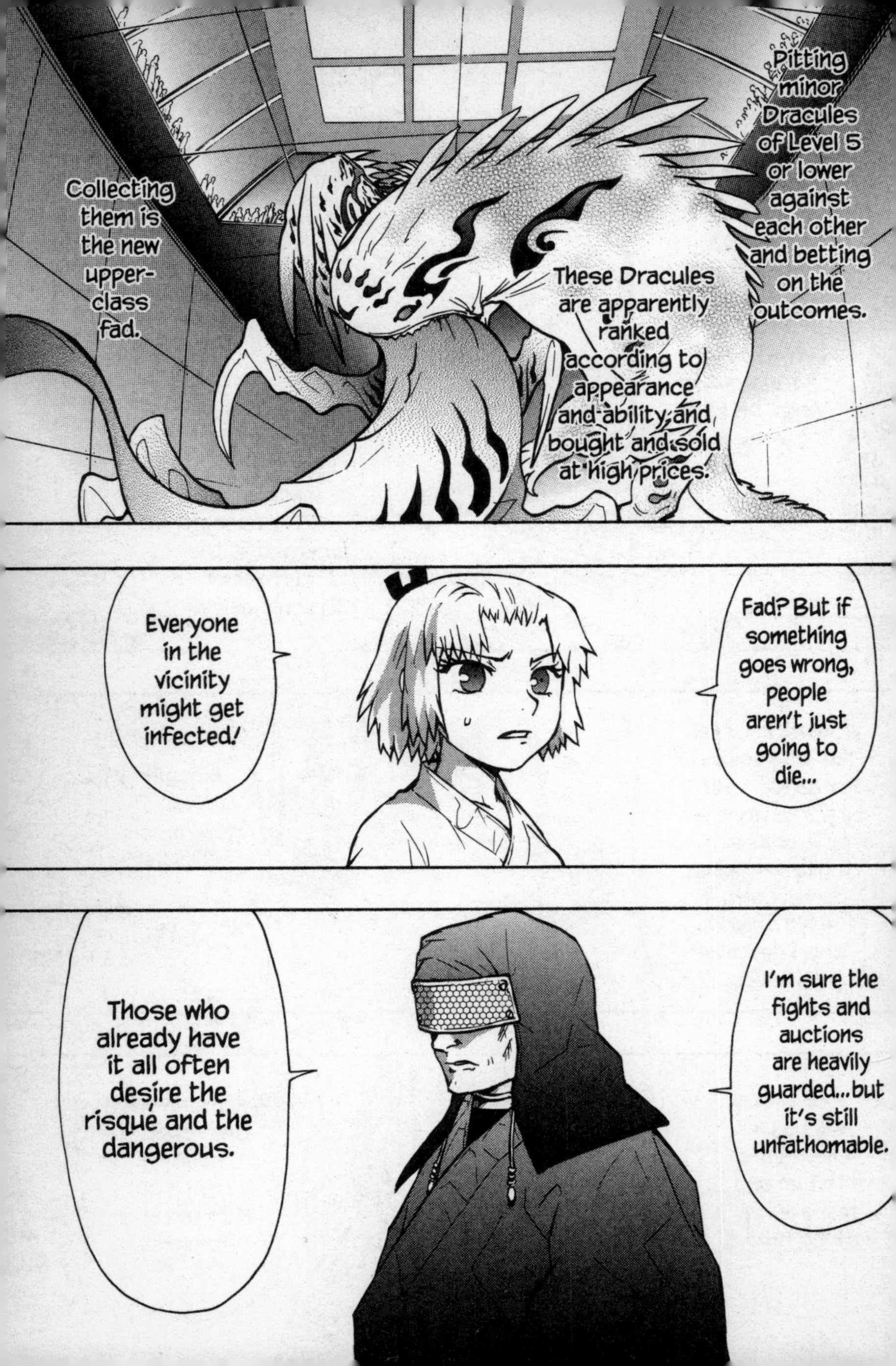
Pitting minor Dracules of Level 5 or lower against each other and betting on the outcomes.
These Dracules are apparently ranked according to appearance and ability and bought and sold at high prices.
Collecting them is the new upper-class fad.
Fad? But if something goes wrong, people aren't just going to die...
Everyone in the vicinity might get infected!
I'm sure the fights and auctions are heavily guarded...but it's still unfathomable.
Those who already have it all often desire the risqué and the dangerous.

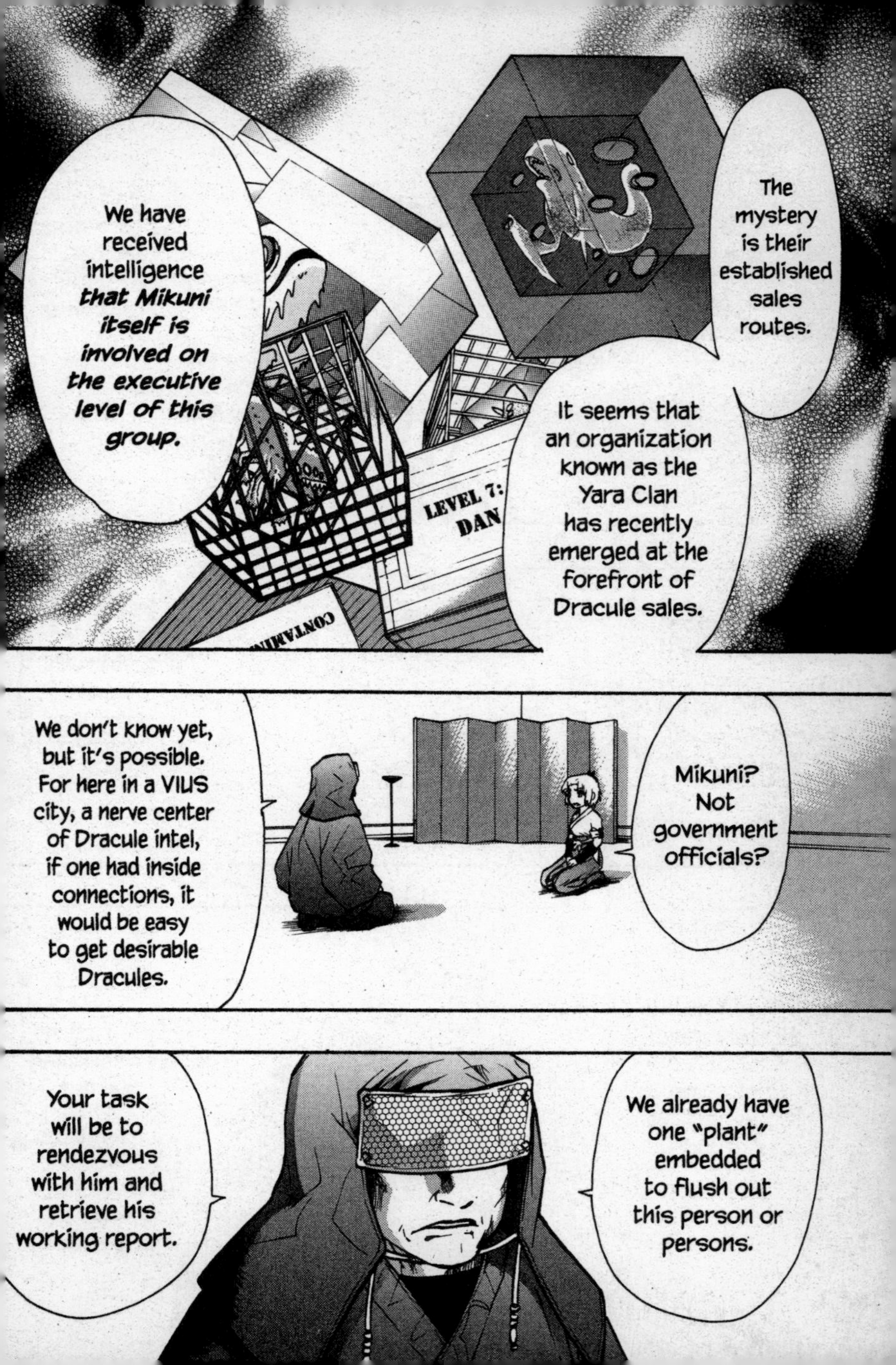
The mystery is their established sales routes.
It seems that an organization known as the Yara Clan has recently emerged at the forefront of Dracule sales.
We have received intelligence *that Mikuni itself is involved on the executive level of this group.*
LEVEL 7: DAN
CONTAMIN
Mikuni? Not government officials?
We don't know yet, but it's possible. For here in a VIUS city, a nerve center of Dracule intel, if one had inside connections, it would be easy to get desirable Dracules.
We already have one "plant" embedded to flush out this person or persons.
Your task will be to rendezvous with him and retrieve his working report.

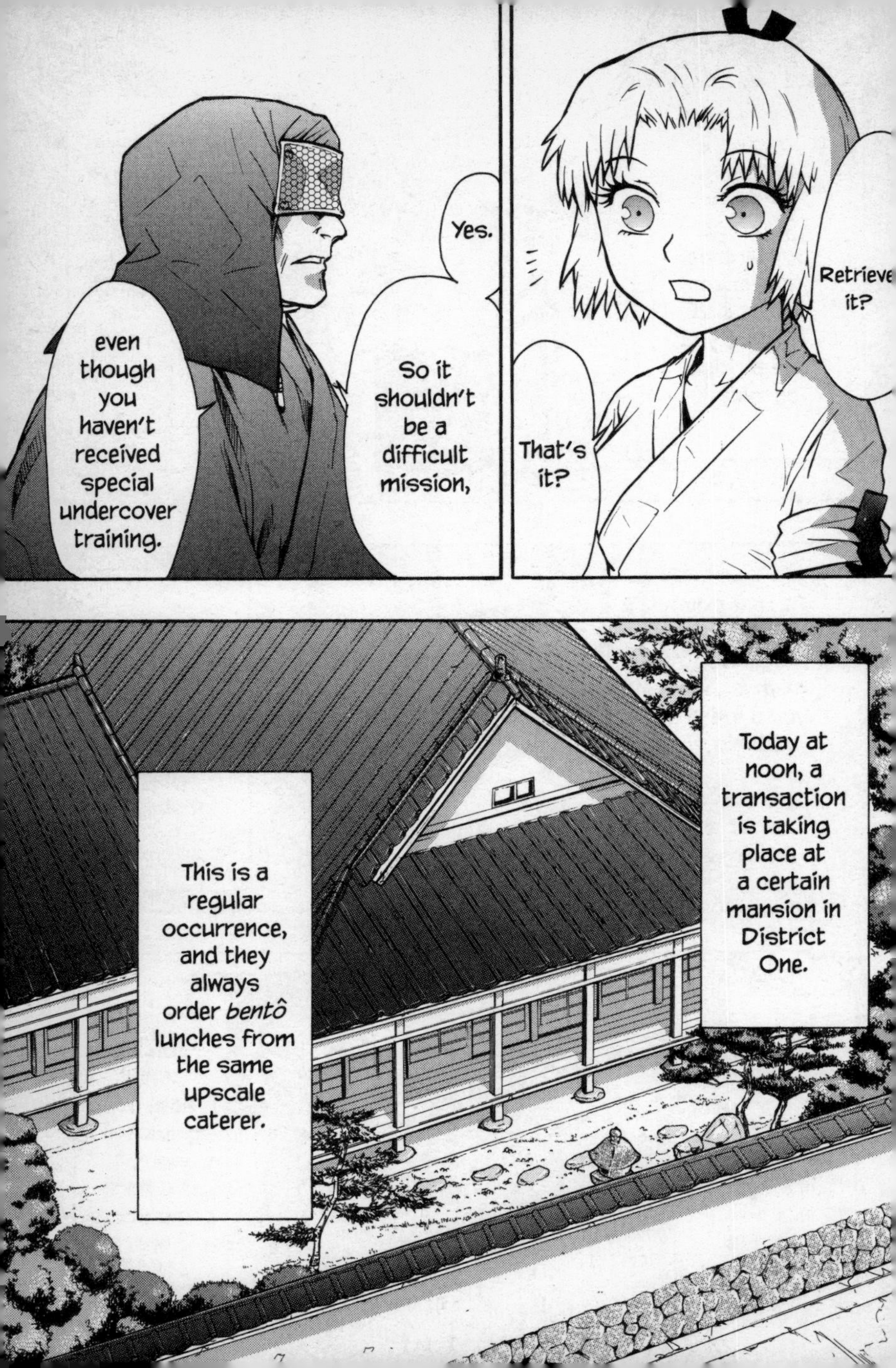

Retrieve it?
That's it?
Yes.
So it shouldn't be a difficult mission,
even though you haven't received special undercover training.
Today at noon, a transaction is taking place at a certain mansion in District One.
This is a regular occurrence, and they always order *bentô* lunches from the same upscale caterer.

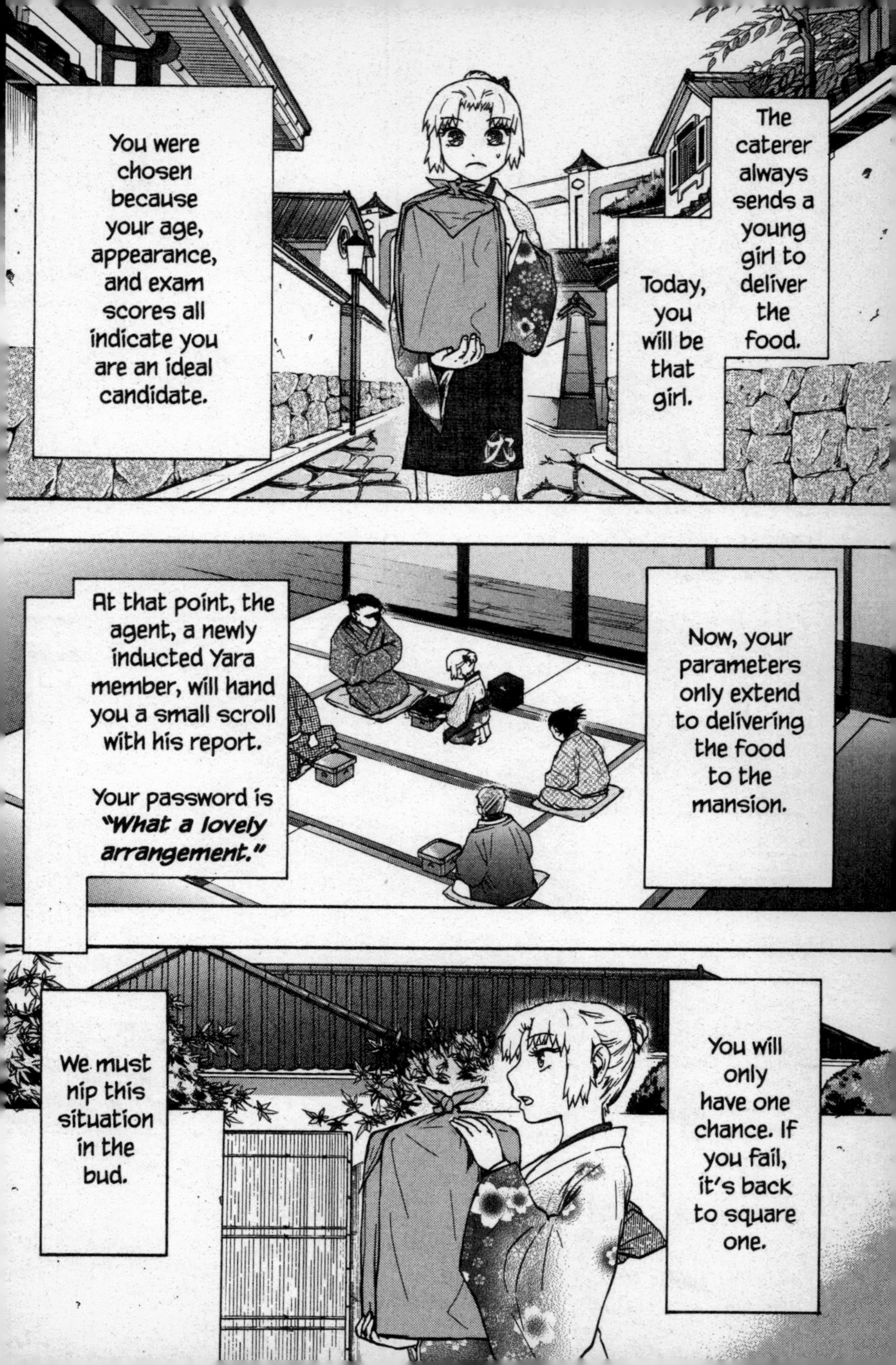
The caterer always sends a young girl to deliver the food.
Today, you will be that girl.
You were chosen because your age, appearance, and exam scores all indicate you are an ideal candidate.
Now, your parameters only extend to delivering the food to the mansion.
At that point, the agent, a newly inducted Yara member, will hand you a small scroll with his report.
Your password is *"What a lovely arrangement."*
You will only have one chance. If you fail, it's back to square one.
We must nip this situation in the bud.

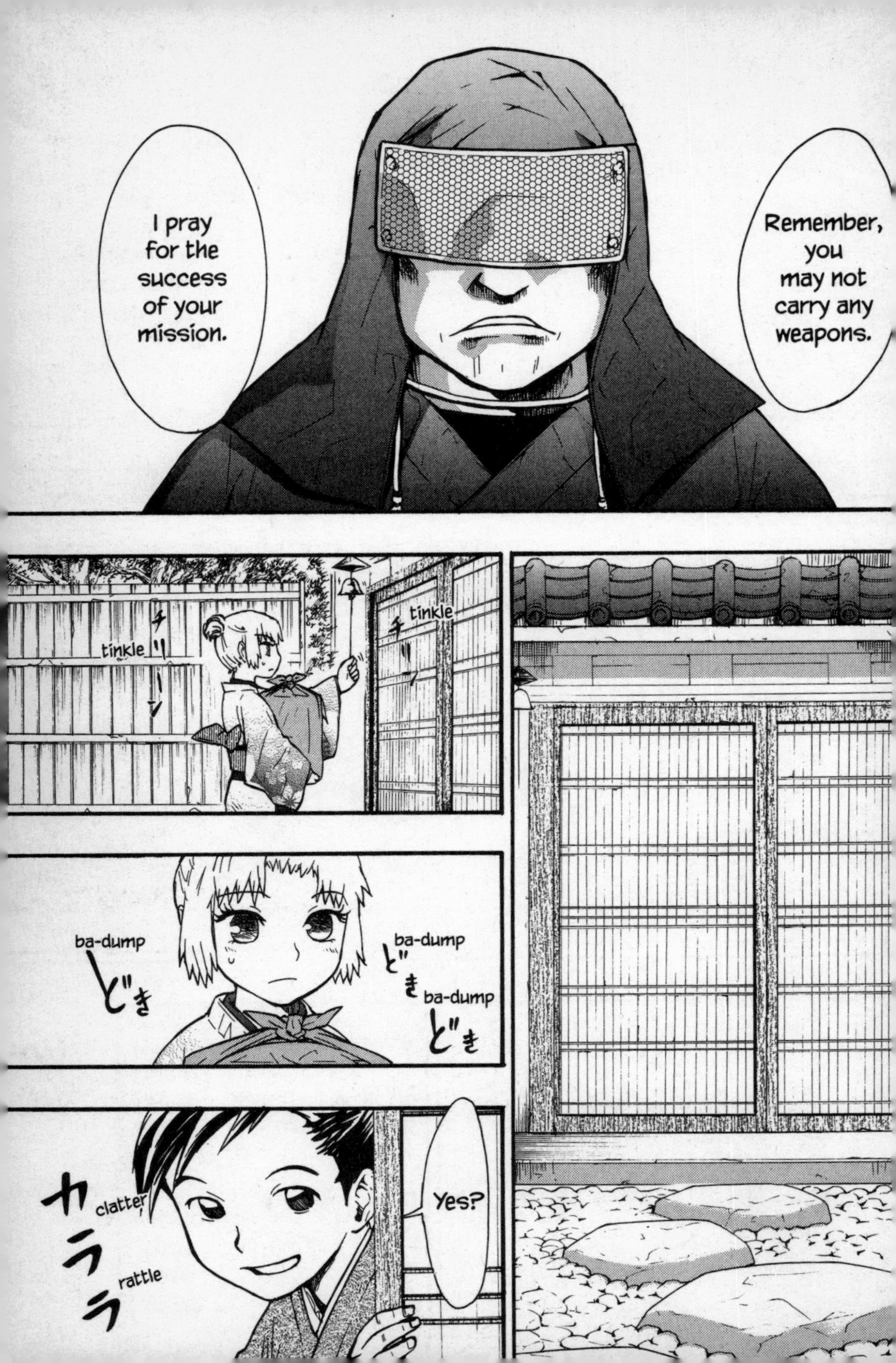
Remember, you may not carry any weapons.
I pray for the success of your mission.
チリーン tinkle
チリーン tinkle
ドキ ba-dump
ドキ ba-dump
ドキ ba-dump
カララ clatter, rattle
Yes?

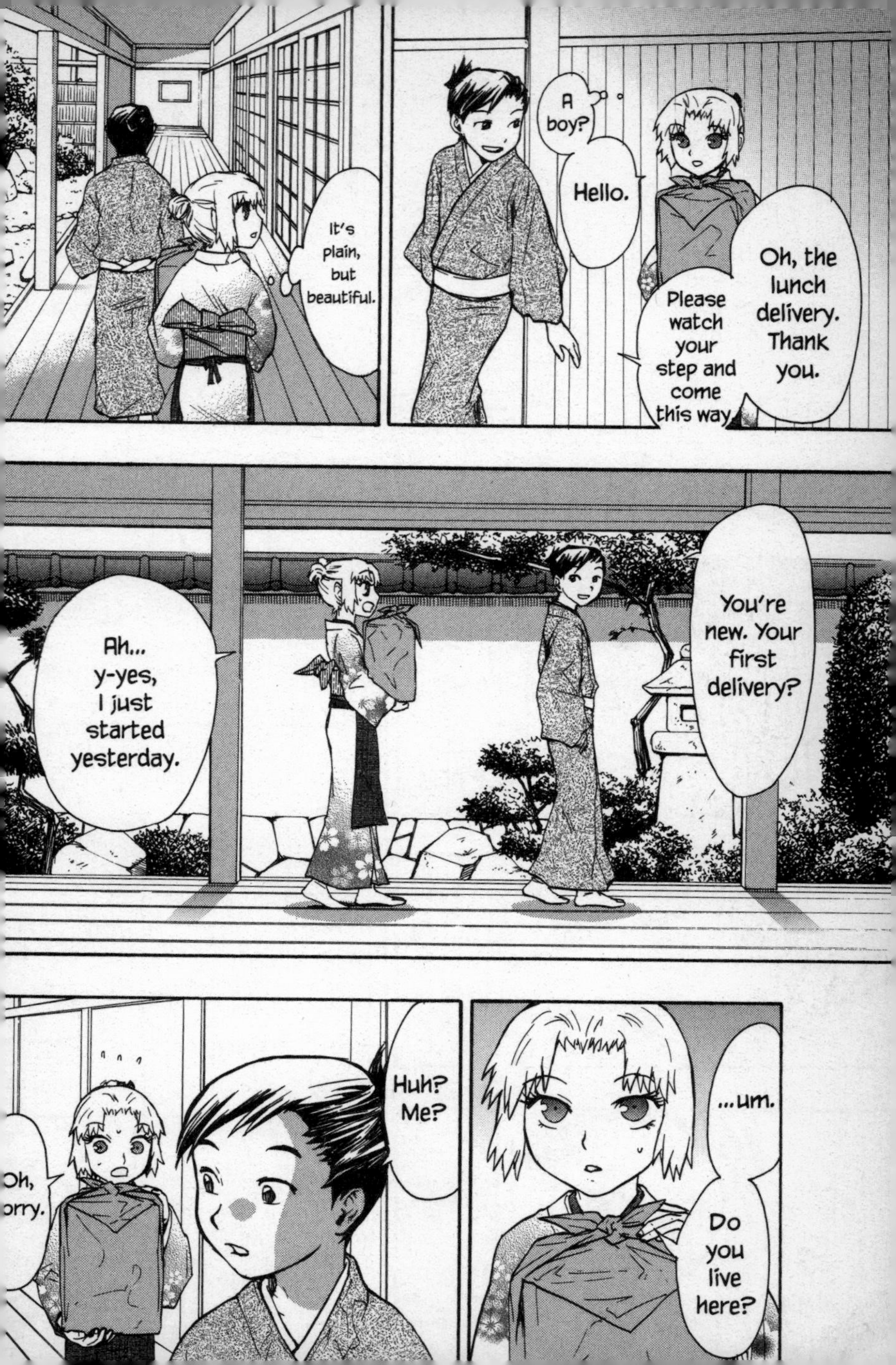
Oh, the lunch delivery. Thank you.
Please watch your step and come this way.
Hello.
A boy?
It's plain, but beautiful.
You're new. Your first delivery?
Ah... y-yes, I just started yesterday.
...um.
Do you live here?
Huh? Me?
Oh, orry.

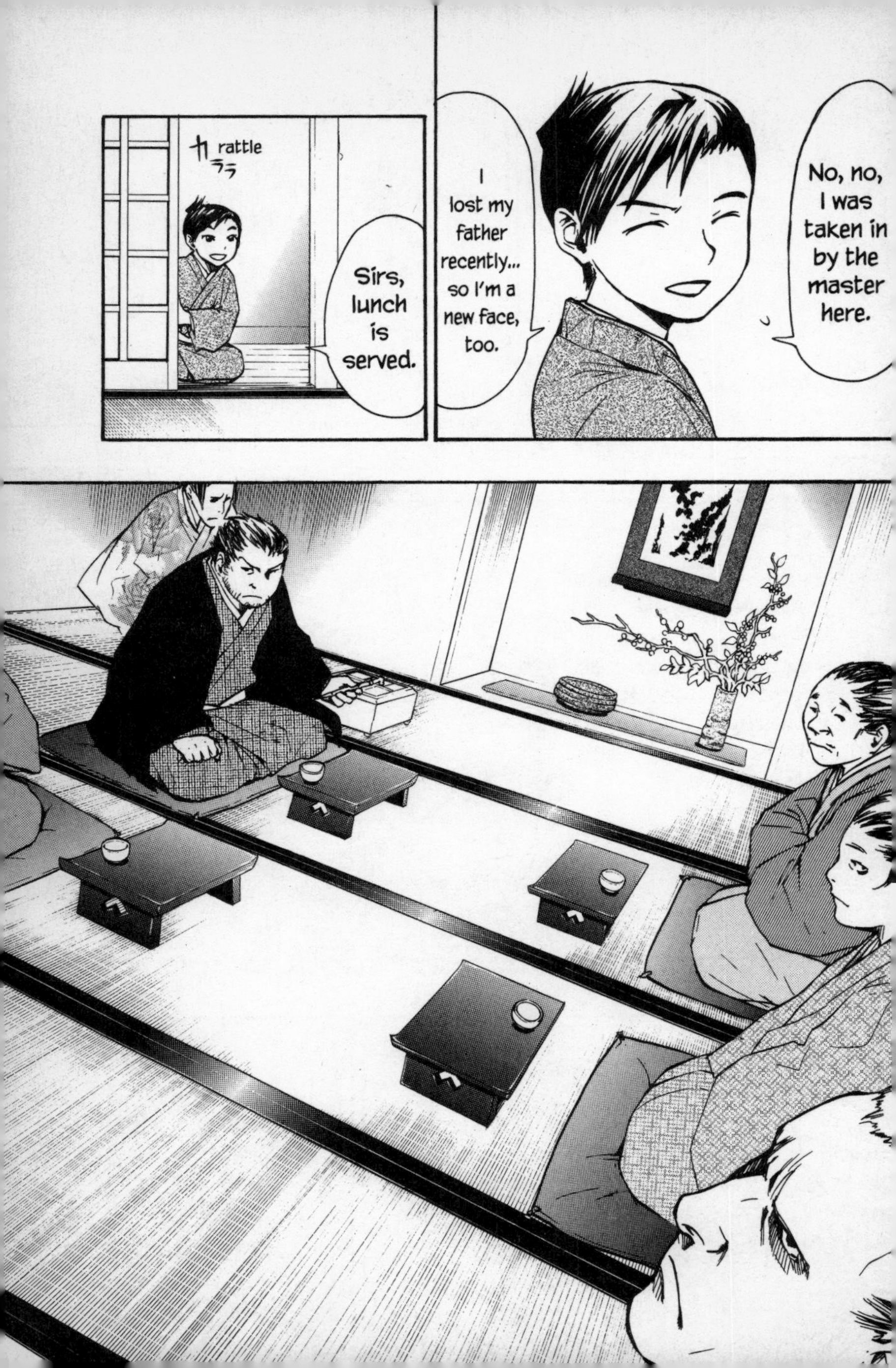
No, no, I was taken in by the master here.
I lost my father recently... so I'm a new face, too.
rattle
Sirs, lunch is served.

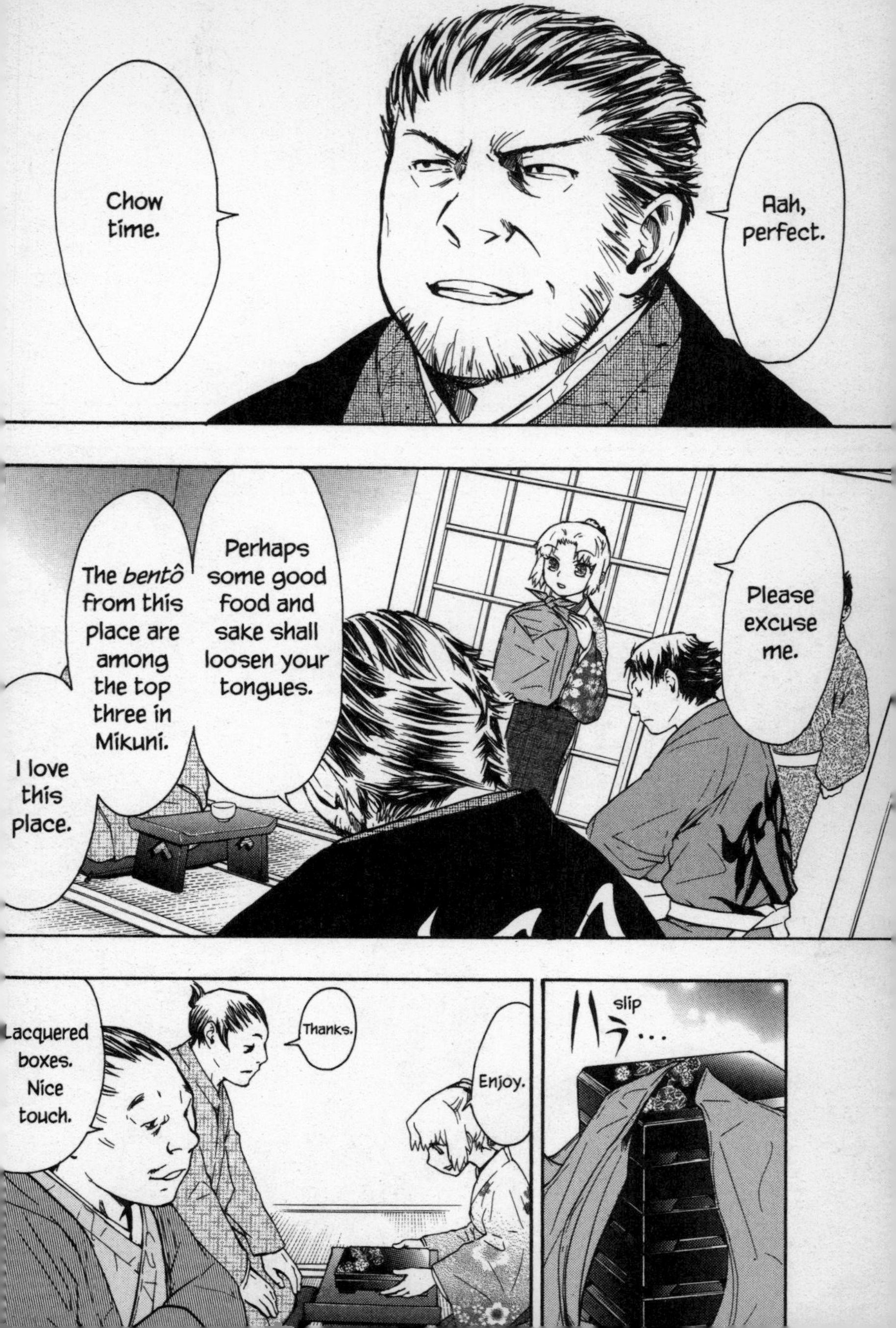
Aah, perfect.
Chow time.
Please excuse me.
Perhaps some good food and sake shall loosen your tongues.
The *bentô* from this place are among the top three in Mikuni.
I love this place.
slip
ハラ…
Enjoy.
Thanks.
Lacquered boxes. Nice touch.

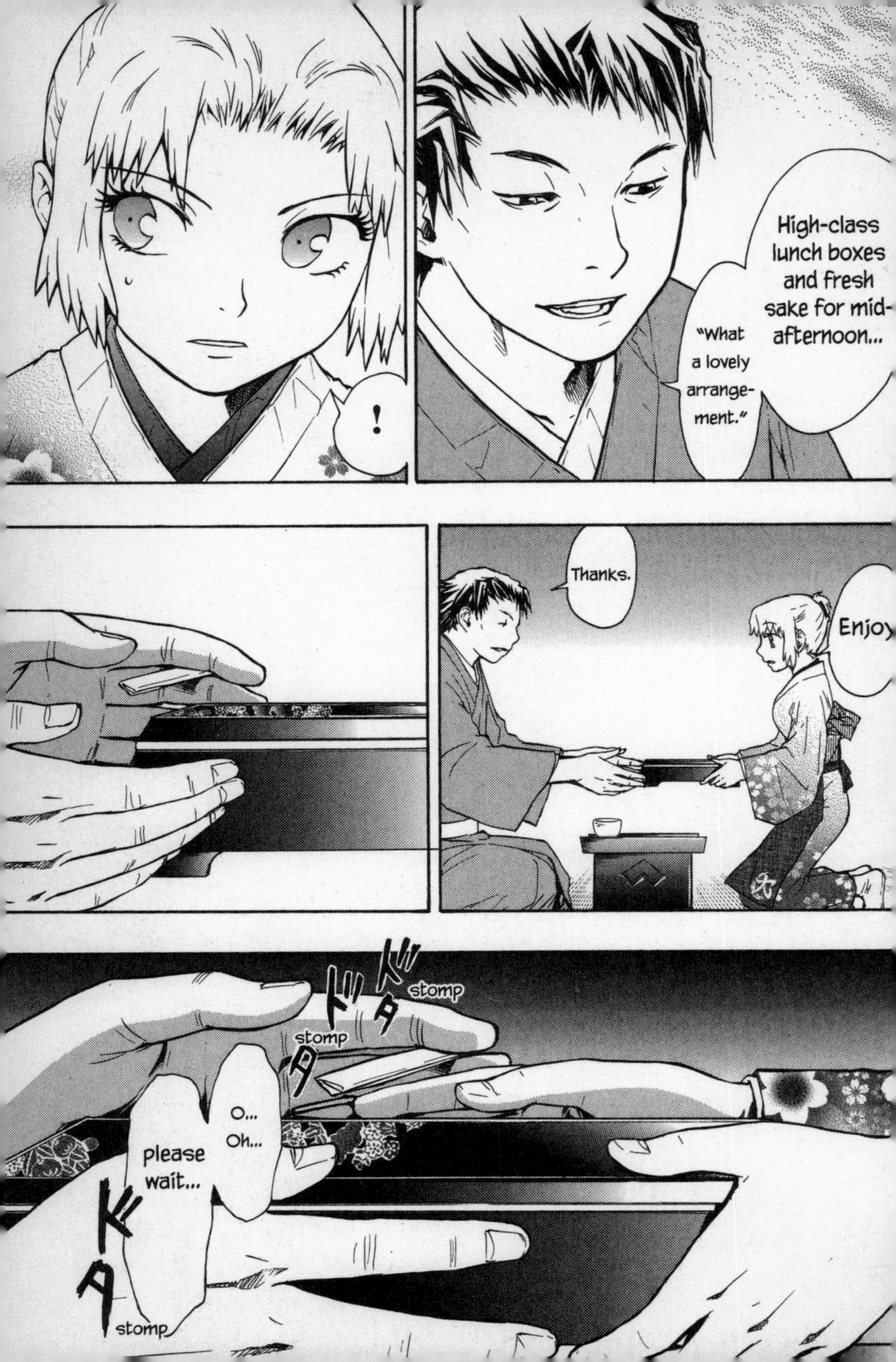
High-class lunch boxes and fresh sake for mid-afternoon...
"What a lovely arrange-ment."
!
Enjoy
Thanks.
stomp
stomp
O... Oh...
please wait...
stomp

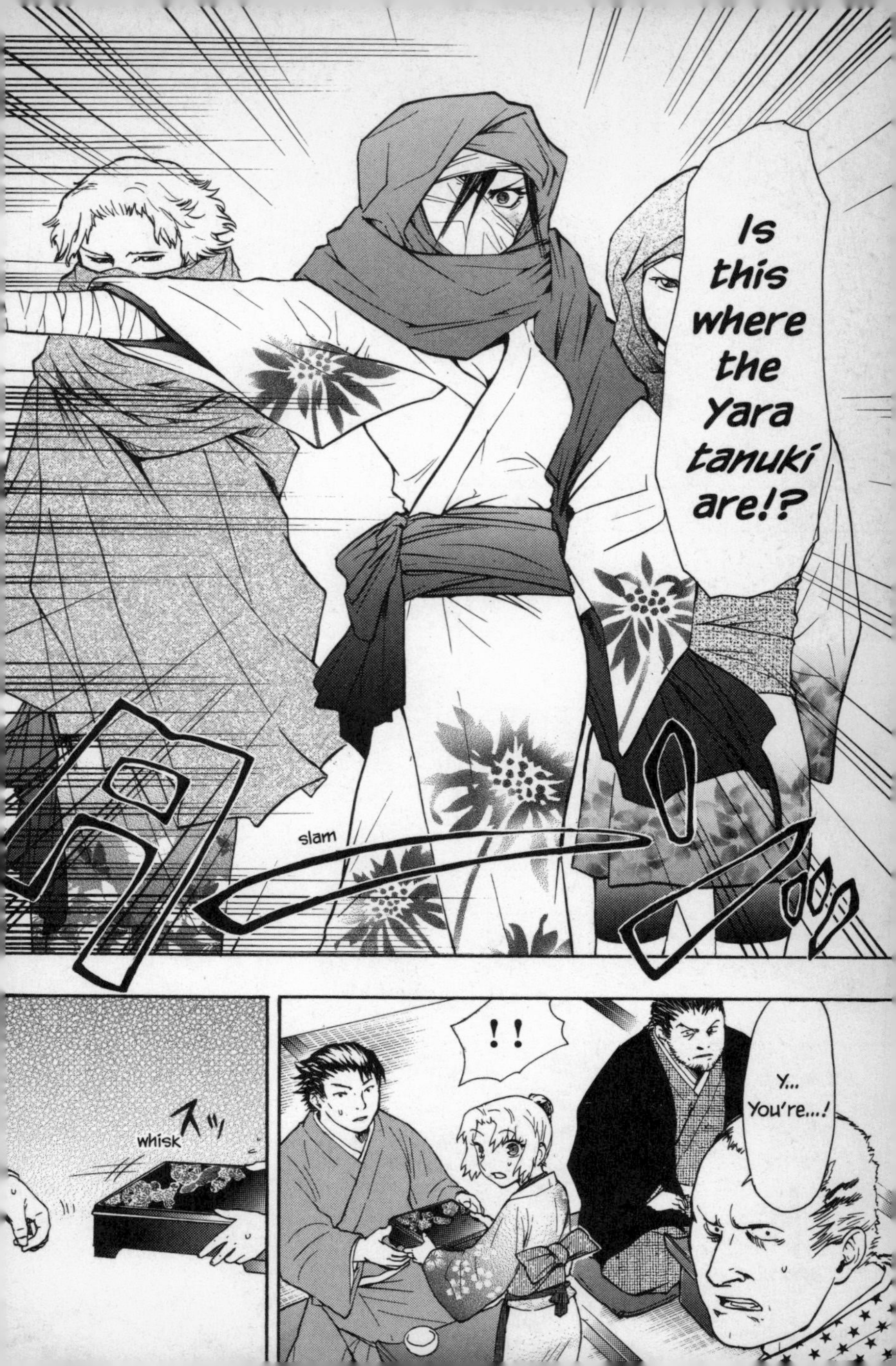
Is this where the Yara tanuki are!?
slam
Y... You're...!
!!
whisk

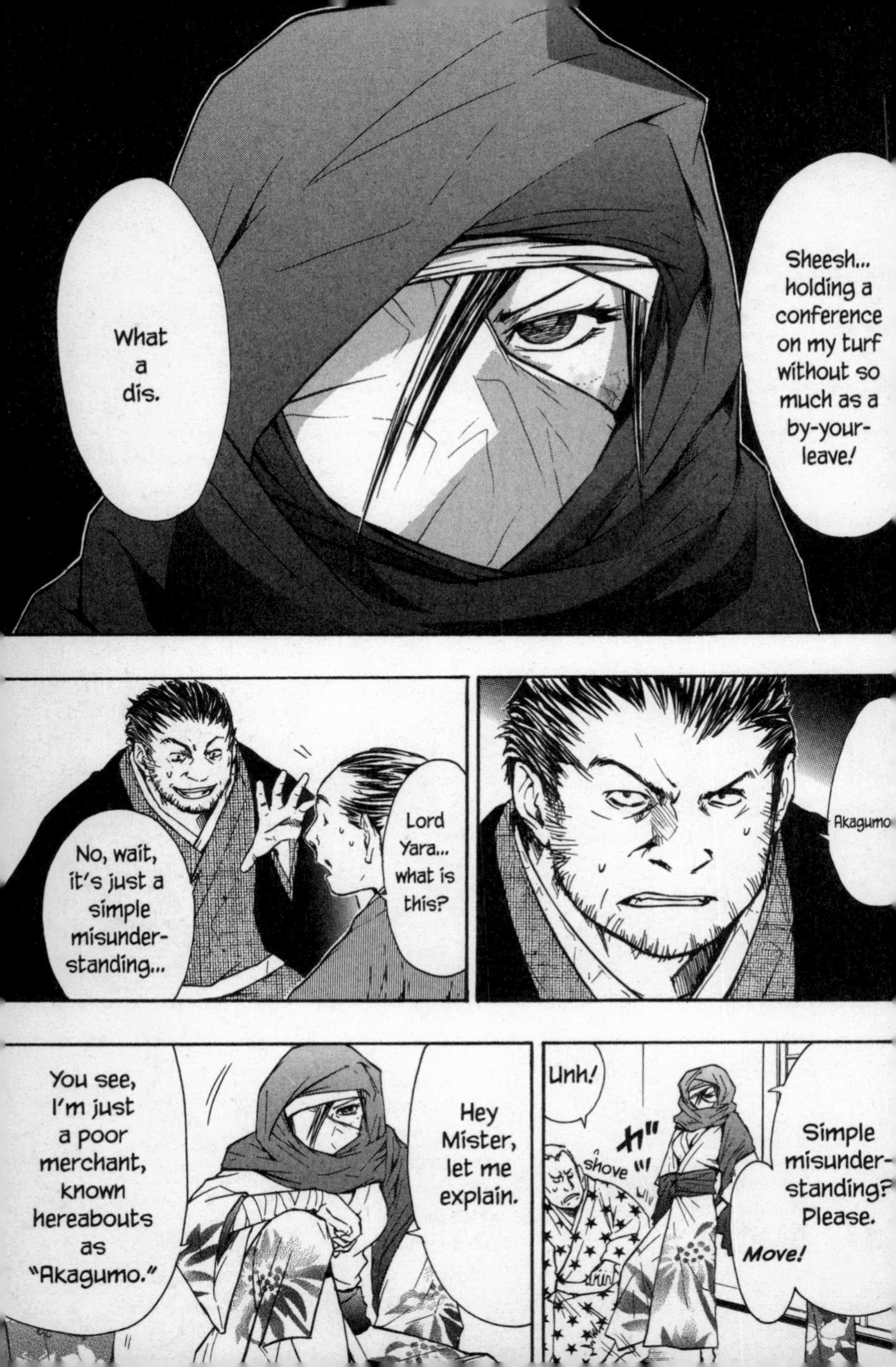
Sheesh... holding a conference on my turf without so much as a by-your-leave!
What a dis.
Akagumo
Lord Yara... what is this?
No, wait, it's just a simple misunder-standing...
Simple misunder-standing? Please.
Move!
Unh!
カ" shove "!
Hey Mister, let me explain.
You see, I'm just a poor merchant, known hereabouts as "Akagumo."

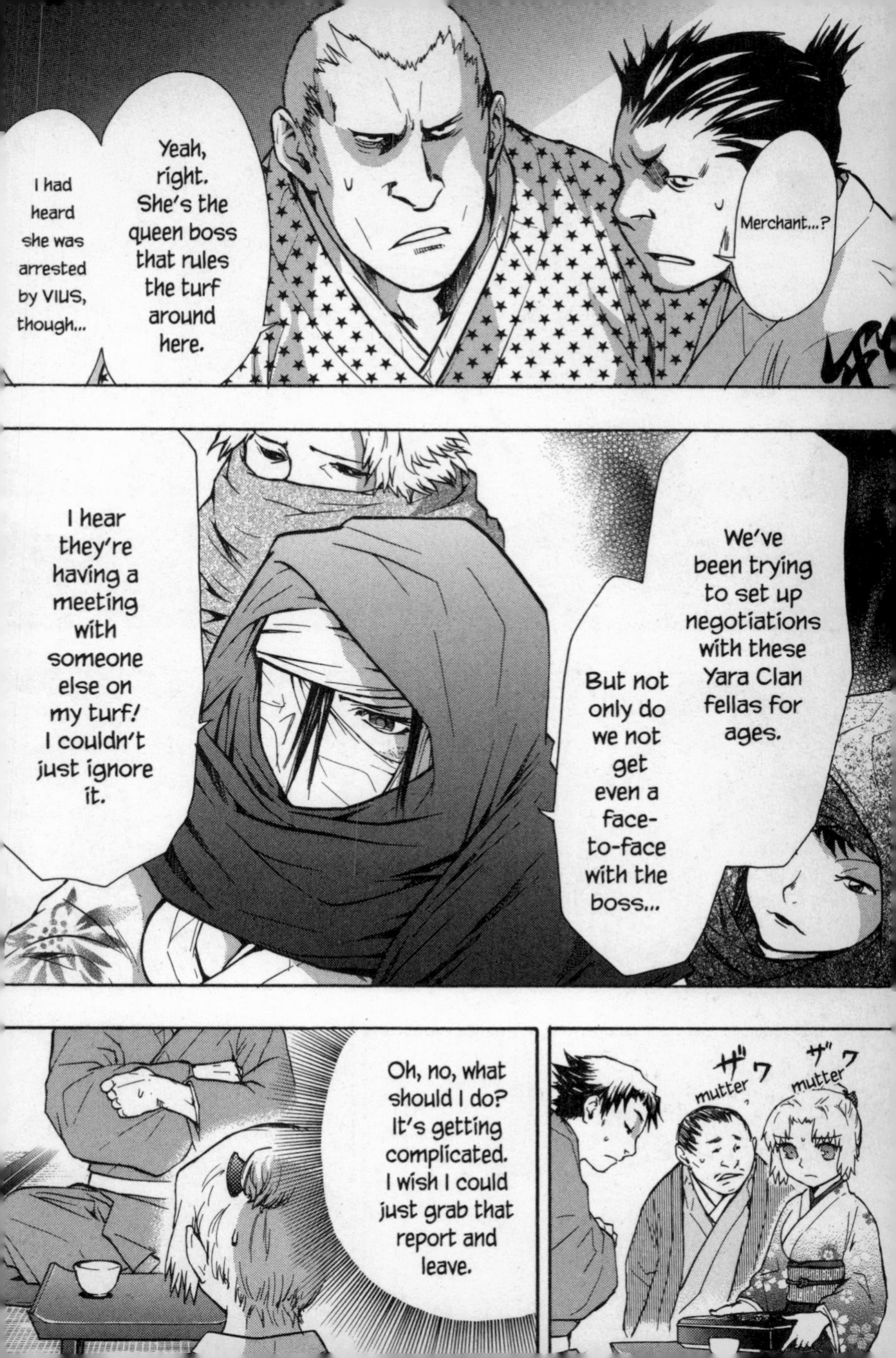
Merchant...?
Yeah, right. She's the queen boss that rules the turf around here.
I had heard she was arrested by VIUS, though...
We've been trying to set up negotiations with these Yara Clan fellas for ages.
But not only do we not get even a face-to-face with the boss...
I hear they're having a meeting with someone else on my turf! I couldn't just ignore it.
ザワ mutter
ザワ mutter
Oh, no, what should I do? It's getting complicated. I wish I could just grab that report and leave.

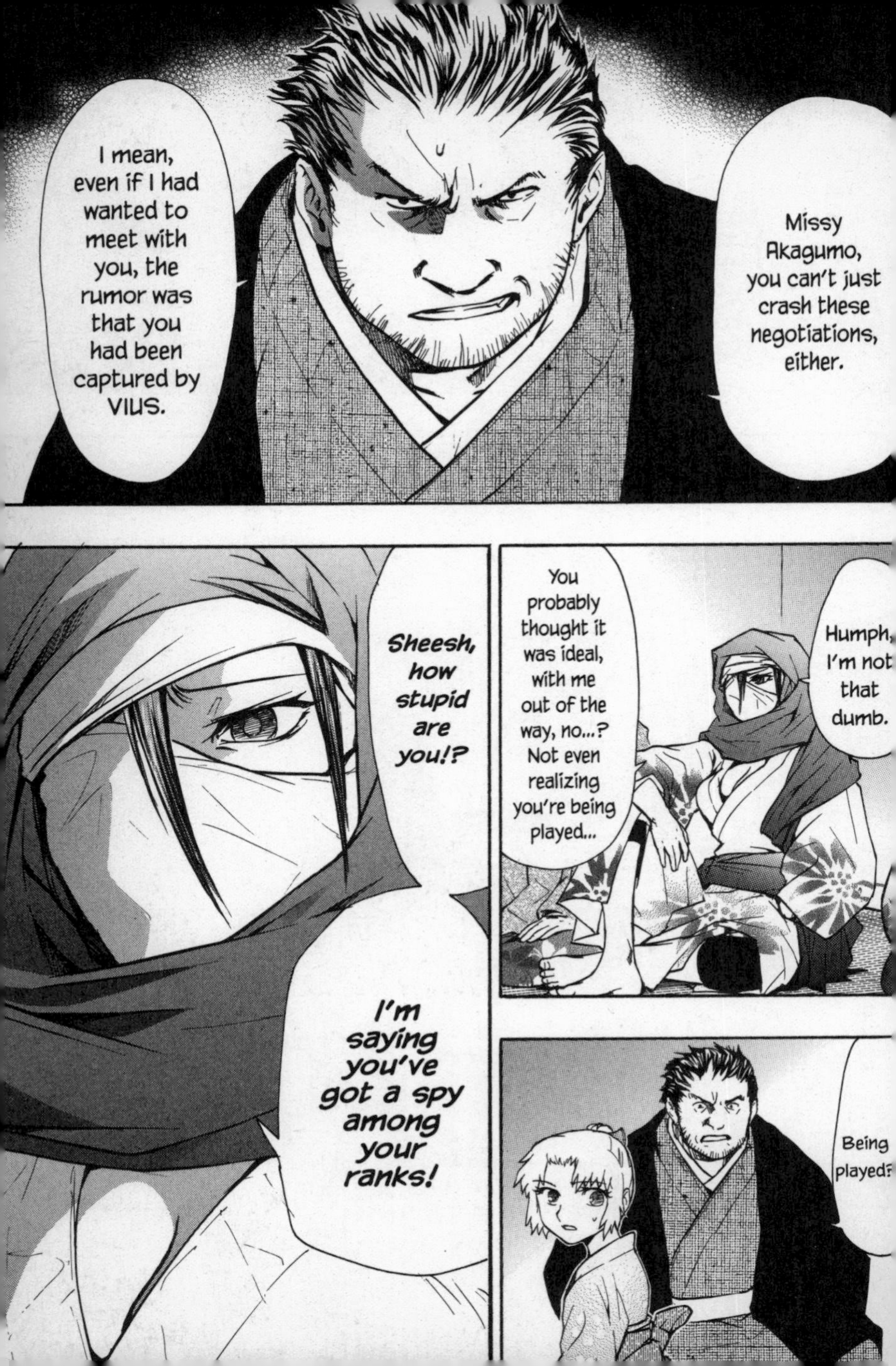
Missy Akagumo, you can't just crash these negotiations, either.
I mean, even if I had wanted to meet with you, the rumor was that you had been captured by VIUS.
Humph, I'm not that dumb.
You probably thought it was ideal, with me out of the way, no...? Not even realizing you're being played...
Being played?
Sheesh, how stupid are you!?
I'm saying you've got a spy among your ranks!

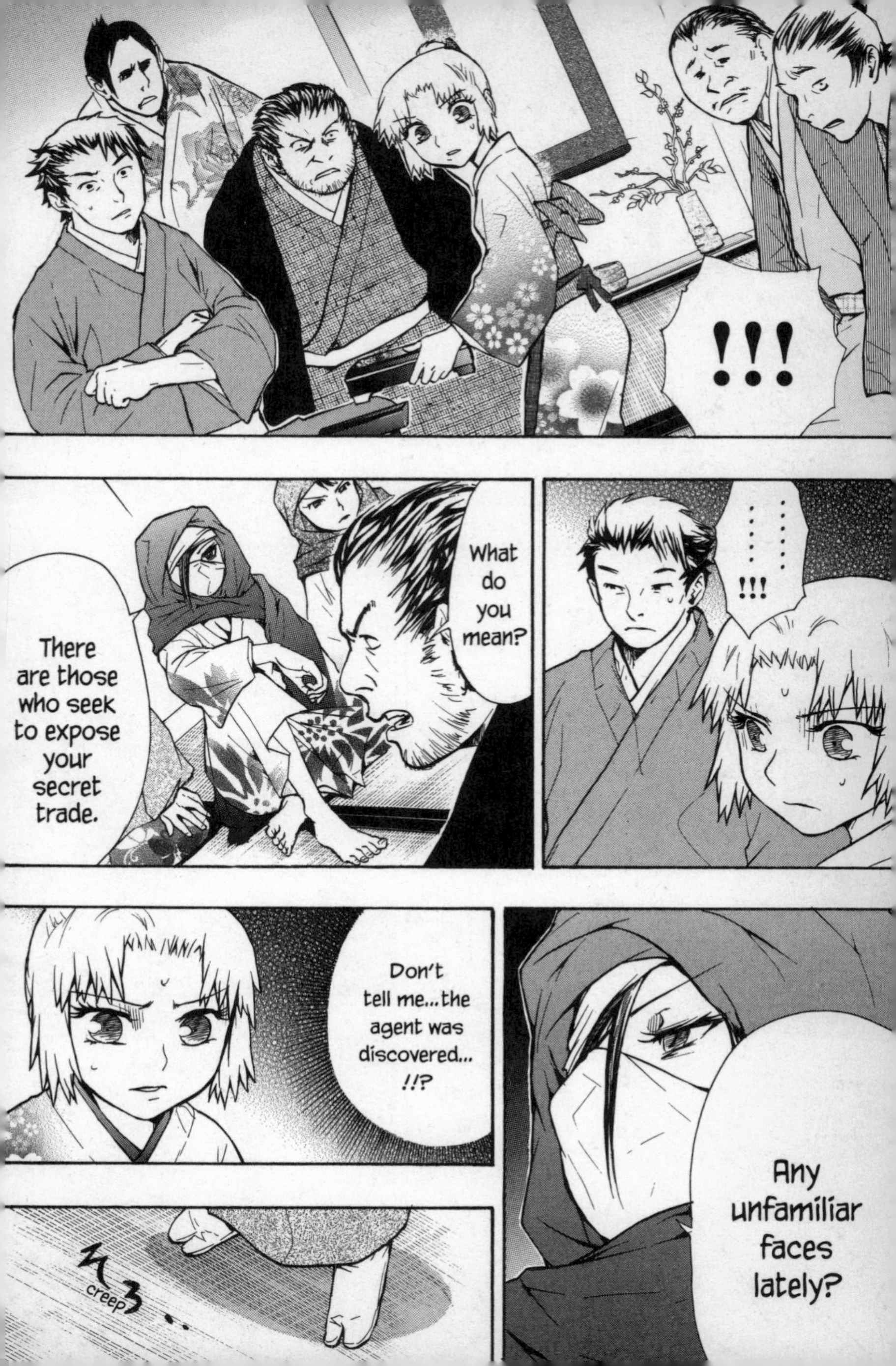
!!!
......
!!!
What do you mean?
There are those who seek to expose your secret trade.
Any unfamiliar faces lately?
Don't tell me...the agent was discovered...!!?
creep

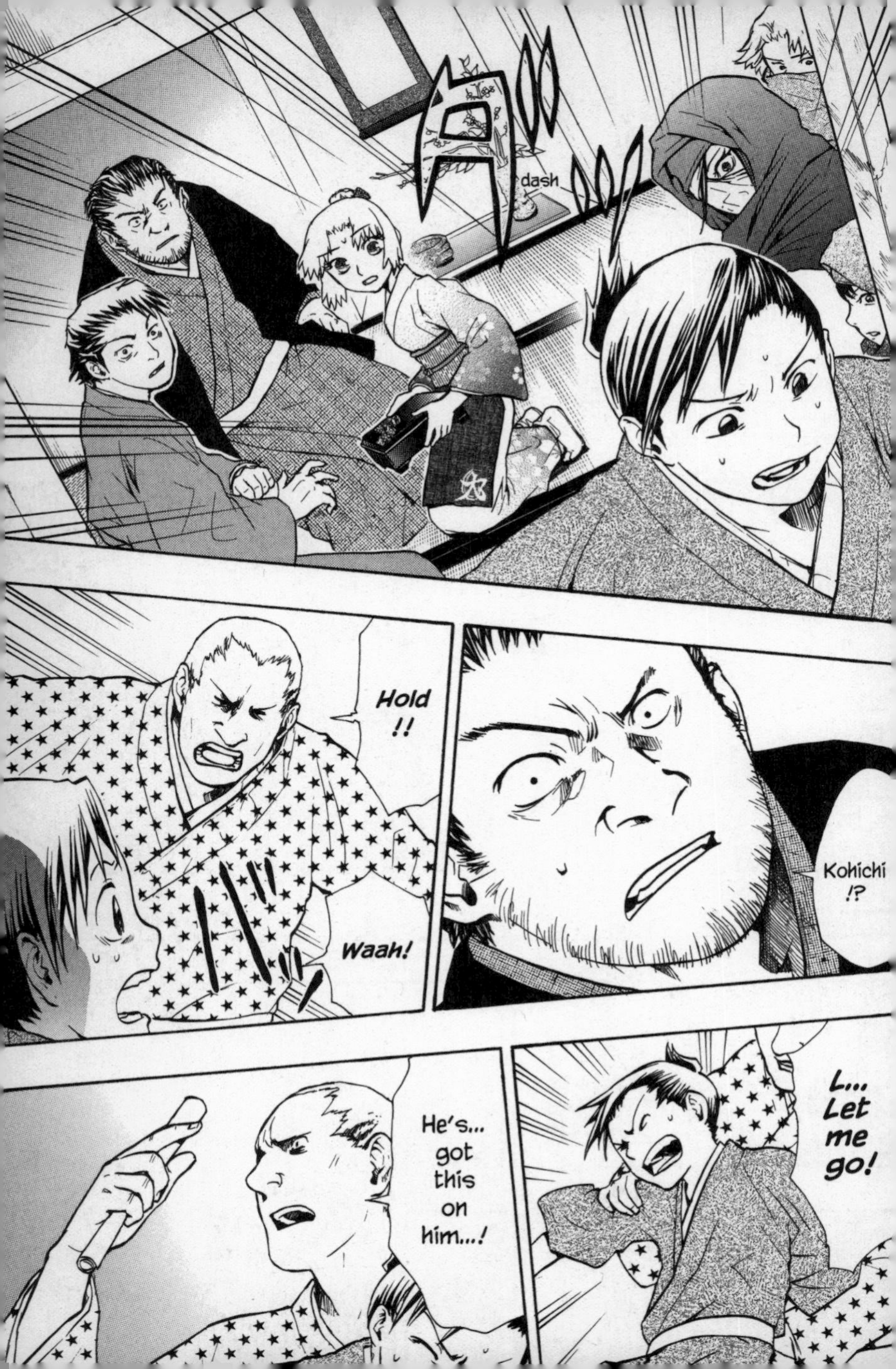
dash
Kohichi !?
Hold !!
Waah!
L... Let me go!
He's... got this on him...!

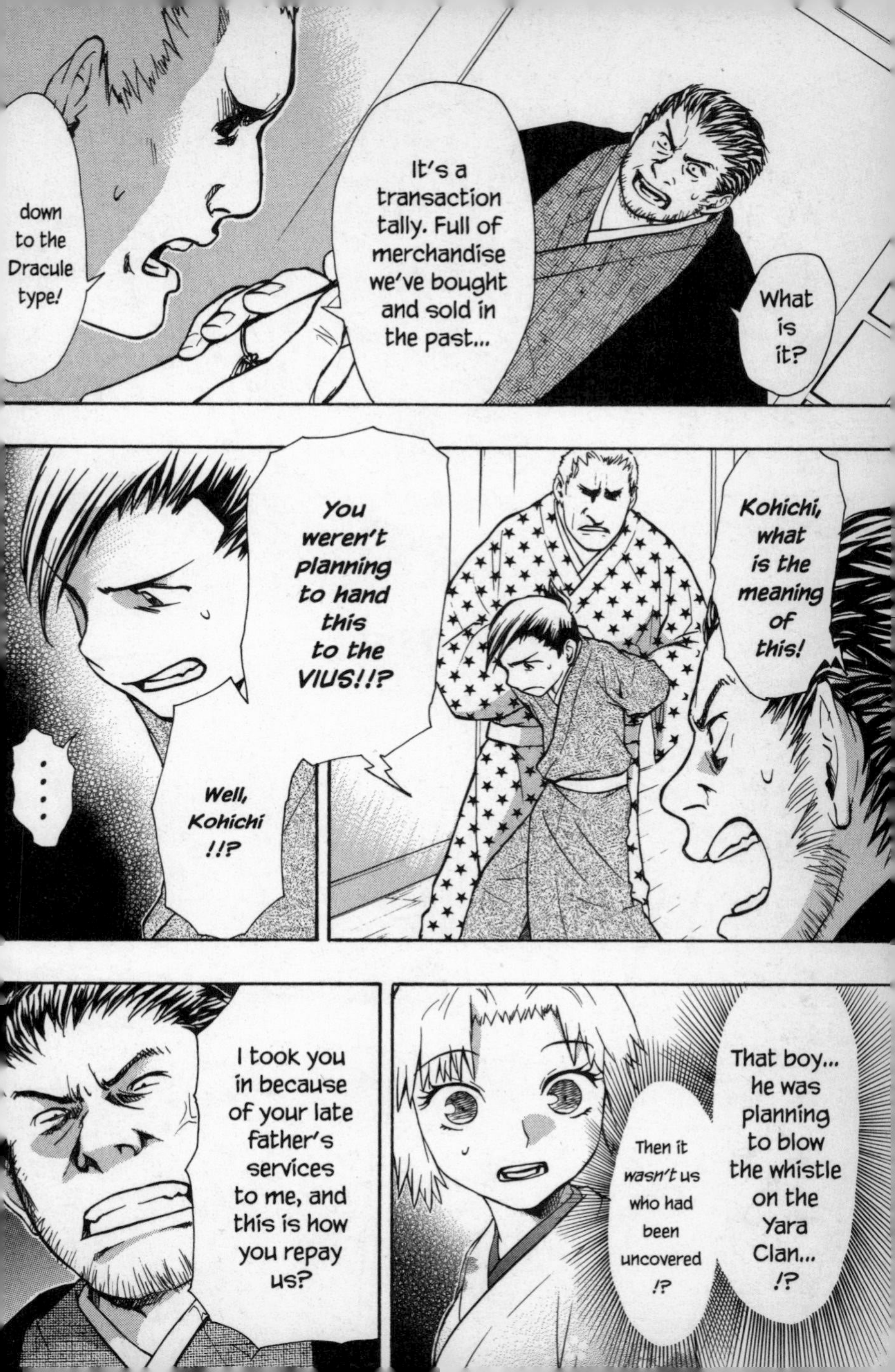
What is it?
It's a transaction tally. Full of merchandise we've bought and sold in the past...
down to the Dracule type!
Kohichi, what is the meaning of this!
You weren't planning to hand this to the VIUS!!?
Well, Kohichi !!?
....
That boy... he was planning to blow the whistle on the Yara Clan... !?
Then it wasn't us who had been uncovered !?
I took you in because of your late father's services to me, and this is how you repay us?

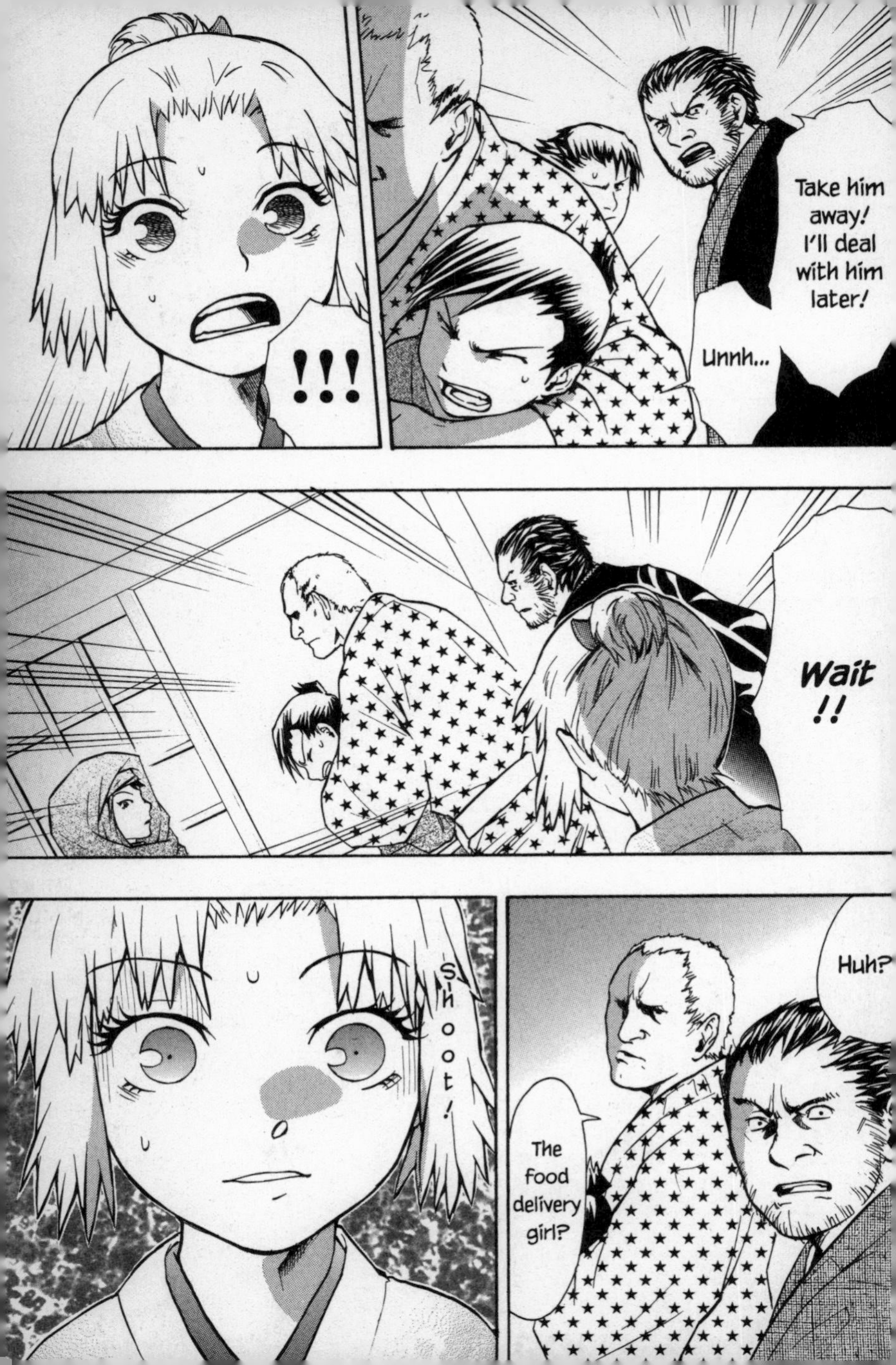
Take him away! I'll deal with him later!
Unnh...
!!!
Wait !!
Huh?
The food delivery girl?
Sh oot!

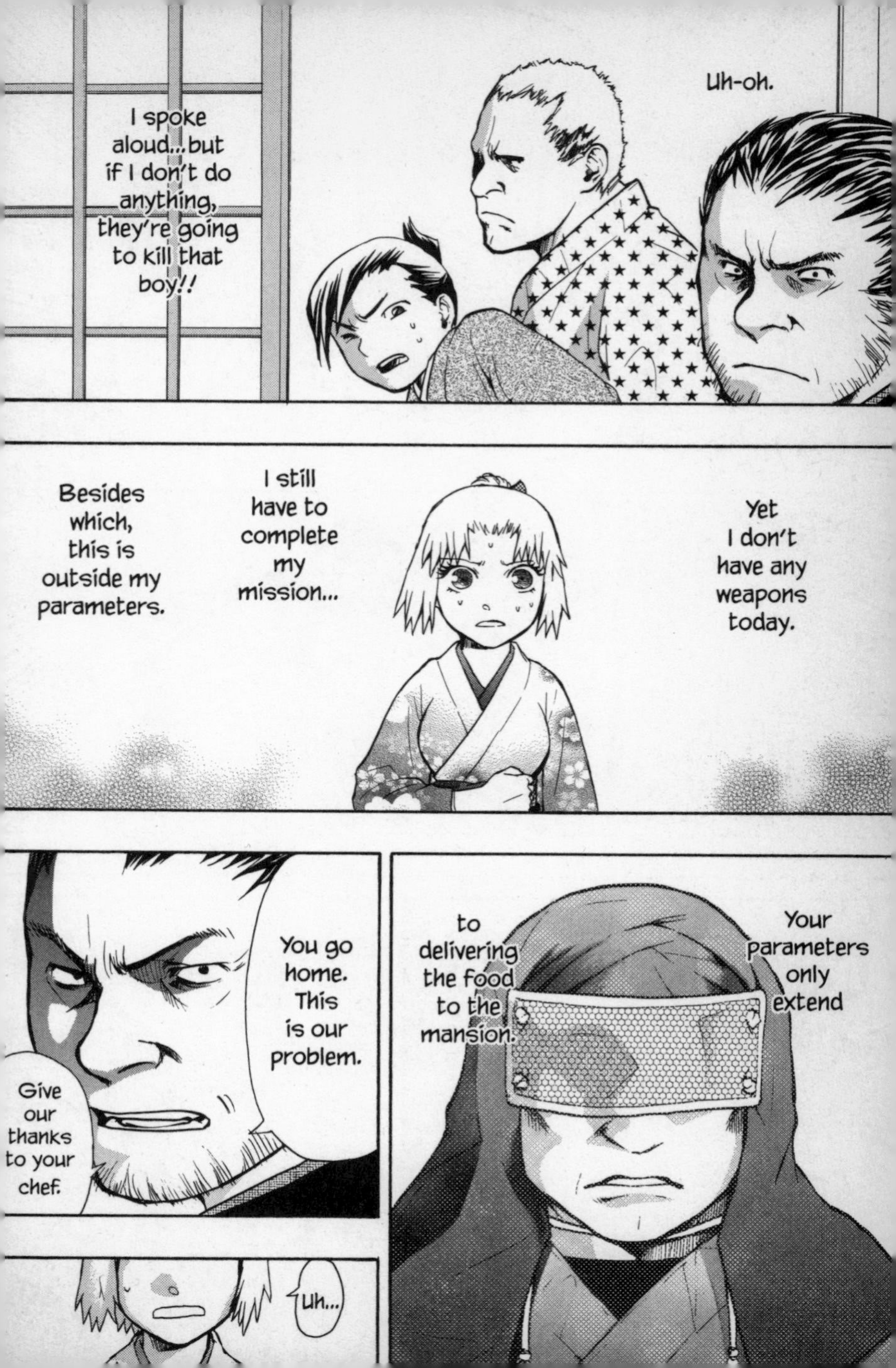
Uh-oh.
I spoke aloud...but if I don't do anything, they're going to kill that boy!!
Yet I don't have any weapons today.
I still have to complete my mission...
Besides which, this is outside my parameters.
Your parameters only extend
to delivering the food to the mansion.
You go home. This is our problem.
Give our thanks to your chef.
Uh...

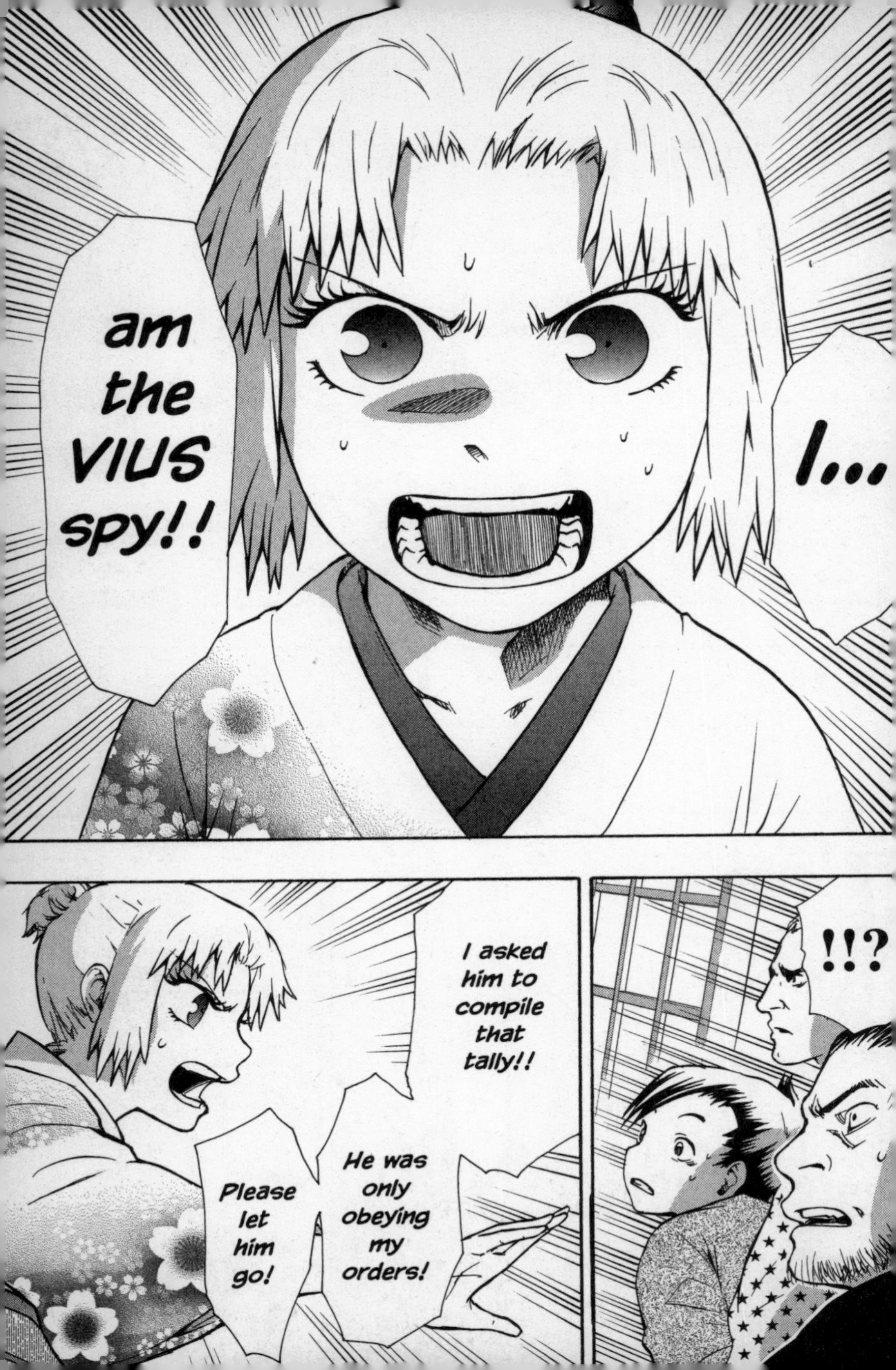
I...
am the VIUS spy!!
!!?
I asked him to compile that tally!!
He was only obeying my orders!
Please let him go!

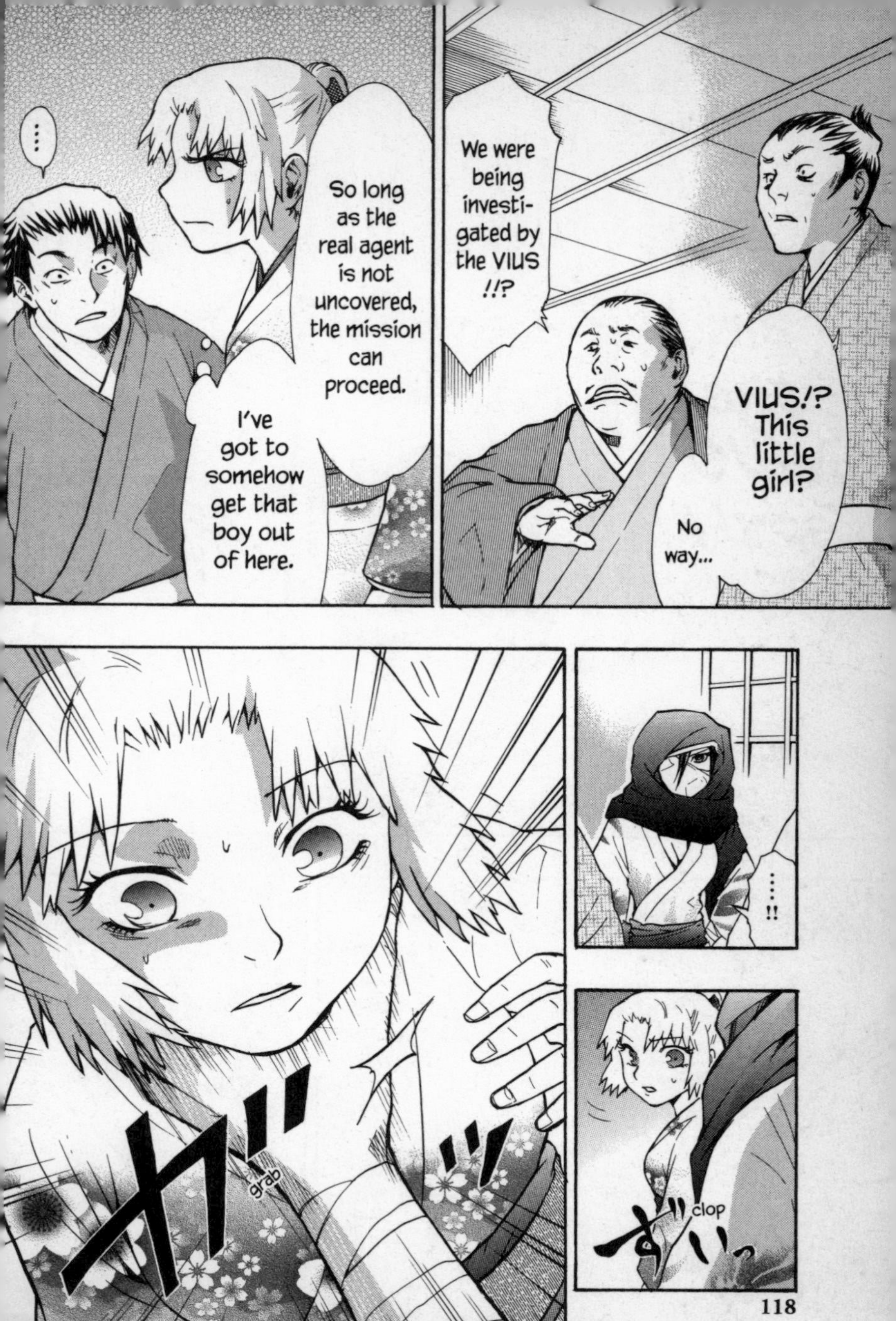
VIUS!? This little girl?
No way...
We were being investi-gated by the VIUS !!?
So long as the real agent is not uncovered, the mission can proceed.
I've got to somehow get that boy out of here.
......
......!!
clop
grab

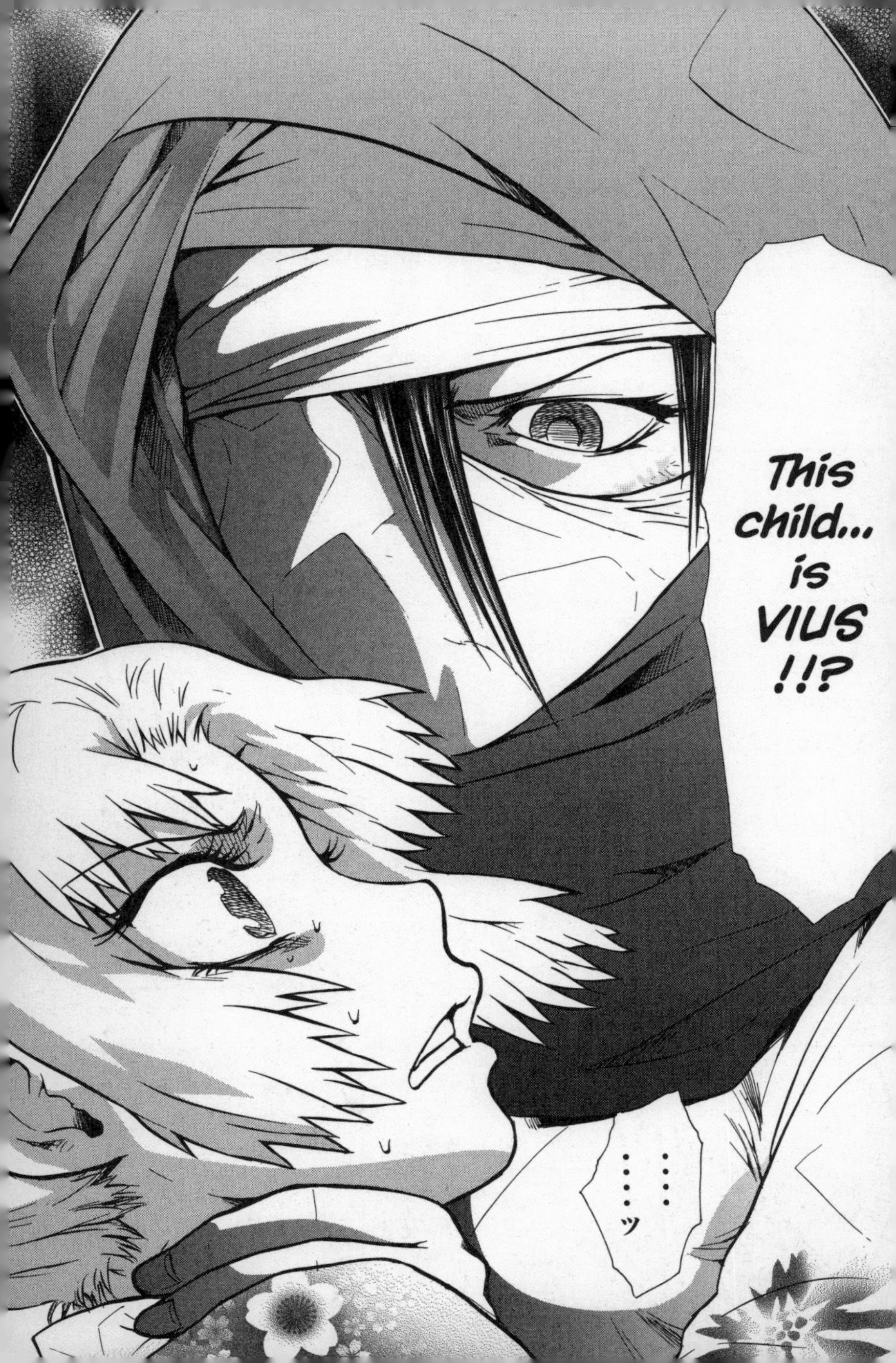
This child... is VIUS!!?
......ッ

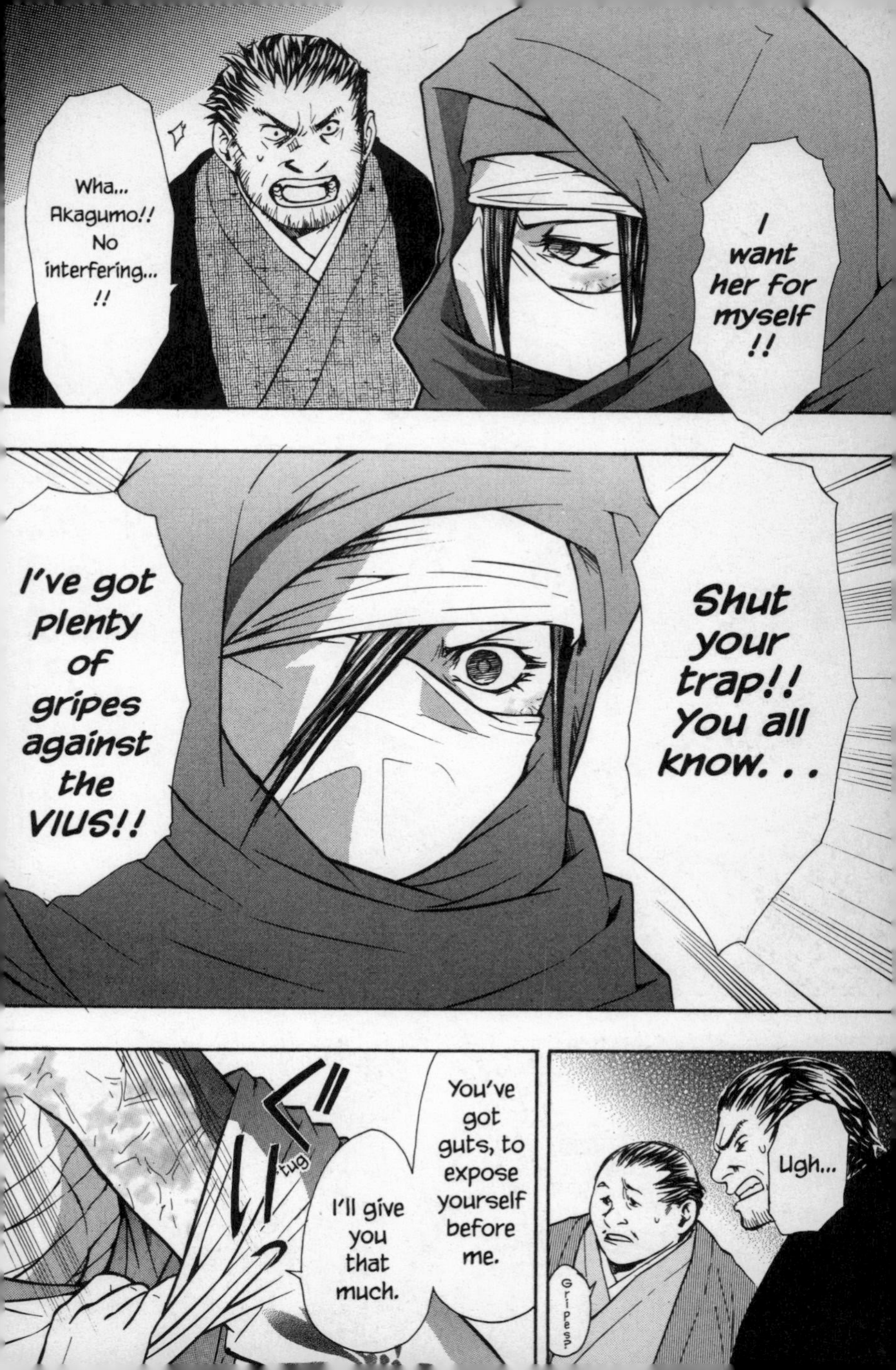
I want her for myself !!
Wha... Akagumo!! No interfering... !!
Shut your trap!! You all know. . .
I've got plenty of gripes against the VIUS!!
Ugh...
Gripes?
You've got guts, to expose yourself before me.
tug
I'll give you that much.

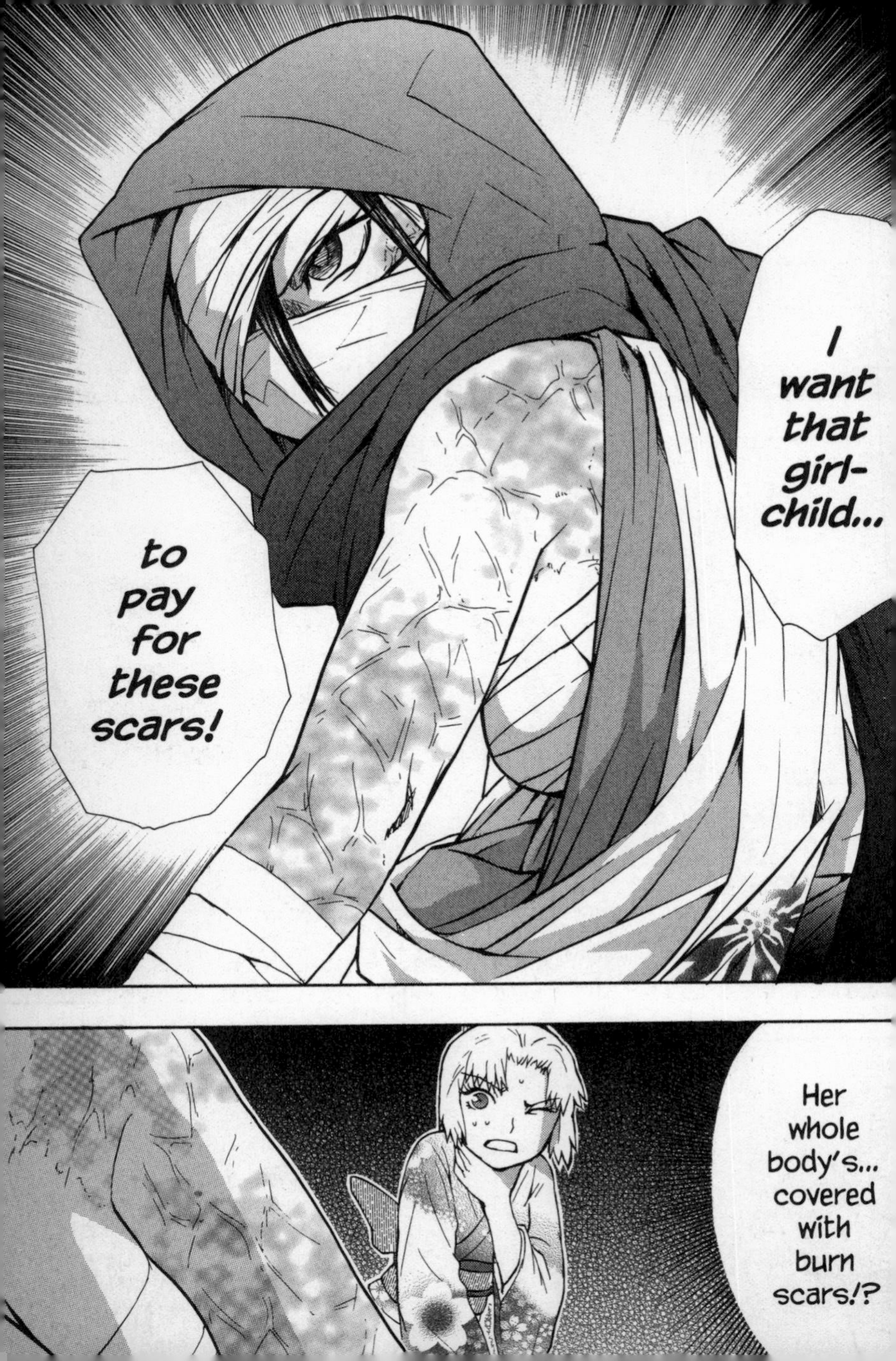
I want that girl-child...
to pay for these scars!
Her whole body's... covered with burn scars!?

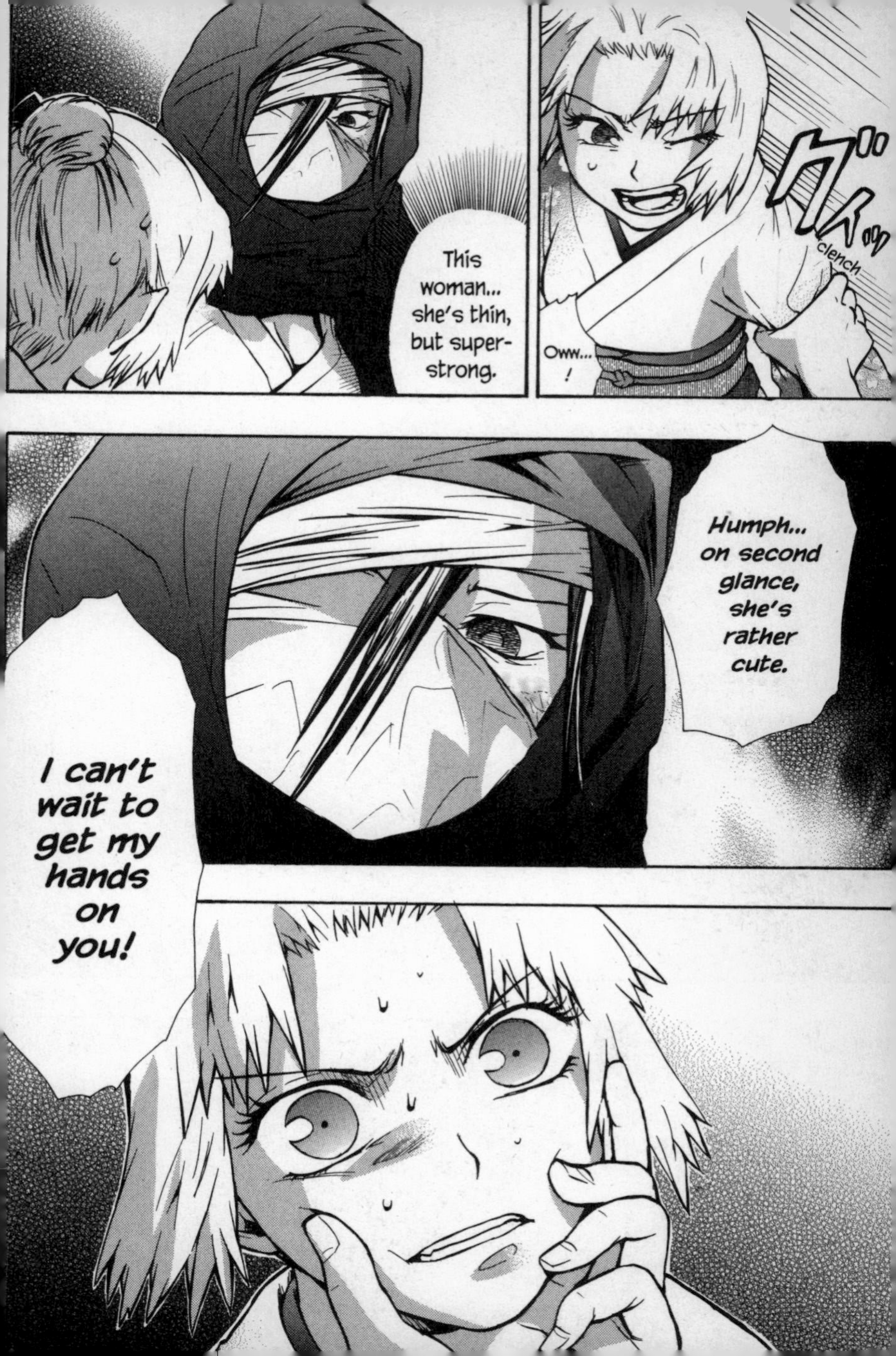
clench
Oww... !
This woman... she's thin, but super-strong.
Humph... on second glance, she's rather cute.
I can't wait to get my hands on you!

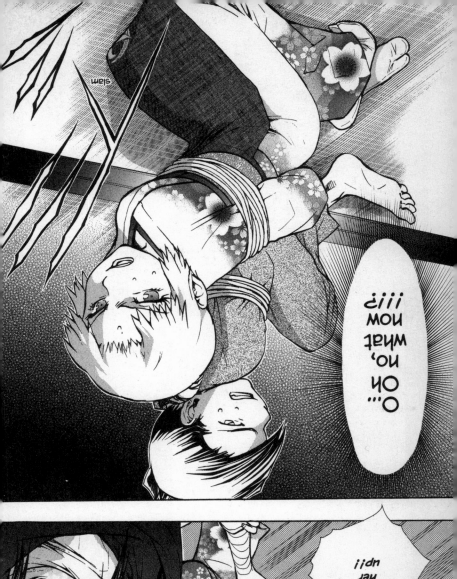

slam

O...
oh no,
what now‼‽

Tie her
up‼

◊ Dragon Eye Tidbits ◊

These are the cover page of and one page
within Mission 11. This time, I want to show
you some of the trial and error that goes into
making a *name* (kind of a rough sketch before
one starts on the actual draft).

These are rough draft copies from Mission 11.
I always procrastinate on the cover art, so I
tend to draw a little, then start inking a different
page. As you can see, I haven't drawn in all of
the houses or roofs yet, nor Leila or Kajiyama.

On the page to the left, I've only partly inked
in the Elder Vice-Director. I sometimes tweak
dialogue halfway through as well, and as you
can see, I did not originally have introductions
for Sakuraba and Issa.

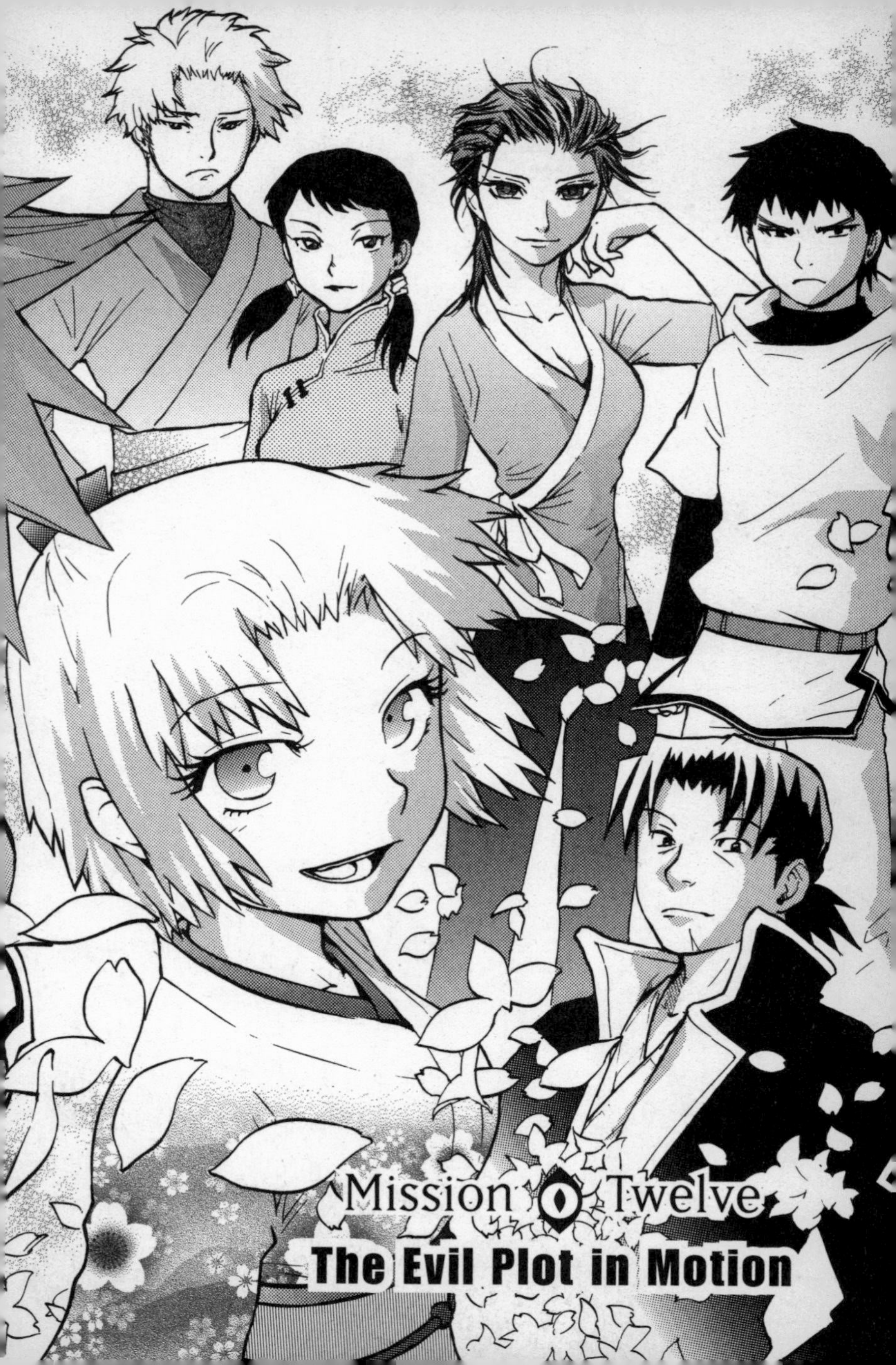
Mission Twelve
The Evil Plot in Motion

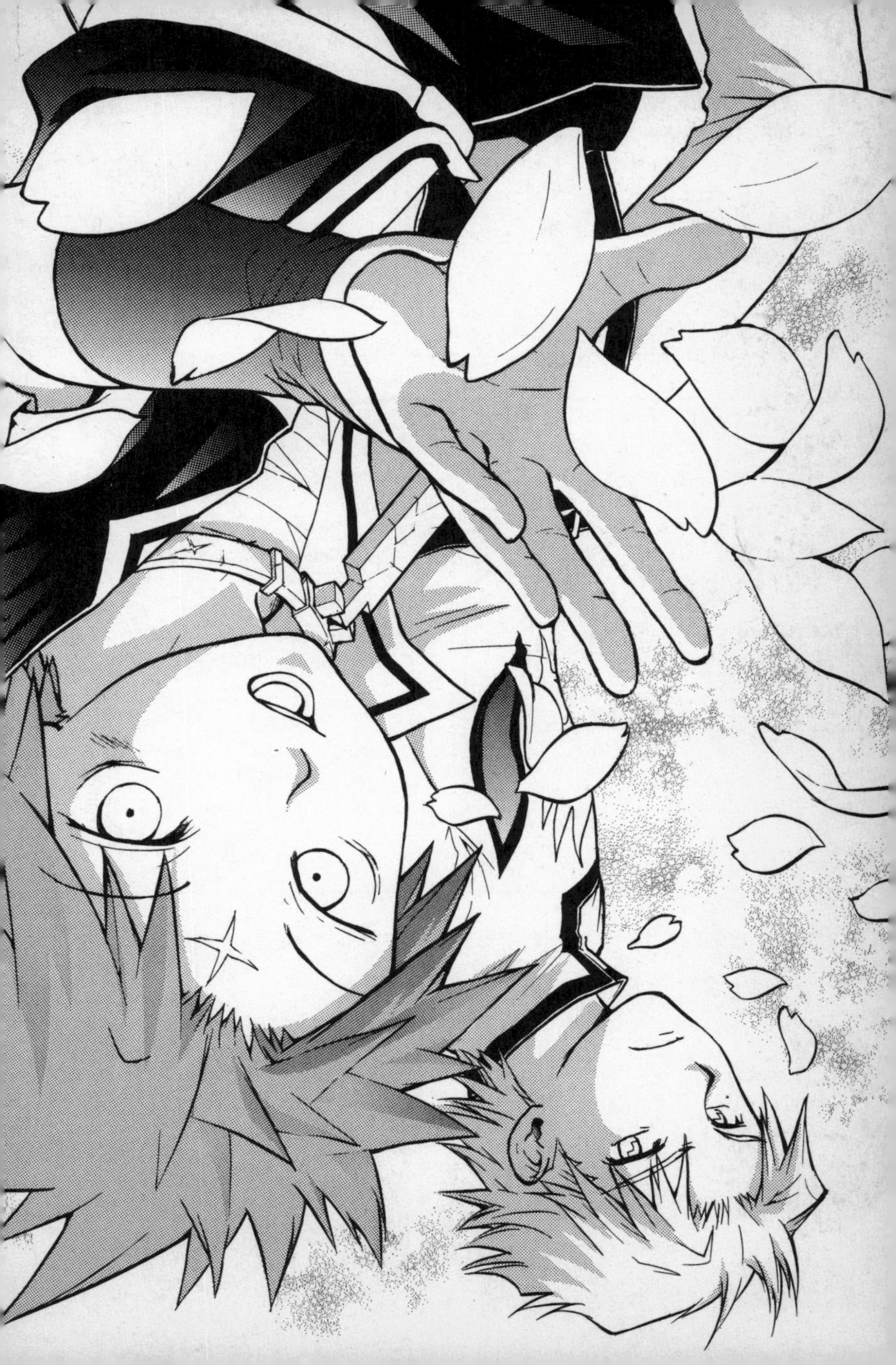

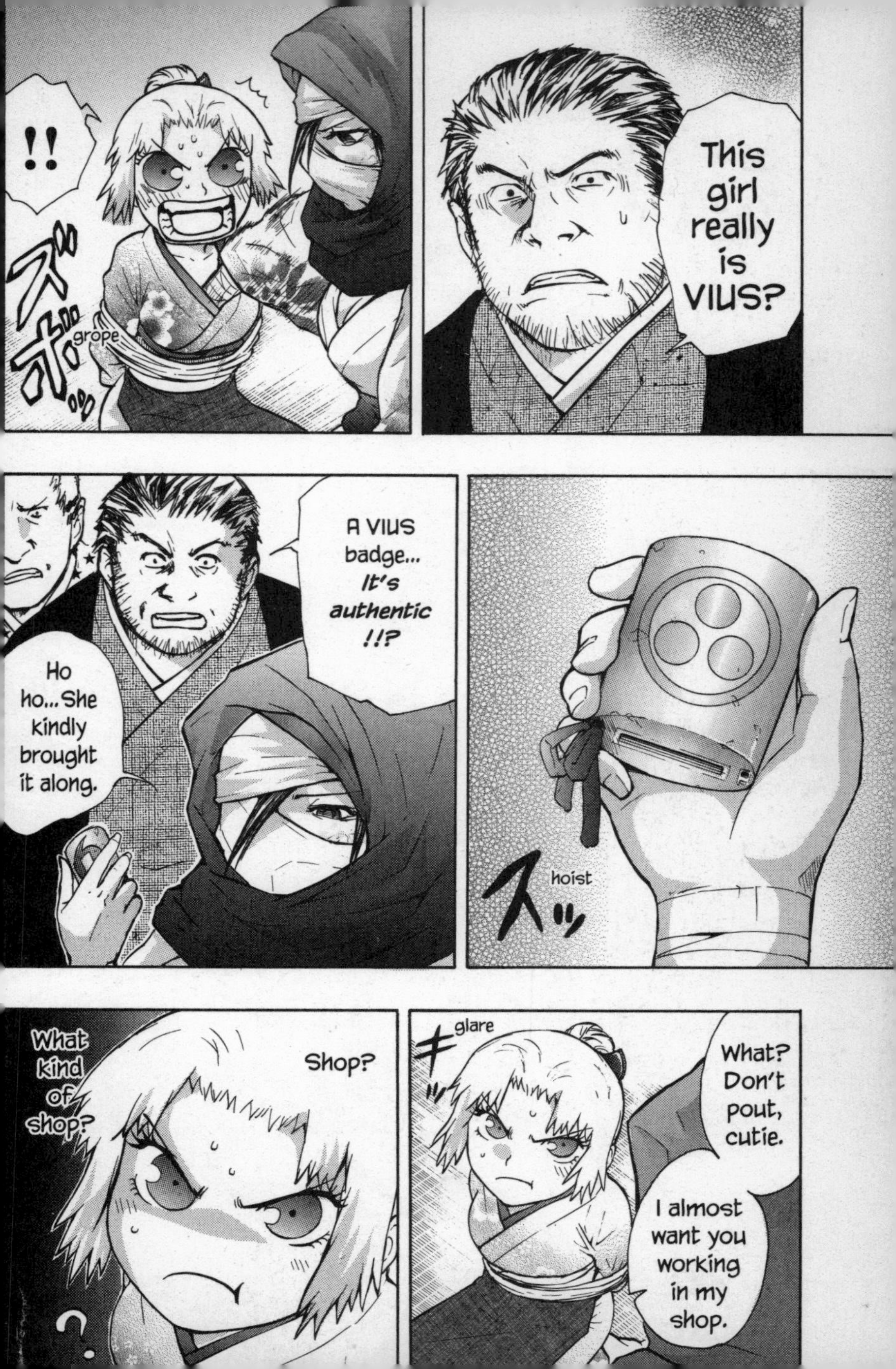
This girl really is VIUS?
!!
grope
hoist
A VIUS badge... It's authentic !!?
Ho ho...She kindly brought it along.
glare
What? Don't pout, cutie.
I almost want you working in my shop.
Shop?
What kind of shop?

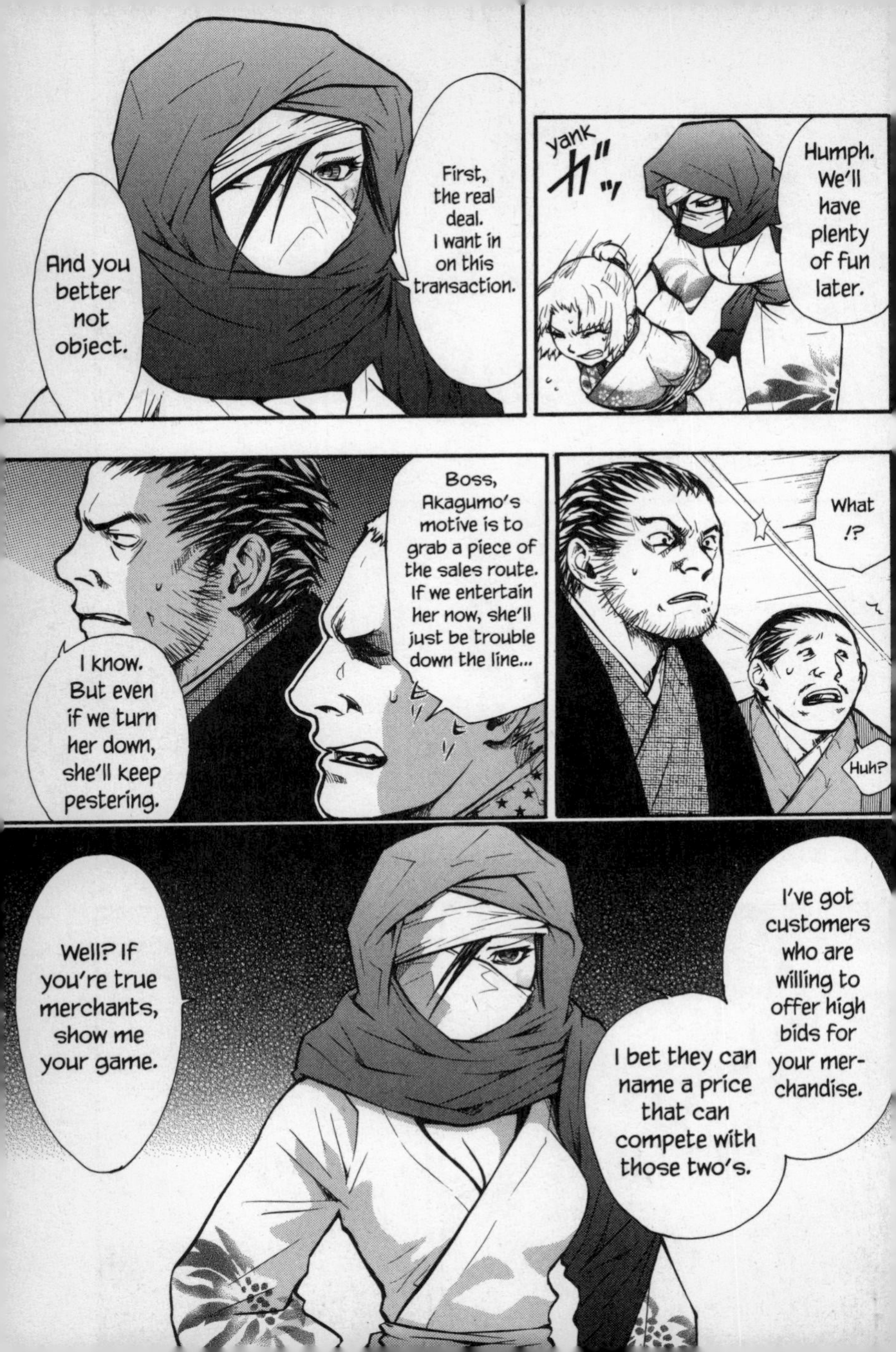
Humph. We'll have plenty of fun later.
yank
First, the real deal. I want in on this transaction.
And you better not object.
What !?
Huh?
Boss, Akagumo's motive is to grab a piece of the sales route. If we entertain her now, she'll just be trouble down the line...
I know. But even if we turn her down, she'll keep pestering.
I've got customers who are willing to offer high bids for your merchandise.
I bet they can name a price that can compete with those two's.
Well? If you're true merchants, show me your game.

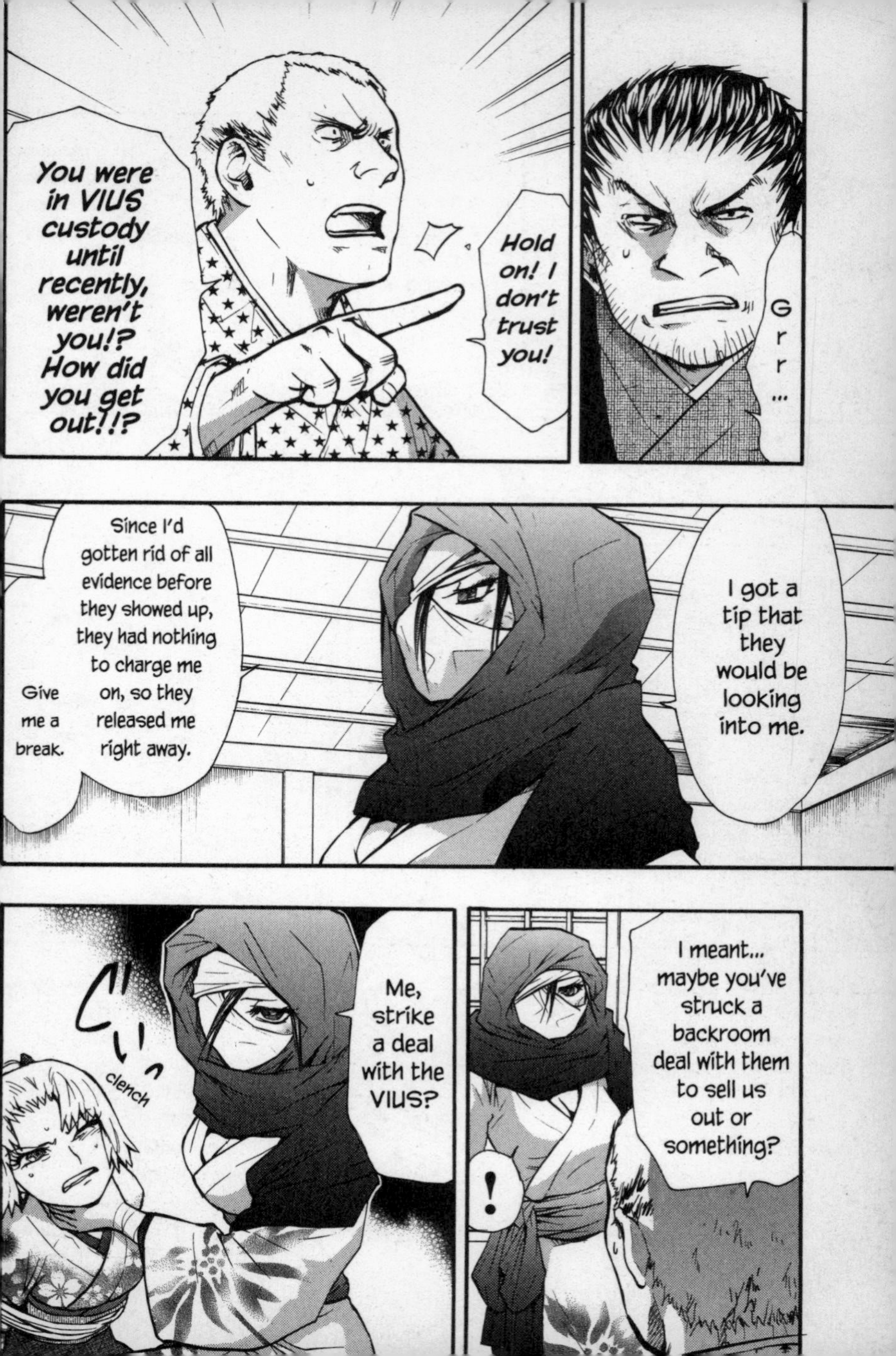
Grr...
Hold on! I don't trust you!
You were in VIUS custody until recently, weren't you!? How did you get out!!?
I got a tip that they would be looking into me.
Since I'd gotten rid of all evidence before they showed up, they had nothing to charge me on, so they released me right away.
Give me a break.
I meant... maybe you've struck a backroom deal with them to sell us out or something?
!
Me, strike a deal with the VIUS?
clench

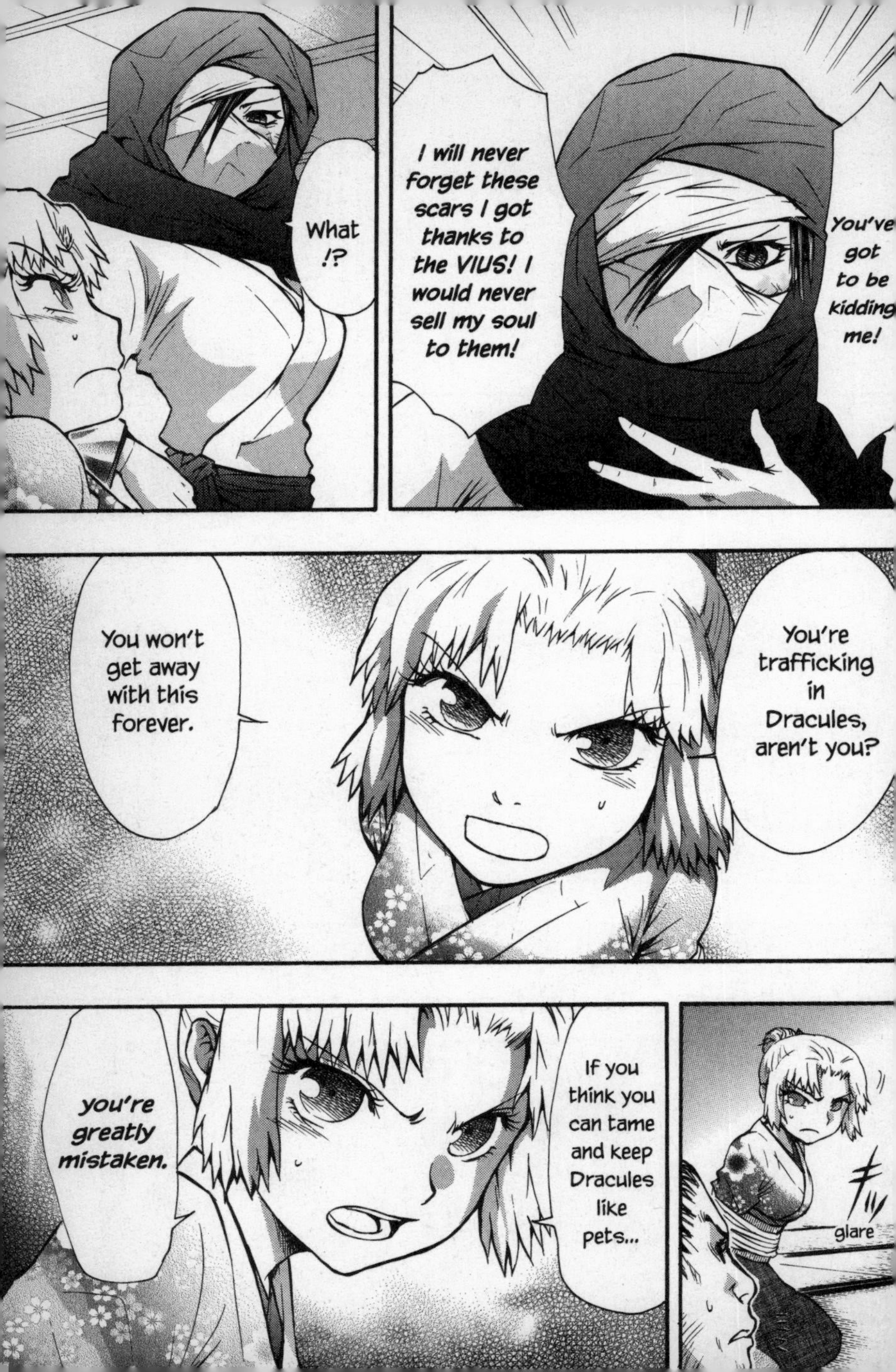
You've got to be kidding me!
I will never forget these scars I got thanks to the VIUS! I would never sell my soul to them!
What!?
You're trafficking in Dracules, aren't you?
You won't get away with this forever.
glare
If you think you can tame and keep Dracules like pets...
you're greatly mistaken.

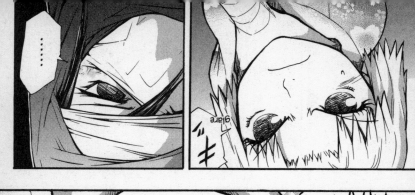

グイッ
yank
You sure are a chatty one, girl-child. Acting all high and mighty...
You all don't know the fearsomeness of Dracules!
By the time you regret it... it'll be too late!!
......
キッ
glare

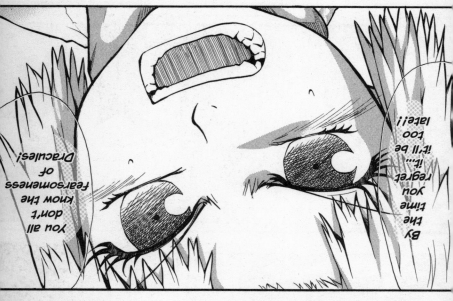

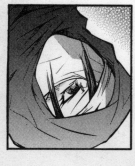

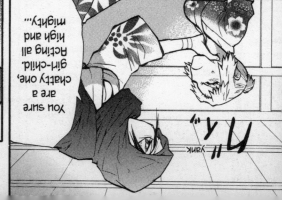

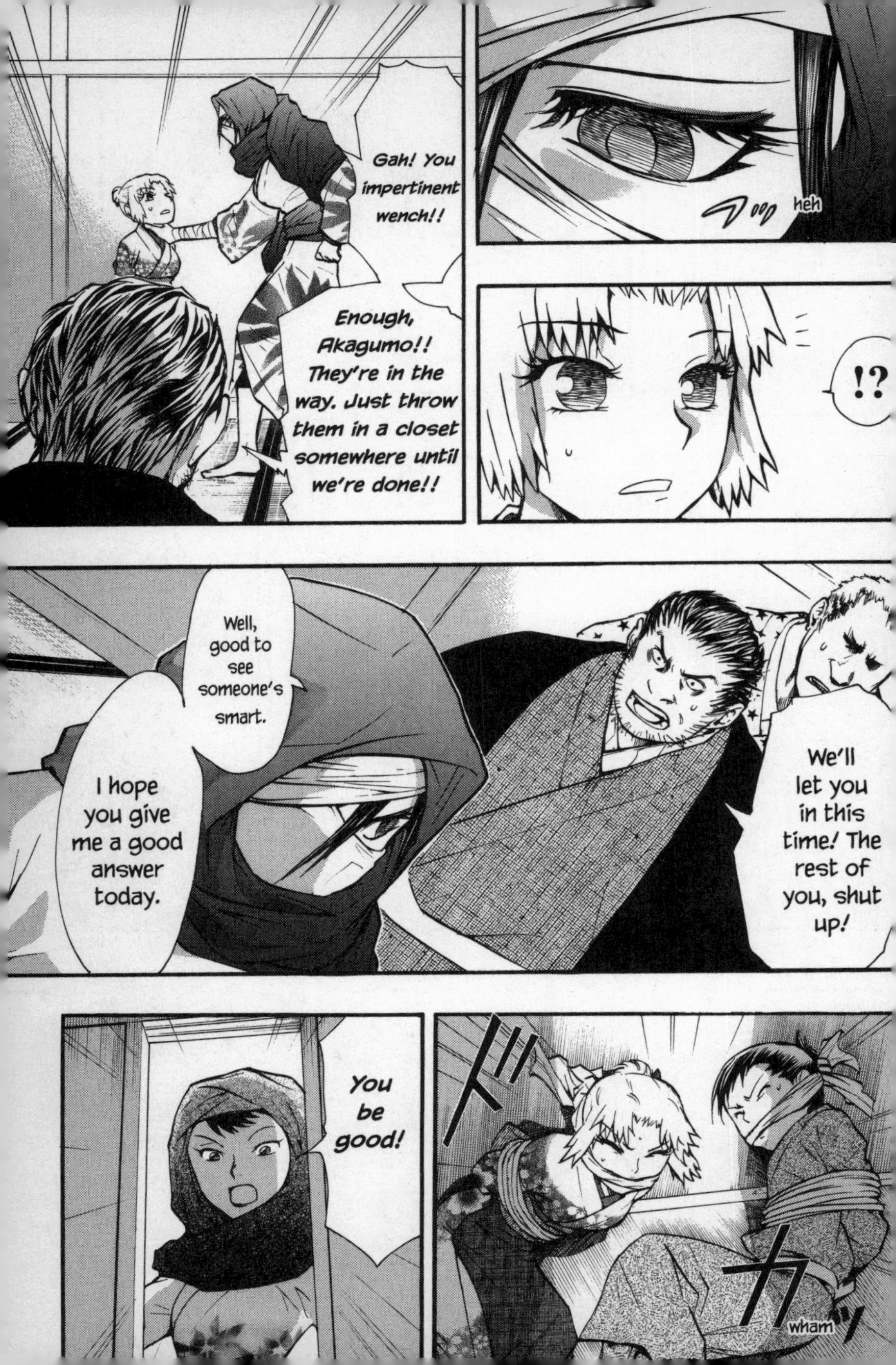
heh
!?
Gah! You impertinent wench!!
Enough, Akagumo!! They're in the way. Just throw them in a closet somewhere until we're done!!
We'll let you in this time! The rest of you, shut up!
Well, good to see someone's smart.
I hope you give me a good answer today.
wham
You be good!

Ummh ummh!
Mmph !
バタンッ
slam
silence
?
くるっ
whirl
ニコッ
grin
!?
Mm... mmm...
スル!...
slip...

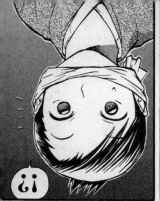

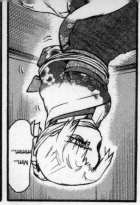

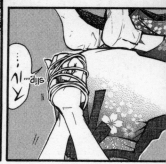

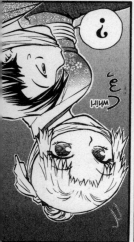

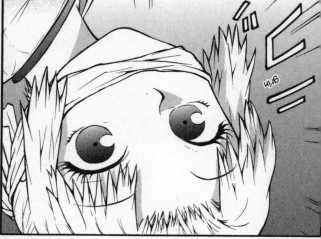

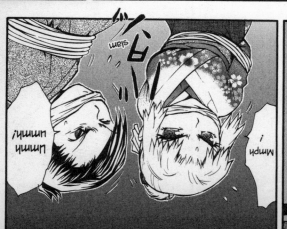

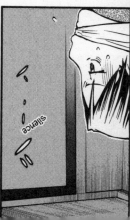

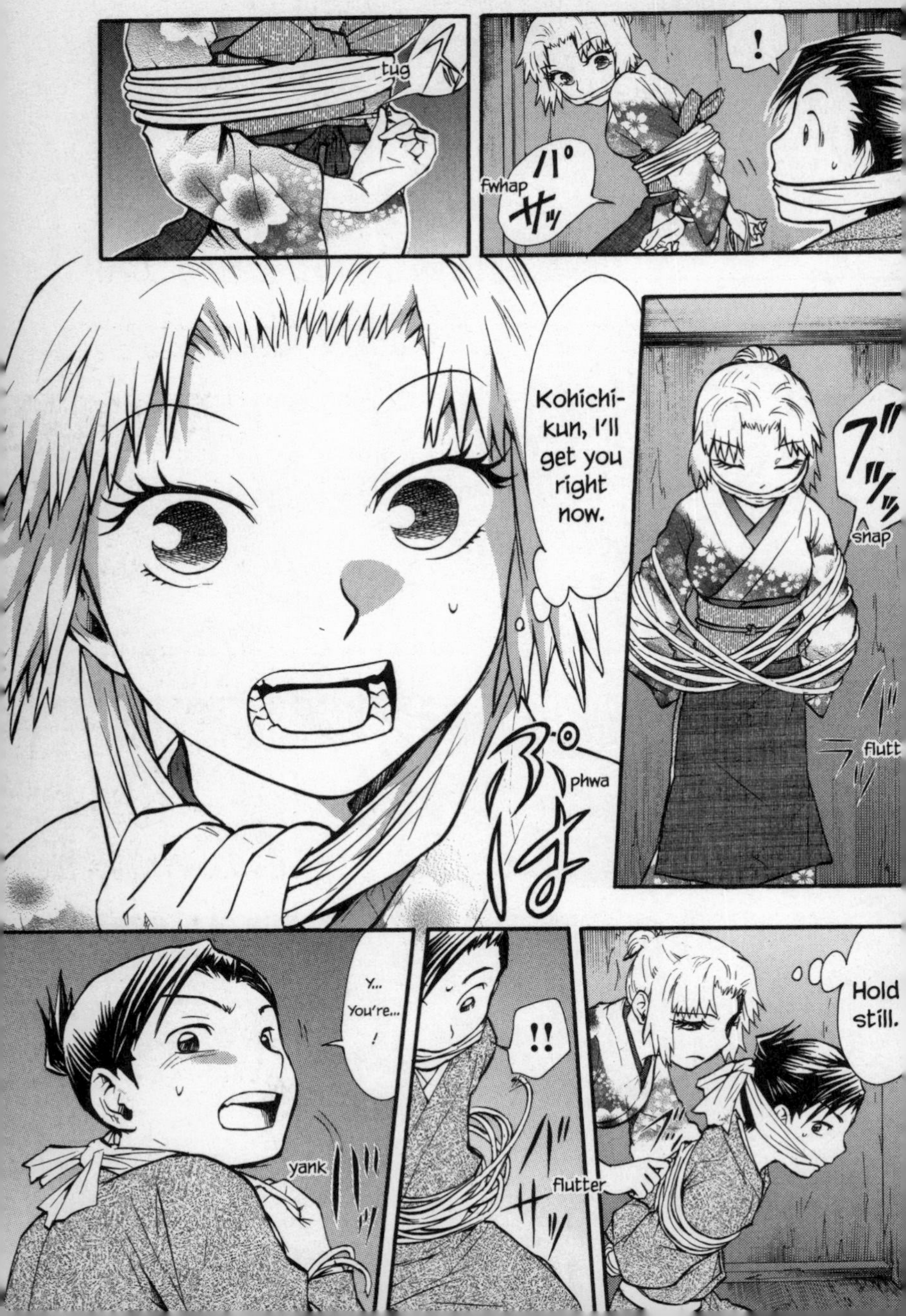
!
パサッ
fwhap
tug
ブツッ
snap
flutt
Kohichi-kun, I'll get you right now.
phwa
Hold still.
!!
flutter
Y... You're...!
yank

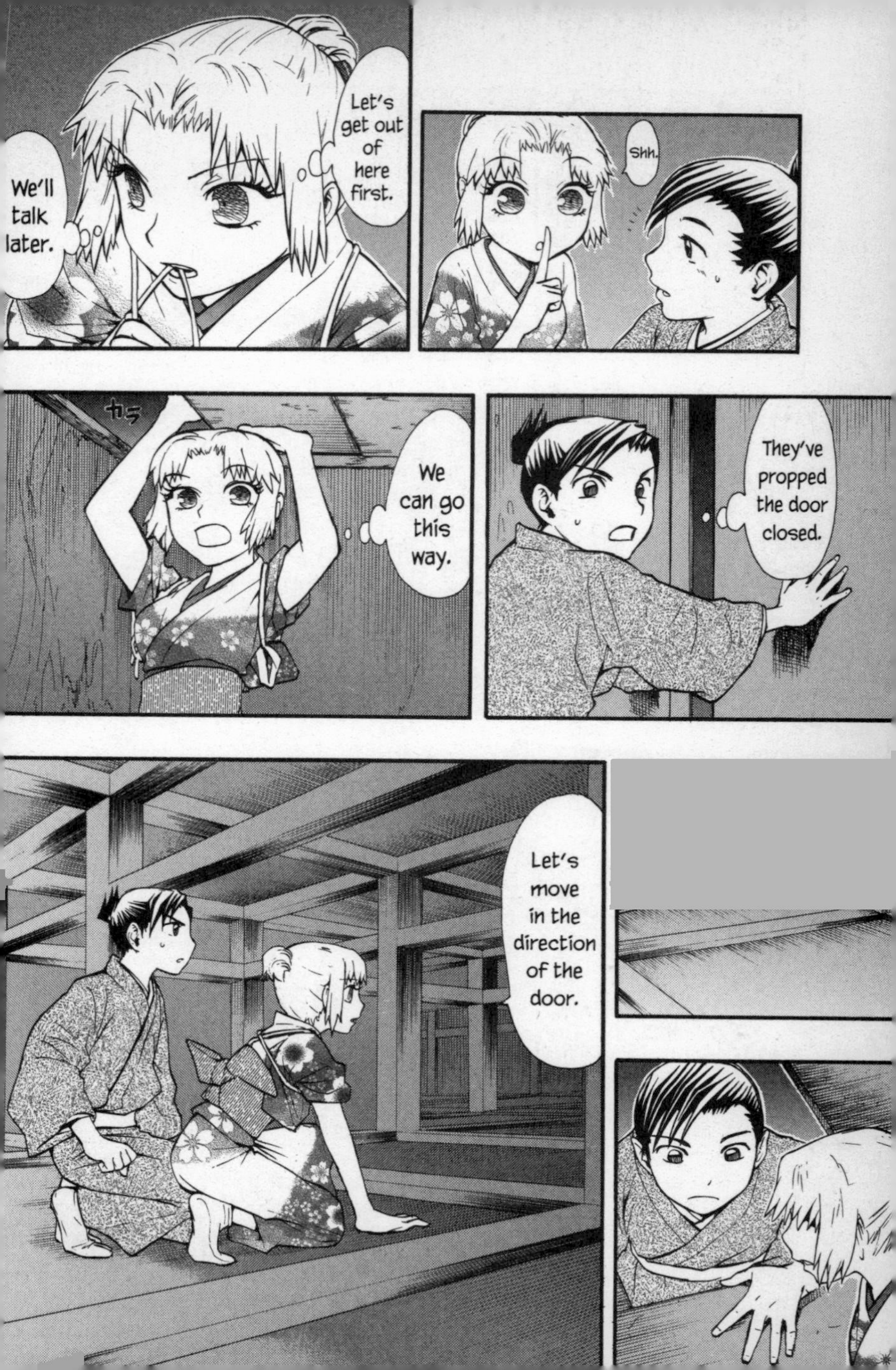
Shh.
Let's get out of here first.
We'll talk later.
They've propped the door closed.
We can go this way.
カラ
Let's move in the direction of the door.

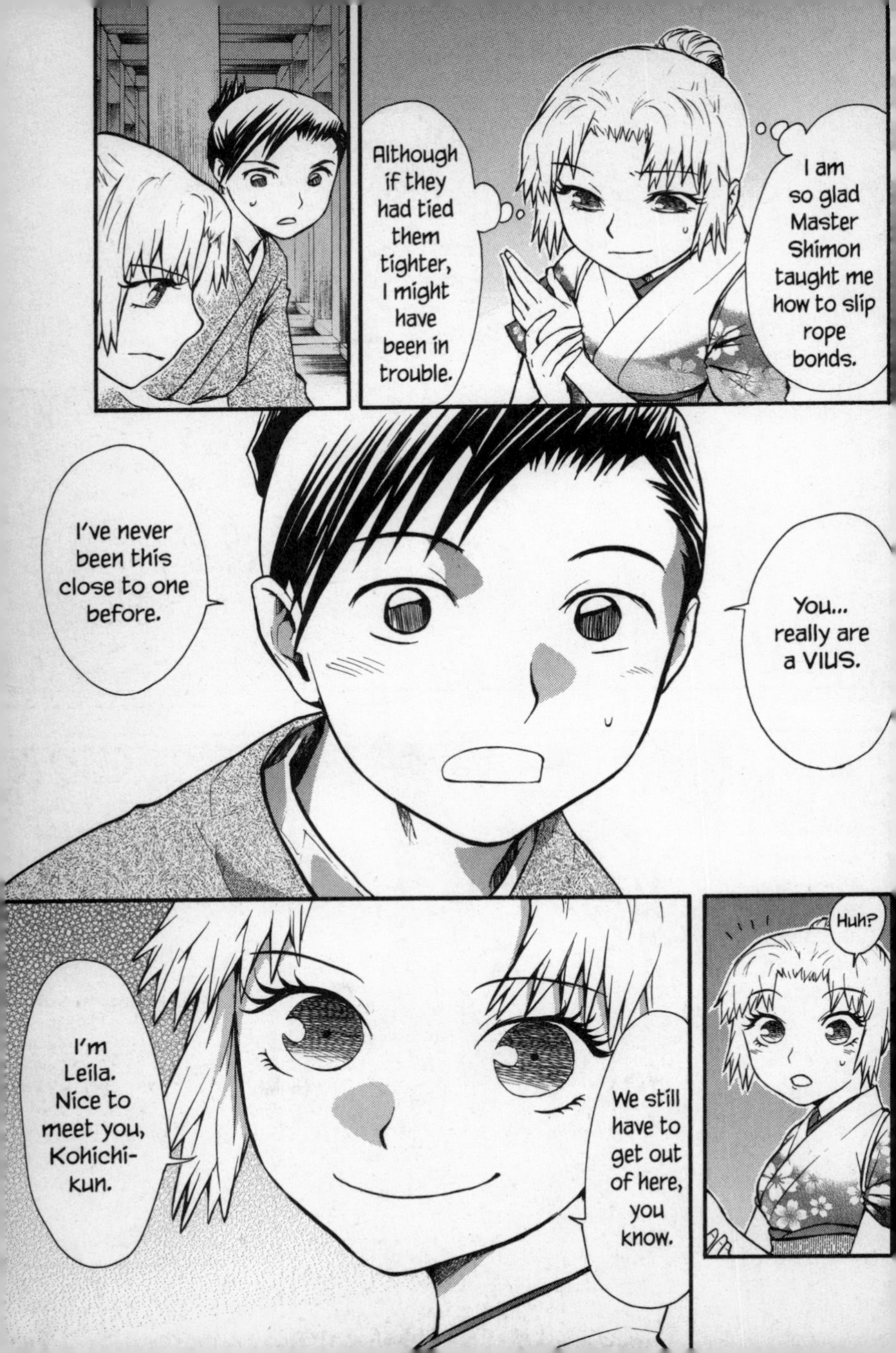
I am so glad Master Shimon taught me how to slip rope bonds.
Although if they had tied them tighter, I might have been in trouble.
You... really are a VIUS.
I've never been this close to one before.
Huh?
We still have to get out of here, you know.
I'm Leila. Nice to meet you, Kohichi-kun.

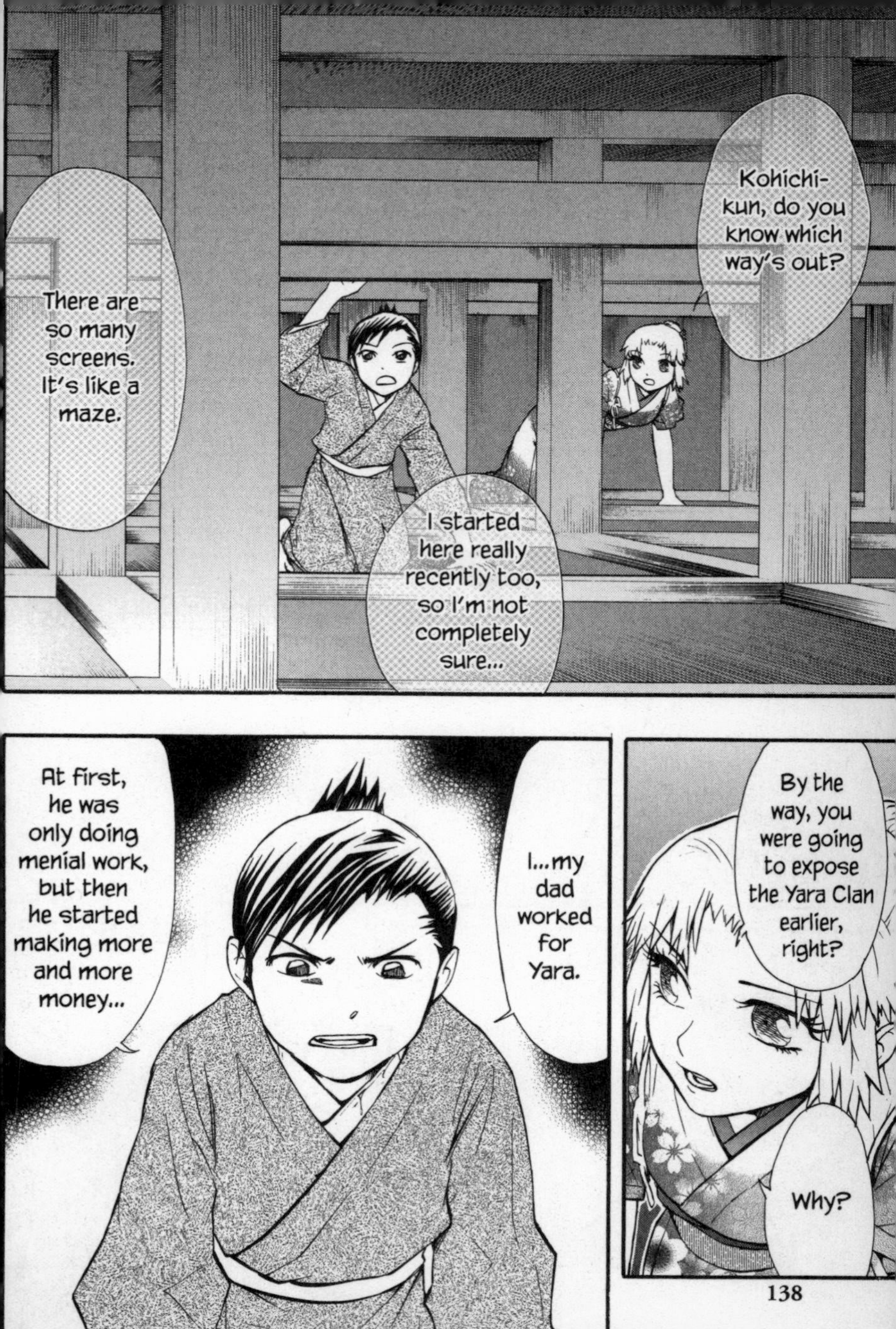
Kohichi-kun, do you know which way's out?
I started here really recently too, so I'm not completely sure...
There are so many screens. It's like a maze.
By the way, you were going to expose the Yara Clan earlier, right?
Why?
I...my dad worked for Yara.
At first, he was only doing menial work, but then he started making more and more money...

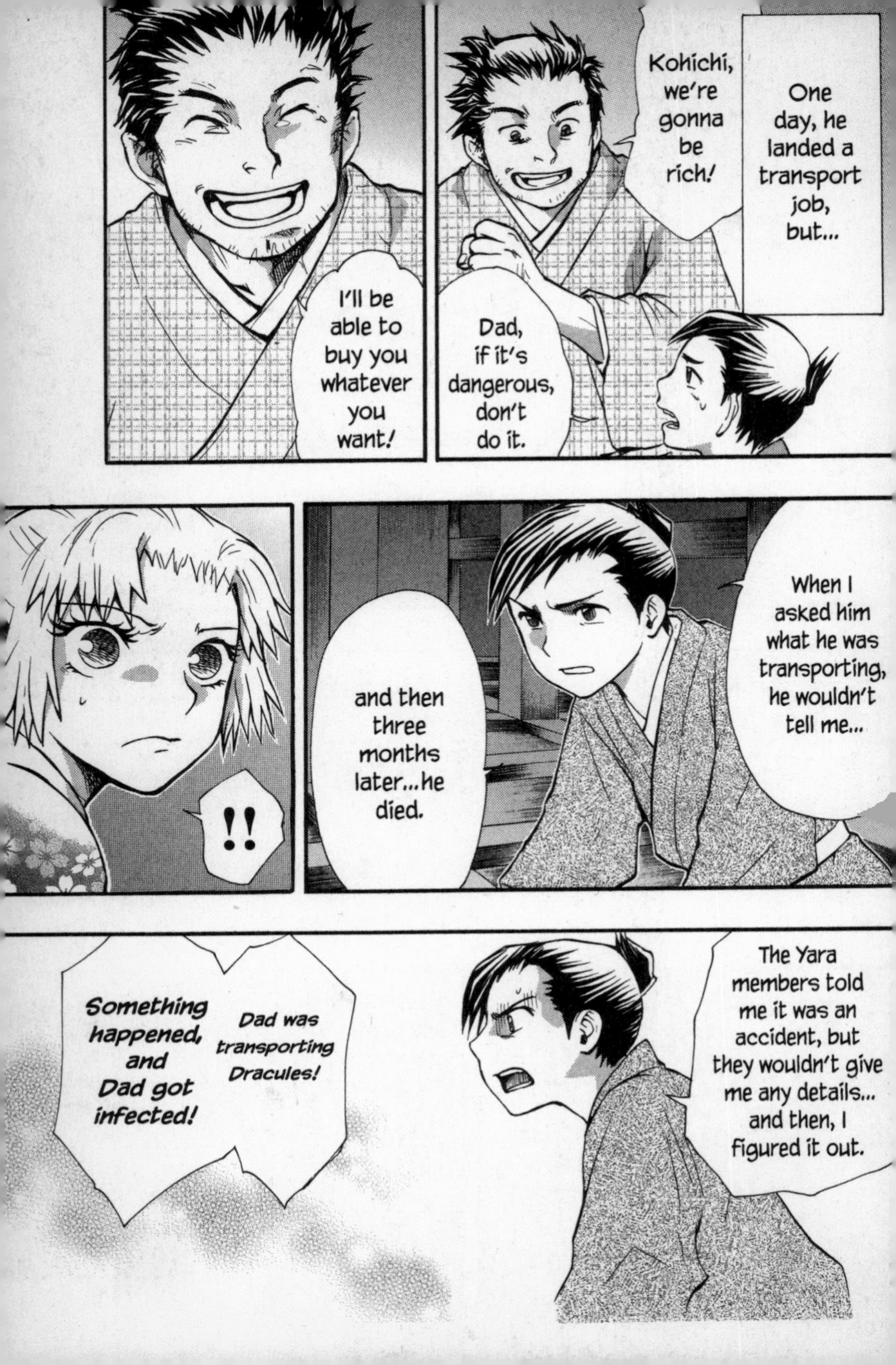
One day, he landed a transport job, but...
Kohichi, we're gonna be rich!
Dad, if it's dangerous, don't do it.
I'll be able to buy you whatever you want!
When I asked him what he was transporting, he wouldn't tell me...
and then three months later...he died.
!!
The Yara members told me it was an accident, but they wouldn't give me any details... and then, I figured it out.
Dad was transporting Dracules!
Something happened, and Dad got infected!

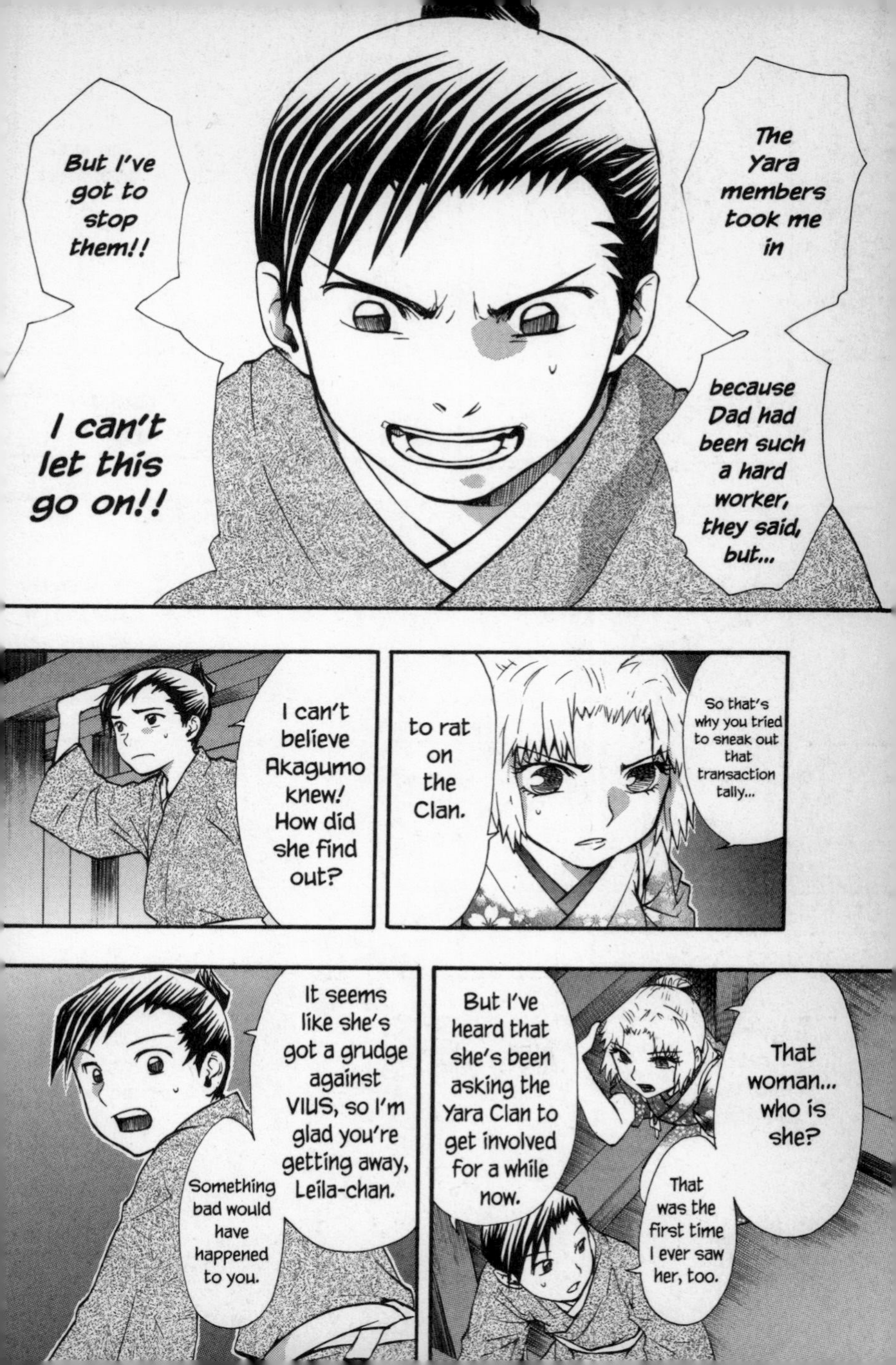
The Yara members took me in
because Dad had been such a hard worker, they said, but...
But I've got to stop them!!
I can't let this go on!!
So that's why you tried to sneak out that transaction tally...
to rat on the Clan.
I can't believe Akagumo knew! How did she find out?
That woman... who is she?
That was the first time I ever saw her, too.
But I've heard that she's been asking the Yara Clan to get involved for a while now.
It seems like she's got a grudge against VIUS, so I'm glad you're getting away, Leila-chan.
Something bad would have happened to you.

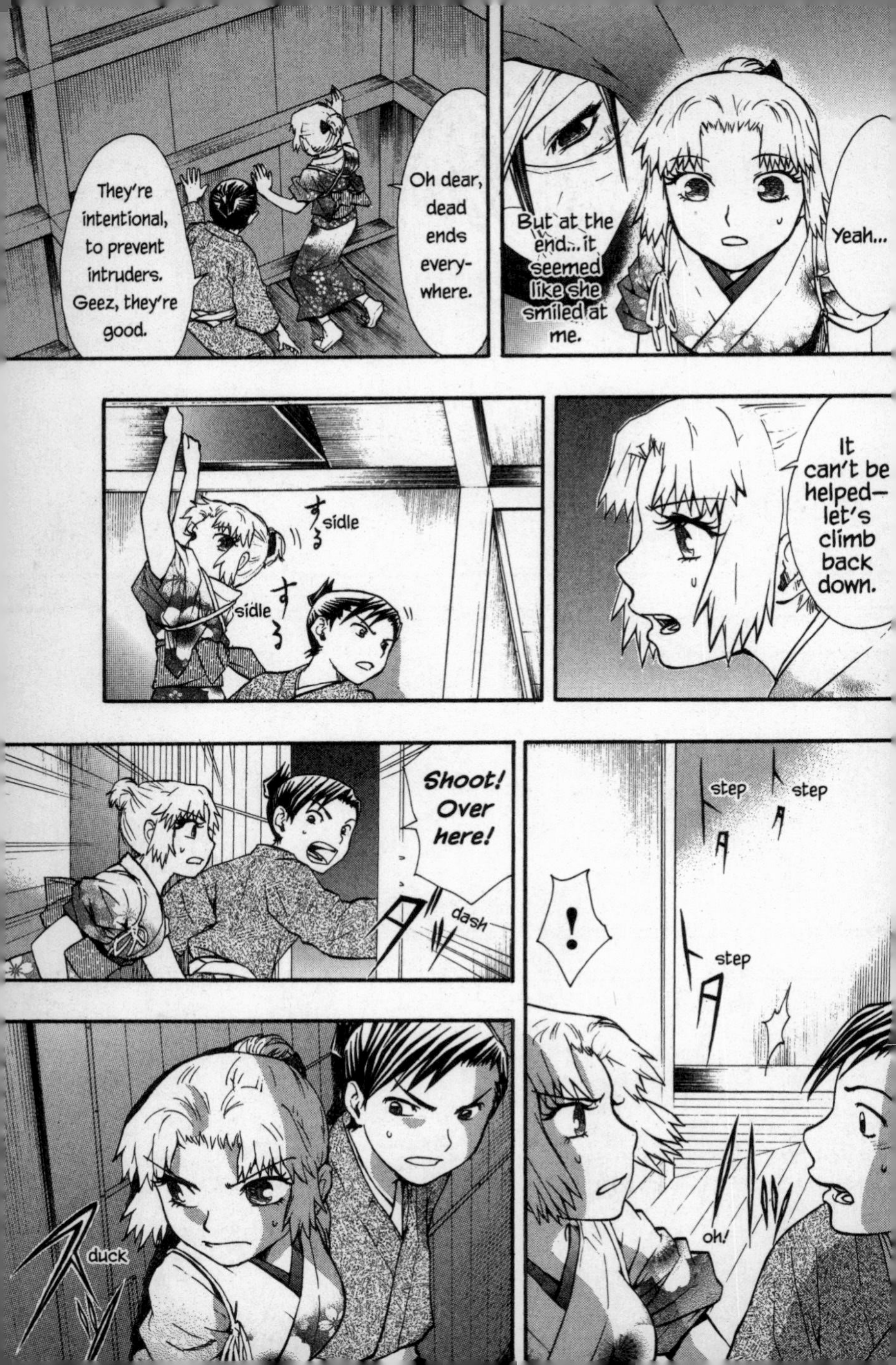
Yeah...
But at the end... it seemed like she smiled at me.
Oh dear, dead ends every-where.
They're intentional, to prevent intruders. Geez, they're good.
It can't be helped—let's climb back down.
する sidle
する sidle
step
step
!
step
oh!
Shoot! Over here!
dash
duck

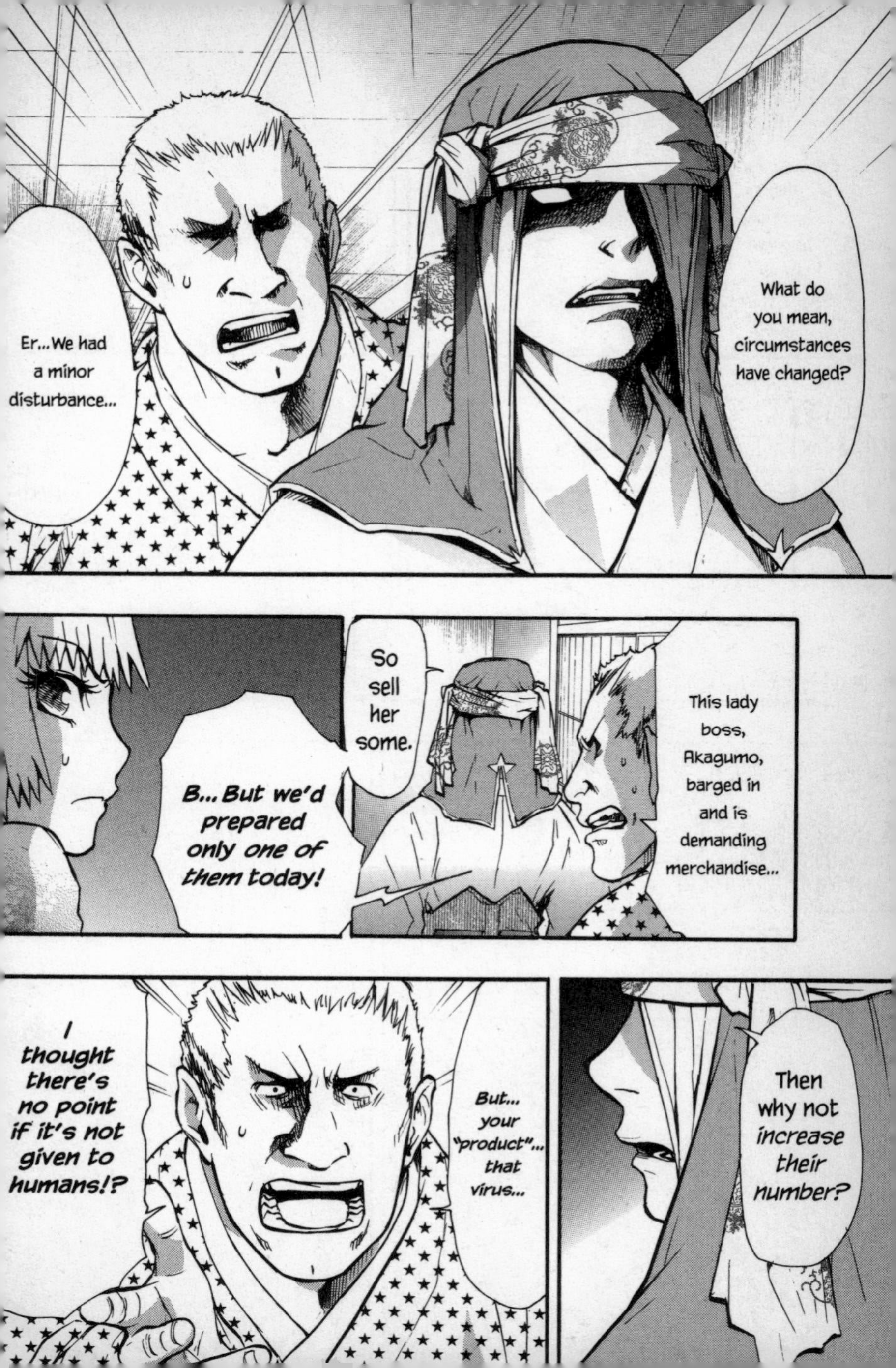
What do you mean, circumstances have changed?
Er...We had a minor disturbance...
This lady boss, Akagumo, barged in and is demanding merchandise...
So sell her some.
B...But we'd prepared only one of them today!
Then why not increase their number?
But... your "product"... that virus...
I thought there's no point if it's not given to humans!?

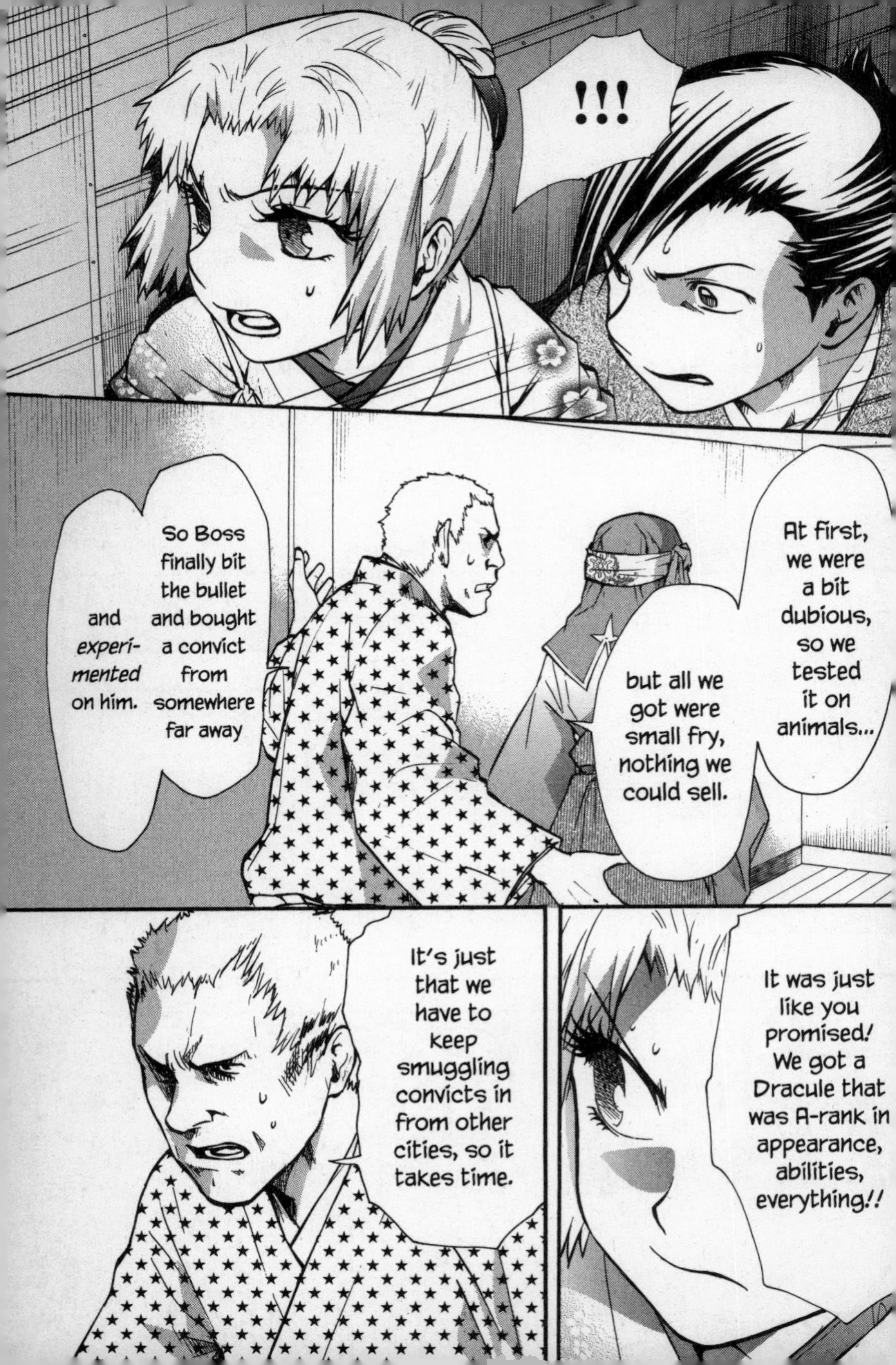
!!!
At first, we were a bit dubious, so we tested it on animals...
but all we got were small fry, nothing we could sell.
So Boss finally bit the bullet and bought a convict from somewhere far away
and *experimented* on him.
It was just like you promised! We got a Dracule that was A-rank in appearance, abilities, everything!!
It's just that we have to keep smuggling convicts in from other cities, so it takes time.

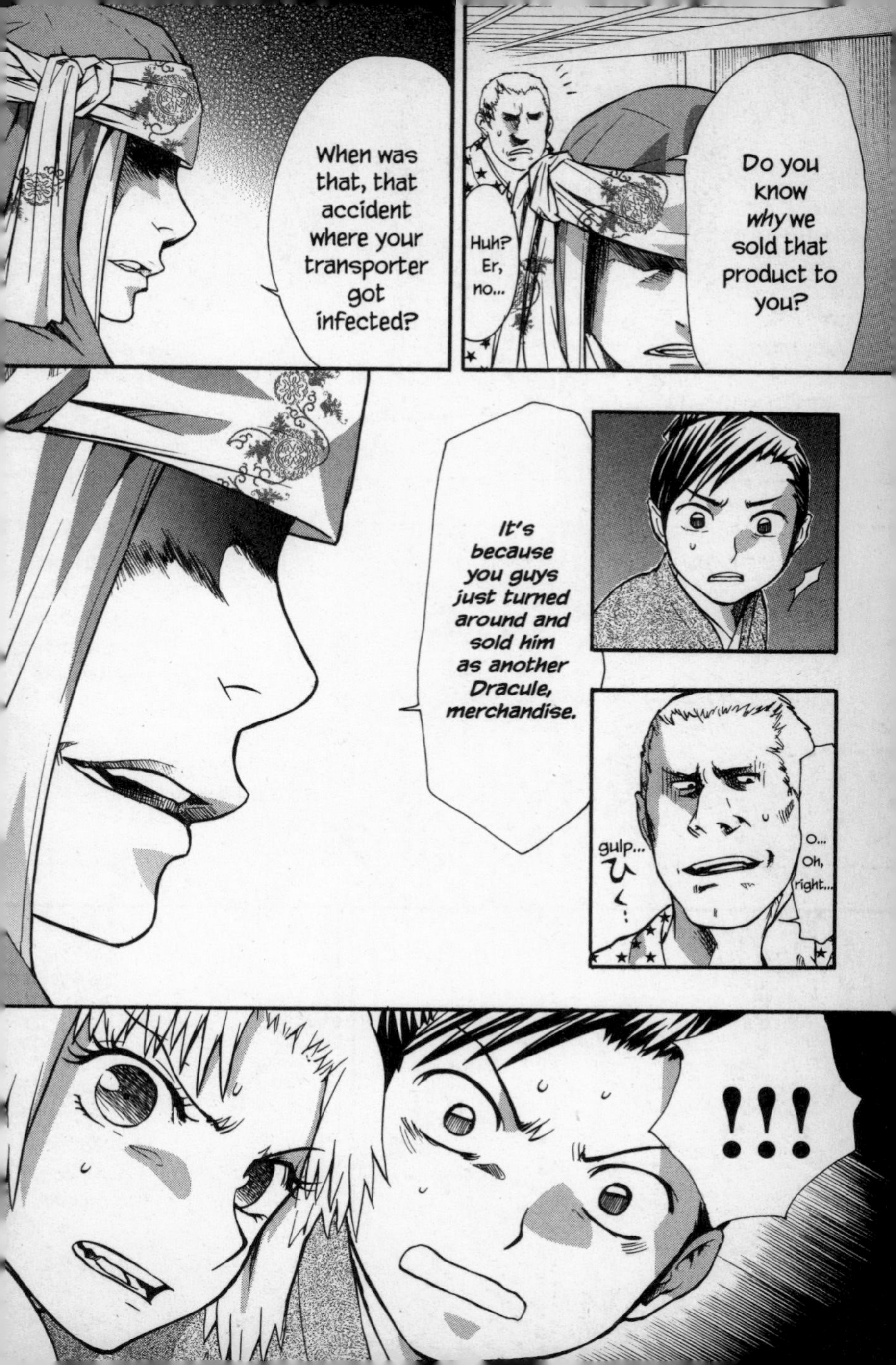
Do you know *why* we sold that product to you?
Huh? Er, no...
When was that, that accident where your transporter got infected?
O... Oh, right...
gulp...
ひく...
It's because you guys just turned around and sold him as another Dracule, merchandise.
!!!

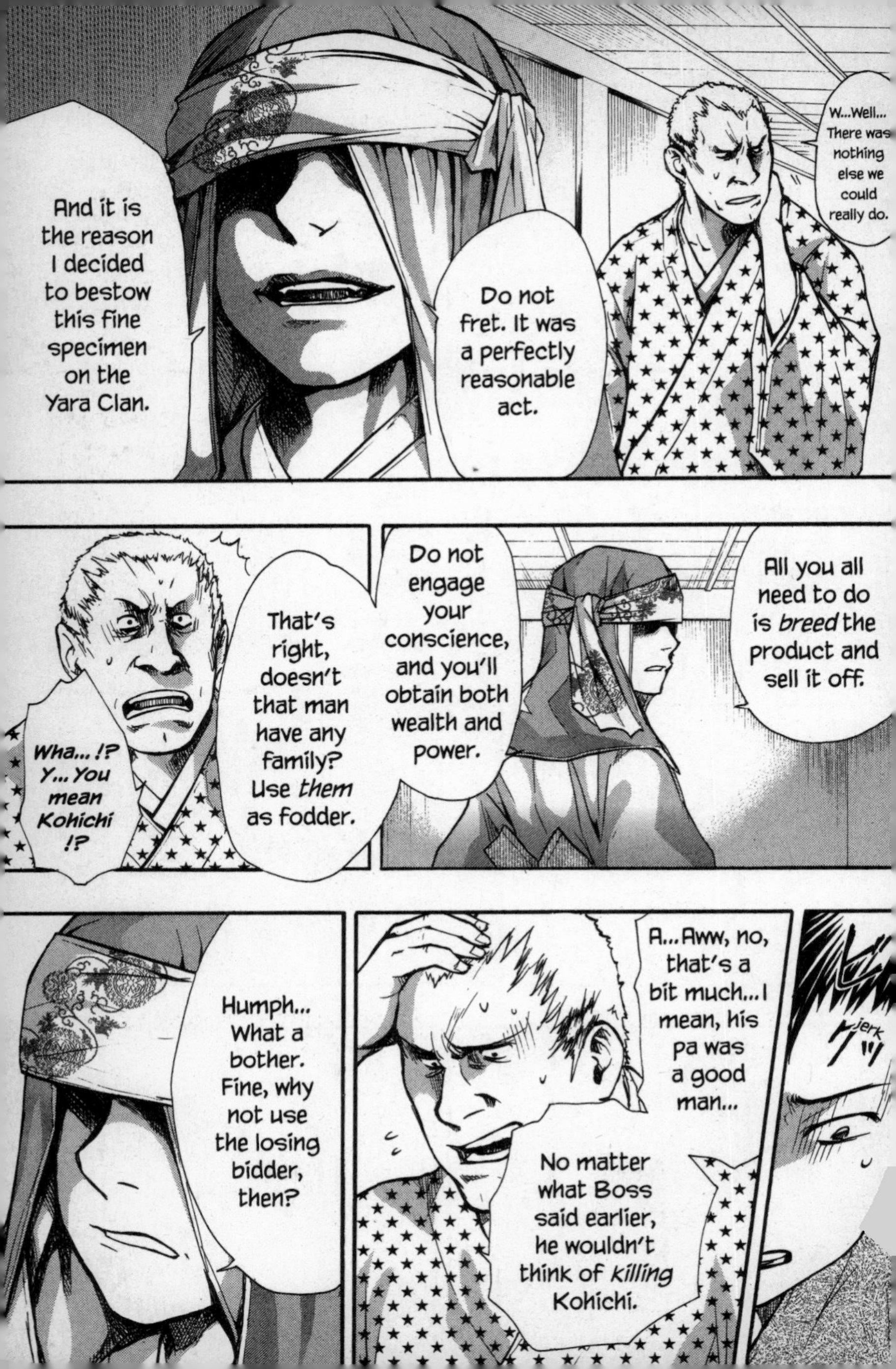
W...Well... There was nothing else we could really do.
Do not fret. It was a perfectly reasonable act.
And it is the reason I decided to bestow this fine specimen on the Yara Clan.
All you all need to do is *breed* the product and sell it off.
Do not engage your conscience, and you'll obtain both wealth and power.
That's right, doesn't that man have any family? Use *them* as fodder.
Wha...!? Y...You mean Kohichi!?
jerk
A...Aww, no, that's a bit much...I mean, his pa was a good man...
No matter what Boss said earlier, he wouldn't think of *killing* Kohichi.
Humph... What a bother. Fine, why not use the losing bidder, then?

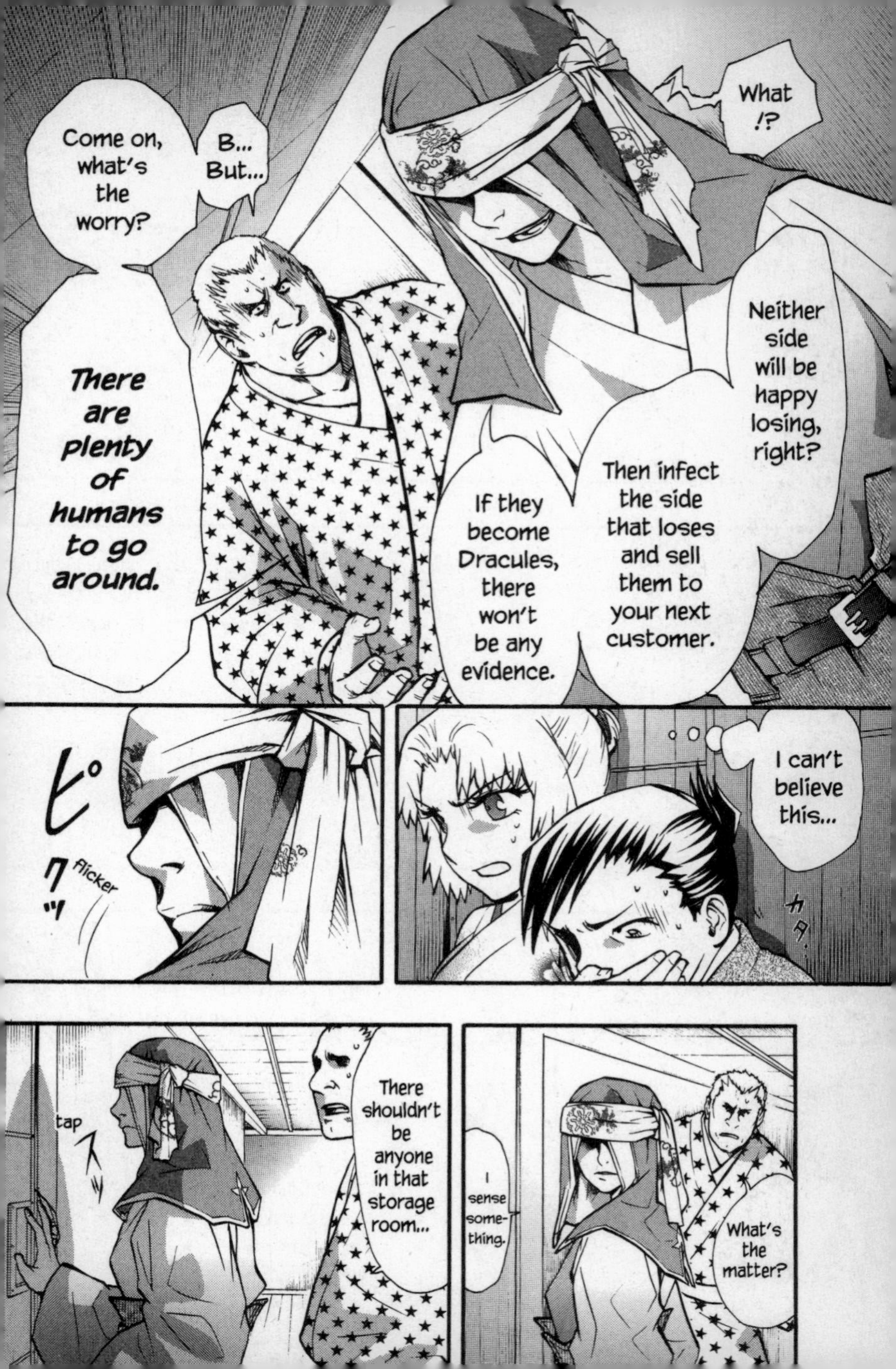
What !?
Neither side will be happy losing, right?
Then infect the side that loses and sell them to your next customer.
If they become Dracules, there won't be any evidence.
B... But...
Come on, what's the worry?
There are plenty of humans to go around.
I can't believe this...
flicker
What's the matter?
I sense some-thing.
There shouldn't be anyone in that storage room...
tap

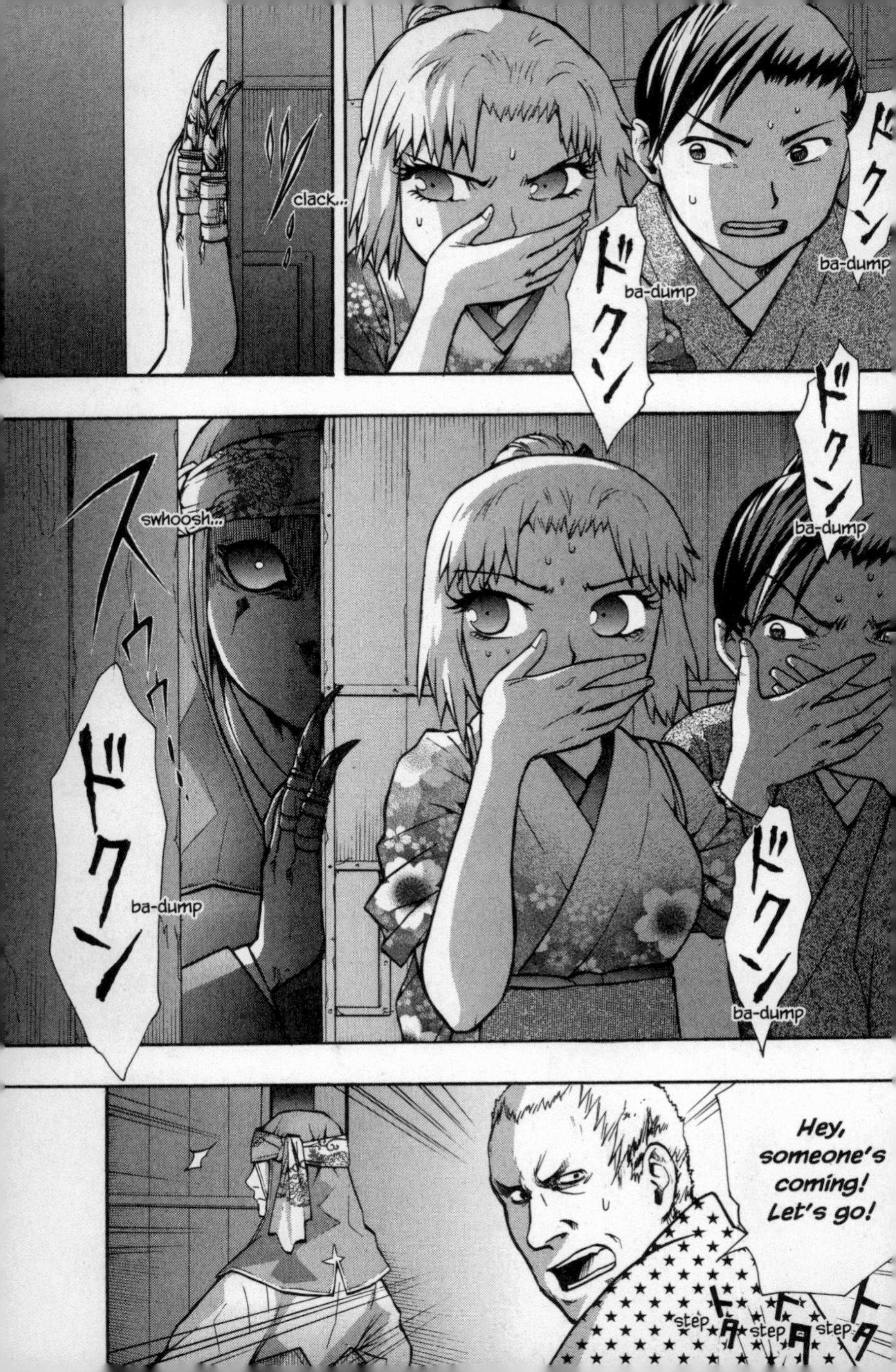
ドクン
ba-dump
ドクン
ba-dump
clack...
ドクン
ba-dump
ドクン
ba-dump
swhoosh...
ドクン
ba-dump
Hey, someone's coming! Let's go!
トタ
step
トタ
step
トタ
step

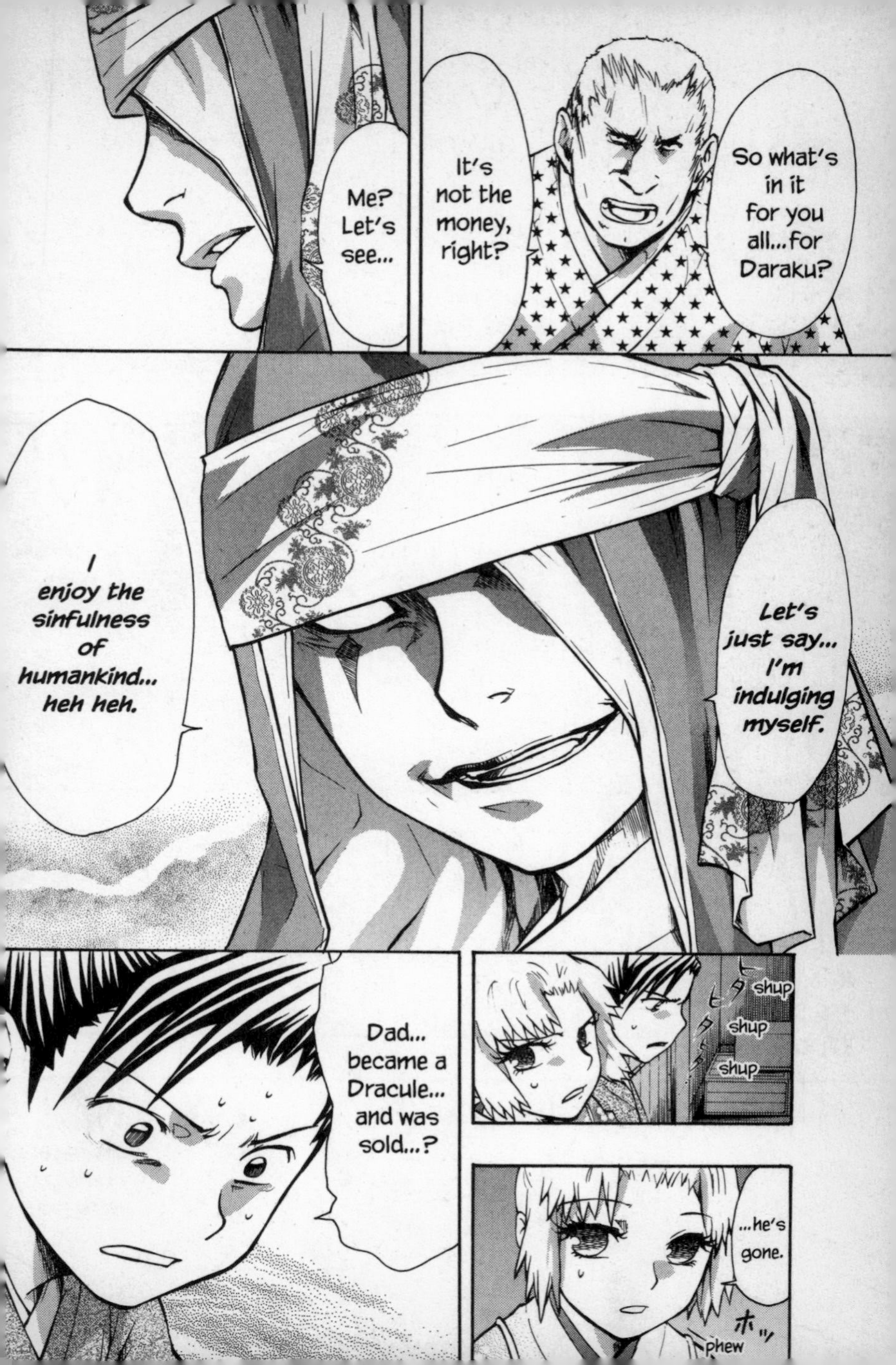
So what's in it for you all...for Daraku?
It's not the money, right?
Me? Let's see...
Let's just say... I'm indulging myself.
I enjoy the sinfulness of humankind... heh heh.
shup
shup
shup
...he's gone.
phew
Dad... became a Dracule... and was sold...?

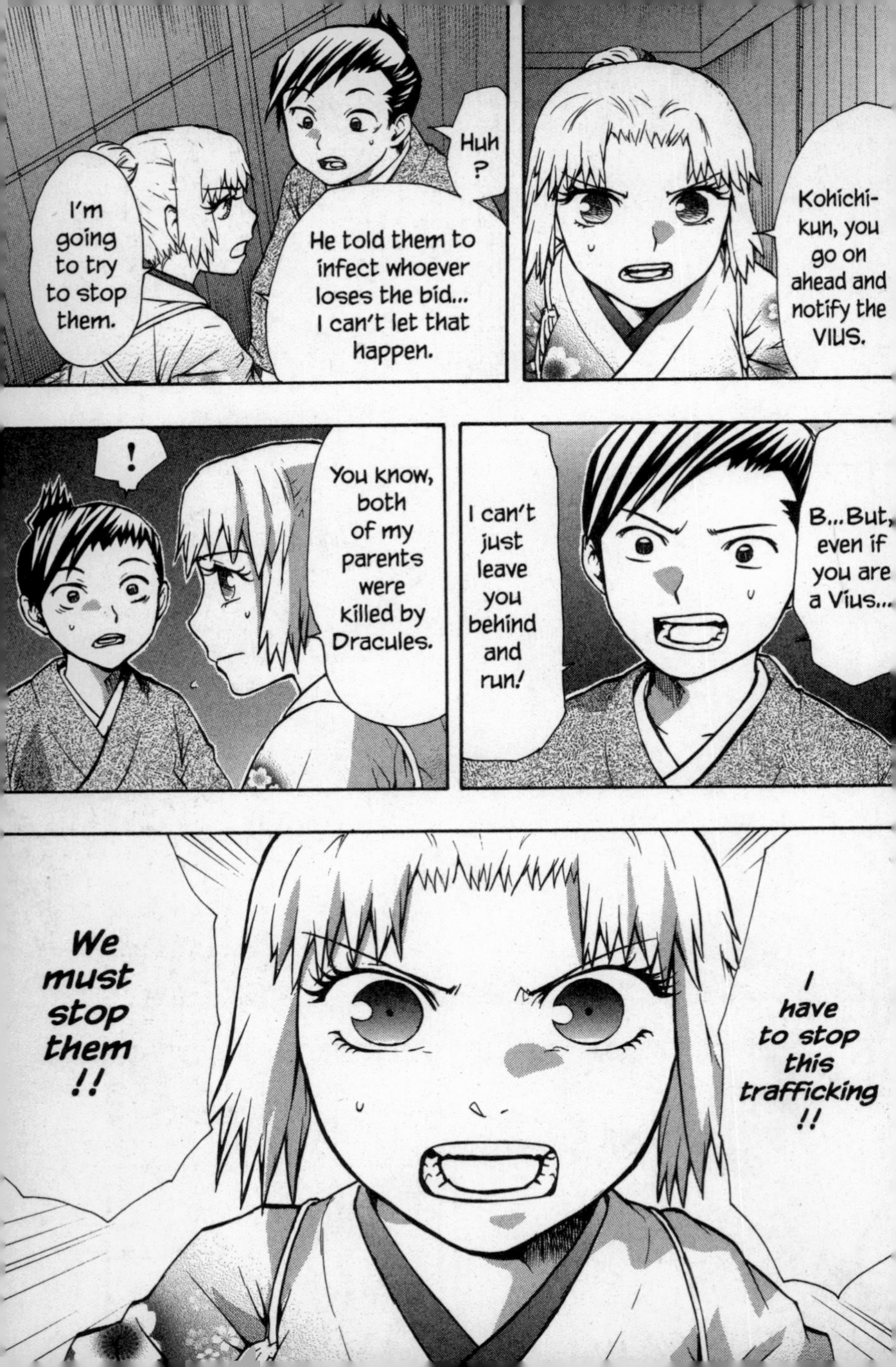
Kohichi-kun, you go on ahead and notify the VIUS.
Huh?
He told them to infect whoever loses the bid... I can't let that happen.
I'm going to try to stop them.
B...But, even if you are a Vius...
I can't just leave you behind and run!
You know, both of my parents were killed by Dracules.
!
I have to stop this trafficking!!
We must stop them!!

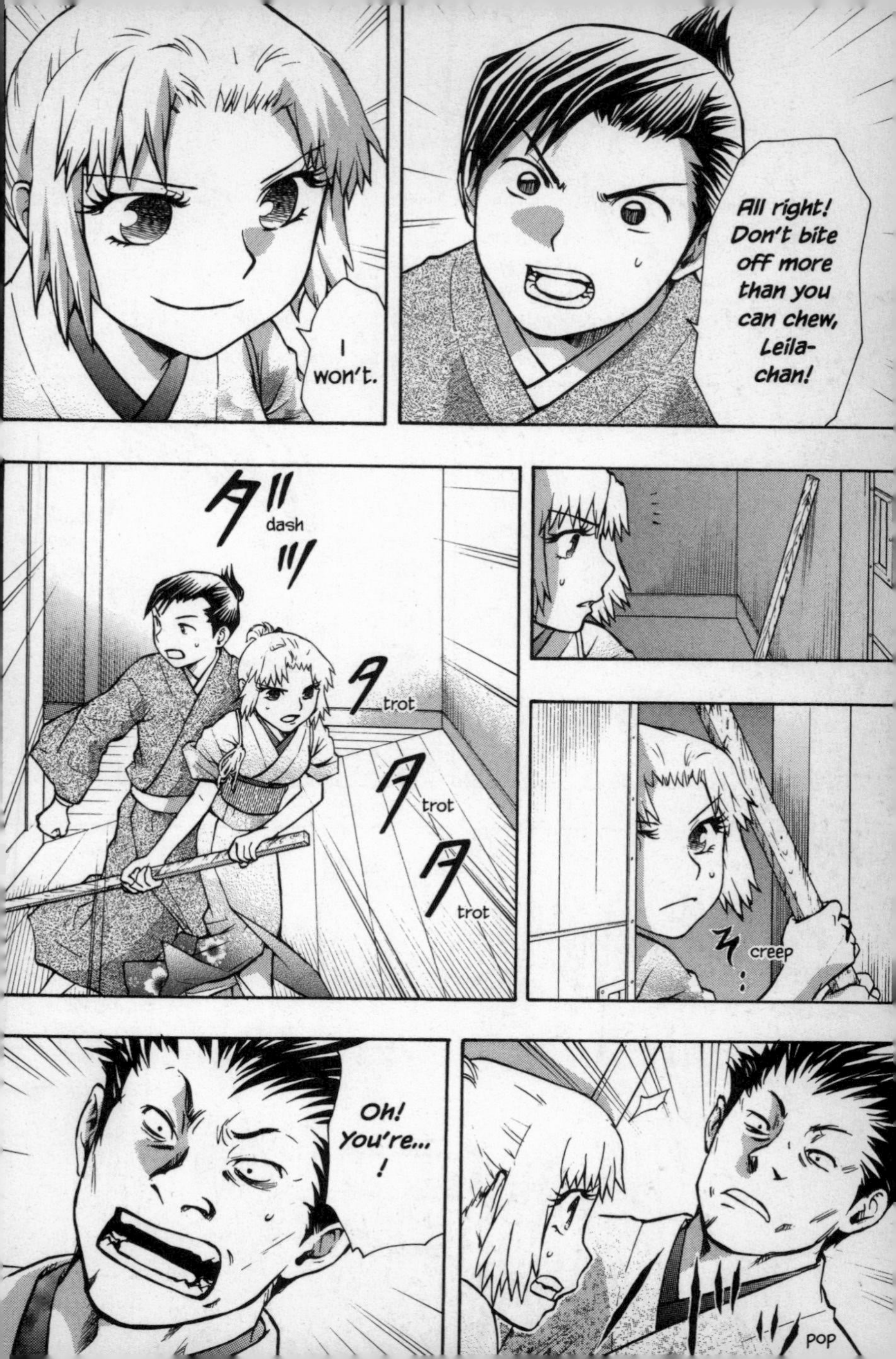
All right! Don't bite off more than you can chew, Leila-chan!
I won't.
creep
dash
trot
trot
trot
pop
Oh! You're... !

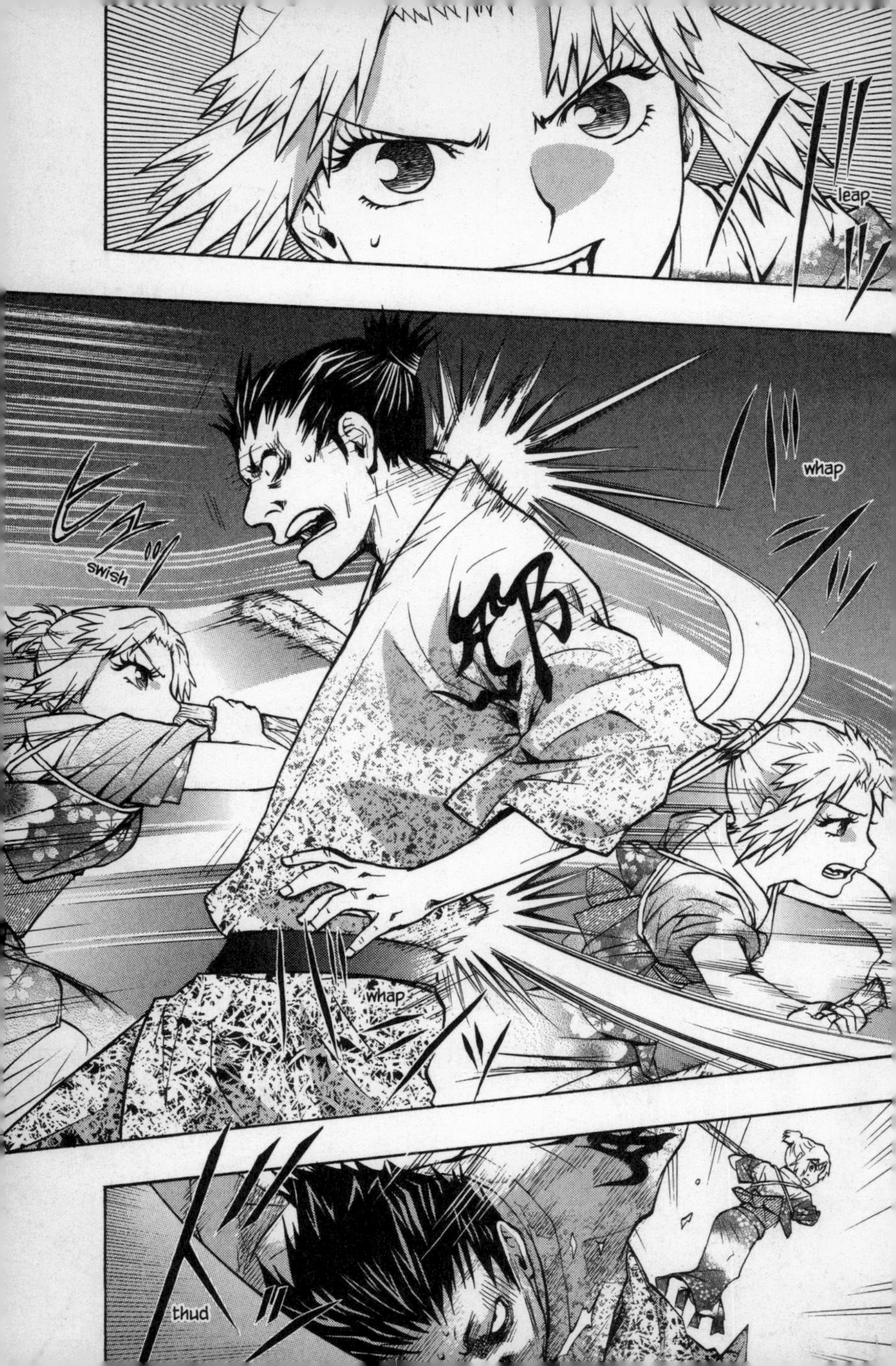
leap
whap
swish
whap
thud

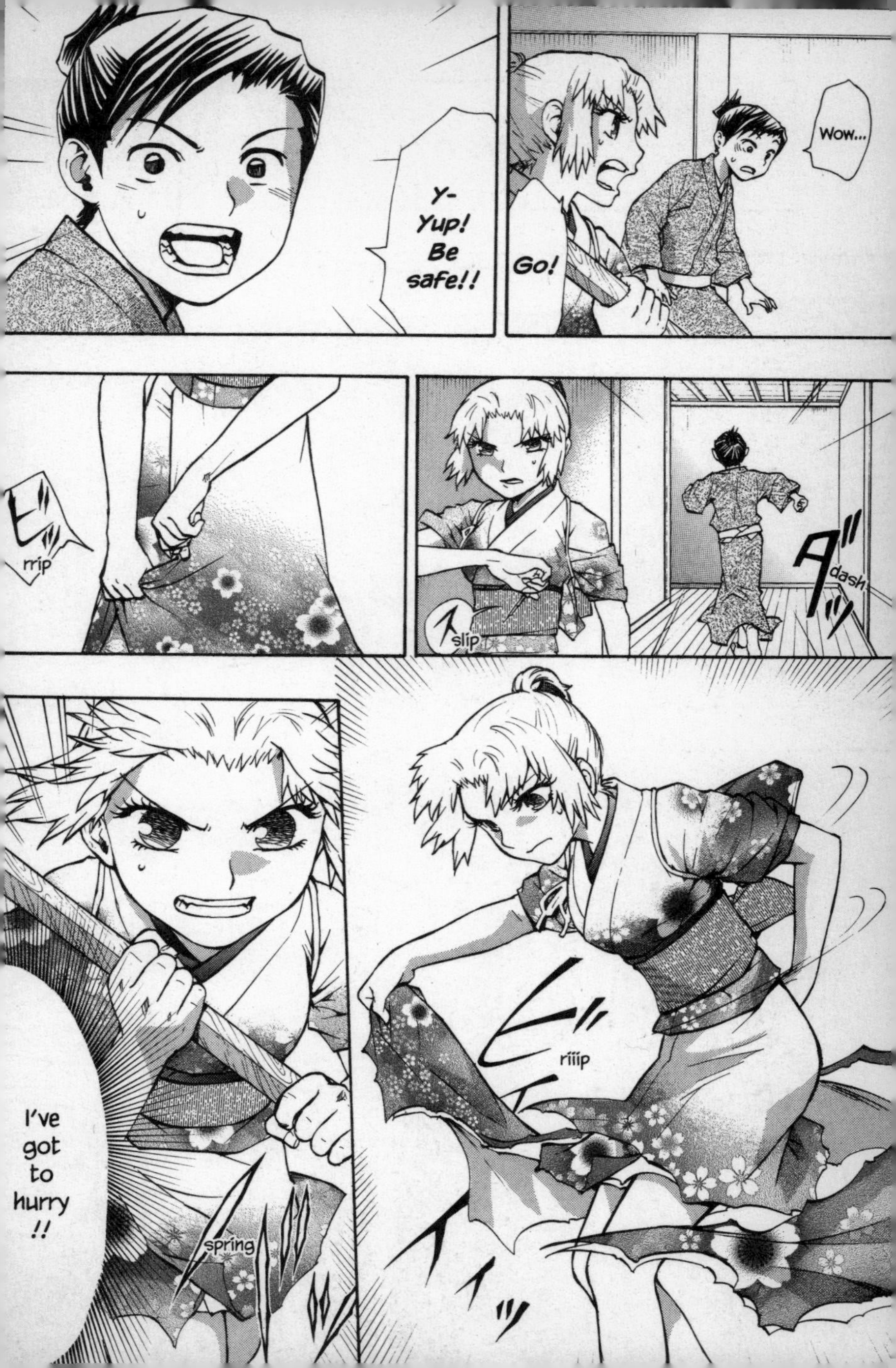
Go!
Wow...
Y-Yup! Be safe!!
dash
slip
rrip
riiip
I've got to hurry!!
spring

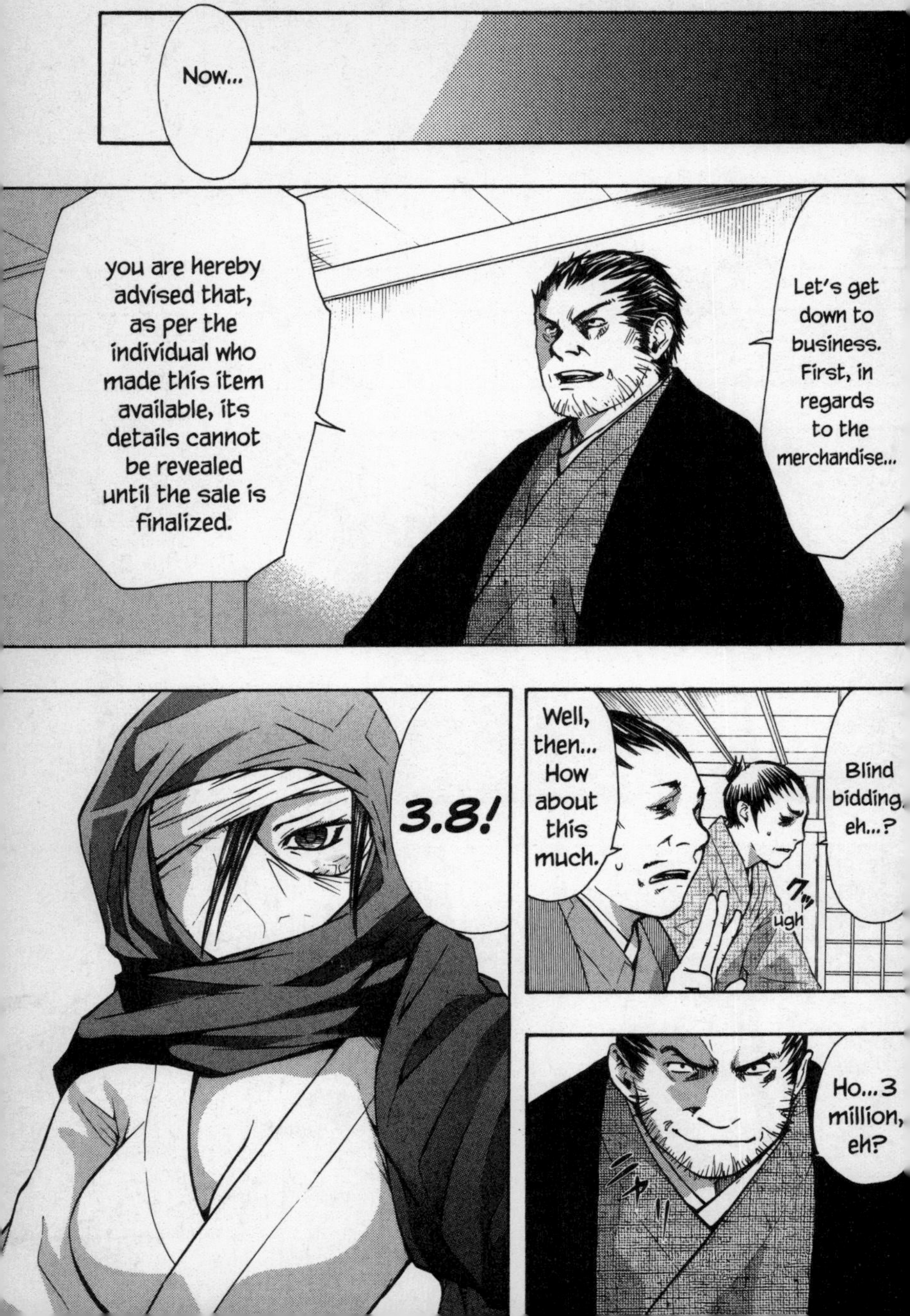
Now...
Let's get down to business. First, in regards to the merchandise...
you are hereby advised that, as per the individual who made this item available, its details cannot be revealed until the sale is finalized.
Blind bidding, eh...?
ugh
Well, then... How about this much.
Ho...3 million, eh?
3.8!

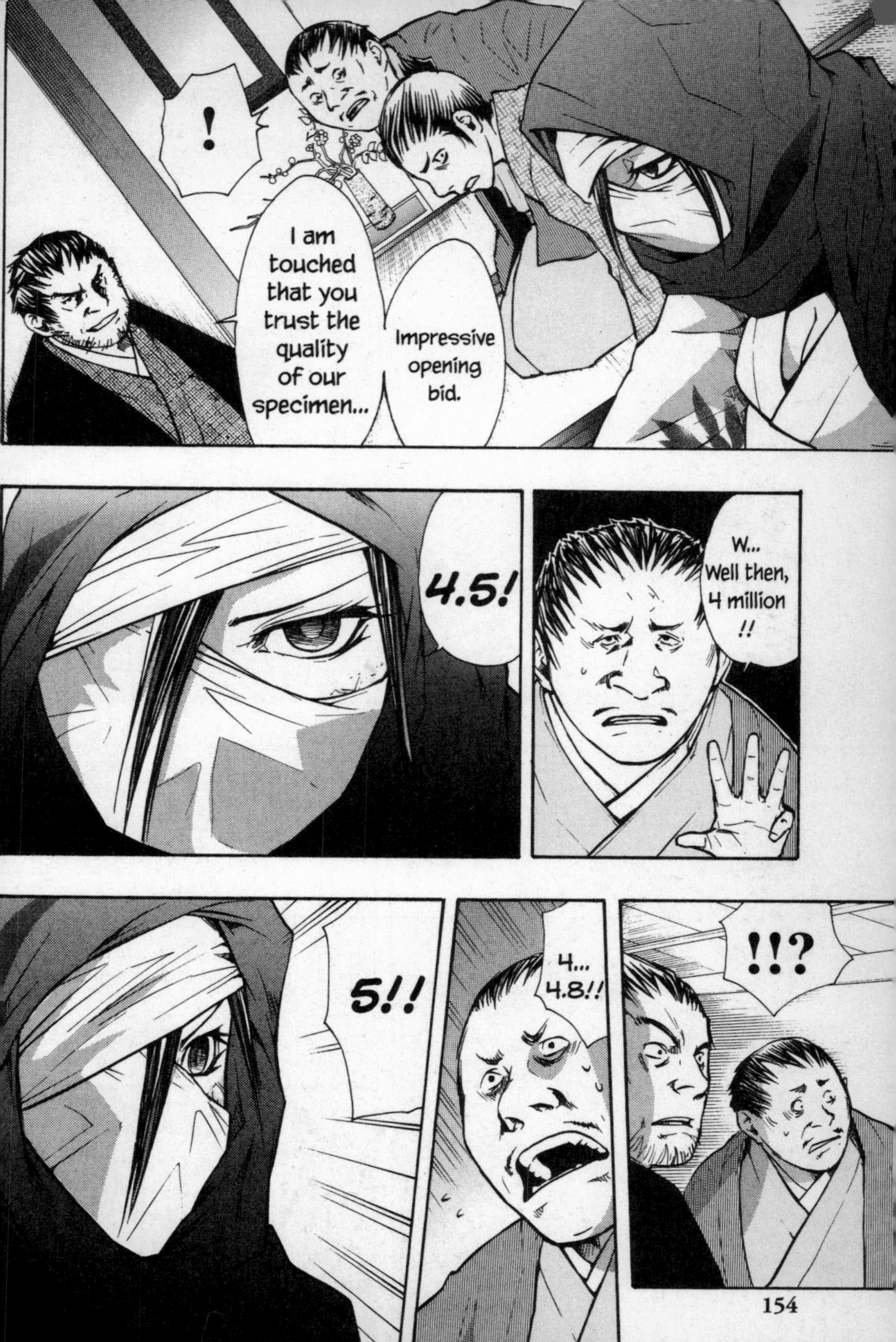
Impressive opening bid.
I am touched that you trust the quality of our specimen...
!
W... Well then, 4 million !!
4.5!
!!?
4... 4.8!!
5!!

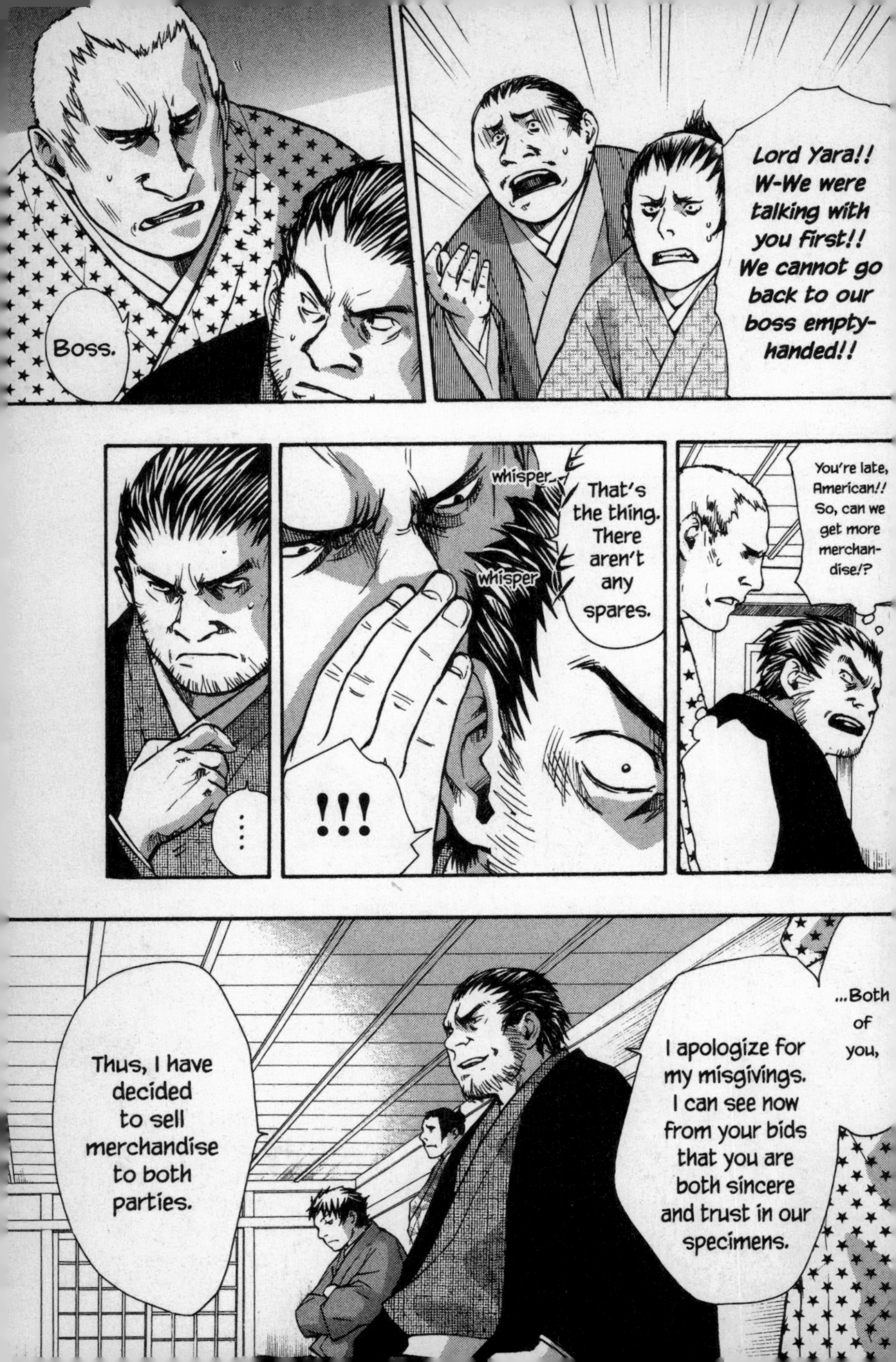
Lord Yara!! W-We were talking with you first!! We cannot go back to our boss empty-handed!!
Boss.
You're late, American!! So, can we get more merchan-dise!?
whisper
whisper
That's the thing. There aren't any spares.
!!!
....
...Both of you,
I apologize for my misgivings. I can see now from your bids that you are both sincere and trust in our specimens.
Thus, I have decided to sell merchandise to both parties.

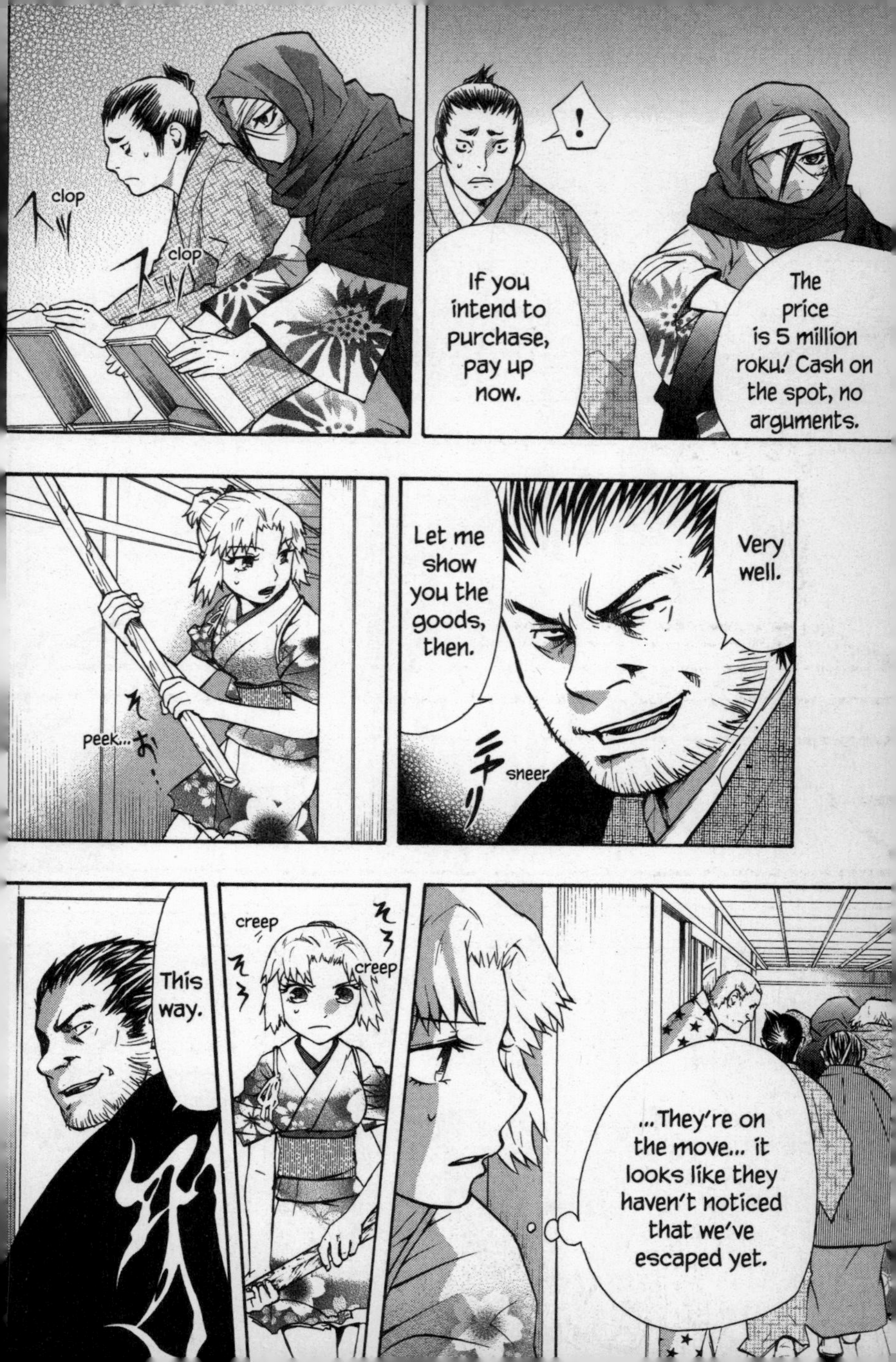
The price is 5 million roku! Cash on the spot, no arguments.
If you intend to purchase, pay up now.
!
clop
clop
Very well.
Let me show you the goods, then.
sneer
peek...
...They're on the move... it looks like they haven't noticed that we've escaped yet.
creep
creep
This way.

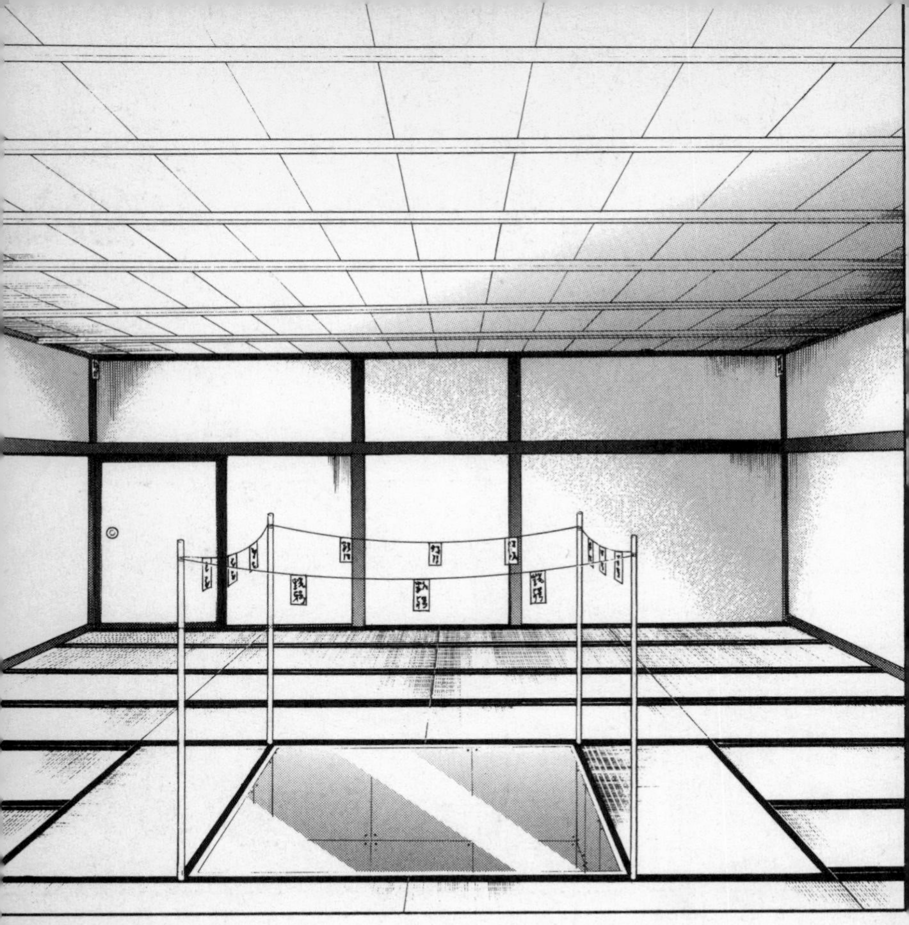

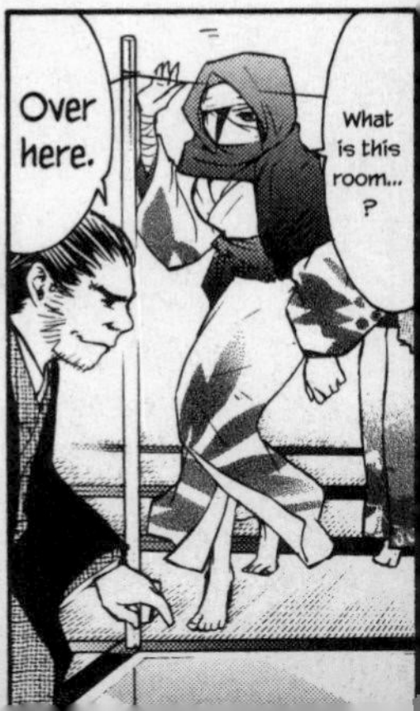
What is this room... ?
Over here.

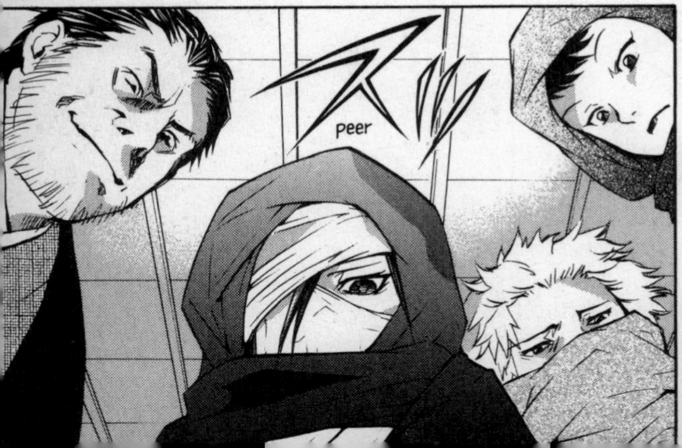
peer

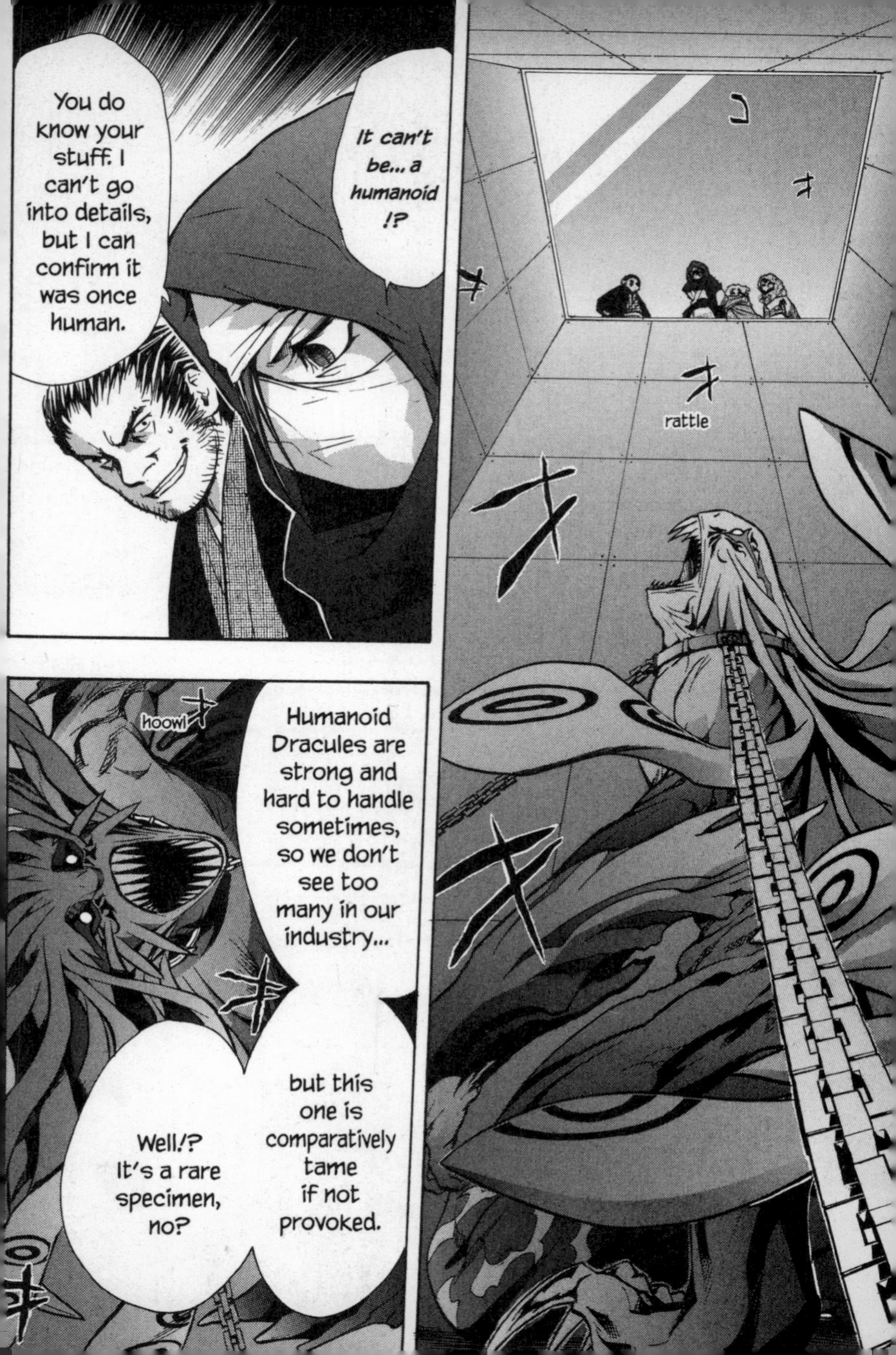
rattle
It can't be... a humanoid !?
You do know your stuff. I can't go into details, but I can confirm it was once human.
hoowl
Humanoid Dracules are strong and hard to handle sometimes, so we don't see too many in our industry...
but this one is comparatively tame if not provoked.
Well!? It's a rare specimen, no?

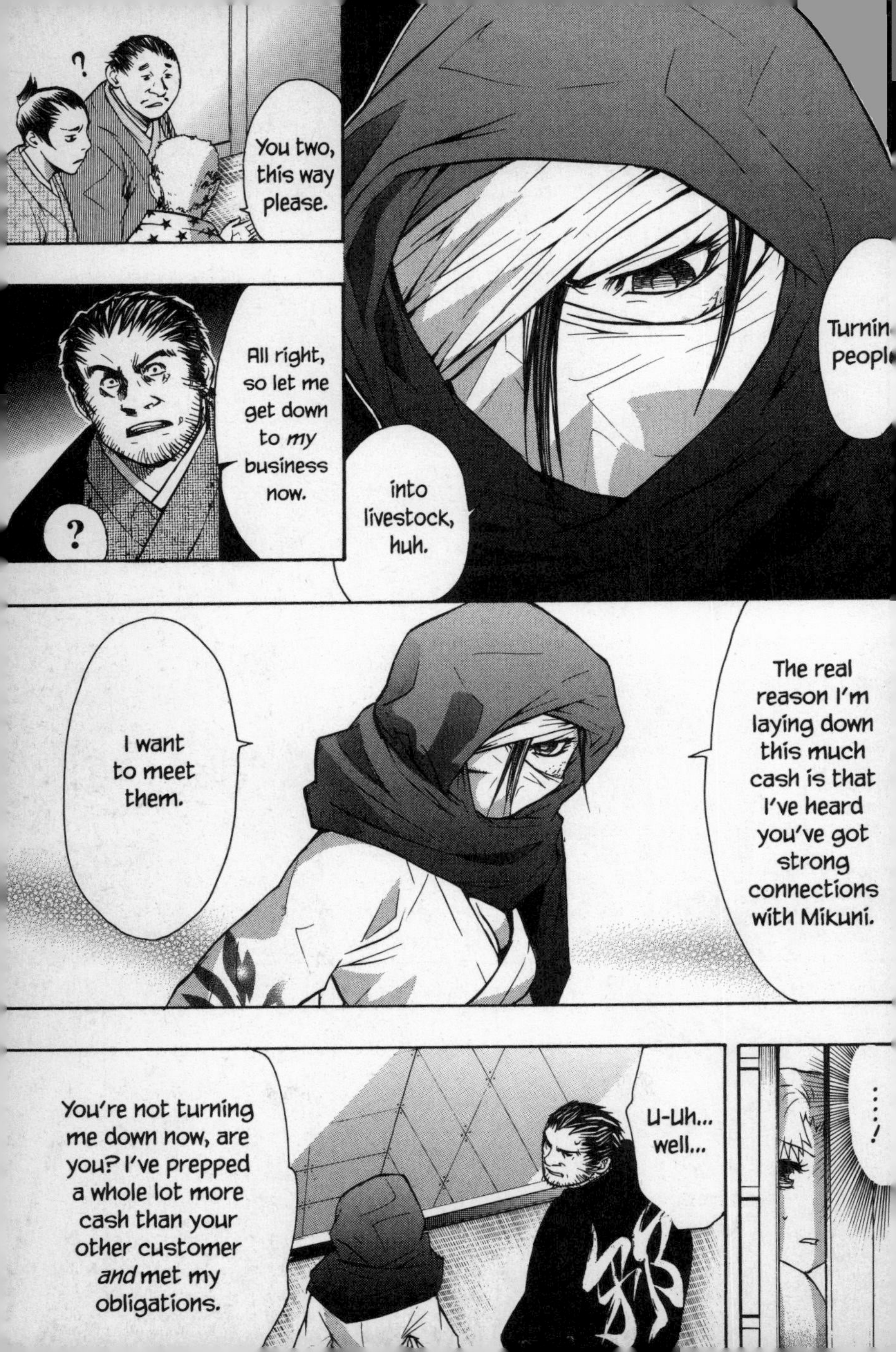
Turnin
peopl
into livestock, huh.
?
You two, this way please.
All right, so let me get down to *my* business now.
?
The real reason I'm laying down this much cash is that I've heard you've got strong connections with Mikuni.
I want to meet them.
...!
U-uh... well...
You're not turning me down now, are you? I've prepped a whole lot more cash than your other customer *and* met my obligations.

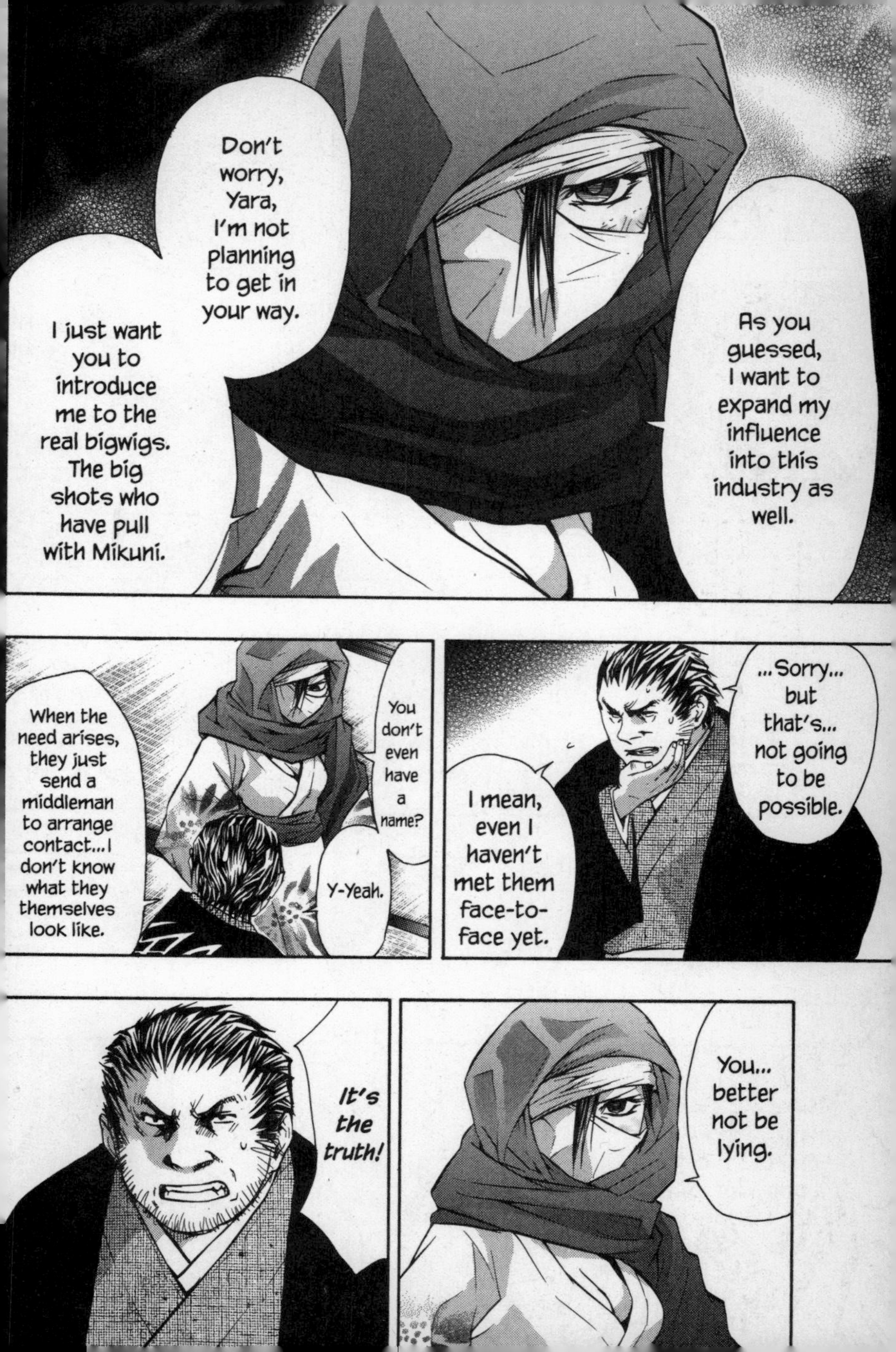
Don't worry, Yara, I'm not planning to get in your way.
As you guessed, I want to expand my influence into this industry as well.
I just want you to introduce me to the real bigwigs. The big shots who have pull with Mikuni.
...Sorry... but that's... not going to be possible.
I mean, even I haven't met them face-to-face yet.
You don't even have a name?
Y-Yeah.
When the need arises, they just send a middleman to arrange contact...I don't know what they themselves look like.
You... better not be lying.
It's the truth!

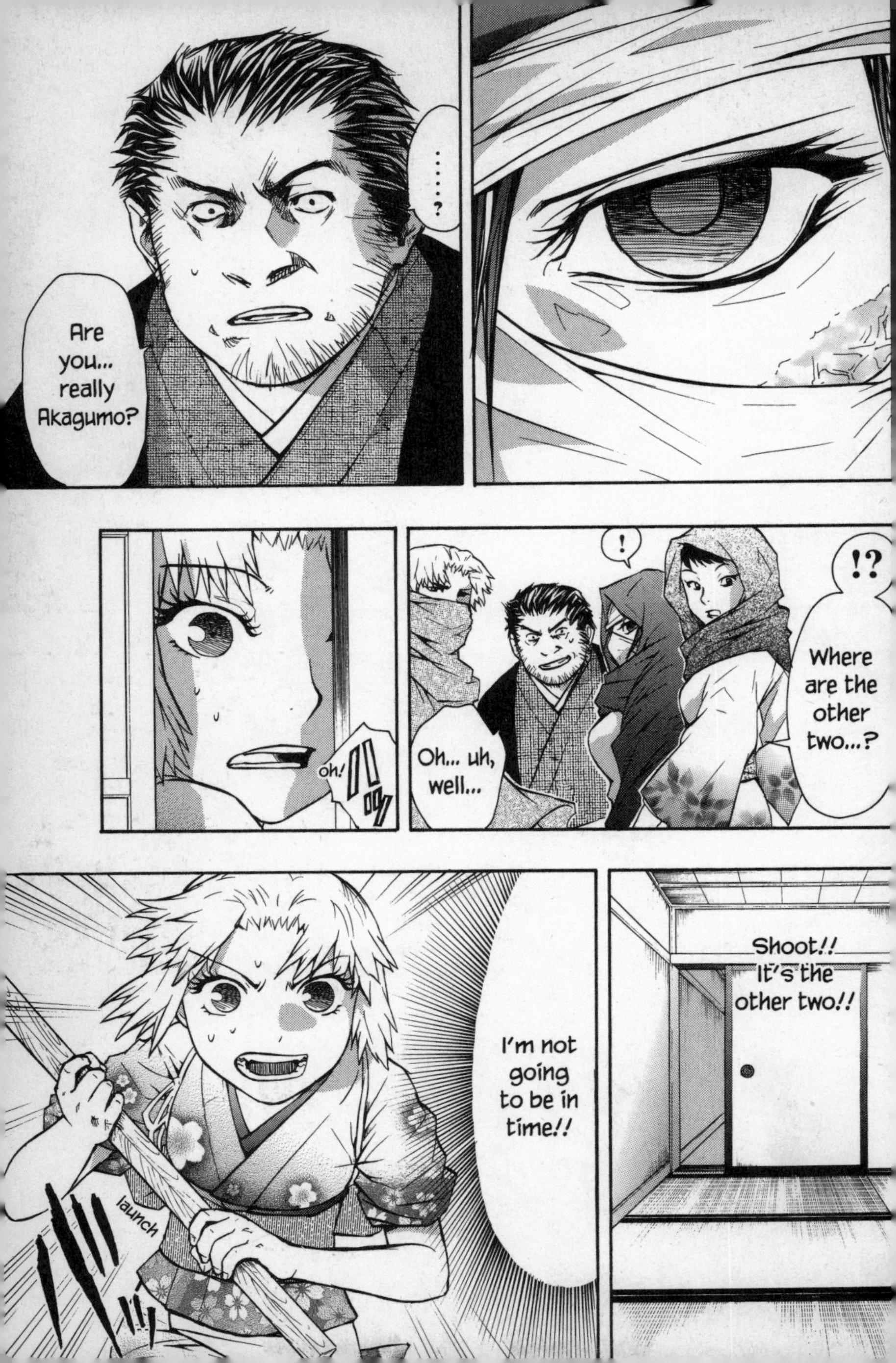
.....?
Are you... really Akagumo?
Where are the other two...?
!?
!
Oh... uh, well...
oh!
Shoot!! It's the other two!!
I'm not going to be in time!!
launch

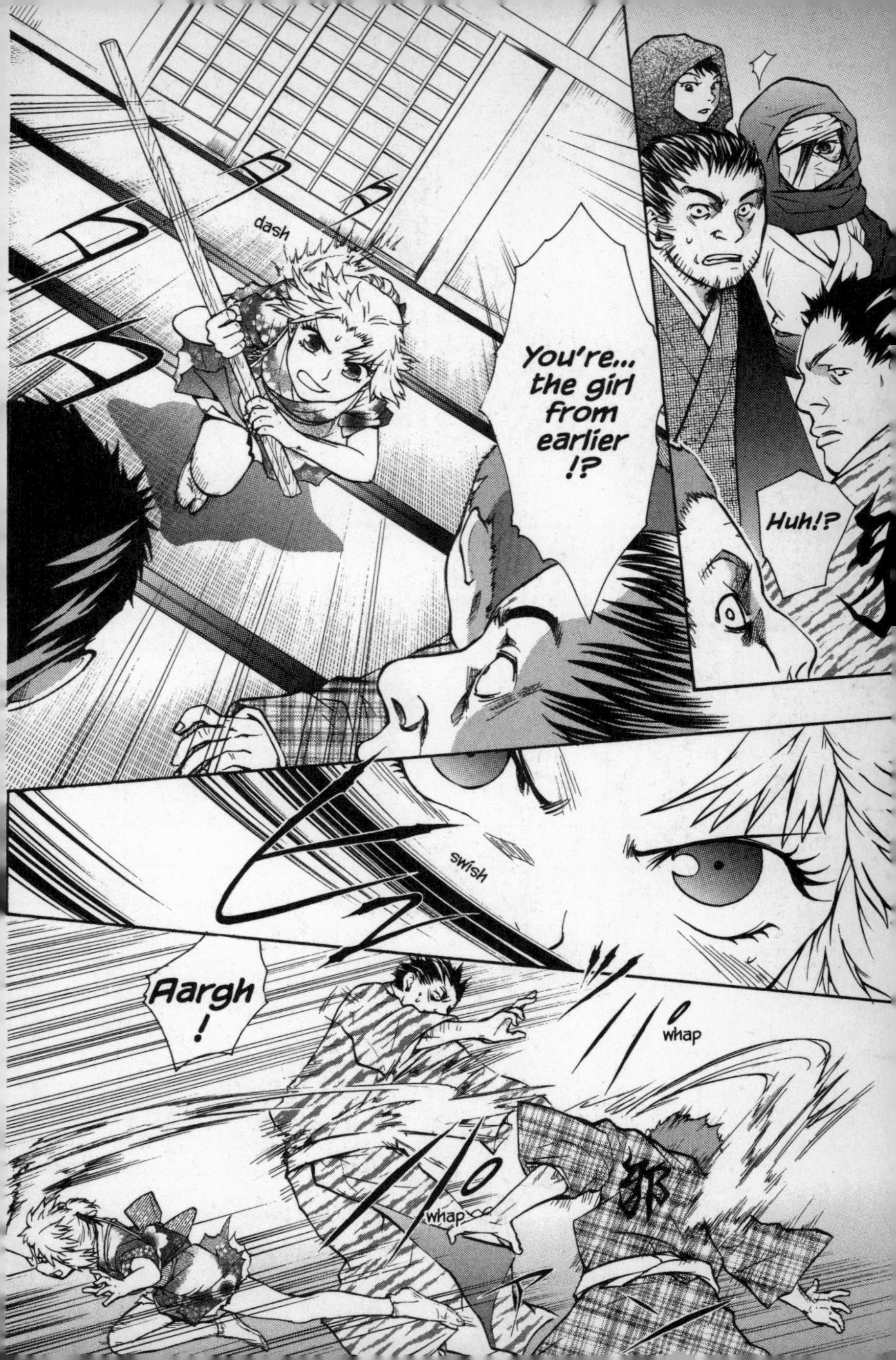
Huh!?
You're... the girl from earlier !?
dash
swish
whap
Aargh !
whap

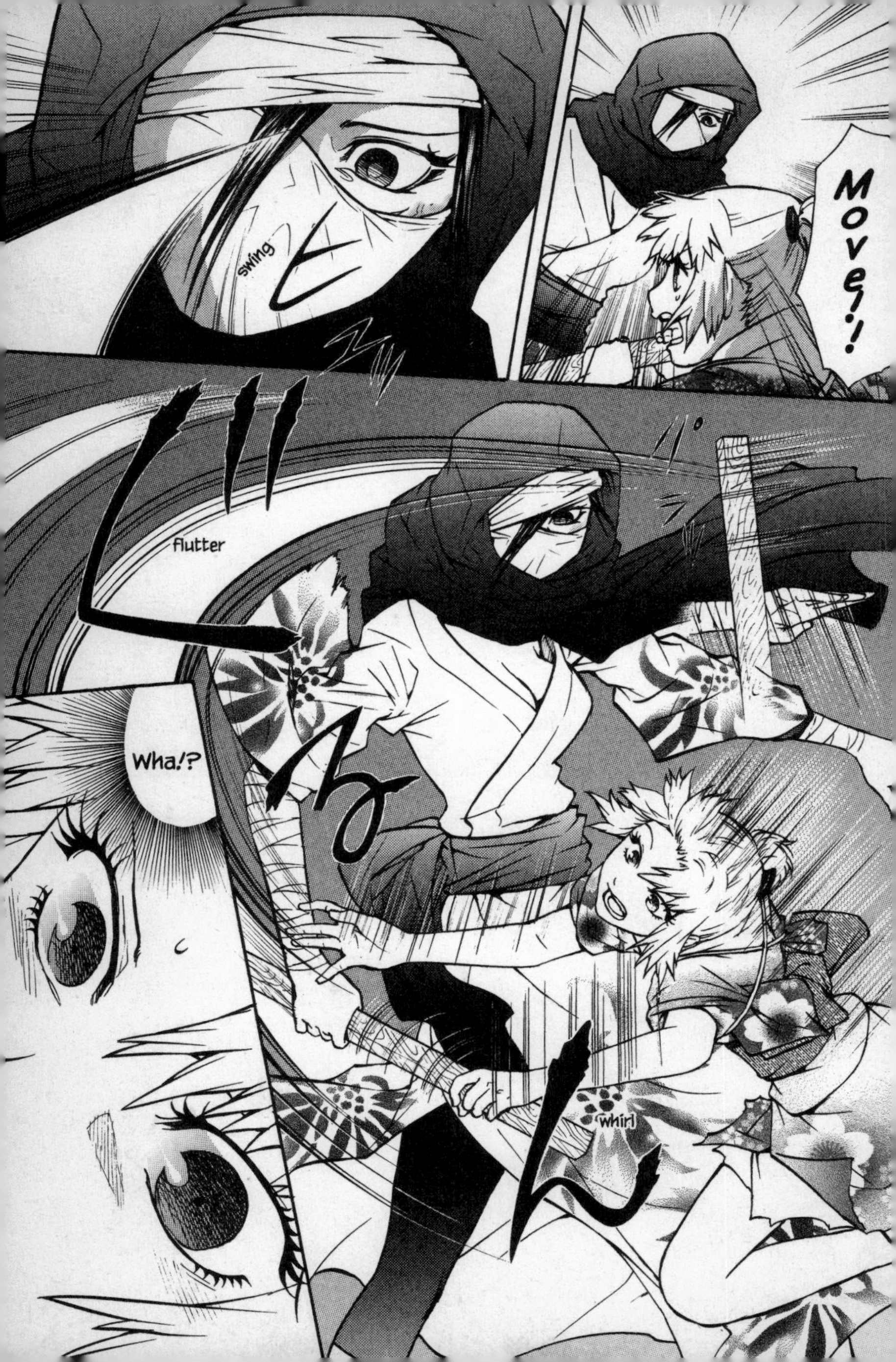
Move!!
swing
flutter
Wha!?
whirl

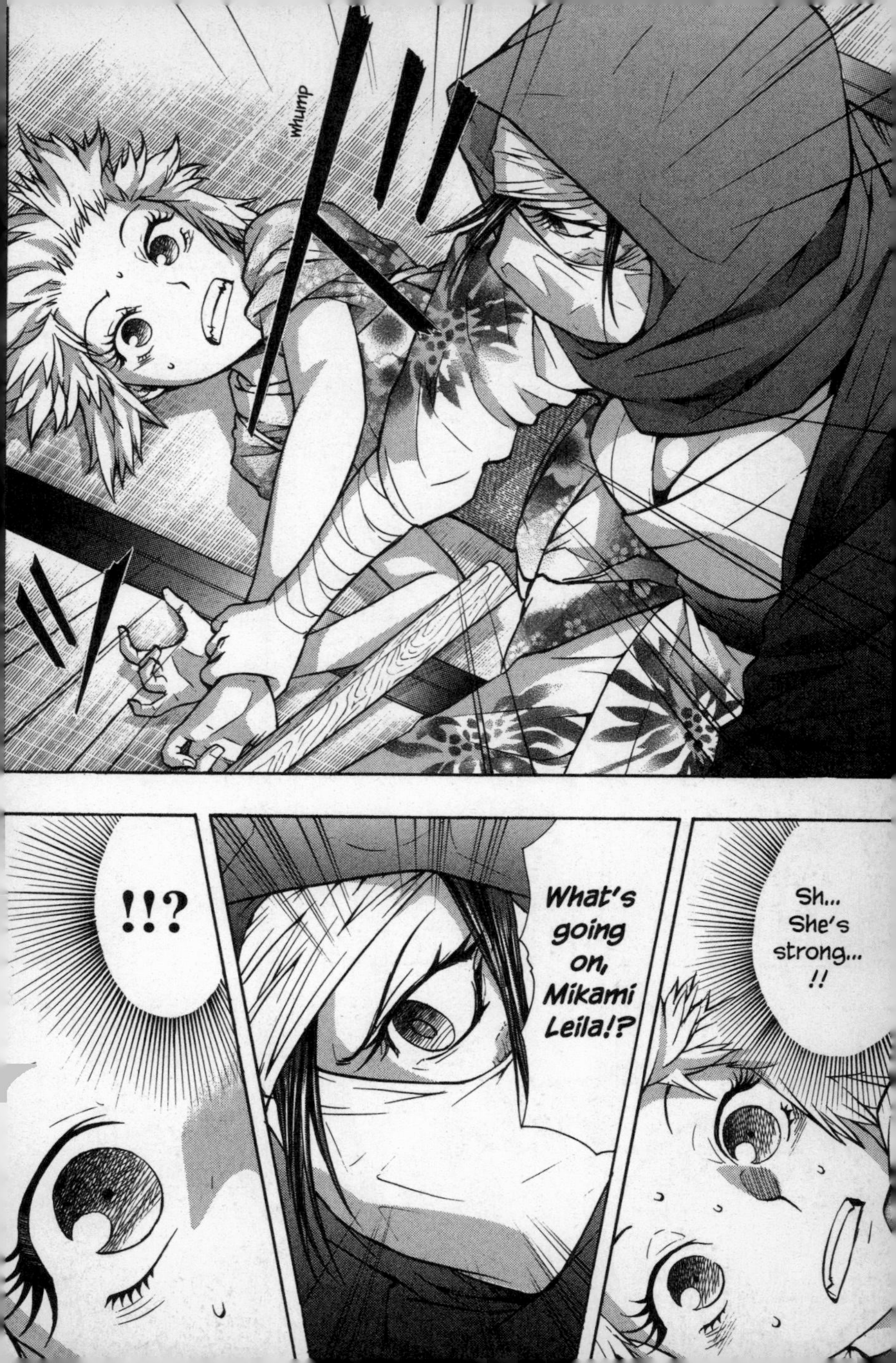
whump
Sh... She's strong... !!
What's going on, Mikami Leila!?
!!?

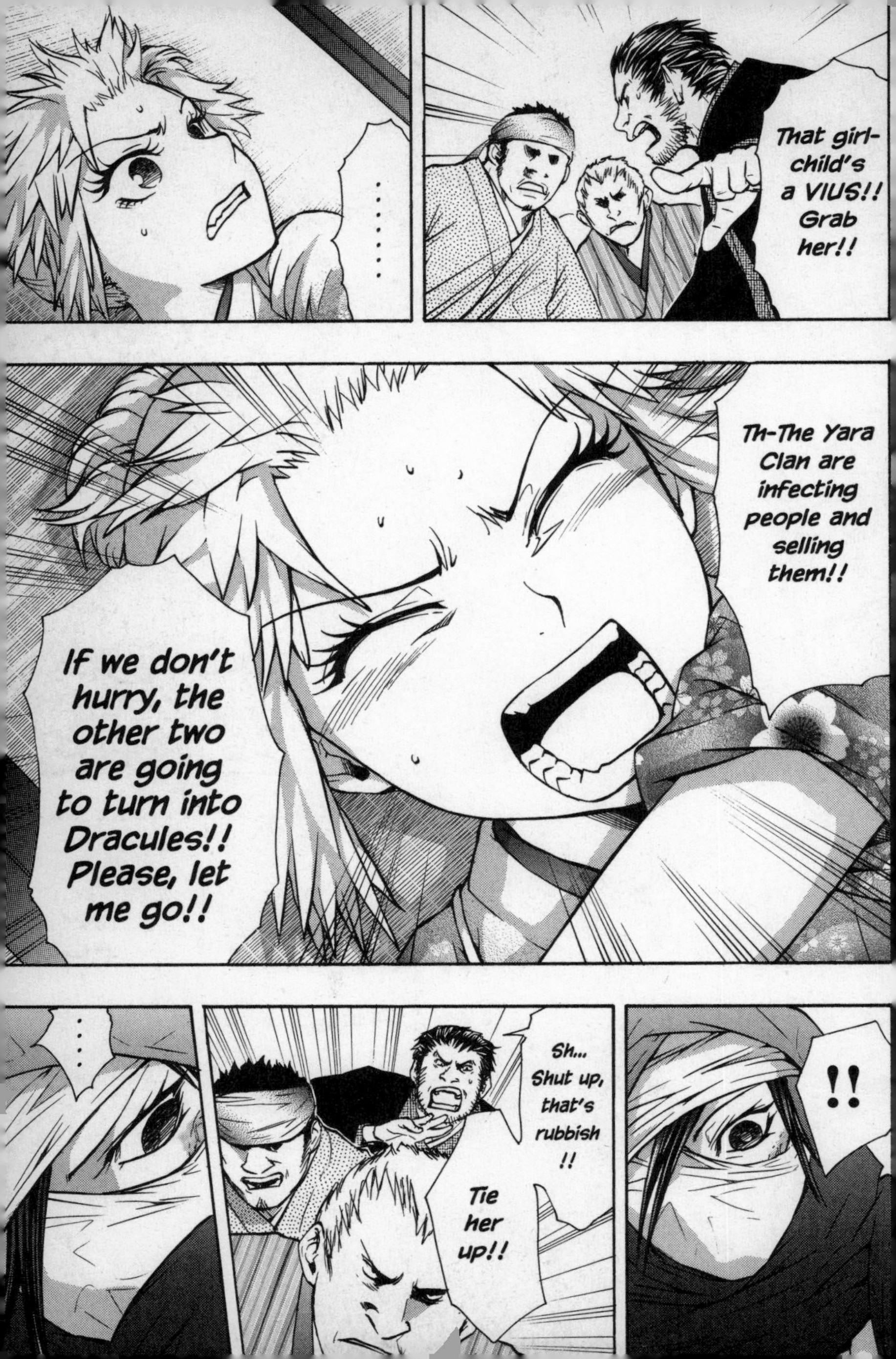
That girl-child's a VIUS!! Grab her!!
......
Th-The Yara Clan are infecting people and selling them!!
If we don't hurry, the other two are going to turn into Dracules!! Please, let me go!!
!!
Sh... Shut up, that's rubbish!!
Tie her up!!
....

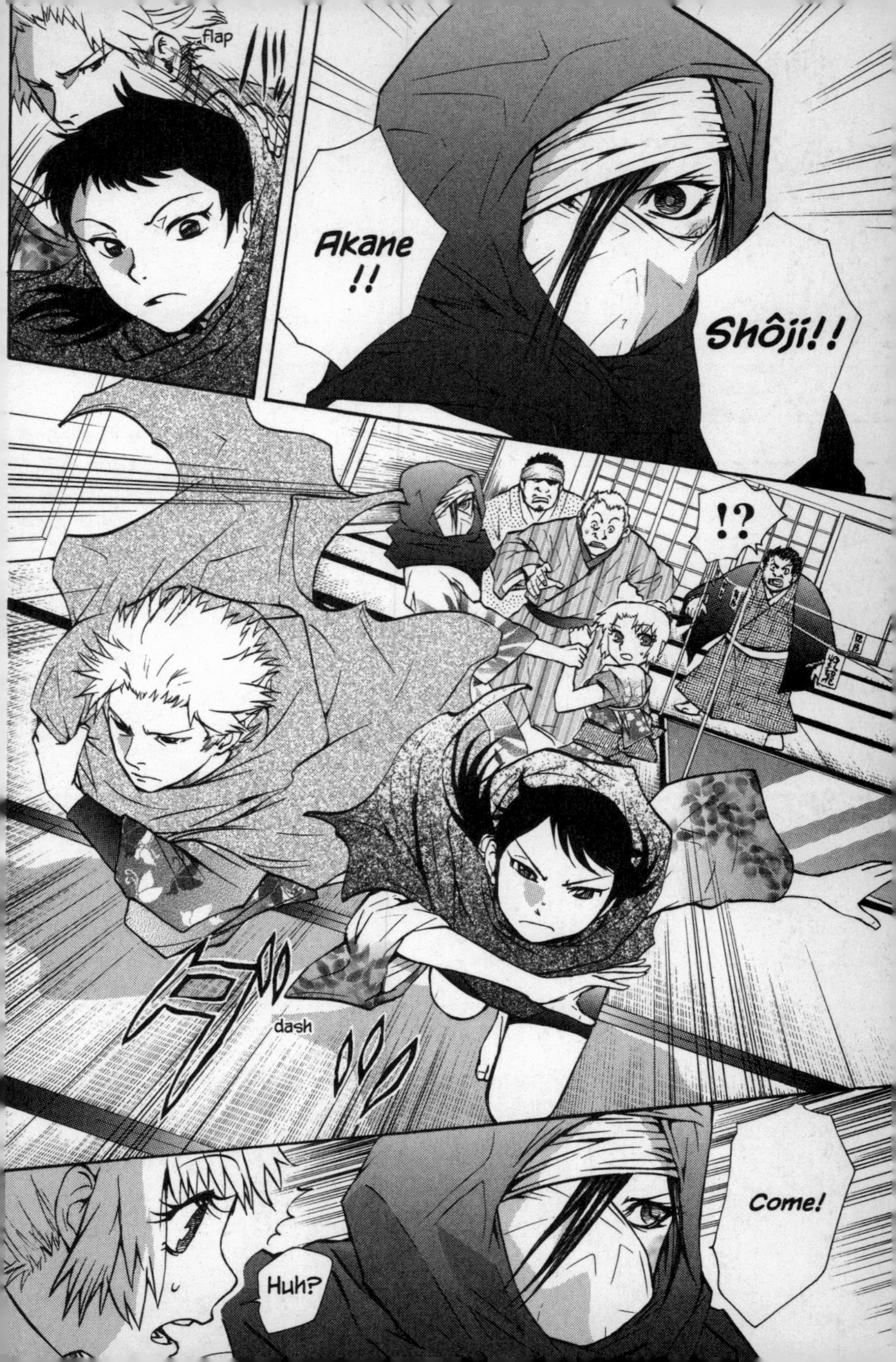
Shôji!!
Akane !!
flap
!?
dash
Come!
Huh?

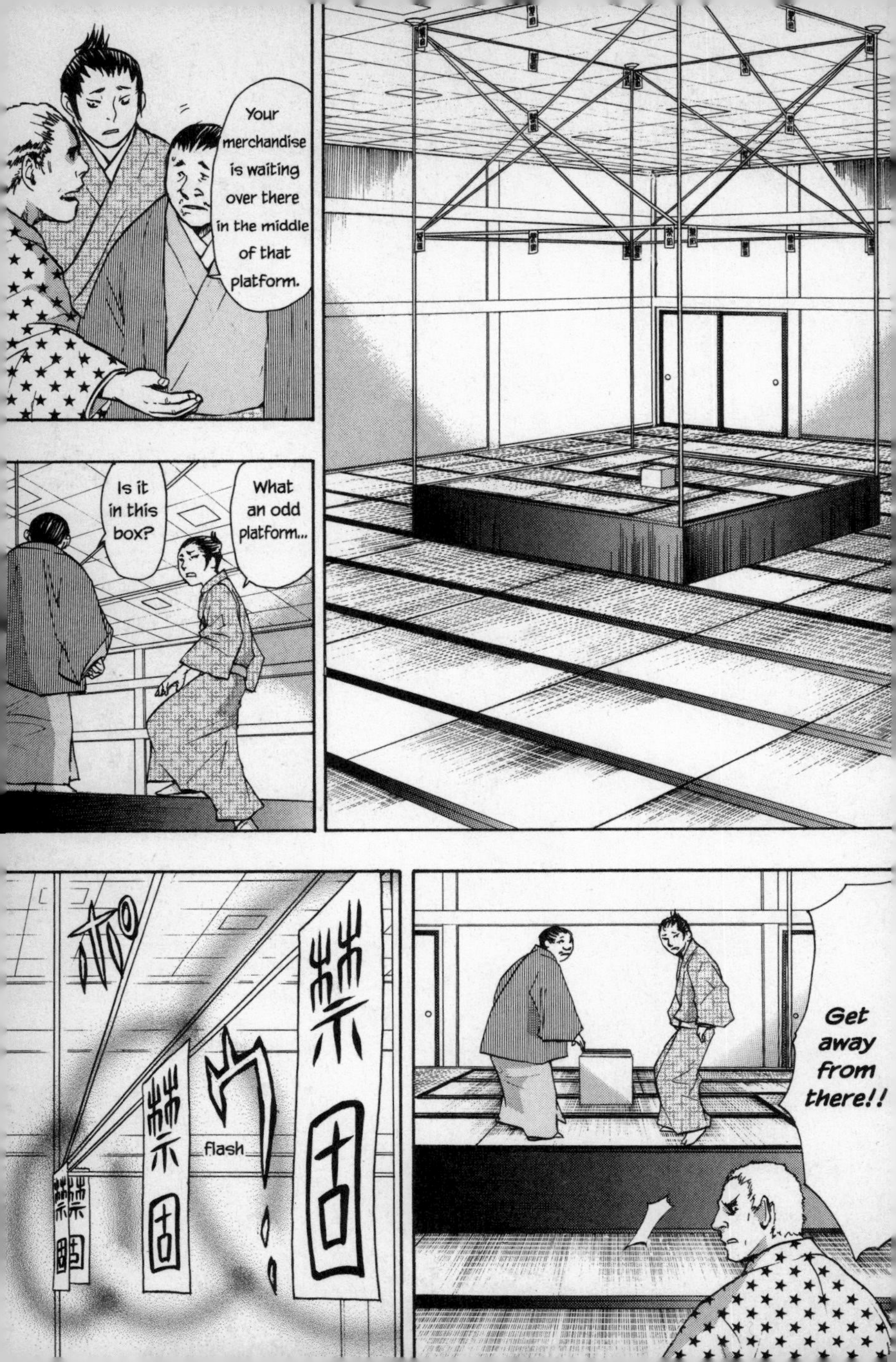
Your merchandise is waiting over there in the middle of that platform.
What an odd platform...
Is it in this box?
Get away from there!!
flash

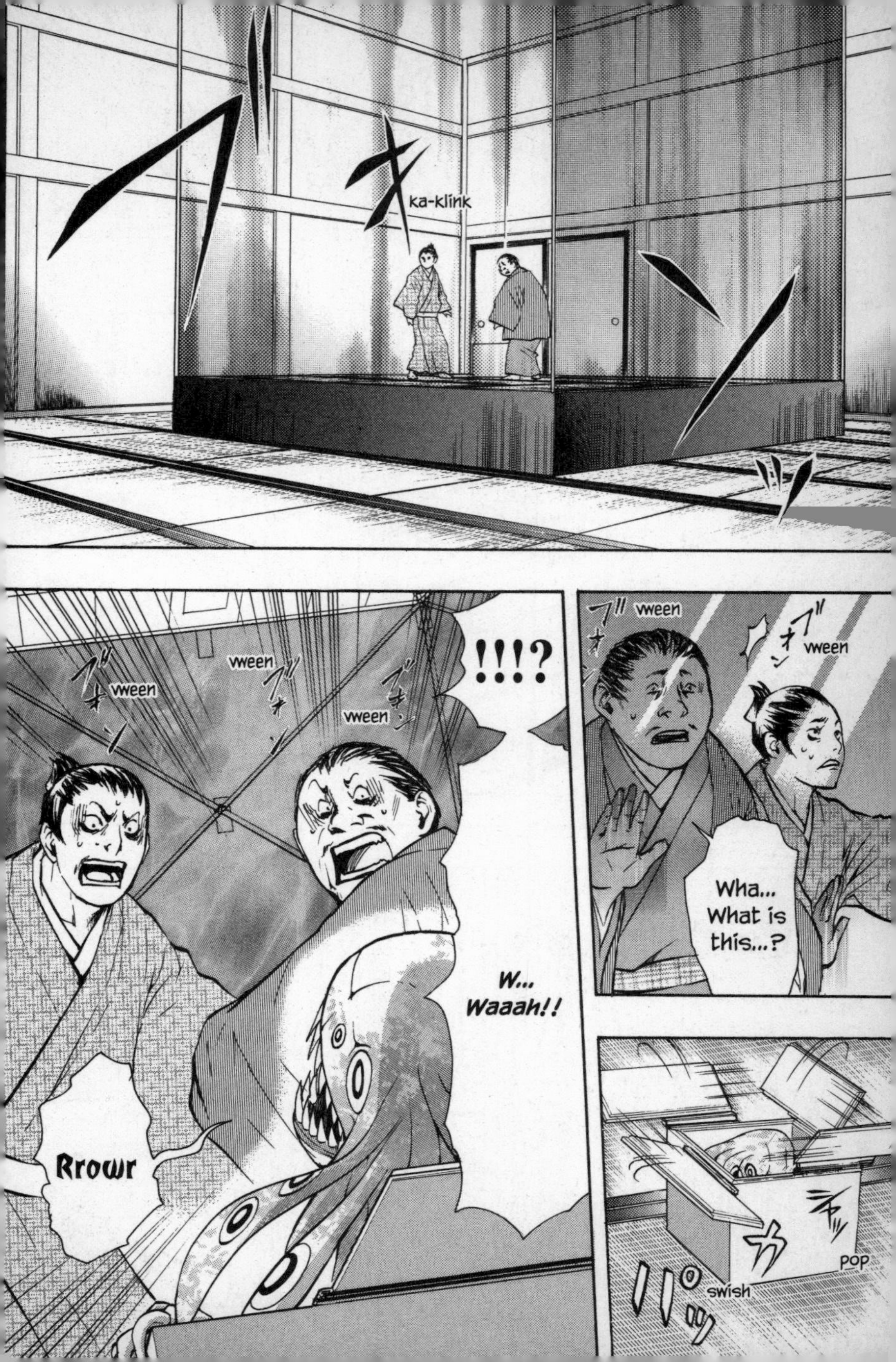
ka-klink
vween
vween
Wha... What is this...?
pop
swish
!!!?
vween
vween
vween
W... Waaah!!
Rrowr

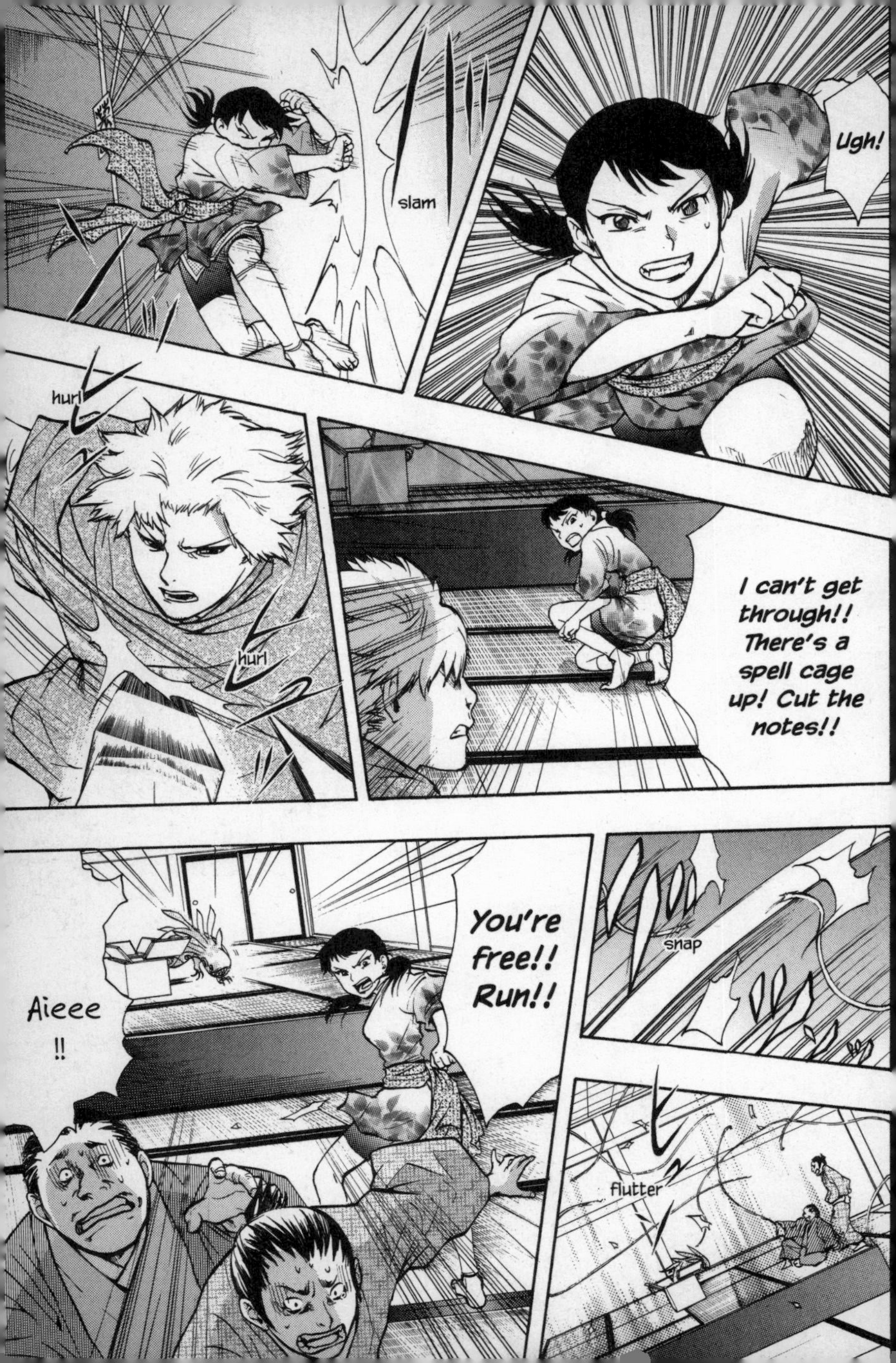
Ugh!
slam
I can't get through!! There's a spell cage up! Cut the notes!!
hurl
hurl
snap
flutter
You're free!! Run!!
Aieee !!

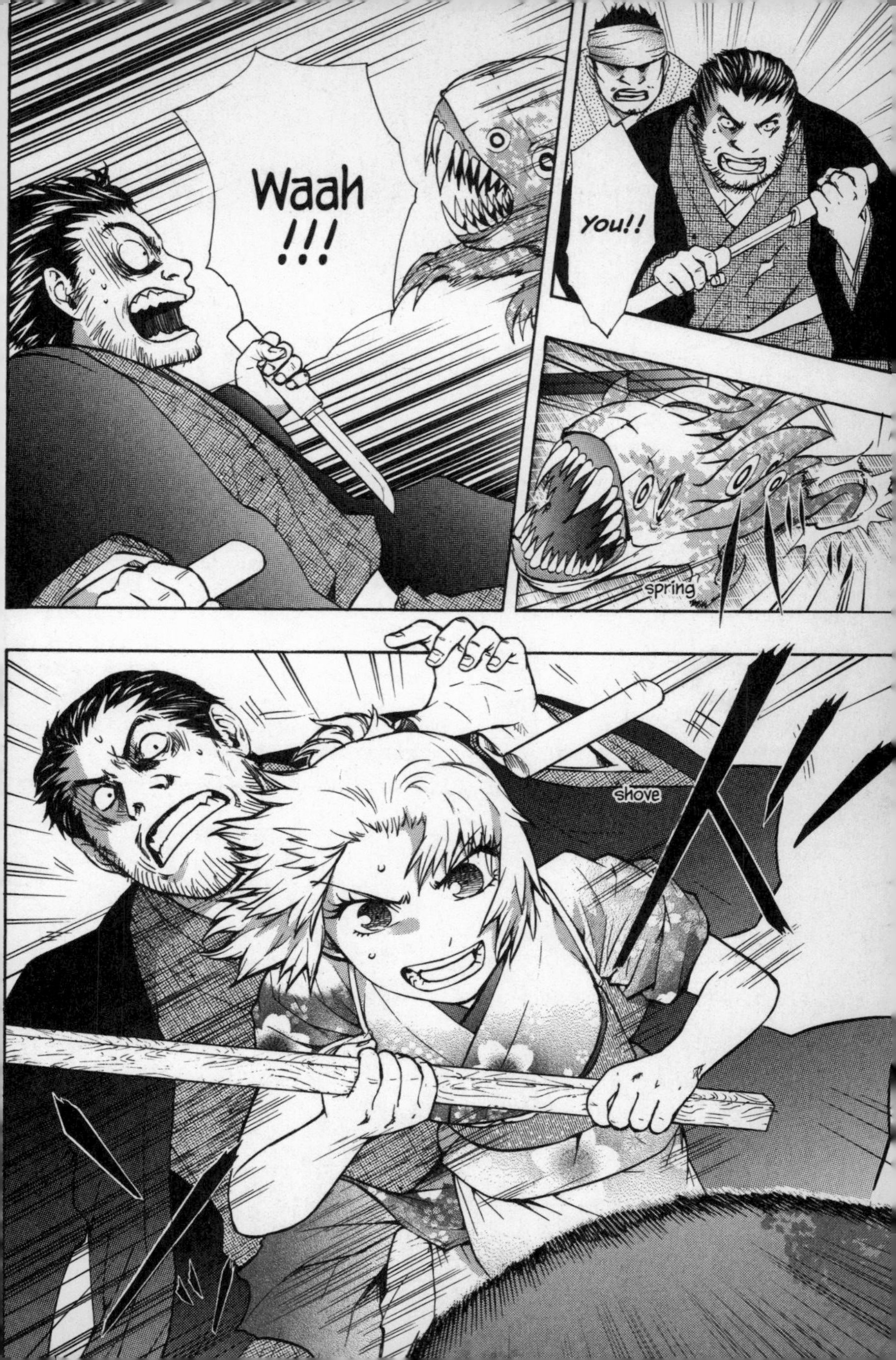
You!!
spring
Waah !!!
shove

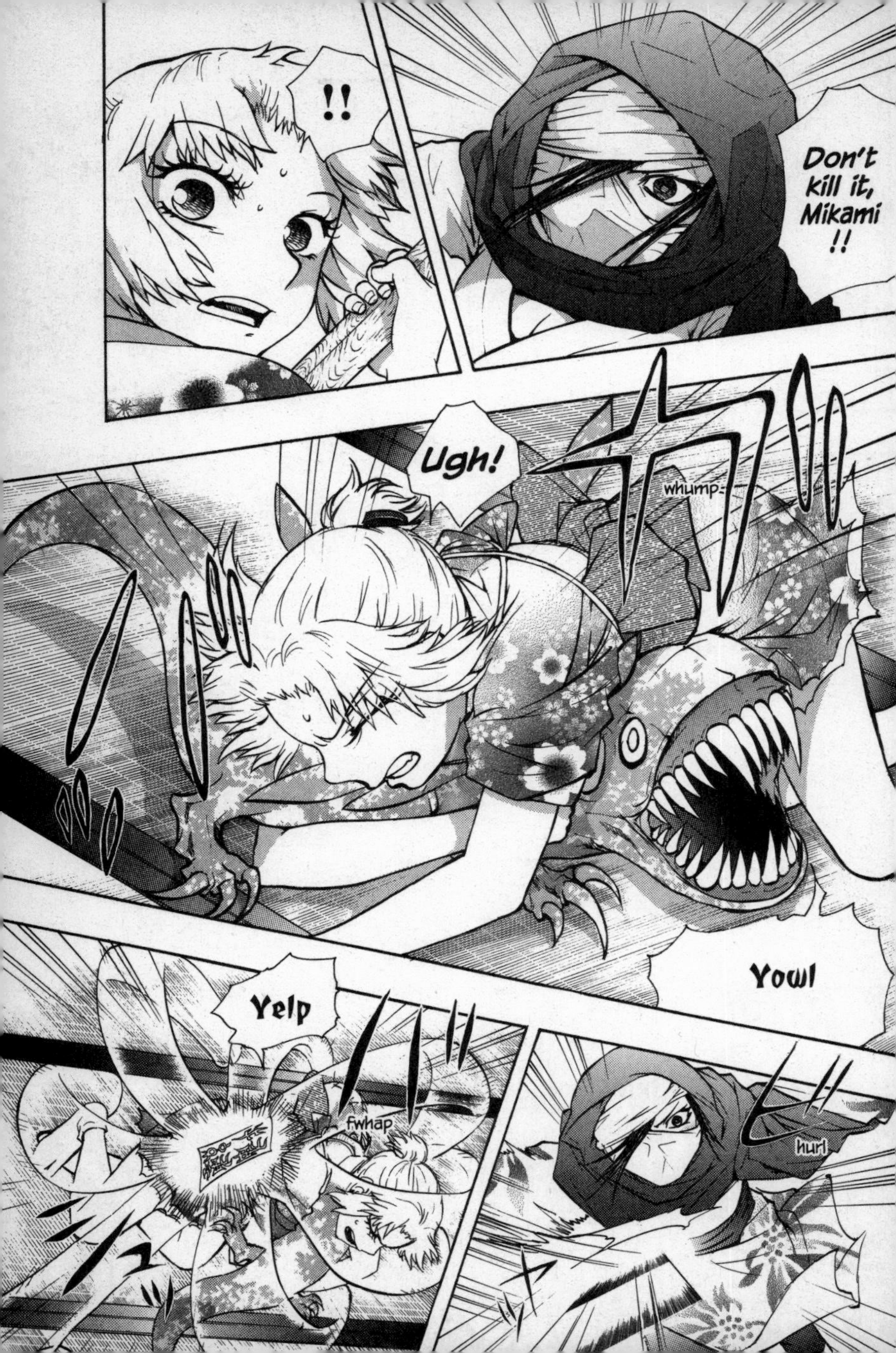
Don't kill it, Mikami !!
!!
Ugh!
whump
Yowl
hurl
Yelp
fwhap

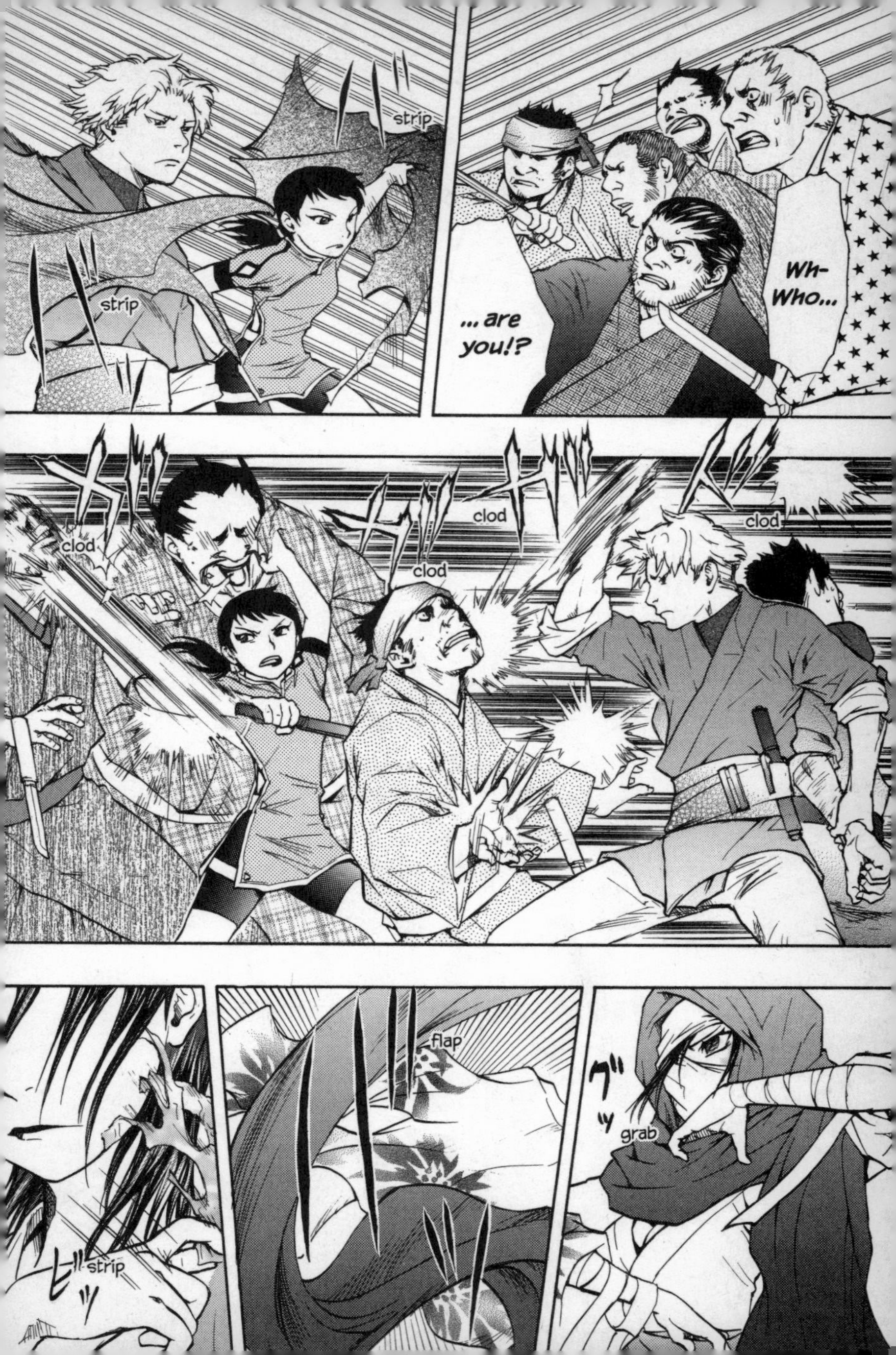
Wh-
Who...
... are
you!?
strip
strip
clod
clod
clod
clod
grab
flap
strip

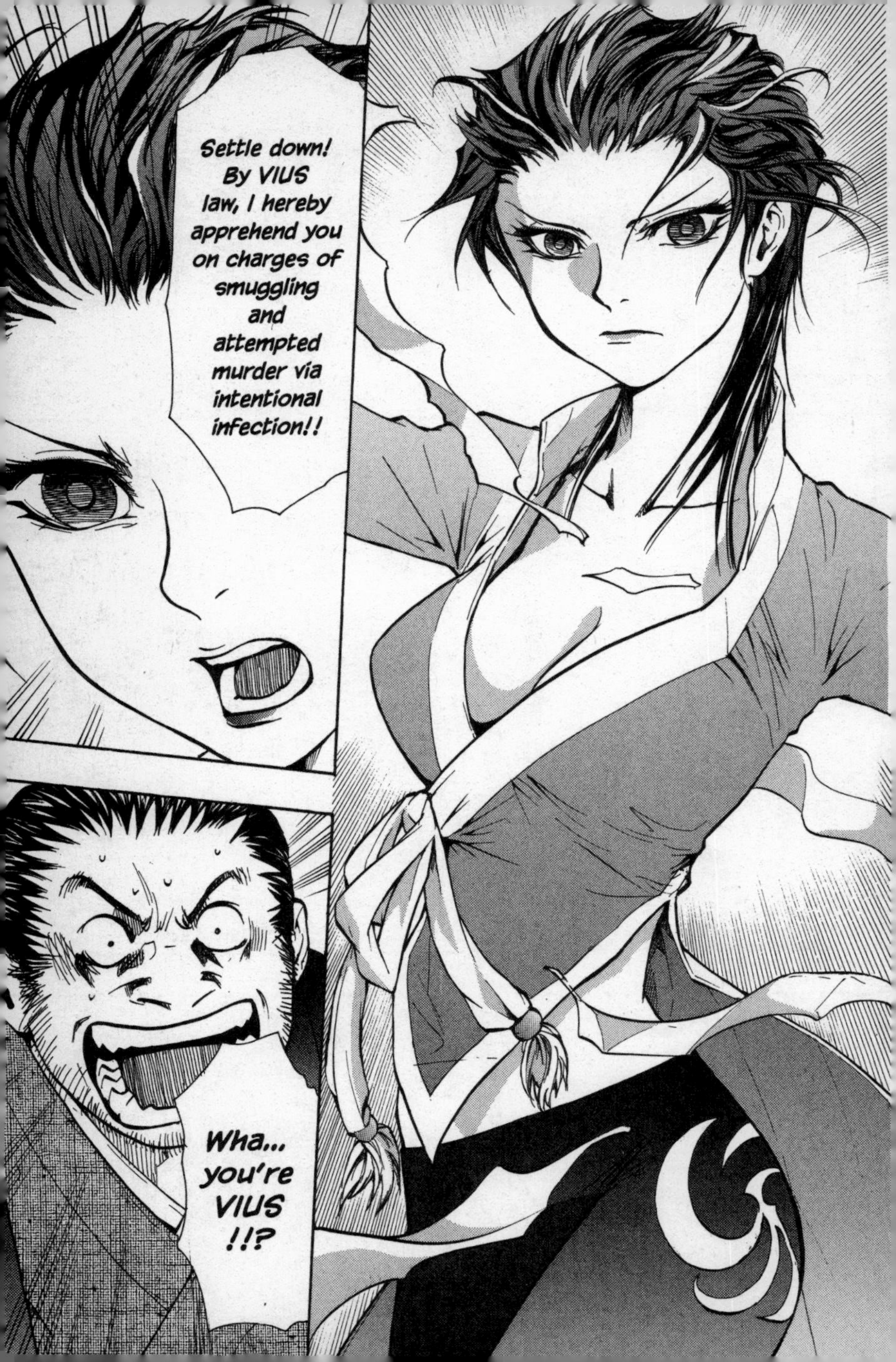
Settle down! By VIUS law, I hereby apprehend you on charges of smuggling and attempted murder via intentional infection!!
Wha... you're VIUS !!?

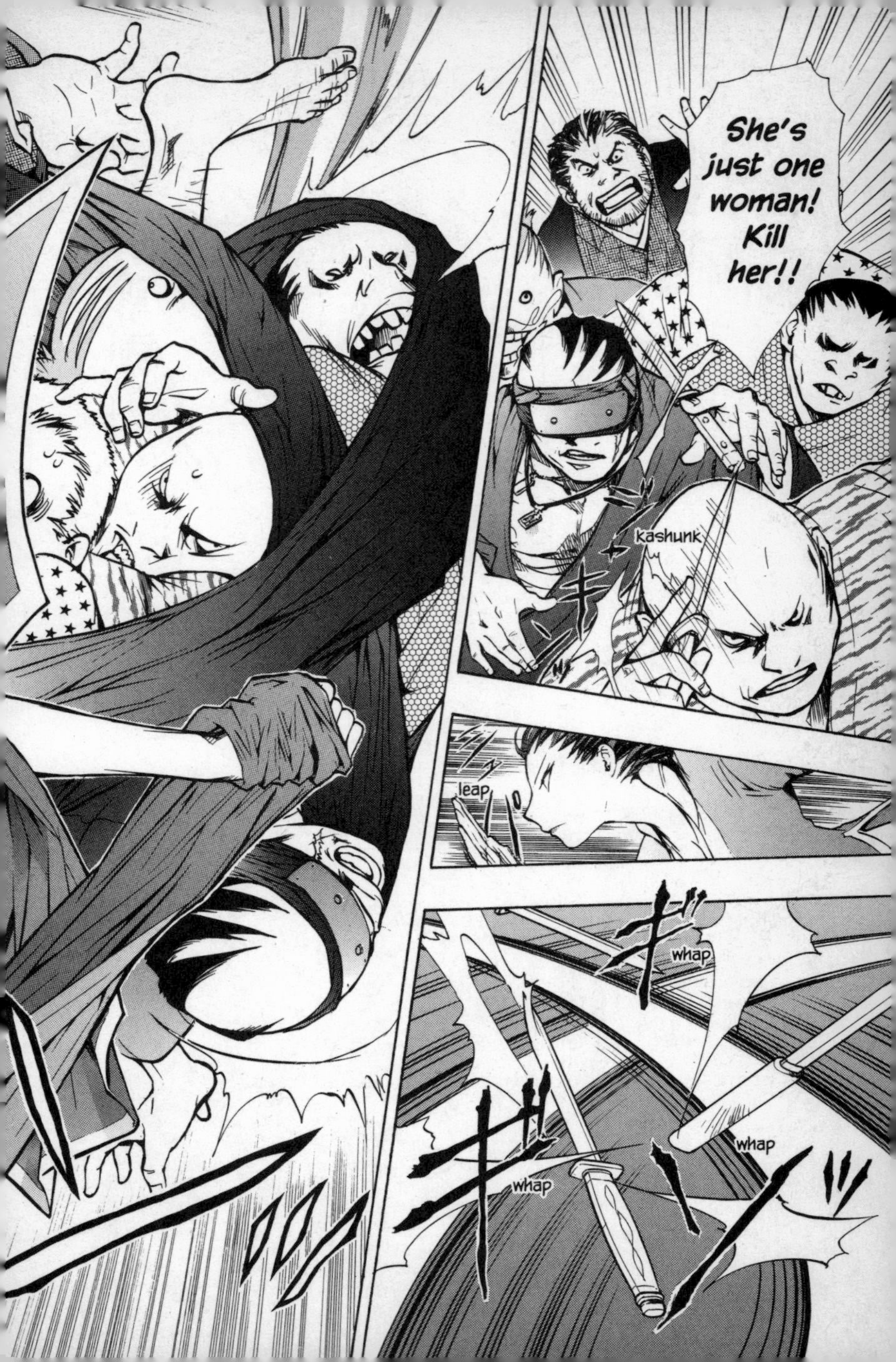
She's just one woman! Kill her!!
kashunk
leap
whap
whap
whap

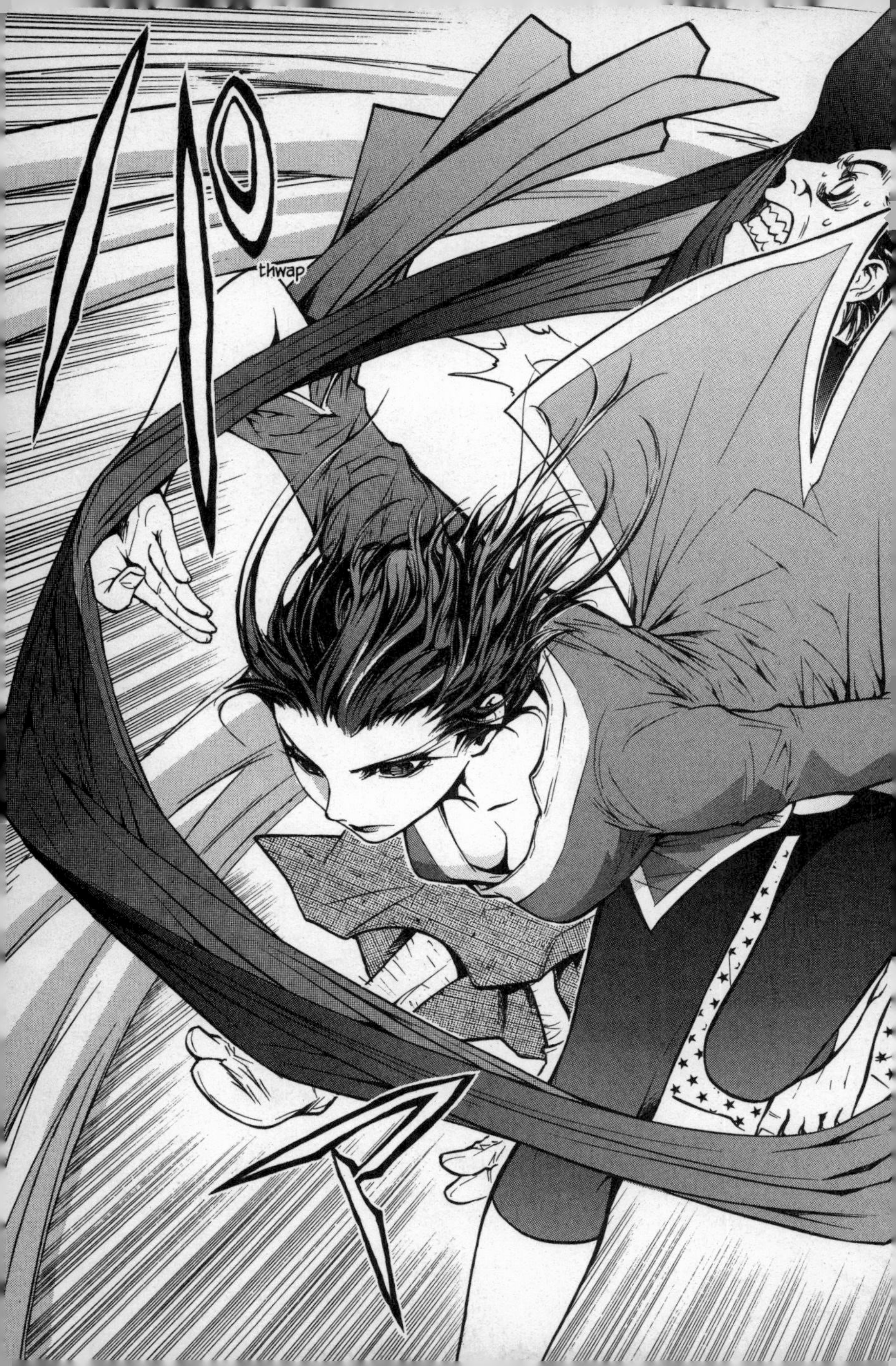
thwap

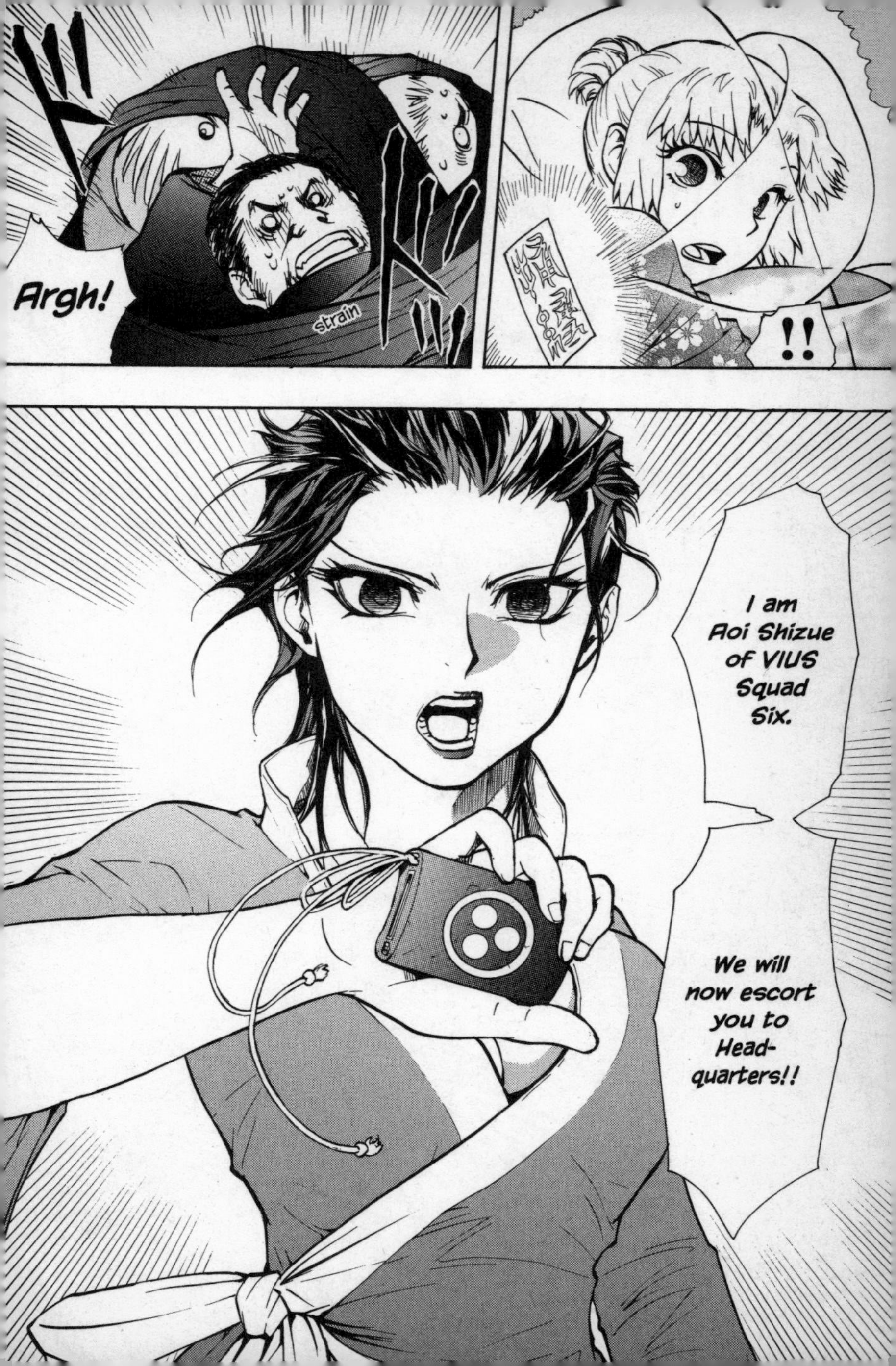
!!
Argh!
strain
I am Aoi Shizue of VIUS Squad Six.
We will now escort you to Head-quarters!!

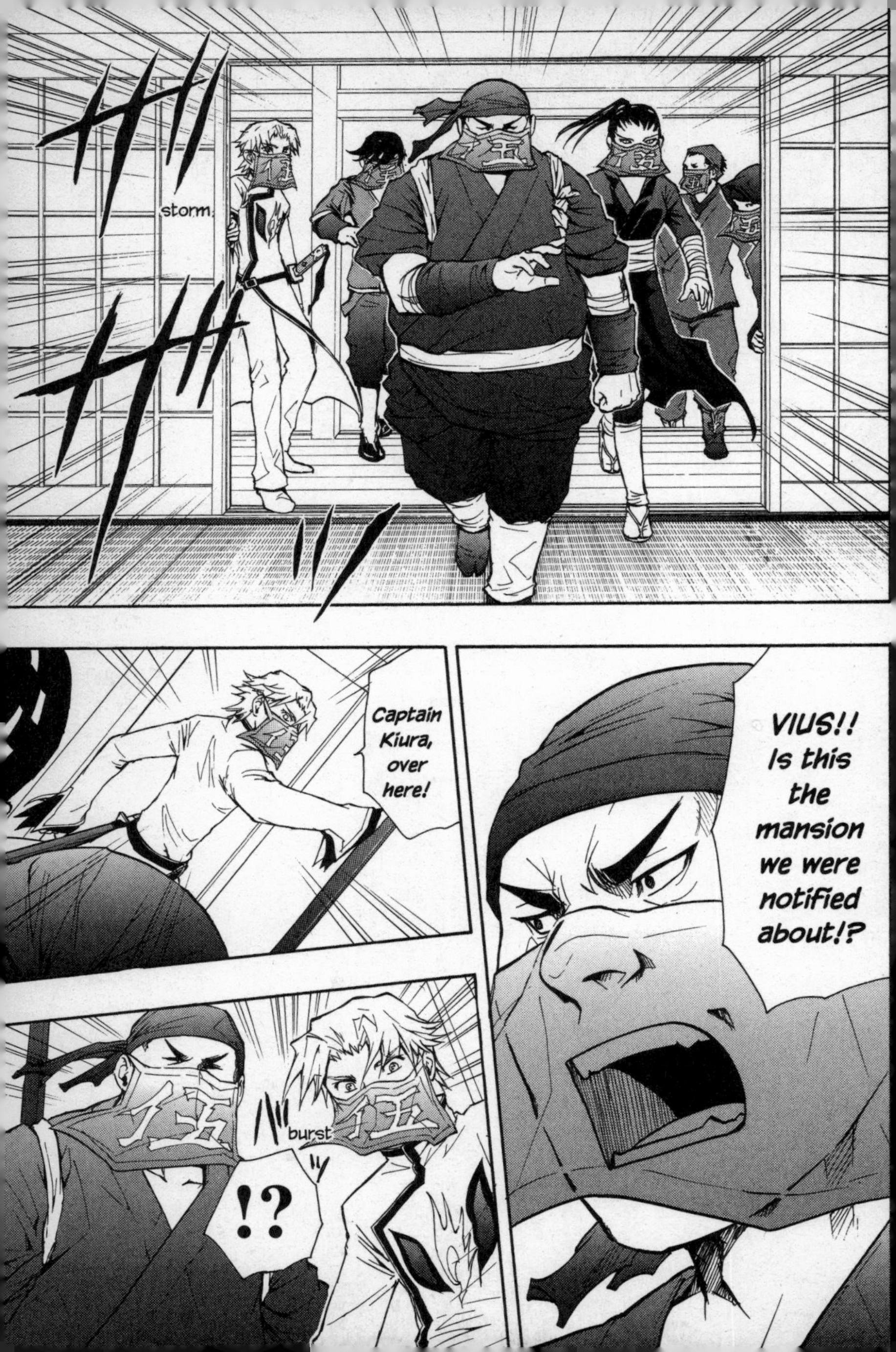
storm
VIUS!! Is this the mansion we were notified about!?
Captain Kiura, over here!
burst
!?

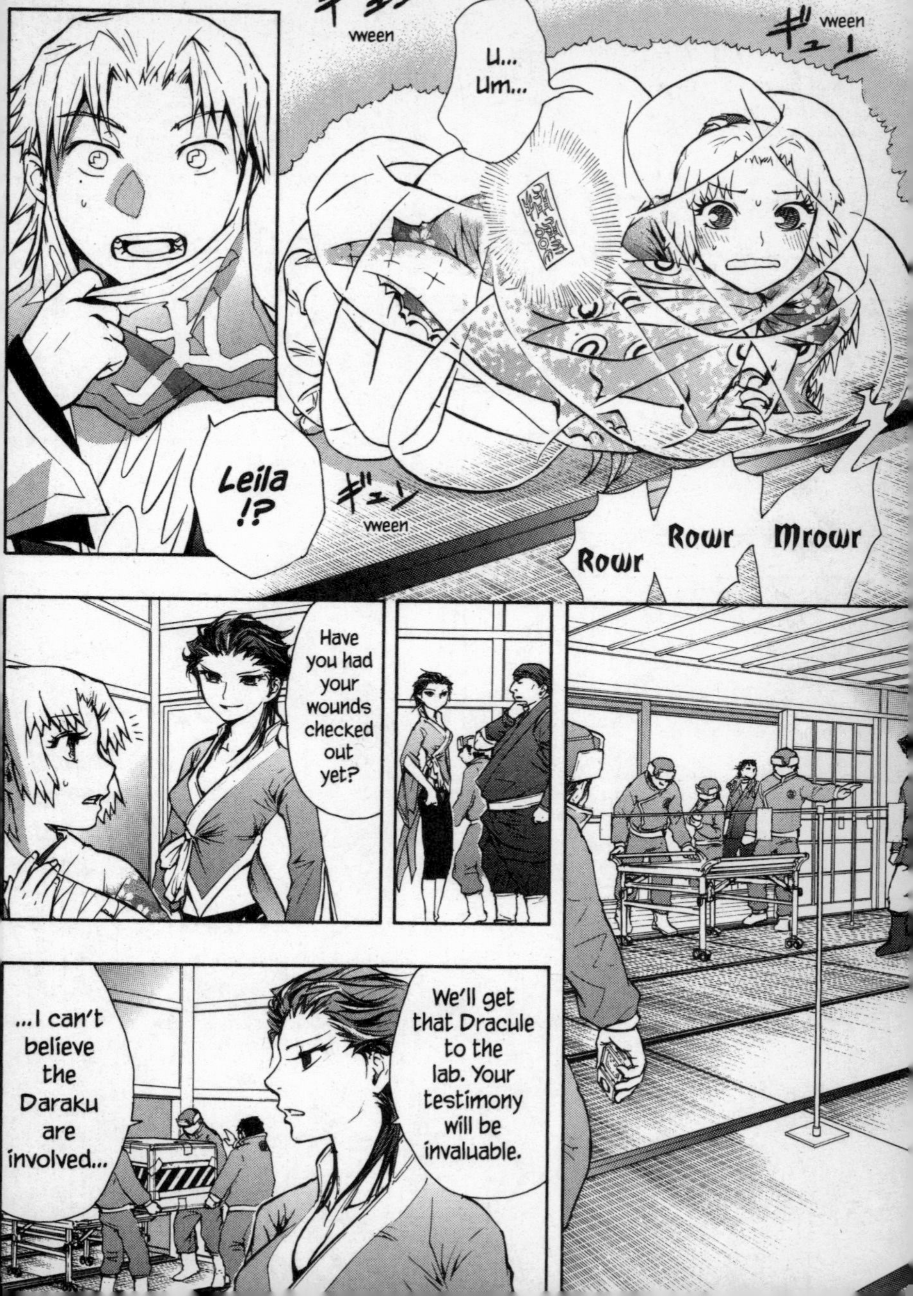

ギュン
vween
U...
Um...
ギュン
vween
Mrowr
Rowr
Rowr
Leila
!?
ギュン
vween
Have you had your wounds checked out yet?
We'll get that Dracule to the lab. Your testimony will be invaluable.
...I can't believe the Daraku are involved...

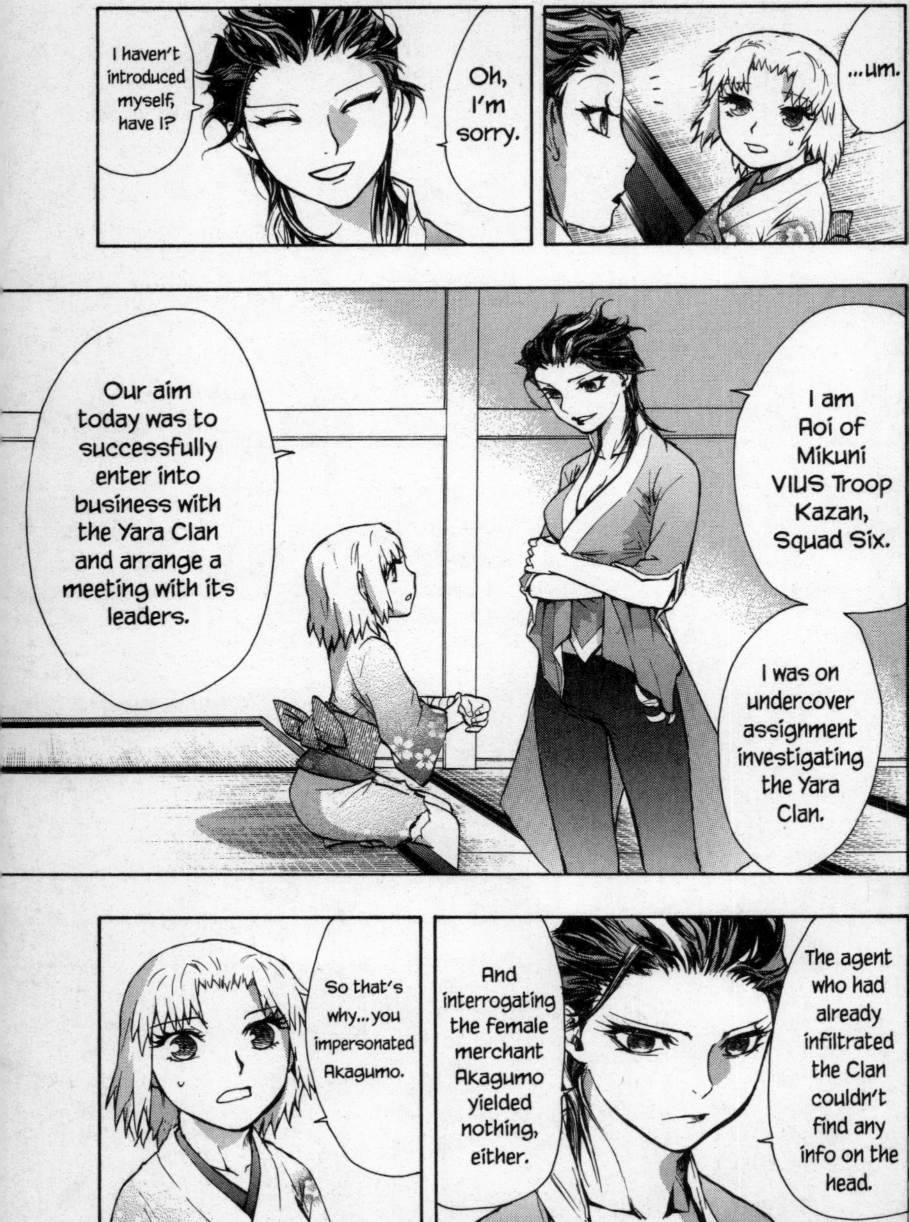
...um.
Oh, I'm sorry.
I haven't introduced myself, have I?
I am Aoi of Mikuni VIUS Troop Kazan, Squad Six.
I was on undercover assignment investigating the Yara Clan.
Our aim today was to successfully enter into business with the Yara Clan and arrange a meeting with its leaders.
The agent who had already infiltrated the Clan couldn't find any info on the head.
And interrogating the female merchant Akagumo yielded nothing, either.
So that's why...you impersonated Akagumo.

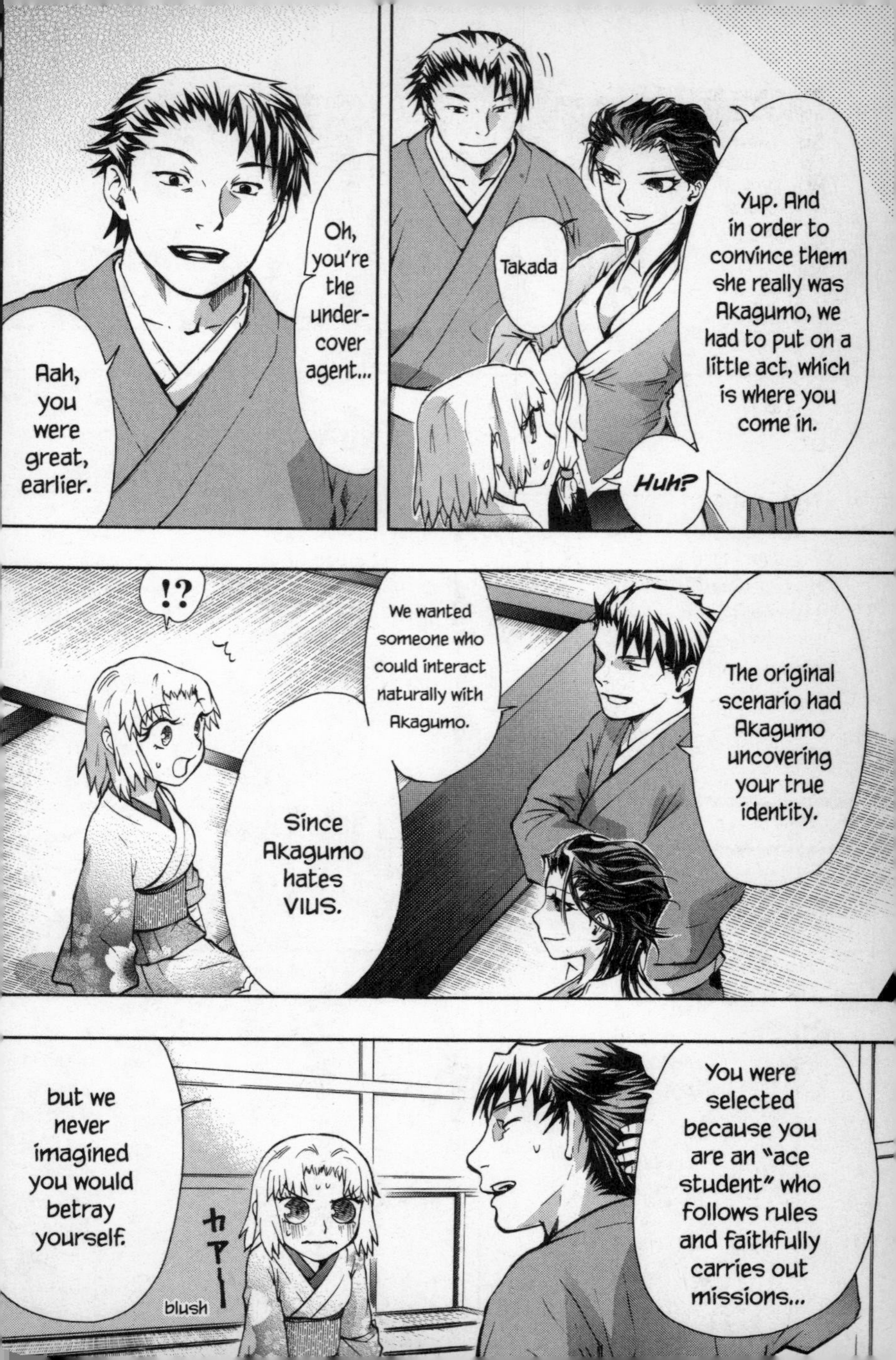
Yup. And in order to convince them she really was Akagumo, we had to put on a little act, which is where you come in.
Takada
Huh?
Oh, you're the under-cover agent...
Aah, you were great, earlier.
The original scenario had Akagumo uncovering your true identity.
We wanted someone who could interact naturally with Akagumo.
Since Akagumo hates VIUS.
!?
You were selected because you are an "ace student" who follows rules and faithfully carries out missions...
but we never imagined you would betray yourself.
blush

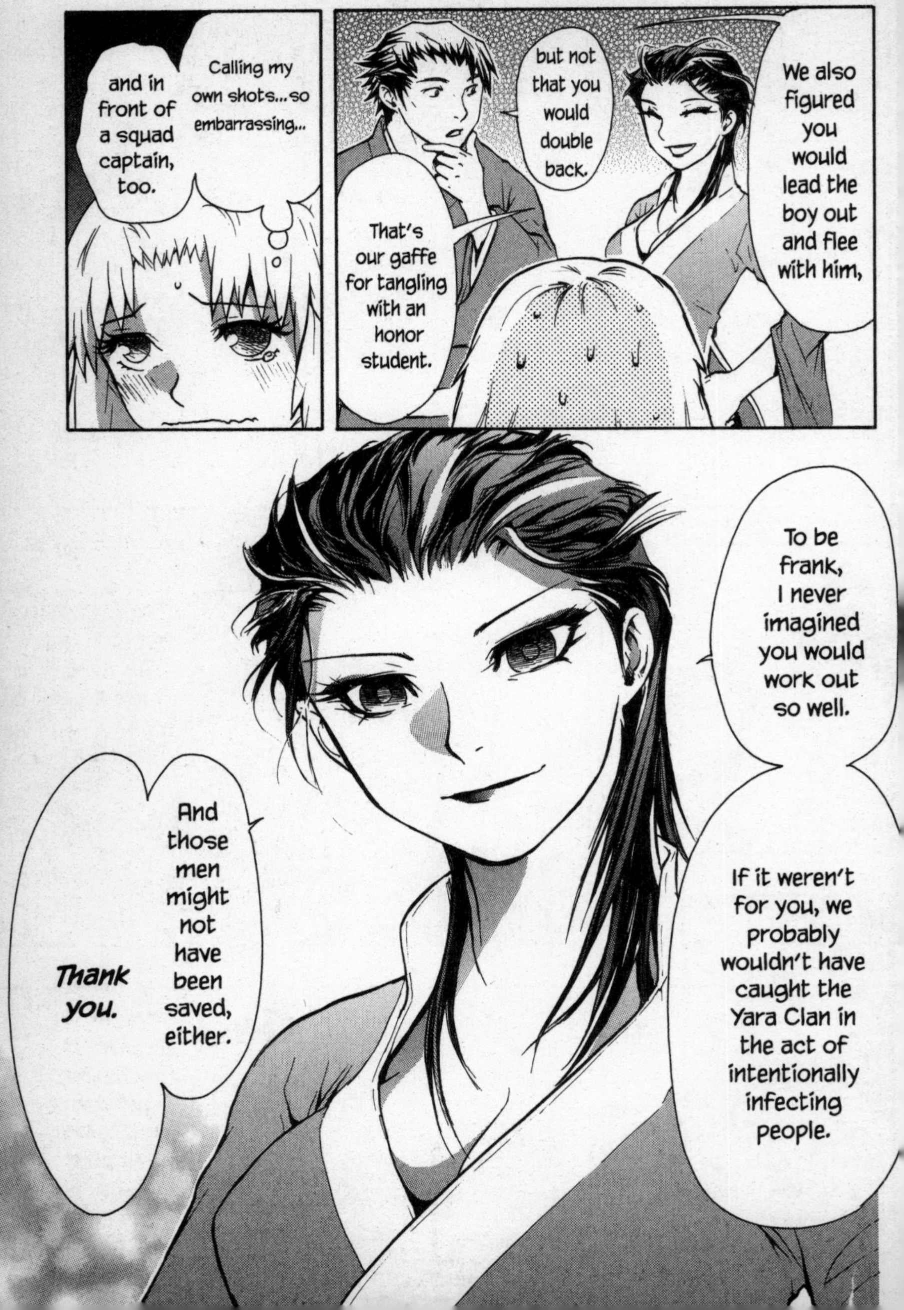
We also figured you would lead the boy out and flee with him,
but not that you would double back.
That's our gaffe for tangling with an honor student.
Calling my own shots...so embarrassing...
and in front of a squad captain, too.
To be frank, I never imagined you would work out so well.
If it weren't for you, we probably wouldn't have caught the Yara Clan in the act of intentionally infecting people.
And those men might not have been saved, either.
Thank you.

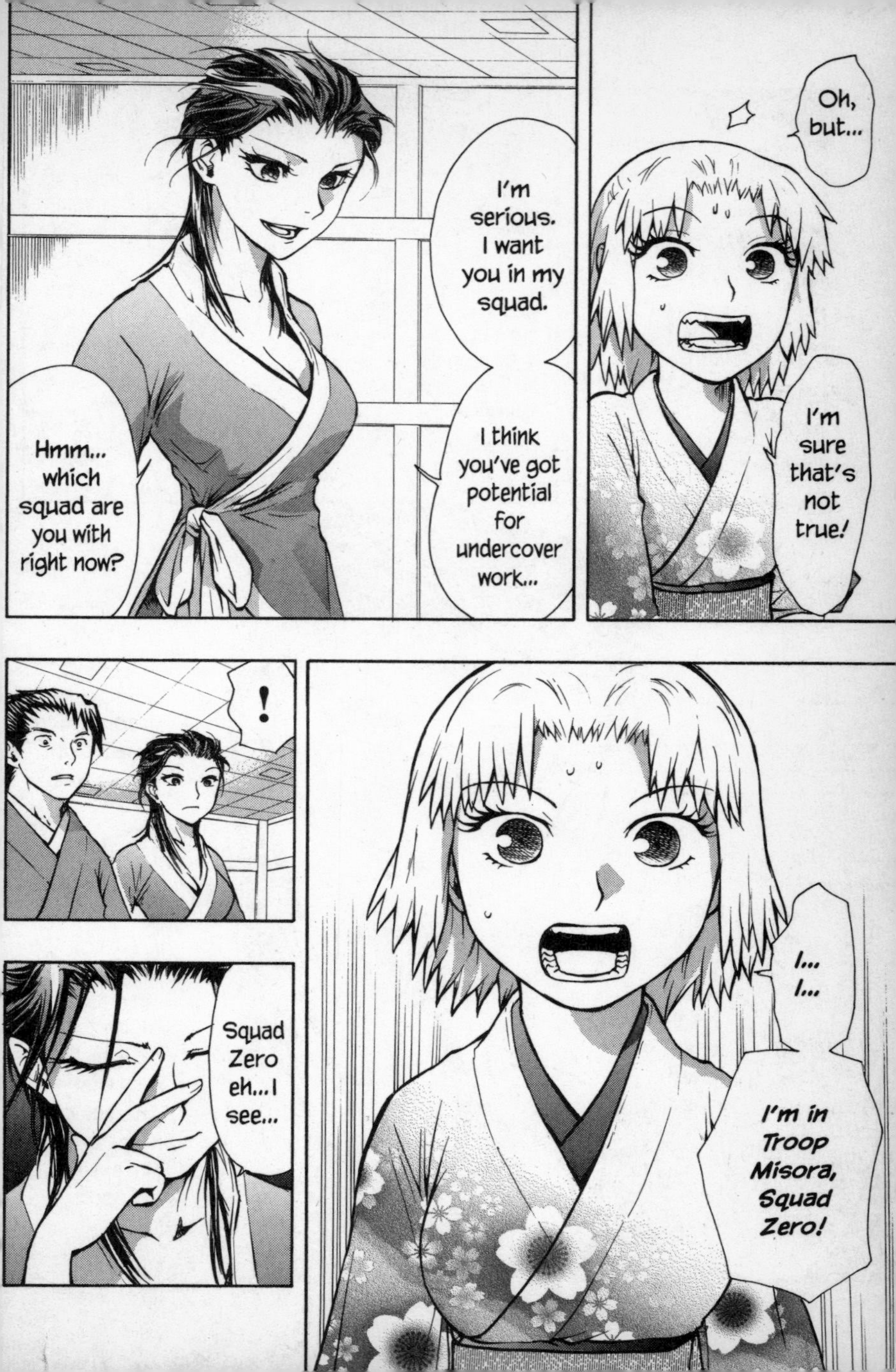
Oh, but...
I'm sure that's not true!
I'm serious. I want you in my squad.
I think you've got potential for undercover work...
Hmm... which squad are you with right now?
I... I...
I'm in Troop Misora, Squad Zero!
!
Squad Zero eh...I see...

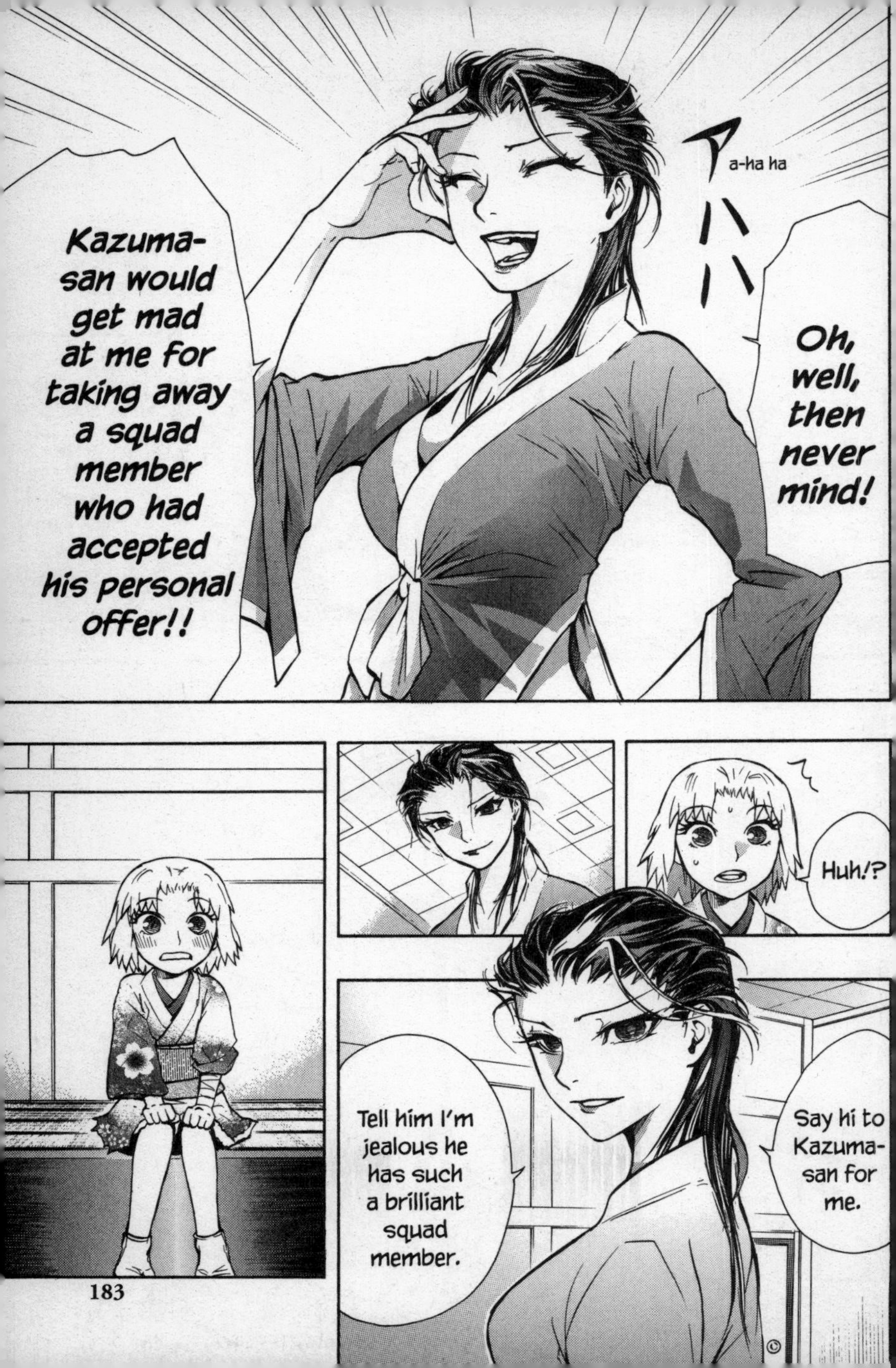
Oh, well, then never mind!
a-ha ha
Kazuma-san would get mad at me for taking away a squad member who had accepted his personal offer!!
Huh!?
Say hi to Kazuma-san for me.
Tell him I'm jealous he has such a brilliant squad member.

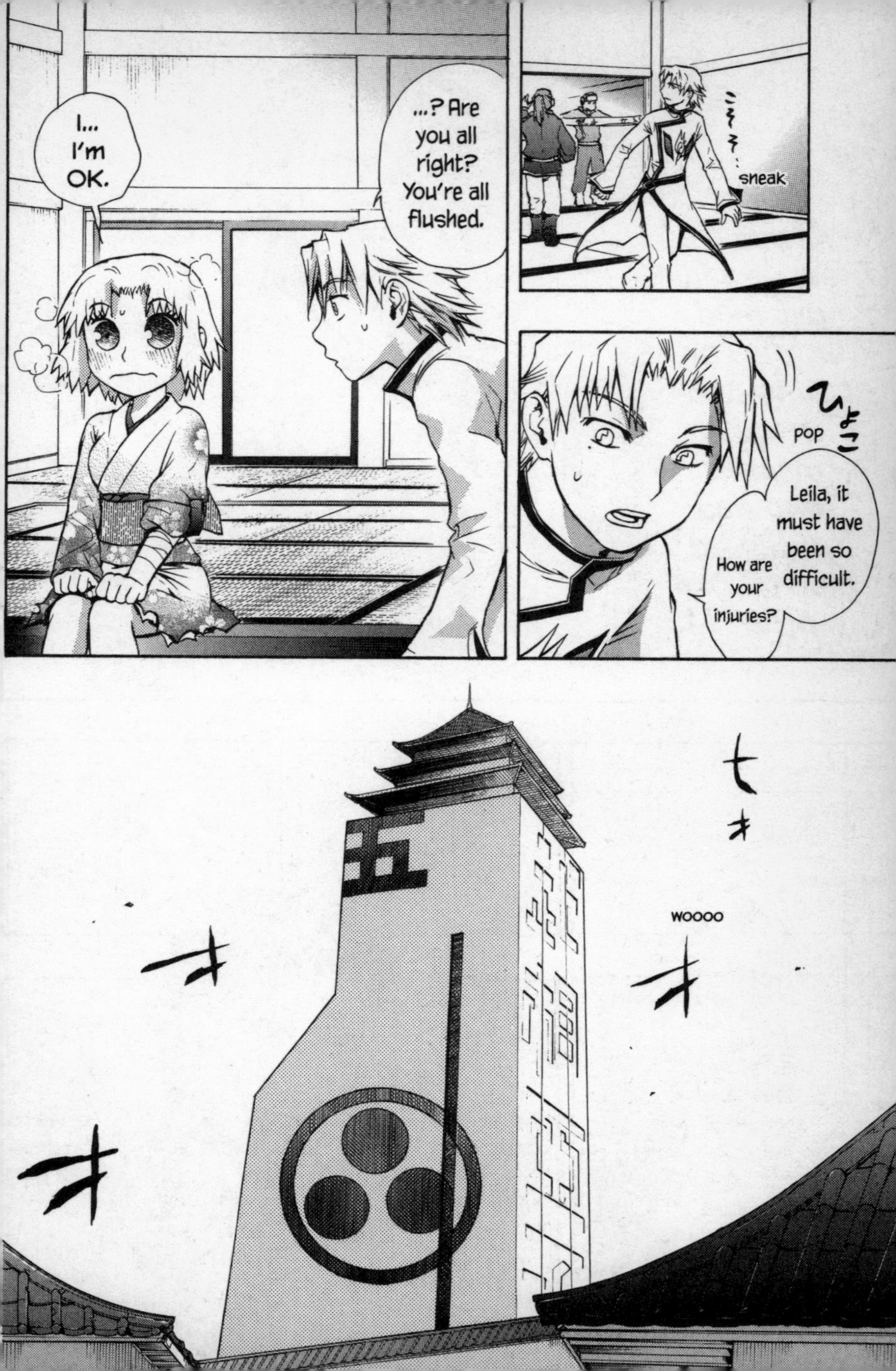
sneak
ひょこ
pop
Leila, it must have been so difficult.
How are your injuries?
...? Are you all right? You're all flushed.
I... I'm OK.
woooo

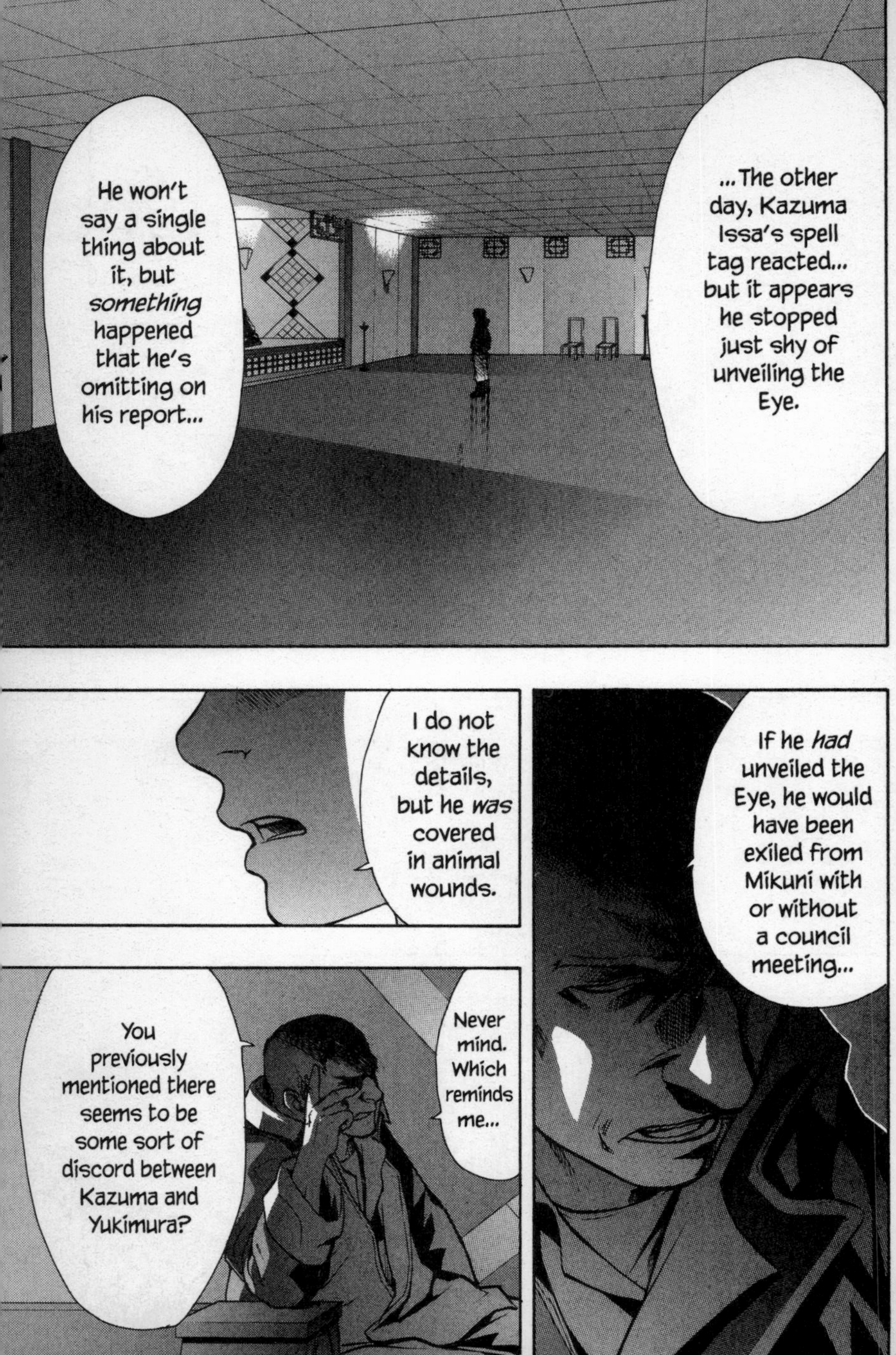
...The other day, Kazuma Issa's spell tag reacted... but it appears he stopped just shy of unveiling the Eye.
He won't say a single thing about it, but *something* happened that he's omitting on his report...
If he *had* unveiled the Eye, he would have been exiled from Mikuni with or without a council meeting...
I do not know the details, but he *was* covered in animal wounds.
Never mind. Which reminds me...
You previously mentioned there seems to be some sort of discord between Kazuma and Yukimura?

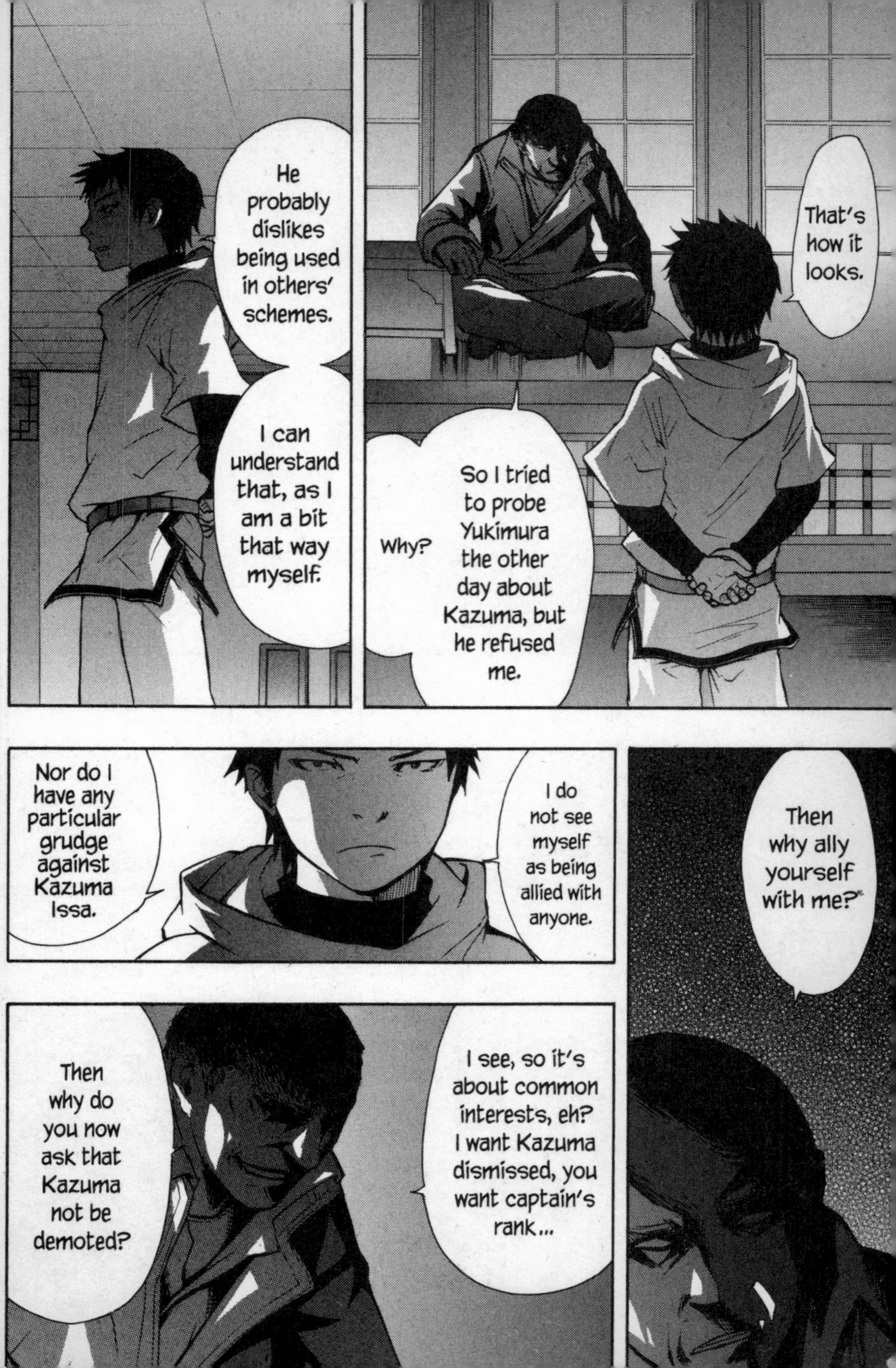
That's how it looks.
So I tried to probe Yukimura the other day about Kazuma, but he refused me.
Why?
He probably dislikes being used in others' schemes.
I can understand that, as I am a bit that way myself.
Then why ally yourself with me?
I do not see myself as being allied with anyone.
Nor do I have any particular grudge against Kazuma Issa.
I see, so it's about common interests, eh? I want Kazuma dismissed, you want captain's rank...
Then why do you now ask that Kazuma not be demoted?

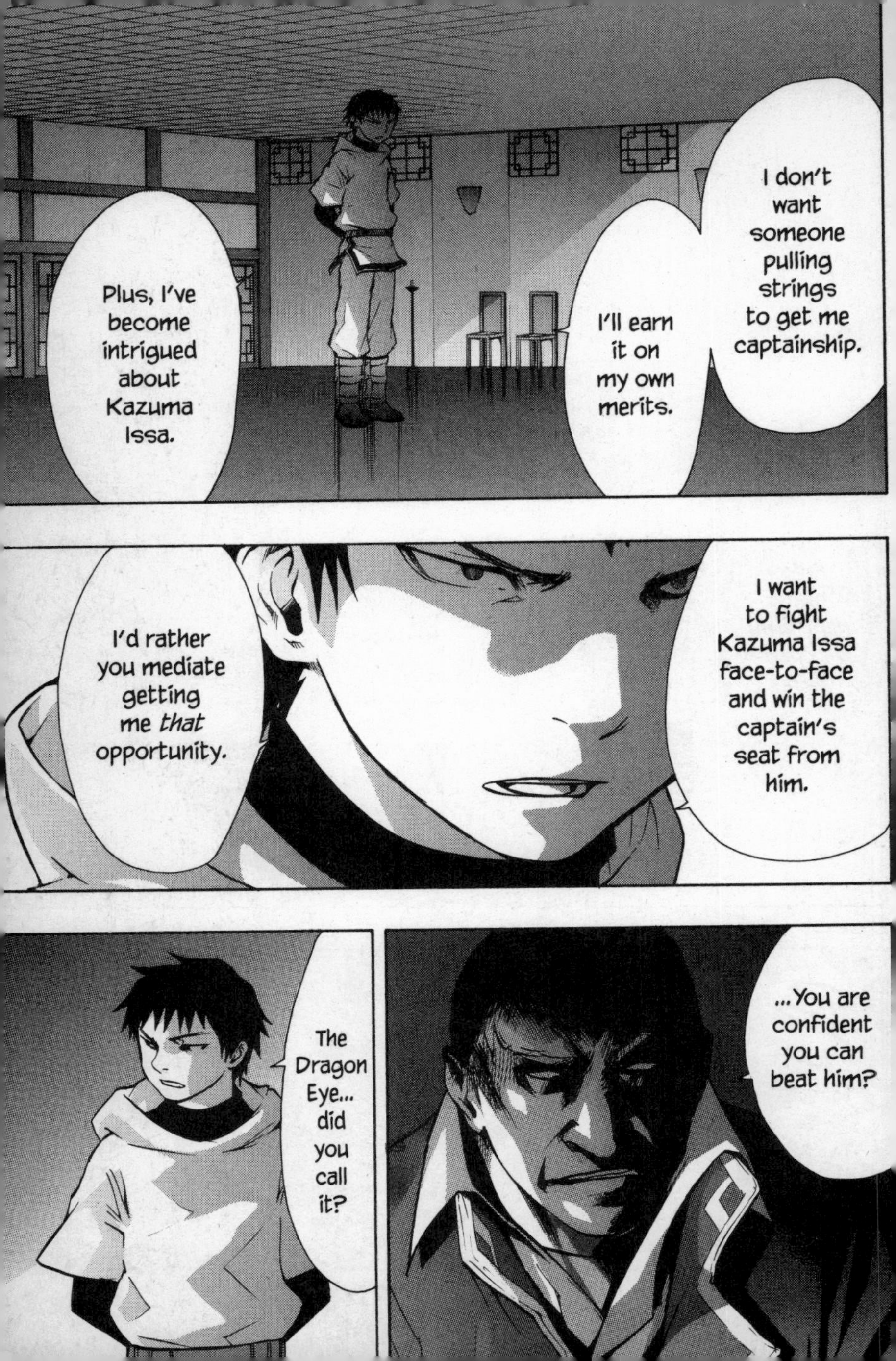
I don't want someone pulling strings to get me captainship.
I'll earn it on my own merits.
Plus, I've become intrigued about Kazuma Issa.
I want to fight Kazuma Issa face-to-face and win the captain's seat from him.
I'd rather you mediate getting me *that* opportunity.
...You are confident you can beat him?
The Dragon Eye... did you call it?

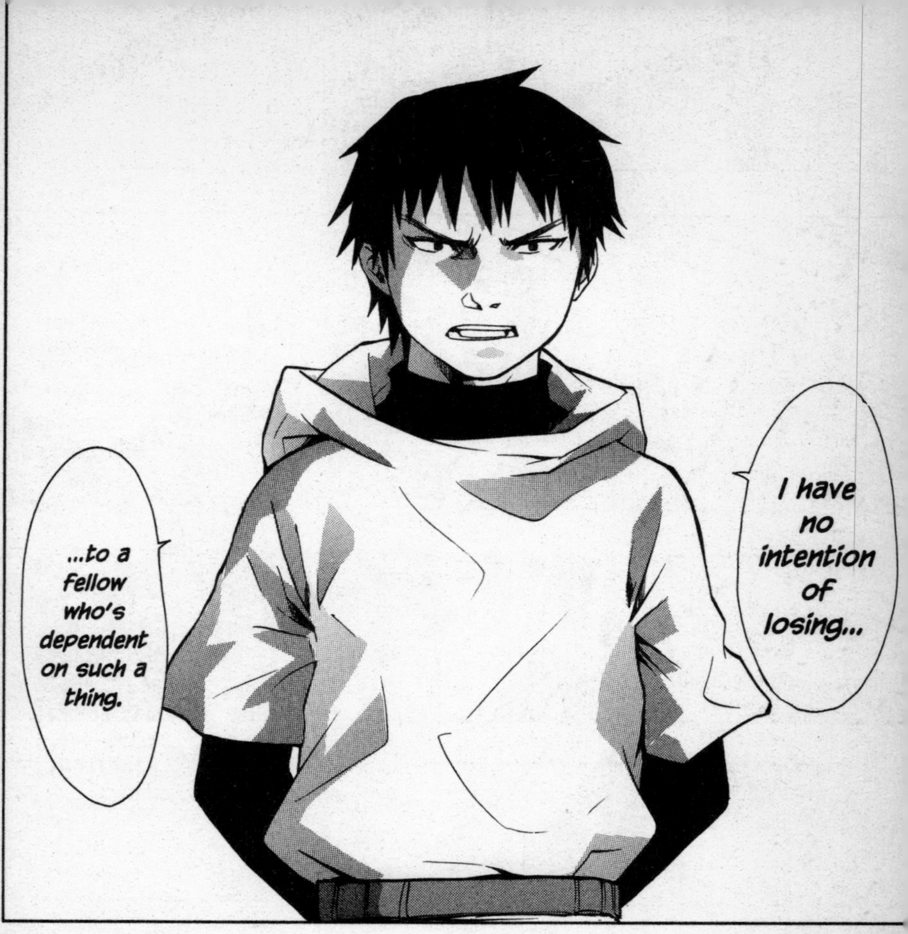
I have no intention of losing...
...to a fellow who's dependent on such a thing.

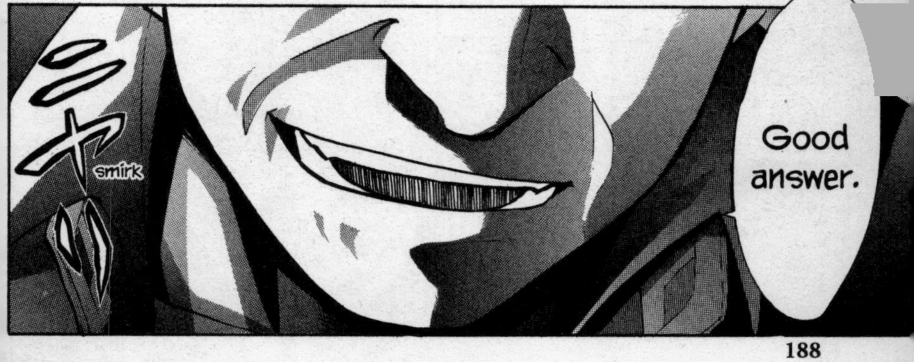
Good answer.
smirk

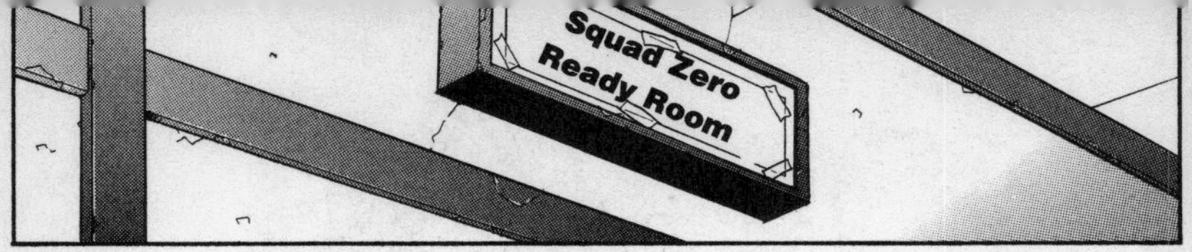
Squad Zero
Ready Room

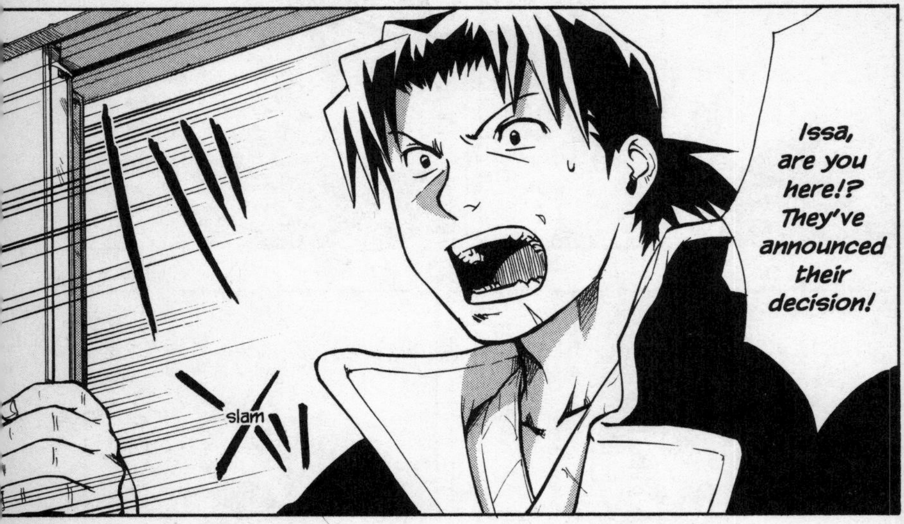
Issa, are you here!? They've announced their decision!
slam

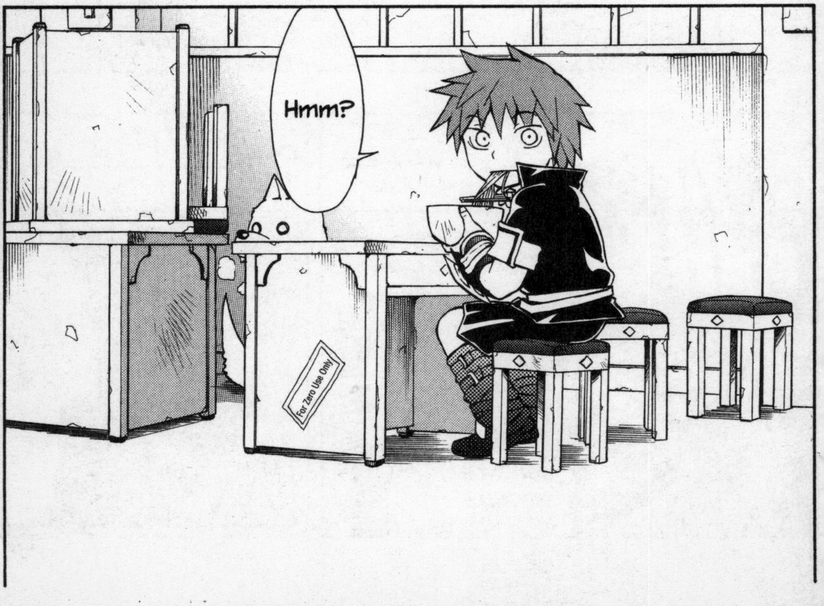
Hmm?
For Zero Use Only

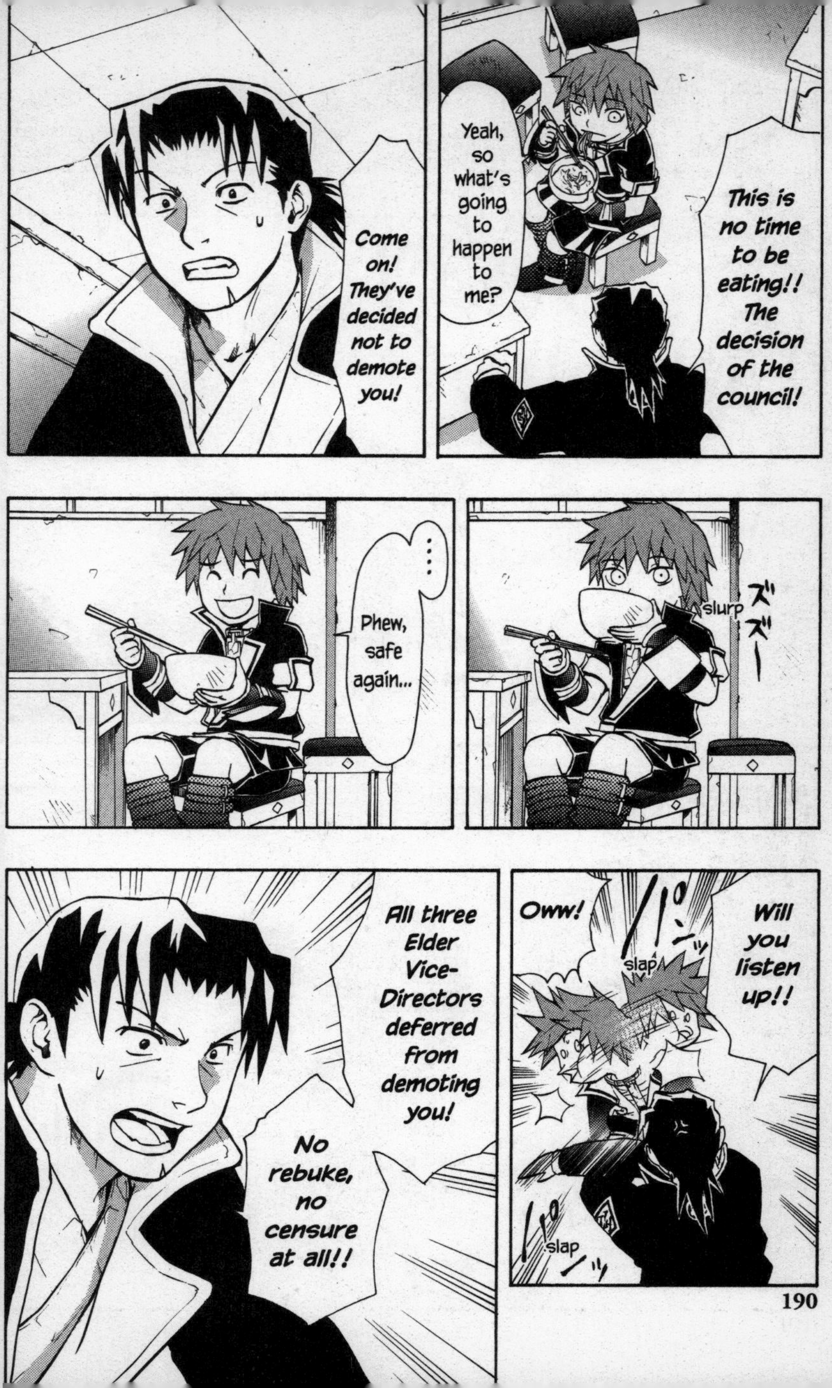
Yeah, so what's going to happen to me?
This is no time to be eating!! The decision of the council!
Come on! They've decided not to demote you!
slurp
ズズー
Phew, safe again...
....
Will you listen up!!
Oww!
slap
slap
All three Elder Vice-Directors deferred from demoting you!
No rebuke, no censure at all!!

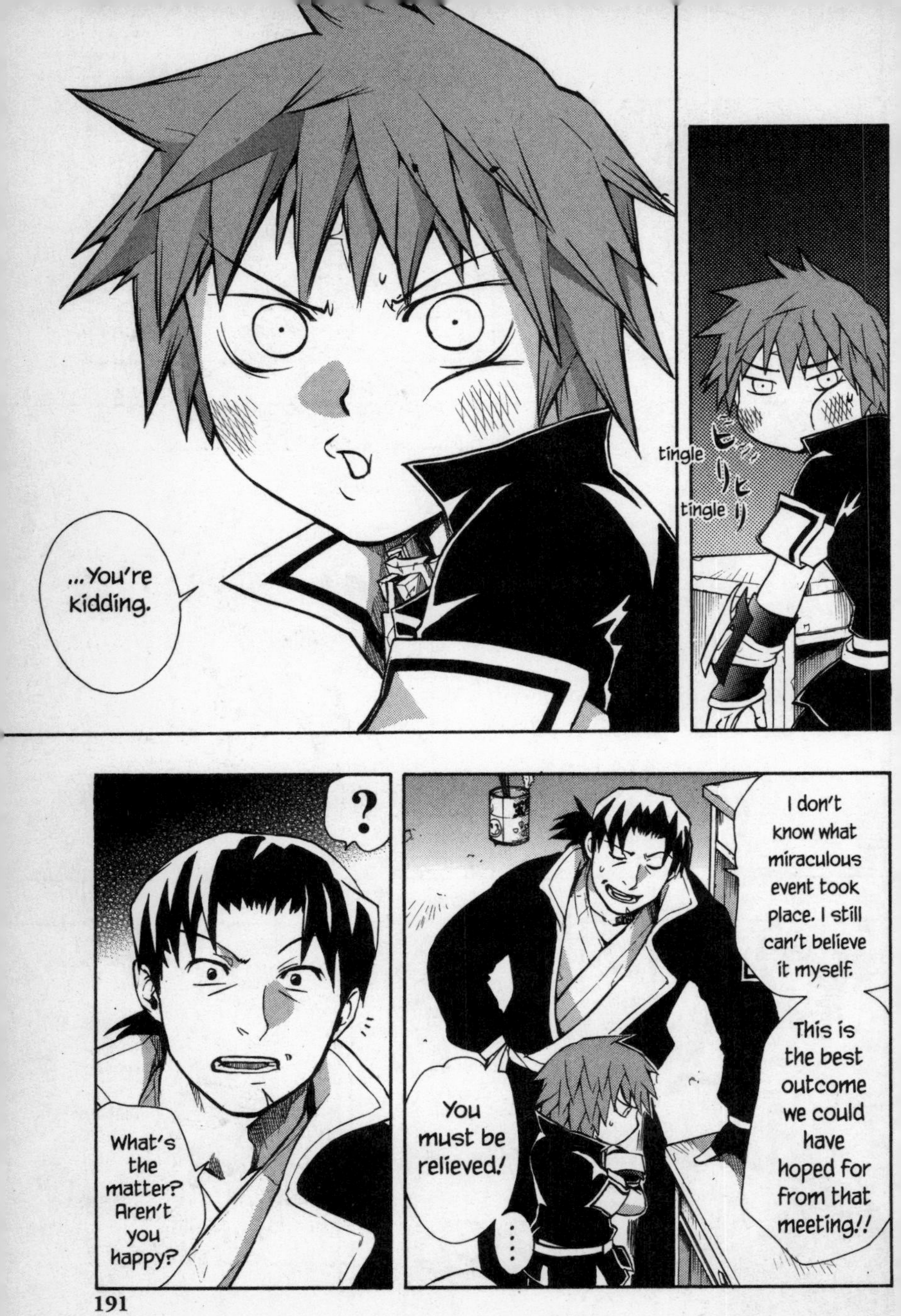
tingle
tingle
...You're kidding.
I don't know what miraculous event took place. I still can't believe it myself.
This is the best outcome we could have hoped for from that meeting!!
You must be relieved!
...
?
What's the matter? Aren't you happy?

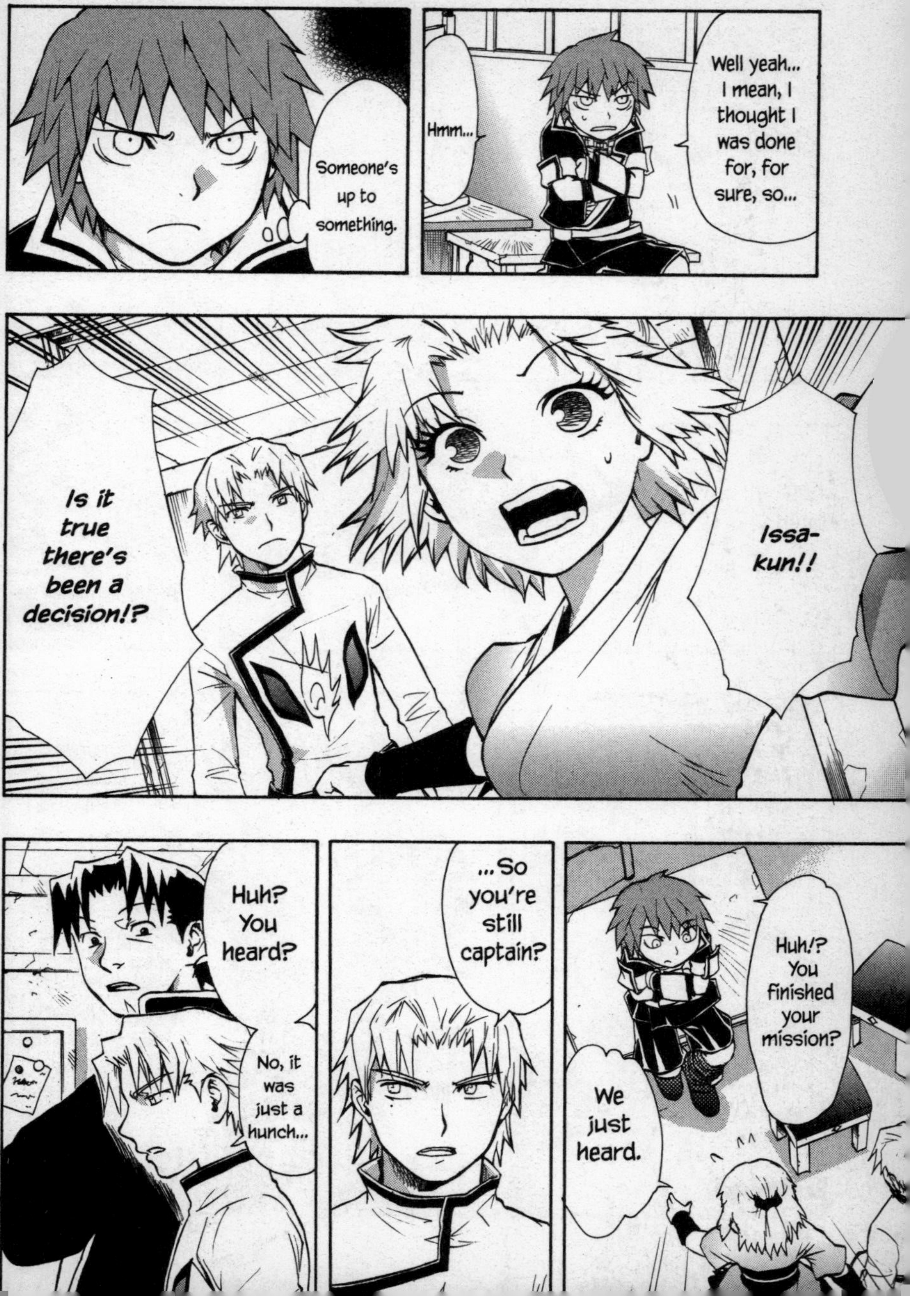
Well yeah... I mean, I thought I was done for, for sure, so...
Hmm...
Someone's up to something.
Issa-kun!!
Is it true there's been a decision!?
Huh!? You finished your mission?
We just heard.
...So you're still captain?
Huh? You heard?
No, it was just a hunch...

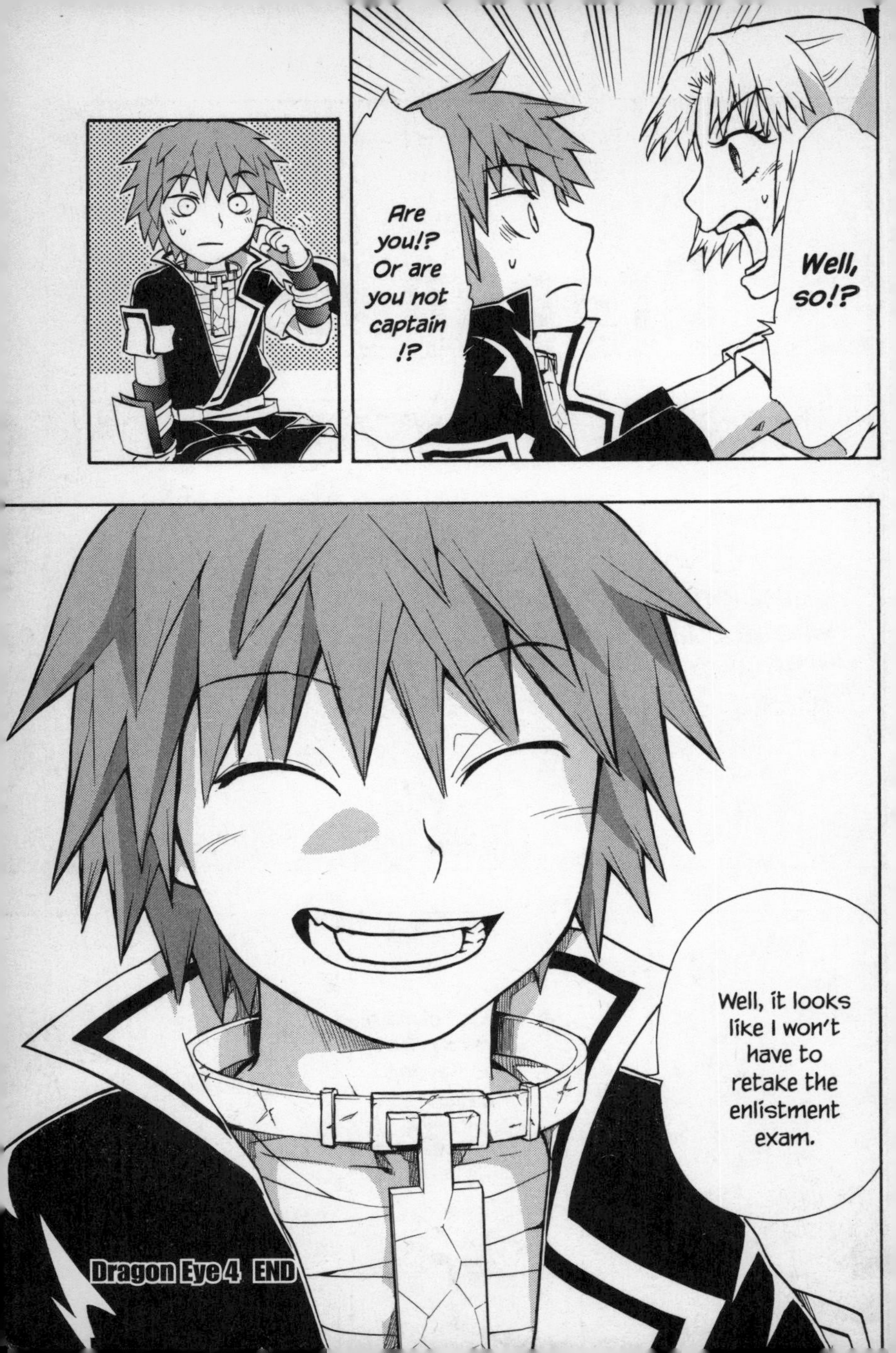
Well, so!?
Are you!? Or are you not captain!?
Well, it looks like I won't have to retake the enlistment exam.
Dragon Eye 4 END

Dragon Eye

Thank you very much to everybody that bought
volume 4!!

For this volume, Issa will answer some of the
questions that you all have sent in! Those
whose queries have been printed shall receive
a small gift! But don't expect anything too
grand! And please buy volume 5!

Fujiyama

My wonderful staff
· Uemura Erika
· Ueda Satomi
· Kamimura
· Dantani Ai

 Hi all, thanks for sending in so many letters! So here goes with the first question! Which reminds me, there were quite a few questions for Sakuraba.

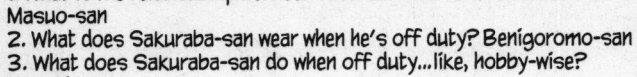

 1. What is the relationship between Issa-kun and Sakuraba-san like? Masuo-san
2. What does Sakuraba-san wear when he's off duty? Benigoromo-san
3. What does Sakuraba-san do when off duty...like, hobby-wise? Nozaki-san

 I don't really think you'll get interesting answers asking Sakuraba about his hobbies!? On the other hand, I'd tell you all sorts of things about me. Well, never mind. He and I have known each other since we took the same enlistment exam. So we're classmates, year mates! In terms of what he wears off duty... he's always wearing the same thing. I bet he even goes to bed in his uniform!? Plus, he's been working nonstop recently, so he doesn't seem to have any hobbies. He's really boring!! Next question!

 Where does the Squad Zero dog usually sleep? Also, how old is Aoi-san? Sakiware Spoon-san

 That dog is always in Zero's Ready Room, so I think he sleeps in there too. But it's not like anyone keeps an eye on him, so maybe he wanders around at night... The only command he knows is sit, so. In terms of Aoi... I wonder. I don't think she'd tell me if I asked. Hmm... as far as I can remember, she enlisted later than I did.

 A question for Issa! Can you see with the Dragon Eye? Also, if one were to touch the scar on your forehead, would it feel squishy like an eyeball? If so, I bet it would hurt if someone snapped his or her finger there. Amber Cateyes

 Hey! Finally, a question for me... all I can say is that the Dragon Eye is not one of my eyes, so I've never used it to look at anything. Also, my scar is not squishy! The Eye was implanted using very special surgery, so to most folk it just looks like a plain old scar. Either way, I wouldn't let anyone snap his or her finger at my forehead anyway!

 I love the battle scenes in **Dragon Eye!!** I especially like Yukimura because I think his two-sword technique is real cool. Oh, so my question is, did Yukimura train under a certain style like Leila's "Shimon School Sacred Blade"?

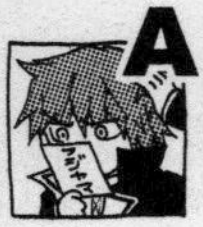
A

Hmm, I think I better ask Fujiyama this one. Give me a sec... (3 minutes pass) OK, huh, "Yukimura is self-trained, so he doesn't actually follow any particular school or style." So he's like me!

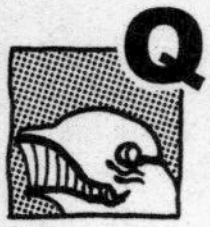
Q

Are there VIUS other than just Sôsei-san who have the Vius emblem sewn on their uniforms? Oda-san

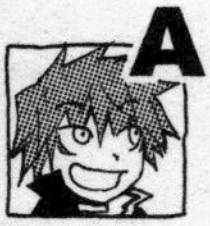
A

Oh! I can answer this one. If I remember correctly, what he wears is a special dress uniform issued to those who score especially high on their enlistment exam. There are several different emblems, so I'm sure there are other folks who have them too.

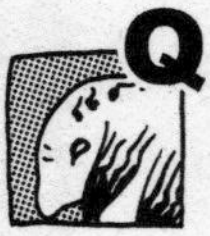
Q

Please explain the how-to of the strap for Issa's *Kongôreitetsu* [Diamond Sacred Steel] and what happened to it (it disappears around page 58 of volume 3), and how the anti-virus masks work. And what is the prospective retail price of the *Hikaritsûshin* Twin Sticks of Light? Blue Uniform-san

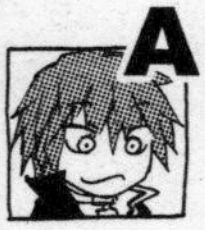
A

Interesting question! How the masks and my blade's strap work...I've enclosed diagrams, so take a look at them! And, where my strap went, huh. You've got sharp eyes! I'm always losing it. Once in a while, the Clean-up Division folks find it and bring it back to me. I've got a ton of replacement straps in my room, and when I run out, I just have them make more. But because I go through so many of them, I have to pay for them myself! I wonder if that's why I can't seem to save up much money.... We should ask Kajiyama about the *Hikaritsûshin* Twin Sticks of Light.

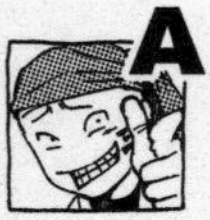
A

Keep those questions coming! What, you want to buy the *Hikaritsûshin*? It's patent is still pending, you know! But for those willing to put down an advance deposit, I'll sell you a set of 5 for the special price of 1000 roku! Although I eventually plan to sell them at a flat rate of 100 roku each! By then, they'll be such a mega-hit that they'll be continuously sold out!

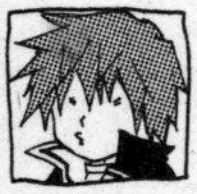

So he says. Uh, onto the final question...

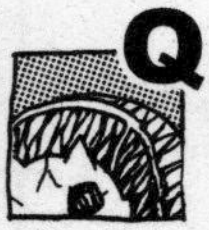
Q

Please show us more of Kajiyama-san's other inventions! I-want-to-see-***Dragon Eye***-animated-san

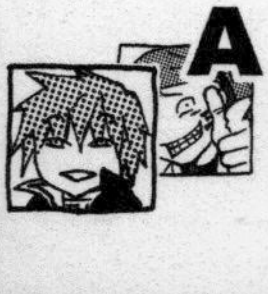
A

Good one...

Once you get him started, he'll go on forever, so just look at the diagram, OK? Well then, thanks, all of you!

Kajiyama's Wondrous Invention!

"*Shintaisokutei* Height Stretcher Rack"! Trial Model

A miracle product for those of you plagued by short stature! Strap yourself in when you go to bed, and flip on the switch!

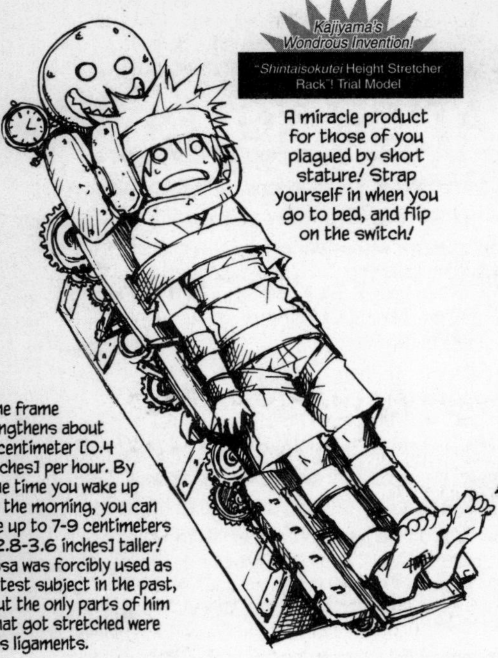

The frame lengthens about 1 centimeter [0.4 inches] per hour. By the time you wake up in the morning, you can be up to 7-9 centimeters [2.8-3.6 inches] taller! Issa was forcibly used as a test subject in the past, but the only parts of him that got stretched were his ligaments.

Diagram of *Kongôreitetsu* [Diamond Sacred Steel]'s Strap

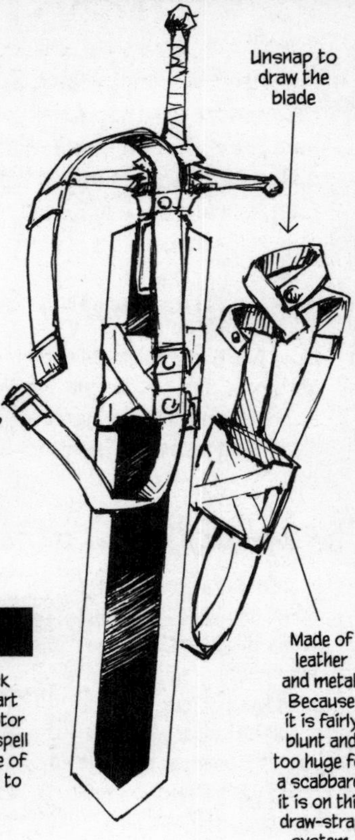

Unsnap to draw the blade

Made of leather and metal. Because it is fairly blunt and too huge for a scabbard, it is on this draw-strap system.

Simplified Diagram of the Anti-Viral Masks

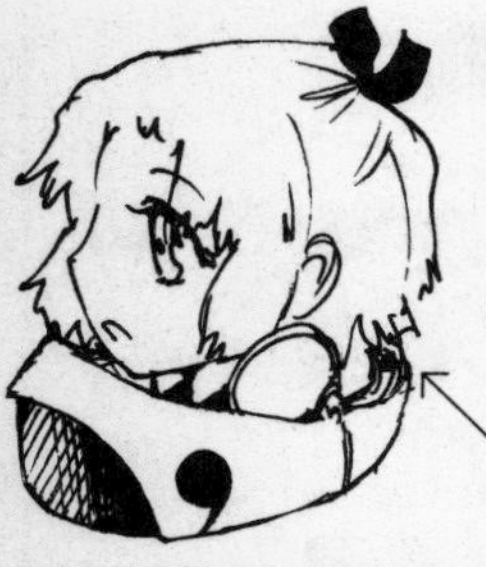

Once the switch in the back is pressed on, an internal part called the Rotating Spell Motor starts spinning and a small spell film forms at its head. Inside of the spell film, the air is safe to breathe.

Switch

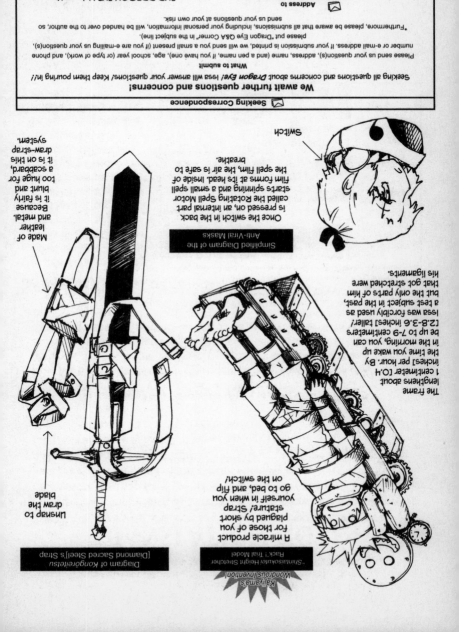

Seeking Correspondence

We await further questions and concerns!

Seeking all questions and concerns about ***Dragon Eye!*** Issa will answer your questions! Keep them pouring in!!

What to submit

Please send us your question(s), address, name (and a pen name, if you have one), age, school year (or type of work), and phone number or e-mail address. If your submission is printed, we will send you a small present (if you are e-mailing us your question(s), please put "Dragon Eye Q&A Corner" in the subject line).

*Furthermore, please be aware that all submissions, including your personal information, will be handed over to the author, so send us your questions at your own risk.

Address to
112-8001 Tokyo City Bunkyô District
Otowa 2-12-21 Kôdansha Monthly
Shônen Sirius Attn: "Dragon Eye Q&A Corner" sirius@kodansha.co.jp

END DRAGON EYE Volume 4.

TRANSLATION NOTES

Japanese is a tricky language for most Westerners, and translation is often more art than science. For your edification and reading pleasure, here are notes on some of the places where we could have gone in a different direction in our translation of the work, or where a Japanese cultural reference is used.

Troop designation symbols, various pages

Most VIUS members wear their troop designations somewhere on their uniforms, and equipment and objects sometimes bear stamps as well. For example, on the cover, Issa's sleeve has Troop Misora stitched on it, and he also has a flag with the character "zero" tied around his left arm.

Funerary rites, page 49

In Leila's dream sequence, Sôsei and Issa were killed in the initial earthquake. Their photographs have been hung before a makeshift altar where a pair of flower vases and a bowl with burning incense have been offered, and the sound heard in the background is that of a Buddhist altar bell being struck.

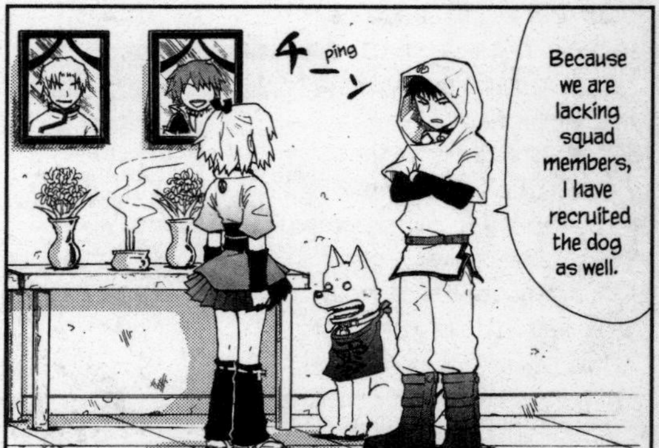
Because we are lacking squad members, I have recruited the dog as well.
ping

Street stalls, page 72

Open-air food stands are still very common in Japan, especially in commercial districts and around train stations. They allow people to grab a quick and often very cheap meal. Some don't even have seating, giving new meaning to the phrase "eating on the go."

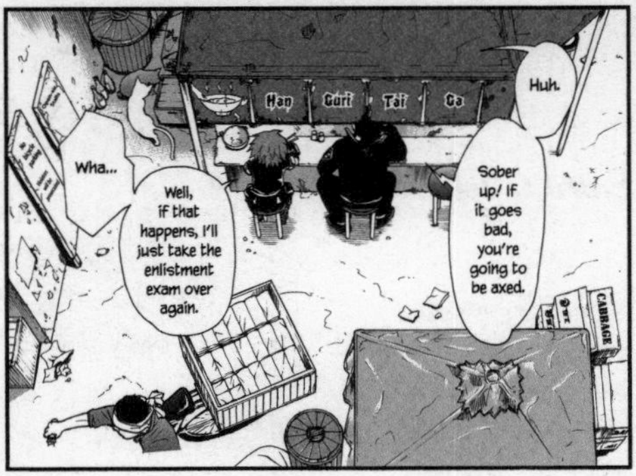

Huh.
Sober up! If it goes bad, you're going to be axed.
Well, if that happens, I'll just take the enlistment exam over again.
Wha...
Han
Guri
Tai
Ga
CABBAGE

Geta, page 97

Geta are traditional Japanese wooden clogs that have been around for centuries and visually resemble flip-flops or sandals. They have a wooden base of variable height (those low to the ground are more commonly known as *zôri*) and shape with a fabric or rope thong. Although associated more with *kimono* or *yukata*, men especially can be seen wearing *geta* with Western clothing. The usual two "teeth" attached to the base result in the distinctive clacking or clopping sound made when walking in *geta*.

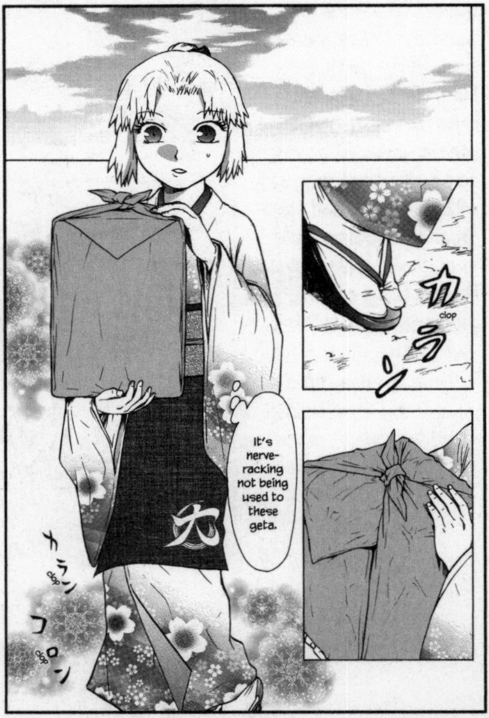

clop
It's nerve-racking not being used to these geta.
clop
clop

Bentô lunches, page 101

Bentô are single-portion boxed meals associated in the United States with take-out and eat-in Japanese restaurants, but they actually have a long history that dates back to the 12th century. Wooden lacquer boxes were first used for these meals around the 16th century. *Bentô* can also refer to home-packed meals. Catered boxes can be quite elaborate, with food cut and/or arranged to resemble seasonal flowers or leaves, or to make pictures and patterns.

Today at noon, a transaction is taking place at a certain mansion in District One.
This is a regular occurrence, and they always order *bentô* lunches from the same upscale caterer.

Enjoy.
Thanks.
Lacquered boxes. Nice touch.